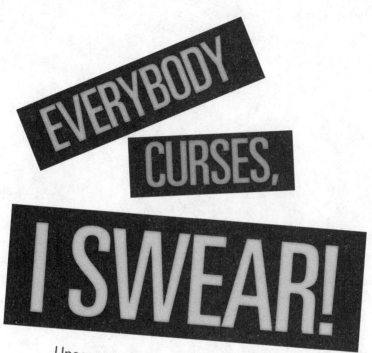

EVERYBODY CURSES, I SWEAR!

Uncensored Tales from the Hollywood Trenches

CARRIE KEAGAN

with DIBS BAER

ST. MARTIN'S PRESS
NEW YORK

www.stmartins.com

Designed by Omar Chapa

The Library of Congress Cataloging-in-Publication Data is available upon request.

ISBN 978-1-250-02620-0 (hardcover)
ISBN 978-1-250-02619-4 (e-book)

Our books may be purchased in bulk for promotional, educational, or business use. Please contact your local bookseller or the Macmillan Corporate and Premium Sales Department at 1-800-221-7945, extension 5442, or by e-mail at MacmillanSpecialMarkets@macmillan.com.

First Edition: January 2017

10 9 8 7 6 5 4 3 2 1

FOR

KOUROSH

THERE IS NO SHE WITHOUT HE

CONTENTS

ACKNOWLEDGMENTS

To all the people who believed I wasn't doing porn
when I told them I was making uncensored online videos.
To those who understood that no good didn't mean not good.
To those who used kind words when talking about my dirty ones.
To those who made me a part of their family.
To those who had no choice about who's part of their family.
To all of you reading this.
From the bottom of my fucking heart,
THANK YOU.

Many thanks to my editors, Michael Homler and Lauren Jablonski, Steve Cohen and everyone at St. Martin's Press whose patience, guidance, and graciousness made this book possible. I'd also like thank Kourosh Taj, Dibs Baer, Josh Wolf, Beth Spruill, Emily Carroll, David Komurek, Matt Sayles, and Sue Carswell for their talent and contributions.

I am endlessly grateful for the support and guidance of my indefatigable and dedicated partners in crime—David Sherman, Jason Hodes, Strand Conover, and Eric Lupfer at William Morris Endeavor; Bob Lange, Esq., and Jill Smith, Esq., at Kleinberg Lange Cuddy & Carlo; Lauren Auslander and Janelle Nazario at PMK·BNC; Seth Gettleson and Larry Witzer at Gettleson, Witzer & O'Connor; and Christian Herles and Sabine Zygmanowski at REBEL Media GmbH—along with my inspirational consultants: Hans Zimmer, Harry Gregson-Williams, Leah Horwitz, Rick Krim, W. G. Snuffy Walden, Aaron Sorkin, Jimmy Fallon, and Sylvester Stallone.

Much love to my wonderful family. Thanks for giving me the strength and courage to reach far beyond my grasp: Mom and Dad; Sean, Jill, and Piper; Katie, David, Alexis, Kira, and Rhys; Keith Jeffery; George, Peggy, Dan and Virginia; Willie Nile, Margie, Lucas, JoJo, Mary, Bob, and Isadora; Maryanne, Alfonso, Alicia, and Claire; Barbie, Dave, Erin, Lauren, and David; Brian, Trevor, Crystal, Altar, Terry, Michael, Dennis, Patty, Kevin, and Bobby; Danny, Carol, Colleen, and Kathleen; Guy, Florence, Clint, Vicky, Guy, and Janet Carbonneau; Parto Seyed-Kazemi; Iraj and Shirin Hamidi; Simin Daneshvar; Natasha Hamidi; Norman, Scarlett, Kianshah, and Junior Patten; Tania Hamidi; Hasti Ebadati, Nazanin and Aseman.

And a heartfelt debt of gratitude to my dear friends for being crazier than me so I could feel normal: Kenneth Stroscher; Quentin Owens; Michael Ore; Hannah McCarthy; Avi, Lori, and Doron Kipper; Jessica Hoffman; Niki Schwan; Richard Rudy; Troy and Melissa Hardy; Mo Nakamoto; Rich Jacobellis; Brian Richards; Bruno Roussel; Cameron Malin; Gino Bona; Michael Markarian; Johnny Hunt; Paul & Chuck "The Movie Guy" Thomas; Pete LoPiccolo; Kevin Rubio; Leo Quinones; Colin Malone; Peter and Candy Judson; Mike, Traci, Cassie, and Ryan Nugent; Dave Greenhalgh; Lynn Lovallo Ferenc; Jesse Farber; and Brian Yurko.

INTRODUCTION

THE ENCYCLOPEDIA HYSTERICA FOR THE
CURSING CONNOISSEUR

Cock-juggling thunder cunt.

That's my favorite curse word. So vile, so visceral, so poetic. It feels like a Vivienne Westwood ensemble from the seventies. Rebellious, absurd, tasteless, precarious, and powerful, all wrapped up into one plaid, pleated, and politically incorrect pantsuit. You can't get the image out of your mind just like you'll never forget this curse word. I heard it for the first time in one of my favorite guilty-pleasure movies, the 2004 masterpiece *Blade: Trinity*. In it, Ryan Reynolds's character, Hannibal King, was being held captive by a demented vampire queen played by Parker Posey. Tied up and maybe a little turned on, Hannibal spat at her, "You cock-juggling thunder cunt!" My eyes widened, my jaw dropped, I felt a slight tingling sensation, and I believe I had my very first *sweargasm*. It was like witnessing the triple Salchow of cuss-outs—dazzling yet dangerous—and oh, so inspiring. I immediately put it into regular rotation in my vocabulary. If you don't think cock-juggling thunder cunt really rolls off the tongue nicely, you're either lying or you're doing it wrong! Like the one night I got a little elegantly elevated (aka drunk) and hit my head on a parking meter. It came flying out of my mouth so organically and effortlessly: "cock-juggling thunder cunt." On a side note, I do find it funny that the man who helped craft Chris Nolan's *Batman* trilogy and Zack Snyder's adventures with the Justice League was the creative genius who gave birth to the cock-juggling thunder cunt, at Marvel of all places: David S. Goyer, my hero!

Before we go any further . . . if you're offended by the idea of a cock-juggling thunder cunt, or that sometimes I get shitfaced and fall down, I'm afraid this book is not for you. Just close the cover or tap that [x] right now. Go back to your local/digital bookstore and choose something safer. Might I suggest the incredibly charming *Games You Can Play with Your Pussy* by Ira Alterman, or there's the wonderful coffee-table book by Graham Johnson, entitled *Images You Should Not Masturbate To*—a personal favorite.

For the rest of you, welcome to my wonderful world of potty-mouthed depravity! By the way, most of us live in this world. The average person swears eighty times a day, according to a thing I found on Wikipedia that I choose to believe. Sounds like a lot, but it really isn't considering it's only about 0.7 percent of the estimated sixteen thousand words you speak all day. Here's what eighty curse words looks like. It's surprisingly small:

Arse. Asshat. Ass-jabber. Assmuncher. Asswipe. Ballbuster. Bastard. Bitch. Blowjob. Boner. Bullshit. Bumfuck. Bumblefuck. Buttfucker. Camel toe. Carpetmuncher. Clitface. Clusterfuck. Cockburger. Cockjockey. Cocksucker. Cooch. Cooter. Cumguzzler. Dickwad. Dickweed. Dildo. Dingleberry. Dipshit. Dookie. Douchebag. Douche nozzle. Dumbass. Dyke. Fartface. Fat-ass. Felching. Fistfuck. Flamer. Fuckface. Fuckstick. Fuckwad. Hard-on. Hair pie. Hand job. Jagoff. Jizz. Kiss-ass. Knob-polisher. Lameass. Lardass. Lezzie. Muffdiver. Nutsack. Peckerhead. Pencil-dick. Pissflaps. Polesmoker. Poon. Prick. Pube. Pussy. Queef. Rimjob. Schlong. Shitbag. Shitface. Shithead. Shithole. Shitbreath. Shitstain. Shit-for-brains. Slut. Snatch. Spooge. Titty-fuck. Twat. Twatwaffle. Wanker. Whore.

Okay, so maybe those are the eighty creative curses I might say in a day—sometimes by 10 A.M. Truth is, I actually have a really big vocabulary for someone who says fuck so often. I'm not saying I'm sesquipedalian for sesquipedalian sake, but I happen to agree with Kelly Preston, who once told me, "People think that just because you say fuck, you have a limited vocabulary; well I say fuck that!" Don't feel bad if your bank of bad words is slightly more basic. I've made a career and an art form out of swearing, so my Rolodex is kind of unparalleled. But I assure you that by the time you're done reading this book, you just might become the most colorful person in your school, workplace, community center, synagogue, PTA, or local YMCA. And by colorful I mean blue, lots of shades of blue. So enjoy the added attention, and don't forget to laugh when the door hits you in the ass as they throw you out.

You might know me best as the host and producer of VH1's *Big Morning Buzz Live with Carrie Keagan*, but for the last ten years I've also been the co-creator and lead anchor of the groundbreaking Internet network and YouTube sensation No Good TV (NGTV.com). Before Judd Apatow made "being dirty" mainstream, before Will Ferrell challenged the world to be Funny Or Die, I was doing uncensored, comedy-driven, and raw video interviews with movie stars, rock stars, TV stars and the like. I earned the nickname "the Naughty Critic" after doing more than nine thousand of these things with every A-, B-, C-, and D-lister you can think of: young and old, highbrow, lowbrow, and unibrow. From George Clooney to Cheech & Chong, I've cursed with them all!

I've gone toe-to-toe with virtually every celebrity in Hollywood and lived to tell the "fucking" tale. And luckily, I've been taking notes. Here's what I found out: Stars—they're just like us! They have a penchant for profanity and when given the opportunity, as they are in my interviews, will come up with the most outstanding and creative swear words you could ever imagine. They spend most of their time being on their best behavior during countless other interviews they have to do, so when they're in front of me, and I tell them that anything goes, they happily go for it. And why shouldn't they? Cursing is the tie that binds: the great equalizer. It makes them more relatable, it makes them more human, and it makes us love 'em even more. That's right! If you really think about it, I've been performing a public service by building a bridge between the fans and their idols, a bridge built with the magic fairy dust of coprolalia, which comes from the Greek *kopros*, meaning feces and *lalia*, meaning to talk . . . do the math!

Take Sandra Bullock. For years we couldn't get her to sit down for an interview because she was *"America's sweetheart"* and NGTV didn't exactly vibe with her squeaky-clean persona. But in 2009, when she was promoting the romantic comedy *The Proposal*, her people finally gave us the green light. It was the beginning of a beautiful, filthy friendship that has, on at least one occasion, resulted in me spanking her ass on camera. Our sit-downs feel so good because, free at last, she's able to be herself, which is, in her own words, a "drunken sailor." For example, during our interview for *The Heat*, with co-star Melissa McCarthy, the conversation naturally turned to girl balls:

Me: Is it fair to say this film is so funny, it will tickle your little girl balls?

Sandra: Yes, it'll *wet* your girl balls, as well.

Melissa: Yes. Yes.

Me: That's our goal: to wet your girl balls. Everyone should be walking around with little wet girl balls.

Sandra: I totally agree. Mine are wet now.

Melissa: I've said it so many times.

Sandra: Yes, you have.

Me: Do they have to be little, though? Because I feel like sometimes I'm walking around with some big sweaty boy balls.

Sandra: The nice thing about girl balls is that we don't want them showing sometimes because of the way the outfit works, so you want to be able to just tuck.

Melissa: She likes a discreet ball.

Sandra: I like a discreet ball. Powerful, yet something that can be tucked away.

Me: You were wearing Spanx in this movie, obviously.

Sandra: My Spanx hold in my girl balls.

Me: They hide your giant girl balls.

Sandra: That's right. You're the first person to bring that up.

Me: I'm so glad, and I don't know how that's possible.

Sandra: Well, some people just don't have the eye . . . for detail. It requires someone with balls themselves to see.

Me: YES! (*Cupping my fake balls in the air.*)

Sandra: My balls! (*Cupping her fake balls in the air.*)

These kinds of interviews are my favorite; when the words coming out of someone's mouth defy any expectations and surprise me into a giggle-fest. I love bringing that out of people. It means that they are truly comfortable with me. To me, the mark of a good interview is when you forget you're watching an interview because it feels like a normal fucking conversation!

(Of course when you see these interviews online or on TV, they are cut up by the promotional film clips provided by the studios, so you don't get quite the full flavor I've enjoyed in person and that you can read in transcript form here.)

You might be asking: What's so hard about that? My answer: Have you ever tried to wash a cat? Well I have and it's pretty fucking hard! And, I have the scars to prove it. Pretty much all celebrity interviews, especially the A-list, take place as part of the well-oiled PR machine that is show business. There is a structure and a format for everything, and all of it takes place in a completely controlled environment behind a towering, burning wall that is impenetrable to all but a select few lucky journalists affectionately referred to as "junketeers." I think of us as a lovable group of misfits, hustlers, and pop-culture poets. Now, *who* gets to go behind this wall and *how* they do it is, if we're being brutally honest, an entire book unto itself. Think *Fifty Shades of Grey* meets *The Little Engine That Could.* So we'll save that for another time.

Now, once you get past the wall and enter this exclusive media speakeasy, you become keenly aware of the rarified air you're now breathing, the incredible access to talent you're getting, and how much you don't want to fuck this up by doing something stupid. The last thing you'd want to do is cross the gatekeepers of this sacred cabal and risk an expulsion handled with the cold indifference of a greeter at Soho House. Trust me: Nobody knows how to make you feel like shit like the low paid, self-entitled misanthropes suffering from club-bouncer syndrome at Soho House. So my personal mission of reinventing the wheel was about to go face-to-face with the inventors of said wheel. The prognosis was murky at best, and by murky I mean I'm bleeding so heavily in the ocean that I can't even see the great white shark blowing air bubbles in my face.

You see, for the most part, celebrity interviews are a bit like bananas. They all kind of look the same. They all kind of taste the same. Some are sweet and mushy while some are noxious and rotten but they all come in the same neat, familiar little package. They are easy to consume, easy to dispose of, and leave very little mess. That's why it's called the perfect fruit. Show business thrives on the comforts of familiarity, and I don't blame them. There's too much money at stake, so there's no room for apples, oranges, or the occasional wild cucumber. I've been doing this for well over ten years, and I've seen them all come and go. I still shed the occasional tear over the wild cucumber. But in the end, you must respect the banana!! The banana is life.

What you may or may not know is that most news and entertainment outlets in the world are banana farms, so this is a perfect system. Everybody gets what they want. My company, No Good TV, and I were new to the scene, we were more "colorful" than most, and we needed to differentiate ourselves if we were to have any chance of surviving. So the challenge was how to stand out in this game of One Banana, Two Banana. We found our answer in a riddle: When is a banana not a banana?

The answer: When it's an apple banana.

So instead of reinventing the wheel, we merely altered the chemistry. My interviews look like a banana, they feel like a banana, they pretty much have the consistency of a banana, but they taste like an apple. And guess what? I discovered that at a typical junket or press event, after a day of being served the same banana, the talent couldn't wait to taste the crisp and refreshing bite of my apple banana. I had become one with the banana, and everybody wanted a nibble.

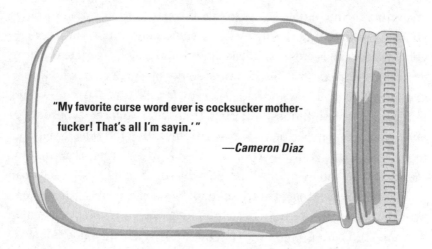

"My favorite curse word ever is cocksucker motherfucker! That's all I'm sayin.' "

—*Cameron Diaz*

Keep an eye out throughout the book for more of these wonderful Swear Jars featuring even more celebrity cursing favorites as told to me by the celebrities themselves!

I know that a lot of people question what I do and how I do it. I've been called vulgar, crass, sophomoric, offensive, dirty, and dumb. And that was just in one article. But, honestly, I don't give a fuck. Those words can never hurt me. I have made a career out of giving people a fun and safe place to verbally let their hair down. And the audience loves it! My interviews for NGTV have more than *TWO BILLION* views online. So how does my banana taste now, haters?!

I worked really hard to get those two billion views. How did I do it, you may wonder? It's about more than my boobs, but thank you for noticing. Some women fucked their way to the top, but I literally "fucked" my way to the top. My journey is no blueprint; it's just my journey. I didn't have it all figured out. In fact, I didn't have any of it figured out. Along the way, my weaknesses became my strengths and my ignorance became my edge. You see, I'm not a trained journalist in the classic sense, or in any sense, and I don't know all of the "DOs and DON'Ts" they teach you in broadcast journalism school. I didn't know much about the decorum of an interview and how things were supposed to be done, and I had no fear because I didn't know any better. All I knew was how to be me. Someone who loves to talk about anything, someone who loves to swear, someone who loves to drink and have a good time. To borrow the immortal words of Andy Samberg from the movie *Hot Rod*, "My name is Carrie and I like to party!" I figured if I could bring who I naturally was into these interviews, I was going to have a lot of fun, and I just might make it out alive.

For your reading pleasure, I'm about to share my journey from bullied kid in Buffalo to Hollywood's most fearless host (it was actually kind of an accident). You're going to get all the juicy, behind-the-scenes stories from my candid interviews, but there are a few more extremely important lessons I'm hoping you'll take away from this book. I'll put them in a *listicle* because that's what all the kids are doing these days:

1. Cursing is as old as time, and like prostitution, is not going away anytime soon. There are entire books written on the history of cursing, and from what I can tell, words like bloody, bugger, and shit were some of the OG cusses. Fuck is relatively new, gaining popularity in the late 1900s and never looking back.

2. Cursing is FUN. I've got a bucketful of words and a laundry list of celebrities saying them to make my case. I mean, when you've got Robert Downey Jr. gleefully shouting out, "You son of a cock-loving whore!" or Leonardo DiCaprio bustin' out "fuckin' retaahded" in a heavy Boston accent, that's some seriously good times. And don't just take my word for

it either. After Jennifer Aniston busted out, "Go see the fuckin' Millers!" with a cute smile on her face to a roomful of laughter, I responded, "It feels good, doesn't it? It makes us just feel good all under," and she replied, "It's tingly!!" with an uncontrollable quiver.

3. Cursing is cathartic. Sometimes the most effective way to communicate a thought is to just let it fly like Kaley Cuoco's "You can say 'fuck'?? Been waiting all day!" or Gillian Anderson bustin' out, "Fuck you, you fuckin' fuck!" 'cause she needed to get it out of her system or director Terry Gilliam, who couldn't help but exclaim, "Fuckin' awesome!" when he realized we were uncensored.

4. Cursing makes you a human thesaurus. *Pulp Fiction* star Samuel L. Jackson believes "motherfucker" is one of the most versatile words in the English language. "It works for so many things," he told me. "I'm on the golf course; people three fairways away know that if I hit a bad shot, '*MOTHERFUCKER!*' Or if I hit a great shot it's, '*YEAH, MOTHERFUCKER, YEEEAH!* That's my friend . . . that's my *motherfucker* right derr.' '*Ay, motherfucker, what's up?*' That's cool. And then you can say something that's really bad. '*Aw, that was a motherfucker . . . horrible.*' Or if it's really cool: '*OOH! That shit's a MUTHAFUCKA!*' Sometimes you have to go 'muh . . . thur . . . fuck . . . er' and sometimes you go 'muhfuhkah.' You know it works."

5. Cursing instigates thoughtful philosophical discussions. Once I interviewed prolific writer Aaron Sorkin about his Oscar-winning script *The Social Network*. In the movie, Facebook-founder Mark Zuckerberg was called a dick and an asshole. I didn't want to do the same standard questions Sorkin had heard before, so I, naturally, asked him, "What's worse? Being a *dick* or an *asshole*?" Instead of being disgusted and walking out, he laughed, and we totally engaged in a tit for tat over the merits of the *D* and *A*. At the *Argo* junket, in response to whether you can unfuck a fucked situation with carefully crafted bullshit, Ben Affleck responded, "Yeah, most things in life require carefully crafted bullshit, it turns out. At least in Hollywood. 'Cause that's what we do. We

make bullshit and we ship it to the world." That's the beauty of cursing . . . and democracy.

Cursing isn't evil. They're just words, and I've always believed that language should **never** be a barrier. Having said that, you're still going to run into a few jackasses out there who see being uncensored as an opportunity to showcase their hate and ignorance. But it's not about the words; it's about the meaning. It's not about the use; it's about the intent. I'll admit I have interviewed more than my fair share of "geniuses" who throw around f****t or n****r like confetti. It's very odd to be so ignorant, especially after being so media-trained and living at a time when we're supposed to be a bit more enlightened. There are two actors that specifically come to mind. One, in particular, is a very well-known white actor who has to be the biggest offender of the N-word, but he appears in like every African-American movie and has adopted a false sense of entitlement to the word. As if, somehow, that makes it okay? WTF! I mean, look how well it worked out for Paula Deen. Another is a moderately famous white TV actor from a former prime-time soap, who shall also remain nameless, who uses the N-word with abandon because, it seems, he's out to prove that just because you're famous, it doesn't mean you're smart. Without his knowledge, we totally saved his ass and edited around his colorful personality. You're welcome!

But, again, they're just fucking words. If you take away all of the outside noise, they mean nothing. They only matter if the people whom they are directed at are offended, and they have a right to be offended if they want to be. Personally, I never use either of those words. On the flip side, I have a lot of gay male friends who call each other f****t affectionately. In fact, my best friend and wardrobe stylist, Quentin Owens, is African American and gay (what a drunk Mel Gibson might call "a double threat"), and he and his friends call each other f****t as a term of endearment. When anyone says he's black or crosses the line and calls him the N-word, he simply shuts them down by saying, "I prefer to be called colored." He decided to own all of it. There's nothing I love more than when people take something that was intended as an insult, reclaim it, and turn it into a powerful statement. Oprah and Jay Z had a big beef about the N-word. Oprah says it shouldn't exist; Jay Z says they're taking the word back from the white man, just like how my gay friends are reclaiming f****t and changing the meaning. Fun fact: Did you know that the word "coffin" used to just mean *box*? But it became so associated with dead people being in them, it ended up only being used in that context. So, if you want to say, "Think outside the coffin" in your next meeting, you wouldn't be wrong.

Anyway, the message I'm trying to convey here is that it's all about context and intent. To borrow from the old adage "It's not the heat; it's the humidity": It's not the words; it's the stupidity. Remember, curse words are not exclusive nor do they discriminate. Unfortunately, people are, and they do. But we can't allow the ignorance of the few to ruin the verbal bliss of the many. When we have so many beautifully descriptive and cathartically wondrous words to choose from in our lexicon of rudeness, why wouldn't we use them all?

Speaking of, we haven't even talked about the word "cunt" yet, and I'm warning you, it's all over this book! Relax, I don't mean literally! I once read this piece about cursing in *The New Republic*, and it said, "Etymologically, *cunt* is more feminist than *vagina*, which is dependent on the penis for its definition, coming from the Latin for 'sword sheath.' Rather than being a taboo word, *cunt* was the general descriptive term for the vagina." Note to self: Use "sword sheath" in my next sext or phone call with my gyno.

Used in an aggressive way, "cunt" can be scary, but, then again, so can any word. Any word can also be dirty. It can be whatever you want it to be. In fact, ever since Steve Carell wooed Elizabeth Banks with "Hope you have a big trunk, 'cause I'm putting my bike in it" in the film *The 40-Year-Old Virgin*, let's just say sliding your *dandy horse* into a *dickie* has never been the same! Case in point, when I interviewed Demi Moore and David Duchovny for *The Joneses,* not one traditional curse word was uttered, but the interview was filthy and engorged with possibilities:

Me: So, the whole gist of this film is you have to make very sure that there's a very strong UNIT. Is that true?

Demi: *(Laughing.)* That our UNIT is working!

David: *(Smiling.)* Ya coined a phrase.

Me: Does the size of the UNIT matter?

David: *(Smiling.)* Oh boy!

Me: Mmhmm.

Demi: You know it's all in how *(Starts laughing.)* you use it *(Then loses it.)* . . . okay. *(Collecting herself.)*

David: *(Playing it up and pretending like his unit is being judged.)* If you guys wanna talk about shoes, I'll leave the room . . . it's fine.

David: *(After taking a second to make him feel better.)* We kind of become, oddly, a real family, you know.

Me: You become a bigger UNIT?!

David: *(David and Demi start chuckling again.)* Yeah, we become a bigger UNIT.

Demi: That's the heart of the movie and it's the dysfunction that . . . um . . . *(Starts laughing realizing she went right back into the hole.)* I think everyone relates to . . .

Me: Nobody wants a dysfunctional UNIT, Demi!

Demi: I don't want a dysfunctional UNIT!

David: I am drawing the line here. That's decadent. *(Demi and I start laughing again.)* There we have it.

Me: *(Triumphantly.)* This is what happens when things go wrong with the UNIT!

As you can plainly see, much like beauty, cursing is in the eye of the beholder.

One thing you should know about me is I curse out of love, not hate. I choose to make curse words fun and funny. It's not always easy. During a press junket for *The Departed*, starring Matt Damon, Leonardo DiCaprio, and Jack Nicholson, I had to make a conscious decision about how to make something funny instead of just raunchy. The movie was a serious Oscar contender for Best Picture, so everyone was taking it all very seriously. There was a scene where Jack Nicholson's character pulls out a big black dildo in a theater, and there was no way I wasn't going to ask about it! It was a big question in my head: Do I specifically say in the interview, "Jack pulls out his cock," or do I refer to it in some other way? "Cock" could come off a little extreme in this sensitive scenario. In the end, I asked Matt Damon about "Jack's junk." The alliteration made it cute instead of crude. He got so excited to talk about "Jack's junk" that it ended in him doing an impersonation of Jack in that "Jack voice" saying, the *scene* could use a big black *cock*! It ended up becoming this beautifully blue moment. A toast to Jack's junk and . . . a little creative cursing!

Cursing is all about being inventive. With all the interviews I'm doing, I'm always learning new ones. When I hear something I've never heard before, it's a wonderful moment of discovery. Like I recently learned *fartleberry* and *shitweasel* and had to share them immediately on Twitter. Being a mentor is very important to me. I welcome you all to follow me and learn the way of the filth.

With that in mind, if you're a beginner itching to dip your toe into the desert hot spring spa of swearing but are struggling to get comfortable bringing the words to your lips, have no fear for I am here. Start off by learning some harmless words that sound incredibly vulgar. Words so innocuous you can easily incorporate them into your everyday conversations with your boss, your parents, your kids, and even your pastor. Words like bumbailiff, bumboat, bumfiddler, clatterfart, cockapert, cockchafer, cockbell, dik-dik, dreamhole, fanny-blower, fartlek, fuksheet, fuksail, fukmast, invagination, jaculate, jerkinhead, kumbang, kumpit, lobcocked, nestle-cock, nodgecock, pershittie, pissasphalt, sackbutt, sexagesm, sexangle, sexfoiled, shittah, skiddy-cock, tetheradick, titbore, tit-tyrant. Daily use of these words will help you perfect your new verbal toolbox in a guilt-free environment. Think of them as training wheels for your brand-new verbo-cycle! And, in no time at all, you'll graduate from tying a fuksheet to the fukmast to becoming a master of "fucking shit up!" Trust me when I tell you that a dip in the Jacuzzi of juvenile jargon is good for the spirit.

My love of cursing has led me on a quest to find the most original and hilarious swear words. Believe it or not, sometimes I'll sit in my office and write a bunch of swears down to see if anything catches my eye. I know, I know, I need a hobby or a boyfriend. I'd prefer a boyfriend who is a hobby but that's a different book, too.

I like making up new swear words and you can, too. Not feeling that inspired? You're not alone. Facebook actually did a study of their users and found that simple ol' *shit* is the most popular swear word used on their site. Here are some other fascinating stats from their research:

- In a three-day period, *shit* appeared 10.5 million times, *fuck* 9.5 million, and *bitch* 4.5 million. *Douche* only got forty-five thousand mentions (and they were probably all about Justin Bieber but that has not been officially tabulated).

- *Pussy* and *dick* are more common with guys; *cock* is more popular with the ladies.
- *Fuck* is more popular in the West, the only region where it outranks *shit*.
- *Dick* and *pussy* rank highest in the Northeast.
- *Cock* and *pussy* are more popular in the South.
- *Asshole* is the word of choice in the Midwest.
- The older you are, the more likely you are to use *darn, crap,* and *shoot.*

We can do better than this. And to help you, I've developed . . . THE SWEAR GENERATOR!!!!!!!!

(FYI, when you read that, you should hear a very deep voice that echoes.)

THE SWEAR GENERATOR!!!!!! (You definitely heard the voice that time.)

That's right, just like the Web site that will generate your Wu-Tang name, I invented something that works 99 percent of the time. I figure anything that works at a higher percentage than condoms is okay to unleash on the public. It's really simple and fun for the whole family. Well, it's fun for my whole family. I can't assume everyone is as twisted as we are.

The generator works like this . . .

Pick two curse words, a verb, and an adjective. Then arrange them like you see below.

Swear, verb (with "ing" at the end), adjective, swear.

Here are a few examples:

Fuck and *cunt* (two swears), jump (verb), and blue (adjective).

Fuck-jumping-blue-cunt.

That is a pretty good one for our first try! I actually horse laughed by myself at my desk. Let's try one more.

Ass and *motherfucker*, punt and sweaty turns into . . .

Ass-punting-sweaty-motherfucker.

An *ass-punting, sweaty motherfucker* is definitely not someone I want to have lunch with, but it is now in my top ten swears of all time.

This is a good time to bring up the one rule that you should remember when plugging a curse word into the generator. Any time you use swears like *motherfucker/cocksucker/assmuncher* they should come at the end, never at the beginning. Look at me giving lessons in swearing. In the past three months, I've called everyone I know and told them to pick two swears, a verb, and an adjective, and when they spit out their own personal swear, they are way happier than they probably should be. It truly is the gift that keeps on giving. Like herpes, only way better.

Have fun with the Swear Generator and reading *Everybody Curses, I Swear!* If you see me on the street, definitely come up and teach me a new one!

—CK

1

FUCK YOU GRANDMA!

Well-behaved women seldom make history.
—Laurel Thatcher Ulrich

I guess I was always a foul-mouthed little shit, or as my parents would say, "Experimental with my words." I shouldn't have been, considering I had a pretty squeaky-clean upbringing in Buffalo, New York. It wasn't like I was a bad kid from a bad family. Quite the opposite, in our community, my family was considered upstanding, hardworking, and humble. My grandparents on both sides were devout Catholics and went to church dutifully every Sunday. My parents didn't really swear unless it was at an inanimate object or when my dad would try to shave our sheepdog each summer. Both situations were more farcical than anything else. I can still hear my mom throw down with a can of Spam while my dad went all biblical on a pile of hair with legs we called Peppy. My dad, who owned a gym and appeared on local and regional TV and radio shows as a health and fitness expert, was so well-known and well-liked, I call him the unofficial mayor of Buffalo. My mom was an entrepreneur who helped my dad and my uncle start and build their respective businesses, as well as being supermom to me and my brother and sister. Now you can see where I got that fire in my belly from.

I come from a big family. Well, it's actually small for a typical Irish-Catholic family, where size is a direct correlation between drinking and a lack of birth control, but you get my drift. On my mom's side, I have

eight uncles, two aunts, and eight cousins. On my dad's side, I have two
aunts and seven cousins with whom my brother, sister, and I spent a lot
of our time. Most of us kids pretty much lived at my dad's parents'
house, which was right down the street from our grade school. Mind
you, afternoons at my grandparents' weren't the nonstop eighties dance
party you might be imagining right now. It was more like an extension
of school with all the food groups represented. Each afternoon, we
were exposed to a rigid curriculum of gym, study, recess, dinner, and
naptime. All under the watchful eye of my Grandma Peggy, a real
honest-to-goodness teacher who had us in such a state of lockdown
that I'd swear she could conjugate the "chemistry of thought" if given
the opportunity. We were allowed to have fun as long as we were learning something. Which makes it all the more interesting that the very
first entry in my lifelong naughty-word manifesto happened here of
all places.

In order to truly appreciate this defining moment in my life, it's
important to know my grandparents. Grandma Peggy was an English
and French teacher who was as loving as she was strict. When she said,
"Please excuse my French," she actually meant French. Grandpa George
was a gentle soul and a devoted husband, quiet and reserved. A simple
working-class hero who never took any shit from anybody and was a
lifelong loyal employee of the Ford Motor Company. For my grandmother, being a teacher wasn't just a profession; it was a way of life. She
yearned for knowledge the way the Kardashians yearn for attention and
laser hair removal. Well, almost as much. She loved to teach, to talk, to
argue, and to reason. So much so that my grandfather would routinely
turn off his hearing aid in order to escape the daily verbal onslaught
known as light after-dinner conversation. No one was safe. I remember
that any time I would send her a card or write her a letter, I could look
forward to having it mailed back to me all marked up and corrected in
red with a grade. There were days when I felt like I was a supervillain
and my crime was the . . . gasp . . . overuse of the dangling participle.
That's a lot of pressure when you're five.

The point is that Grandma Peggy was such a grammatical gangster,
a stickler, so proper and ultra-conservative that her be-all, end-all
F-word was "fart." Anything beyond that was inconceivable. I do take a
little pleasure in the fact that my grandma had a game-ender curse word,
and I loved her very much for it. Plus, she secretly told me I was her

favorite because I always took my naps right on schedule. Hey, you take the wins where you can get them, okay?!

Having said that, we come to the dawn of my myth, my legend, my reason to pontificate about facts that I am marginally familiar with. The right given to me by the celebrity Gods that bestow anyone who has a brush with fame the belief that what they say matters. It so happens that the beginning of *me* took place on the occasion of my third birthday. It was a Tuesday. An unexceptional Tuesday. It was unremarkable in every way except that it yearned to be a Wednesday. The story, which was told to me by my father through mime and song, as is the tradition of our clan, goes that my entire family had gathered at Grandma Peggy's home for a party. It was a festive occasion, and everyone had gathered around the famous pink table in the kitchen, eating my aunt Maryanne's nacho dip, drinking rum and Cokes out of those old glass Coke bottles that Grandma hid in the garage. I was perched in my high chair, taking in all the activities and enjoying being the center of attention. My grandmother was busy boiling hot dogs on the stove with her back to us. The room was bustling with chatter from the various conversations happening between my cousins, parents, and friends. . . . It was, perhaps, that uncomfortable din that permeated the kitchen that prompted my grandma to firmly tell everyone to "settle down" as if we had all just come into her class from recess. Such moments are often mood killers at a party, like stepping on a dog turd right in the middle of telling your friends just how good the fresh grass feels beneath your bare feet. But today something else quite unexpected happened. As the noise in the room quickly died down, suddenly and out of the blue, I dropped three words that changed the course of history:

"Fuck you Grandma!" I exclaimed.

As if it were pierced by the falling blade of a guillotine, the room, abruptly, became deathly quiet. The air became as thick as Jell-O—or whatever else it is that Bill Cosby serves you—and time turned to slow motion with everyone dodging each other's silent thoughts and stares like Neo in *The Matrix*. Fearing that a laugh could die of loneliness, my cousins bolted out of the room, fighting their tears. Moments after, like dominos on the fall, the adults lost control, and the room erupted in laughter. To her credit, the old lady didn't slap the snot out of me. She just ignored it and kept making those wieners. As I stared at the back of my grandma's head and basked in the glory of the cackles I heard around me and in the next room, I had an epiphany. The kind of epiphany that only a distracted three-year-old can have. I decided that I wanted a hamster. Oh yeah . . . also, swearing is FUNNY. Sure, Grandma was obviously disappointed in me but I was three and I had no idea what I was saying but my cousins thought I was the *coolest kid that still crapped their pants*. From then on, cursing just came naturally to and out of me.

I wasn't the only *badass* in our family, come to think of it. Despite our commitment to God and Grandma, there was a rebellious streak in my clan. My dad is a straightlaced stand-up guy but loves to tell a dirty joke, like, "What do an easy woman and a good bar have in common? Liquor in the front and poker in the back!" I didn't say they were good. I just said they were dirty. It doesn't matter. He always makes me laugh. (Except when he's whistling Nazareth songs while we're at the grocery store. That's just embarrassing.) My mom is a smart and kindhearted woman who doesn't take kindly to being taken advantage of. Case in point, when I was fairly young, I remember she got fed up with the never-ending stream of "gimme, gimme, gimme" from the Catholic church we attended and told us we didn't have to go anymore if we didn't want to. Um, we *didn't* and therefore *did not*. It's not that she didn't have faith; far from it. It's just that she didn't feel the need to pay for the privilege, especially while she and my dad were struggling to make ends meet. Flash-forward twenty-five years, I took my mom on a trip to Rome, and while we strolled through the Vatican, she blurted out, "This stuff is all bullshit." I was both stunned and in awe. I waited for the thunderbolt to strike us down, but it never happened. My mom considers herself a "recovering Catholic." She believes in God but is still recovering from the associated *mindfuckery*.

Turns out, even "Fuck-You-Grandma" had a secret naughty side. When I was in grade school, my cousin Sito and I rummaged through her extensive book collection and found what some might consider the textbook for sex: the original 1972 version of *The Joy of Sex*. You know, the one where all the explicit pictures are hand-drawn sketches and everyone was so hairy it was like you had stumbled across a book called *Where's Beaver?* and, guess what, Beaver was everywhere. We'd turn on *Scooby-Doo*, and while I'd be making ramen noodles or grilled cheese, he'd sit at her legendary pink kitchen table and read it out loud like passages from the Bible. I'd sporadically glance over his shoulder to look at the dirty illustrations of the lady and her shaggy lover, described perfectly by one reviewer as "a werewolf with a hangover." Looking back, it's hilarious that this book, where every erection looked like it came from Chewbacca's personal dick pic collection, taught me half of the stuff I know about the birds and bees. From how to have sex on a motorcycle—while it's moving (cue Kim and Kanye, or the sexier version with Seth Rogen and James Franco)—to invaluable advice, such as, "Vibrators are no substitute for a penis" and "Never fool around sexually with vacuum cleaners." I will say that it's interesting that today I do have a thing for guys with long hair and/or beards. Is it possible that the Neanderthal humping his way through *The Joy of Sex* was the original mold for all future men who tickled my loins? Hmm . . .

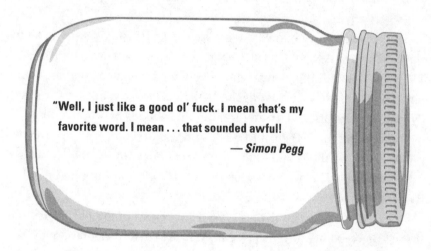

"Well, I just like a good ol' fuck. I mean that's my favorite word. I mean . . . that sounded awful!
— *Simon Pegg*

I also got some of my sex education from my Uncle Kevin. Wait, that came out wrong. But he would appreciate the joke because Uncle Kevin has a really fucked-up sense of humor. Actually, it was more Aunt Barbie with an assist from Uncle Kevin. We used to have family movie nights at my aunt's house when I was pretty young. She had HBO and nobody else did yet, or no one had figured out how to steal it. Back then, in between the wall-to-wall airings of *Eddie and the Cruisers* and *Grease 2*, HBO would throw on what I like to call "classics with a cock-shot." Movies that were there to titillate, but had enough going for them to be called cinematic art instead of soft-core porn, like *American Gigolo* or *Two Moon Junction*. Apparently, not much has changed in the last thirty years in HBO's programming model. Anyway, when the movies would get a little dicey, my uncle Kevin would try to save me from being exiled to another room by my mother. "It's fine," he'd say. "Connie, let her watch." I was always getting kicked out just when the movies would start getting good. Like the time they booted me during the movie *Against All Odds* because Jeff Bridges and Rachel Ward were having some seriously sweaty sex in Mexico. "Okay, punkin' pot, time for bed!" my dad said abruptly as their tan naked bodies writhed on the beach. But, eventually, I wore them down with a three-pronged, foolproof strategy:

1. Pretending to have fallen asleep in front of the TV.
2. My perpetual need for glasses of water after being sent to bed.
3. My insatiable need for yet another bedtime story.

They were putty in my hands. Eventually, it just got easier to let me stay and watch. As a result, I also got to watch a lot of "age-inappropriate" TV shows, including legendary and lecherous British comedian Benny Hill. Hill was sexist, disgusting, and vile; a dirty old man chasing scantily clad women around, trying to grab their boobs and bums. I had no business watching it then, and there's no way it would get past the PC-police today. At the time I hated *Benny Hill*, but funnily enough, I basically grew up to be a dirty old man. A dirty old man trapped inside a Barbie doll body.

On the outside, I've always looked sweet and innocent. The truth is that it's an elaborate disguise I wear. At heart I'm a wannabe Goth girl, a little dark and a lot of weird. But it doesn't come from a place of angst. I'm not pissed off at the world, I'm not on some half-assed pseudo-existential mind trip, I'm actually a happy person. I think it's just part of my DNA. I'm a lot like my crazy great-aunt, Betty. She had super pale skin, like me, long pointy fingernails and jet-black dyed hair. She looked like actress Yvonne De Carlo. I always wanted to dye my hair black, but my mom wouldn't let me. Aunt Betty was bawdy and liked to drink and swear. Sound familiar?

It wasn't just genes; there were environmental factors that helped create my weirdness. My mom collected medieval things like unicorns, but they weren't the sissy *My Pretty Pony* kind and no, this has nothing to do with the swingers' community . . . get your head out of the gutter. She was into some dark shit, like medieval beasties. Now, before you start comparing my mom with your neighbor who has a Hello Kitty gnome collection, please keep in mind that unicorns are mystical crea-tures and the national animal of Scotland. This is some serious fucking shit. She also collected ancient leather-bound books about dragons and graveyard headstone etchings. She was *Game of Thrones* chic before *Game of Thrones*! There was always a cornucopia of intriguing curiosities around our house. Thanks to my mom's influence, I, myself, have a col-lection of gargoyles.

My mom also delighted in reading me the most twisted Grimms' fairy tales, which I loved, and teaching me to sing along to songs like "The Hearse Song." You know how it goes, "The worms crawl in, the worms crawl out . . ." We'd have so much fun together. Funnily enough, the only time I ever got creeped out was the one time she left me home alone for twenty minutes while she went to the store and put *Chitty Chitty Bang Bang* on the TV. That's right, the kid's film. Don't ask me to explain why or how but for some reason the Child Catcher scared the ever-living shit out of me. Saying he could "smell the children," with his big nose, top hat, and greasy black hair. (Which, by the way, I would find attractive now.) I ran around the house in sheer terror, closing every curtain, locking every window, and hiding in a closet until my mom came home. In a strange way, there really is nothing like a children's fairy tale to really fuck you up. Even thinking about that fucker's face now I still get the *ickies* in my *creep-out parts*. I recently forced myself to watch *Shitty Chitty* utilizing the Ludovico Technique from Stanley Ku-brick's classic film *A Clockwork Orange*, with the fucking specula and everything, and it still freaked me out.

That's the only movie that's ever really scared me. And here's why. Good old Uncle Kevin got me hooked on horror with one little white lie that I've now adopted as an absolute truth: that I was named after the Stephen King book/movie *Carrie*. In addition to pervy comedy shows, he used to let me watch classic scary movies, like *Friday the 13th*, *Halloween*, *Night of the Living Dead*, and *The Exorcist*, which has my all-time favorite line from the infamous head-spinning scene: "Did you see what she did? Your cunting daughter!" In the original *Friday the 13th*, there was a scene where the killer drives an arrow right through Kevin Bacon's throat. Instead of covering my eyes, Uncle Kevin slowed the video down, rewound it back and forth, over and over again, and explained to me how they did it in intricate detail. When we were done, that VHS tape had the wear and tear of a teenager's porn collection. His crash course on the intricacies of horror special effects was so profoundly impactful on my personal growth, it was as if I'd just read a treatise on *The Ascent of Man*. From then on I was obsessed with gore, and to this day, I just really get off on blood. The more disgusting, the better. One of my all-time favorite movies is that old *sexy* classic *The Human Centipede*, in which a German doctor surgically connects three kidnapped tourists ass-to-mouth. Need I say more?

The things I'm drawn to are really odd, and sometimes disturbing. I've always had the kind of penchant for the bizarre that Hugh Grant seemed to have for street hookers. I remember highlighting all the bad stuff in the Bible and composing haunting soliloquies in my diary. If you didn't know me, walked into my room, opened up any of my books, and saw the stuff I underlined or scribbled in my journal, you'd think, *This person is obviously going to kill somebody.* It helped earn me the nickname "Basement Creeper" in high school by the select few that knew. Which is why it makes perfect sense that I'm obsessed with vampires and have seen the movie *The Lost Boys* over two hundred times. Now, I'm not saying that classic vampire films weren't the shit because they were. But when you're a teenage girl looking for a make-believe romance with a fictional undead character, Bela Lugosi and Christopher Lee just weren't cutting it! Anyone still reaching for a moist towelette after an all-night *Twilight* marathon can attest to that. I needed the hot, hot heat that Joel Schumacher's snackable sex-boys, I mean *Lost Boys*, provided. I loved that they looked like male models but were evil blood-thirsty killers on the inside. They were a beautiful mystery that could never be solved. The very definition of emotional crack for a teenager.

I remember the very first time I was lured into the vampire's den never to return again. One lazy Sunday afternoon, I was lying on my bed, petting my five-foot iguana, Bela (named after Bela Lugosi), and reading the liner notes from Sting's first album *The Dream of the Blue Turtles*. I found myself enthralled in the backstory behind the song "Moon Over Bourbon Street." It was inspired by a vampire named Louis in the book *Interview with a Vampire* by Anne Rice. I was so captivated that I went to the library and checked it out . . . for eternity. Louis couldn't help his lust and hunger for bloodsucking but felt bad about it afterward. He had a conscience, and it alienated him from the other vampires. At its heart, the book was about loneliness and alienation. Something I could relate to.

2

A TALE OF TWO TITTIES

**What girls do to each other is beyond description.
No Chinese torture comes close.
— Piece by Piece, *Tori Amos***

My breasts have been a blessing and a curse both professionally and personally. I've been hired because of them and I've been fired because of them. I've been ogled by men and criticized by women; been told to push them out and admonished to cover them up. Along the way, I've learned that people have a lot of very strong opinions about *bewbs* regardless of whether they have them or not. And, believe me, I've heard 'em all! To be perfectly honest, I don't really get the fascination. I mean, I sorta get it . . . but you'd think that, at some point in time, they would lose their luster and not be such a big deal. Think about it. Every woman has had them since the beginning of time, so you'd think that, eventually, they'd become old hat, right? Turns out, that's not the case. So I couldn't write a book about myself and not include a chapter about my *boobs*. Not because I want to flaunt them or because I want to draw attention to them (God knows *"Bonnie & Clyde"* do that just fine on their own) but because *"the girls"* have played such a pivotal role in my personal journey. Not a role I necessarily wanted them to play, mind you, but one that, unfortunately, turned an undeniable fact of life into an inescapable torture chamber.

You see, I was bullied mercilessly all throughout middle school and high school. If you can imagine what it must have been like for Andy Dufresne to dodge the sisters in the movie *The Shawshank Redemption*, then you'd have a pretty good idea of what those years of my life were like. It was an endless barrage of humiliation, anxiety, and fear with nowhere to turn for help, no one to talk to, and nowhere to hide. Long before "bullying" became a cause célèbre and "slut shaming" was recognized for the abomination that it is, an untold number of girls, including myself, suffered in silence.

It's been a long and tough row to hoe with *"the twins,"* but I'm happy to say that I'm finally completely comfortable and at peace with them. But to get to where I'm at now, I had to overcome multiple waves of internal turmoil and external conflicts related to my breasts. I spent years ricocheting back and forth between confusion and shame before ultimately finding my way to comfort and pride.

I honestly don't know how I would have made it through those years without my cousin JoJo. She was my best friend, my only real friend. We were pretty much joined at the hip because nothing forges an indestructible bond the way two girls dancing like fools to the mystical acoustic alchemy of Johnny Clegg & Savuka's "Cruel, Crazy, Beautiful World" and Siouxsie and the Banshees's "Peek-a-Boo" over and over and over again, for months on end, can. Plus, we looked like twins, had the same perverse sense of humor, and loved the same things, but always in a complimentary manner. Take *My Own Private Idaho,* for example. It was a film we both loved to consume in order to de-stress. We'd pop that shit like a couple of pill junkies on a Saturday night quaalude bender. But neither of us ever got all *aggro* and grabbed a kitchen knife because I only wanted Keanu Reeves and she only had eyes for River Phoenix. It was always like that with us: effortless. I remember she was going through some personal shit back then, too, so we found solace in each other. There were days when JoJo's kindness was the only shelter I could find from the raging storm that lie ahead. Some things you never forget. Unbreakable were the ties that bound us.

I was eleven years old when it started and, of course, I handled this crisis of confusion with all the great skill and aptitude of any eleven-year-old. That's right; I hid it from the world and turned in on myself as I slowly wandered into teenage isolation. I am still astonished by the capacity we girls have to feel shame and carry the great weight of it over mountains of despair. Looking back, I wish I had known that what I was about to experience would have a profoundly beautiful impact on the person I was to become. During that time, I wish I knew that life is a series of ups and downs and that the journey is the thing. But, unfortunately, all of that was lost on me as I was distracted by the dread of wearing the super maxi pads that my mom had bought a giant box of and placed on my bed. I mean come on, Mom! What the fuck?! The gift of womanhood did not come with a return receipt.

My class, from fifth through eighth grade, had twenty-five girls and only five boys. You'd think with that ratio it would be a girl-power summit and I'd be a total girl's girl, right? Wrong! It was quite the opposite. Just like the various teen-girl cliques that comprise the fan base of boy bands draw lines of demarcation between themselves at concerts as if they were waging a holy war in the Middle East, I found myself isolated in a clique of one . . . and, on top of that, I was wearing the wrong shoes (if you're a girl, you know exactly what I mean). I was stranded on my own personal island and surrounded by a group of mean girls that would follow me around and harass me.

By the time I got to high school the small sanitarium of a middle school I attended had grown into a full-blown asylum where the lunatics had taken over. My expanded peer group had graduated to constantly calling me a "whore" because "slut" and "bitch" had become passé. I remember how they'd corner me in the back of the bus, scream horrible obscenities, and threaten me until I got home. There were days where I felt like I had entered a hot dog eating contest only to realize that I was the hot dog. The older we all got, the more hateful the girls became. Their sole purpose in life was to make my life a living hell, and it worked. I can look back on it now and try to think rationally, *Oh, okay, those girls were just jealous.* Of what, I'm not exactly sure. Although I could make a couple of guesses . . . my boobs?

In many ways, my breasts are the essence of who I am. They are the accompanying musical score to every dramatic moment of my journey. They provide the accent with which my body speaks. No single person I have ever encountered has been able to avoid the allure of their divisive siren song. Homer would have been proud (Not Homer Simpson, you idiot). I have been desired, defined, denigrated, and dehumanized by them; the price I've paid for every *D* in my 32DDDDs. Ultimately, they took me from suffering in silence to finding a blessing in disguise and evolved from being *"Satan's love pillows"* to *"the twins of truth and beauty."* This is their story.

My *cha-chas* will come up a bunch in this book, so let's just kick it off right now. I had the distinct privilege of entering puberty when I was eleven years old and in the fifth grade. It didn't sneak up on me all gentle in the night with the kiss of a fairy; it entered my life like a rigged game of three-card Monte, delivered with the sympathy of a carny street hustler. That's right, it was the perfect trifecta of shit, and I was about to wear two bags of it on my chest. As if to foreshadow their role in my life, first out of the gate were my breasts. It was slightly unnerving at eleven years old but it was still manageable. But then they grew bigger and bigger and bigger than everyone else's. At that point, they were terrifying!

I think most girls hate their bodies when they're growing up. We're too skinny, too fat, too tall, too short, too muscular, too flat, or in my case, too busty. The truth is, when you're young, *nobody* wants to be different. When you're different, it gives the bullies something to aim at, and then all of the other kids who don't want to get picked on pick on you to deflect attention. It's horrible and I was already a target . . . and when I started to develop? It was a nonstop *boob-a-thon* of jokes. Why on earth would an eleven-year-old girl ever want boobs? It was like a cruel joke from up above. And it wasn't the boys who teased me; it was the girls. I knew girls could be mean, but in the Catholic school I went to, they were downright vicious.

"Hey, Carrie! Did two mosquitoes bite you in your sleep?"
Or . . .
"I'm thirsty for milk. Carrie, do you know anyone who might
be carrying some extra milk? Moo!"
Or . . .
"Carrie, you're my breast friend."

Looking back, the "breast friend" one makes me giggle, but at the time I was traumatized. Granted, I inherited my *num-nums* from my lovely mom, whose giant *knockers* are still, thankfully, pretty perfect and not like *National Geographic titties* at all. But at the time it felt like a blight from God. Then came sucker punches two and three as my body continued its sick betrayal: pubes and my period. It all just sort of happened, like a blowjob after prom! "What the fuck is going on?" I remember thinking. *Aliens* on my chest, hair that showed up overnight, and there's blood everywhere. I didn't even tell my mom I'd gotten my period; she figured it out one day doing the laundry.

"Is there something you want to tell me?" she asked gingerly.

"No!" I said like a brat, mortified that she would even ask me such a question.

"Did you get your period?"

"Ugggghhhhh, yessssss!"

"Do you have any questions?"

"No! Wait . . . One . . . How long does this last?"

"Shouldn't be more than seven days."

"Fine!" Then I stomped upstairs and slammed my bedroom door. I had actually become my own horror movie, but this time I was horrified.

Funnily enough, I don't really remember the day my *rack* got installed. They were just there all of a sudden, "like a bastard in a basket," to quote Daniel Day-Lewis's character in the movie *There Will Be Blood* (which, one could argue, could also be the name of this charming chapter in my life). I was always uncomfortable with them. I'd wear baggy clothes and try to hide them, but it didn't work. I just looked like a pregnant teenager.

The worst, the absolute worst, was the day my mom told me I had to go get a bra. My mom has the same *caboodles* that I have now. My sister also has big *butterballs*. We come from a long line of great *Baileys Irish cream dispensers,* so my mom was well versed on what to do and where to go. I remember walking into the department store as my mom grabbed a handful of bras and whisked me off to the dressing room. To say I was not prepared for what was about to happen is an understatement. I've never been a girly-girl, so I didn't look forward to my first bra like a lot of girls did. I remember when my mom put the first one on me; it felt awful. I couldn't breathe, it itched, it pinched my skin, I kept shrugging my shoulders like Rodney Dangerfield, and I told my mom, "I'm never wearing one of these." Then my mom said something that totally ruined my day. Like someone had peed in my Cheerios. She said, "Carrie, starting today, you are going to wear a bra every day for the rest of your life."

"NOOOOOOOOOOOOOOOOOOOO!!!!!!"

Hadn't we become a more civilized society? Didn't we graduate past squeezing women into a corset-like apparatus? I felt like a geisha except she wasn't binding my feet, she was binding my breasts! It was terrible and to make it worse, as comfortable as my mom was with her *Greta Garbos* and wearing a bra, she was no expert when it came to finding the right size. We bought a bra that day, but every time I stretched or reached for something, the bra would come undone. That went over really well in school. To top it off, the bra was sooooo ugly. I mean UUUUHHHH-GLY!! We didn't have much money back then, so we had to buy the bra that was in our price range. It looked like a wife-beater/half-shirt combo with a horrid blue flower that only had two petals on it. Not that a ton of people were seeing my bra when I was eleven, just the people who liked to ridicule me. The locker room was not a fun place.

"Hey, Carrie, did your mom make your bra out of your dad's
   old socks?"

It didn't even make sense and it still made me cry.

A year later, my *oompas* were waaaaaaay bigger. Hooray, right? Nope. The teasing got worse. I did not want the attention and I did not want my *pagodas*. I remember my mom asking me once, "Are you ashamed of your body?"

"Yes, I am," I said.

I felt like a dog wearing a cone. I knew it was for my own benefit, but its constriction caused me to move about as gracefully as I would if I was in a full-body cast. It fucking sucked! In gym class I got in trouble for being squirmy. My shirt was too tight and I had this piece-of-shit bra on and my gym teacher was all, "Carrie, stop adjusting yourself!" Oh. My. God. She called me out in front of everybody, and now they're all staring at me. It was exactly what I was trying to avoid. Fuck. My. Life. I ran and hid in the locker room for the rest of the period. She ended up apologizing later because she realized what she had done was traumatizing. But her apology made it even more awkward because the last thing I wanted to do was keep talking about my *unwelcome guests*.

They were ruining everything! Not only did I get my bra snapped every thirty seconds, and not only did my new *friends* make me feel like a purple, three-legged baboon but they also ruined the only athletic thing that I took part in. Lord knows I'm not the most coordinated person in the world but the one thing I could do was run, and run fast. I know, I know, laugh it up. You're picturing me running right now and envisioning two black eyes and a concussion. Back then, they weren't nearly a big but they were still there, which made the girls laugh and the boys stare.

Up until that point I was the fastest sprinter in school, boy or girl. But when my *speed bags* came 'round, I started getting made fun of. It became less about my dash and more about my flash. The track was situated such that we had to run by the windows of all the classrooms. I wish I could tell you that my experience was exactly like Bo Derek running on the beach in the movie *10* with everyone swooning at the sight of my bouncing bosoms, but in reality it was more like I had just farted on the treadmill at gym. It was so embarrassing. After suffering through a few of those humiliations, I literally stopped running in public for the next *twenty-two* years. Until 2014, when I ran two half-marathons for charity, which were amazing, but to be honest, I don't know who was working harder, me or that beautiful aerodynamic piece of magic we call the "sports bra."

So is it possible the bullying could have had something to do with my *gedoinkers*? In fifth grade, the coolest girl in my class sat behind me, and the first time I wore my *over-the-shoulder boulder holder,* she tapped me on the shoulder and shouted, "Carrie's wearing a bra!" Then later, in high school, some days when I'd walk into a room, another girl would announce, "Hey, everybody, the slut is here!" I hadn't done anything at all to earn a reputation as a slut; it just came with the *lady lumps.* Like that free case of the *herps* my friend got after sleeping with an A-lister. It was mortifying and made me an outcast in every way.

I was embarrassed and incredibly ashamed by it all. I wanted to escape the misery so badly, but I had no clue how to talk to my parents about it or what to tell them. They had worked so hard to afford the tuition and even lied about where we lived so I could attend these well-respected private Catholic schools, and I didn't want to let them down. They were all I had, and I didn't want to risk losing their love and faith in me. I was a teenager, for fuck's sake, not Friedrich Nietzsche . . . this is all the brilliance I could muster at the time.

Sadly, there was no *Breakfast Club* for me to attend where I could solve all my problems by bonding with four strangers over our mutual despair. Plus everything that would happen in my life that was remotely positive would always come with a price at school, like my brief stint in the fast-paced world of modeling in western New York. One of those wonderful *shit sandwiches* that caused me a lot of grief with the girls in school, but was ultimately very rewarding.

I know what you're thinking: *You poor thing, you had to model to make ends meet.* Sounds like something out of *Zoolander* (which in some ways was a frighteningly accurate portrayal of the modeling world, if you think about it). But the truth is, I'm not one that ever sought the spotlight. Not then and not when I started doing NGTV. I was always more comfortable in the background. Plus the reality was that at that point in my life I hated myself. I hated everything about myself. Junior high and high school were a struggle every day and in every way. I was awkward. I felt awkward. I looked awkward with my new body. I was super uncomfortable in my skin. I was always hiding myself in ridiculous clothes. If given the choice, I would have worn a kaftan or a muumuu every day . . . with combat boots, of course. And as much as you might be thinking that the modeling scene in Buffalo was *the dick of the cat,* I just couldn't take it or myself seriously. I was sort of a sad mess, and it was a happy accident that became a wonderful distraction.

Obviously, my mom and dad saw things differently, as moms and dads do. Thankfully for them, it was a way of building my self-confidence and giving me something I could do outside of school. With their plan set in motion, they casually introduced me to a friend of theirs who was a local modeling agent. She was a super-cool lady who really took a liking to me and wanted to put me in some classes. She thought I had potential and gave me some positive attention. After a while, I started to become open to what she had to say. I, of course, wasn't emotionally in a place to do any of it and had not spent my childhood developing my pageant skills like Honey Boo Boo, so it still took more of a push to get me going. Fortunately, my dad, who was a jack-of-all-trades type, had done some modeling and thought it was harmless fun and my mom felt that it might help me find myself. So they both nudged me forward into doing it. In retrospect, I now realize that my parents always saw the swan in me when all I saw was the ugly duckling. I love you guys!

As a kid, I'd had a little bit of practice being in front of the camera, appearing on TV shows with my dad a few times. Like the time I broke my arm and he had me come on so he could talk about children's athletic injuries. But, at this point, I needed a little more help. So we signed me up for a crash course in how to be a model. I remember walking, posing, and practicing being a live mannequin in a store window (which was very popular at the time. Though mine looked more like Scarecrow from *The Wizard of Oz* than Mr. Roboto). I had to learn how to do my own makeup, which I was as skilled at as I was styling my Mattel Barbie Head. You know, the one with the Sharpie eyeliner and a partial skinhead. Then, strangely enough, the unthinkable happened, and I landed some catalog work, runway shows, and a few print campaigns, including one for Fisher-Price toy boxes, and believe it or not, one where I dressed up as Barbie for Mattel. But let me be clear, I was no Kate Moss. I may not have been gracing the cover of *Vogue*, but when upstate New York needed a fresh new face for microwave pizza coupons or poodle sweaters at the local outlet store, they called Megan Kozlowski, and when Megan Kozlowski wasn't available, I crushed it.

In spite of the fact that I had become a professional "clothes hanger" working in the haute couture equivalent of Cleveland, my modeling experience was never about being all glamorous and feminine, or making enough money to treat myself to a sick new double-cassette ghetto blaster. It was about finding my identity and getting a level of confidence I think most girls don't have at that age. At least, I didn't. It was also a major lesson in humility because I got rejected a lot.

One time, I went on a *go-see* (which is sophisticated modeling jargon for going somewhere and being seen for something) for the Valentine's Day version of the Puffalumps, the hottest doll since the Monchhichi. I was very nervous and excited, as I was up against the hottest girl at the agency. She had modeled in Japan, so she was a big deal, and this whole thing could have been a game changer. It ultimately came down to just the two of us, and I literally lost it by a nose. They ended up picking her because her nose matched the male model's nose better than mine. Because that, in a nutshell, is just how random show business is. I'm not going to lie, it sucked. I wanted to be on that box. I wanted them to pick my nose. I recall my dad softened the blow by getting me a Puffalump for Christmas, and in the card he said that I would always be his Puffalump. My dad always knew how to say the right dumb thing just when I needed it the most. At the end of the day, none of it really mattered. Modeling was something that was mine that existed outside of the miserable academic universe that I lived in, and no one could take it away from me. It was a sign of hope that everything did not begin and end in high school and that there was a life beyond it all. Plus, it was really fun, and it prepared me for the constant rejection you deal with in showbiz.

I never flaunted the fact that I was modeling, so nobody ever said anything unkind about it—that I can remember—but it did bring me some unwanted attention. Like when my picture was on those pizza coupons that were delivered to everyone's house in the newspaper. My health teacher thought she was being supportive when she held it up in front of the entire class and said, "Carrie, we have you on our refrigerator at home, and my son wants to know, how much are you by the slice?" Oh God!

I ended up quitting modeling in my senior year, for various reasons. I felt better being in my own skin, but I was far from being sample size with these torpedoes on my chest, and it got frustrating getting turned down for jobs because of them. I wanted to focus my spare time on my then-boyfriend who was battling a serious illness, but that's a story for another chapter. I missed the glamorous life, but as Sheila E. said, "Without love, it ain't much."

When I started high school, I was hoping a fresh start would clean the slate for me. Uh, not so much! Another area in which my *zeppelins* created problems for me with the girls was the obvious added attention it got me from the boys. And I mean the older boys. The smooth, cultured, and sophisticated sixteen-year-olds that young girls covet. The ones who know how to treat a lady. Not those fourteen-year-old "children" who are clueless in the ways of romance and are constantly going at it like a ten-year-old with a pogo stick. Strangely enough, I saw myself as Hatchet-Face from the Johnny Depp film *Cry-Baby*, but apparently, they saw me as more of a *walking magic trick*. Especially because I could peek out from behind my *jumblies* and say, "Now you see me! Now you don't!"

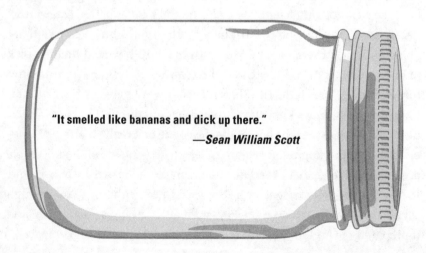

"It smelled like bananas and dick up there."
—*Sean William Scott*

(I'm telling you that move kills at parties.) And girls picked up on that shit to such a degree that the boy drama reached medieval levels of pre- posterousness. They would immediately start spreading rumors about me being a slut. I have to admit, some of the stories I heard about myself were amazing. I wish I had had that much fun in high school!

Believe it or not, on three occasions I literally handed over a guy I was dating to one of the mean girls who also liked him and had threat- ened to give me hell for the rest of my life if I didn't go away. So I'd bow out and say to the guys, "So-and-so likes you. Maybe you should go out with her," and like lambs to the slaughter, they did. It was the relation- ship equivalent of having your lunch money stolen by a bully. I lived in a world where a bunch of high school girls had invoked some sort of half-assed schoolyard *Prima Nocta* on any guy that I happened to like. They were, literally, *taxing that ass.* Honestly, you can't make this shit up! From my perspective, I had to protect myself from any more harass- ment. The guys were absolutely not worth it. Not being beaten up was *way* more worth it to me.

I just wanted the girls to be nice. They just wanted to have someone to hate. I wasn't part of the cool clique, so it was easy to pick on me. I definitely didn't fight back hard enough. In fact, I never threw punches, literal or verbal. I wasn't a master debater, so there was no talking my way out of any of it. I just suffered through it, hoping I would just dis- appear into anonymity, until I couldn't take it anymore.

It got so bad that by the time I was in my sophomore year (that's right, folks, we're not even out of year two yet), I was an emotional wreck with nothing left to lose and at the end of my rope. I mustered up all the courage I could and decided to finally talk to my mom and dad. Then, as if a dam had burst, I unleashed the agony of the last few years on them. It was frightening, cathartic, and ultimately sobering. Instead of understanding and compassion, my words were met with utter dis- belief. I had hidden it all so well and for so long that they thought I was exaggerating and being dramatic. The emptiness and hopeless- ness of that moment has stayed with me to this day. I cried and begged my mom to help me and get me out of that high school only to hear her tell me that she would make a few calls to the school. But I would not be deterred.

The perpetual stomach cramps I had from my crying fits had pushed me to a tipping point, and I began to beg and plead with them daily until they gave in. I'm not sure they ever really understood it all, but they saw all they needed to see in my eyes and the shell of a person I'd slowly become. Then, months later, one day it happened. They took me out of my personal hell by switching me from my all-girl Catholic high school to a coed public high school. Just like that I got a second chance. Don't get me wrong, it was a temporary relief but a welcome one at that. After all, high school is still a proctologist's dream—buildings full of assholes! But at least these were different assholes, and I was now better equipped to deal with them. I have to admit that escaping from the perils of almost drowning in an estrogen-filled kiddie pool was a welcome relief. Gender segregation is archaic and so unnatural. Still, my new school wasn't without its challenges. I had a fresh batch of bullies to face, my own baggage to deal with, and of course, the promise of the perpetual Rock'em Sock'em Robots game known as adolescence.

My sophomore and junior years weren't as bad as before, but they had their highs and lows, most of them served with a generous portion of "not this shit again." My *cans* continued to dominate the news—because, let's face it, high school gossip is essentially *Access Hollywood*, but uglier—still, I did my best to keep my head down and try to fit in. No matter what I did, no matter how good my intentions were, I would always end up the subject of one controversy or another with the girls. It's a gift. The University of Phoenix should offer an online degree in High School Mindfuckery because it would give all those *mingers* who peaked then something to do when they're not asking you if you want fries with that.

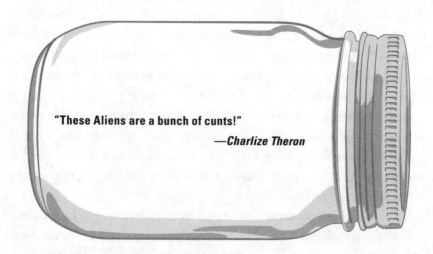

"These Aliens are a bunch of cunts!"
—*Charlize Theron*

In retrospect, I have to admit signing up for the swim team out of the gate, at the advice of my new guidance counselor/swim team coach, probably wasn't the best move. As they say, the road to hell is paved with good intentions.

A couple of years ago, as anti-bullying had finally become a public campaign and I had contributed my story to the conversation, my dad and I went drinking together, and he apologized to me for not understanding how badly I was tormented. He had read my interview about what I had gone through and then had come across an episode of CBS's *60 Minutes* one night where they did an in-depth feature on the subject that ended up being quite the revelation for him. I remember him saying, "I get it now," with tears in his eyes, "and I'm really sorry. If there's anything I could do to go back and change it, I would." It was so sweet, but he really didn't need to apologize to me. Because when it counted, my parents were always there for me. Through the meaningful and meaningless times, even when they didn't quite understand what my teenage mouth was saying (because most parents don't speak *pubescent assclown*), they loved me enough to support me. They were the emotional Wonderbra I always needed. Who could ask for more than that?

Here's the thing: Of course I wish that hadn't happened to me, but I wouldn't be where I am today if it hadn't. It forced me to eventually figure out how to better stick up for myself and prepared me for the bullying I'd get as an adult from female execs in Hollywood, Twitter trolls, and self-righteous celebs (see Chapter 15: *A Kick in the Cunt*). Also, one of the more hurtful insults the mean girls would hurl at me again and again was that I was "worthless." At the time, I believed them. I truly didn't think I was special in any way. The bullying was a source of so much pain, but it pushed me to figure out a new purpose or passion in life. Something that would drive me to get the hell out of Buffalo.

That passion turned out to be music.

I love all music. Period. It was all around me growing up, so I had a well-rounded education. Buffalo has a rich music history, being home to Rick James, Natalie Merchant, Goo Goo Dolls, and Ani DiFranco, to name a few, and of course, there was my uncle Willie Nile, a legend in his own right. A few of my other uncles were in bands, too, and they'd let me hang out while they'd jam. Uncle Kevin had a huge record collection and listened to a lot of David Bowie, Pink Floyd, and Peter Gabriel.

Opera wafted through my other grandma's house at all times. My parents listened to fifties and sixties music, Neil Diamond, Barry Manilow, and Barbra Streisand. My one significant high school boyfriend, Pete, was a skateboarder who had long beautiful hair like Anthony Kiedis from the Red Hot Chili Peppers, he liked punk bands like The Germs and The Damned.

But by far my biggest musical influence was my older brother, Sean. I absolutely worshipped him when I was growing up. I emulated his every move, copied his fashion style, adopted his vernacular, and of course, wholeheartedly embraced his taste in music. Hence the reason why I am now the world's foremost expert on glam metal! I was his mini-me. I'm sure I was the pesky kid sister he couldn't shake who was all over him like a dog with a bone, but he never showed it. He was my hero growing up. He always made time for shenanigans with his little sis. Like when we were kids, we would play air band in the backyard, standing on the picnic table like it was the stage at Madison Square Garden (my sister, Kate, was a preppy teenager who didn't have time for my childish things and quit the family "band," but my big bro and I were always down for a show to an audience of two—my parents). Then there was the time when, after everyone had gone to bed, we snuck downstairs to watch the movie *KISS Meets the Phantom of the Park*. He was the coolest!

I would buy him *Metal Edge* magazine for his birthday, but secretly it was for me. I'd do his chores in exchange for the best pictures he'd collected of his favorite bands. He lived in the attic and plastered his walls with the coolest metal posters, so I swapped out my Michael Jackson and Madonna posters for all my new favorite bands—Skid Row, Poison, Bon Jovi, Warrant, Cinderella, KISS, Mötley Crüe, Guns N' Roses, and Slaughter. My mom was appalled by all of this. She didn't want me taping anything, let alone these boys in drag, to the wall (parents just don't understand).

But there was no stopping me now. I became obsessed with glam metal. The guy-liner, the long hair, the religion-revealing leather pants, it made me swoon. They were so pretty, but they were men, manly men! And they were talented! They were living the lifestyle that I wanted to live: modern day vampires. Up all night, sleep all day, sex, drugs, and rock 'n' fuckin' roll!!

I wasn't old enough to go to concerts when my favorite bands came to Buffalo, so Sean would sneak me into some local clubs. The nightlife felt like home to me. I was born with the DNA to party, but more importantly, this was where I decided I was going to turn my passion for music into my career. My goal would be to work at a major record label in LA, where all the big ones were based, and promote bands. I vowed to myself that nothing would stop me from getting there.

As my senior year began, my priority was getting an internship so I could have a solid extracurricular on my résumé. I set my sights on getting one of only five offered to seniors at my school. It was extremely competitive; you really had to knock the socks off the selection committee to snag a spot. The problem was that I wasn't that good of a student. I wasn't stupid, but school and I got along like oil and water. I was always precocious and took every opportunity to learn and experience new things. I spent most of my time in high school being more nervous than a Winger fan at a Pantera concert. It was hard to focus. I wasn't much of a troublemaker, either, although I did get sent home once for wearing a T-shirt that said MOTHERFUCKER on it. Though I have to admit, that was a high point for my fashion sense back then. Regardless, I knew if I wanted one of these internships, I really had to go balls out and state my case.

To make matters more complicated, my school didn't offer anything relevant like a music internship, which was what I really needed for my plan. They just had standard ones at the local hospital, public defender's office, or working for the Buffalo Bills, which is exciting if picking up sweaty jocks is your idea of a life well lived, but I had my eyes on something entirely different. I realized that I had to get inventive and somehow find a way to blow the committee's minds. What I needed was for them to approve me for an internship at Amherst Records, a reputable local label. To that end, I set upon a mountain of research and legwork in order to create a presentation about how the music industry worked and what I could learn from interning there and how that would then tie into my future academic plans. It was a huge roll of the dice, but when the selection committee realized I had taught *them* something in my presentation, they were totally impressed. I got the internship!!! It was a gloriously fulfilling moment in my life and proof that once I set my mind to something, I will "Rock You Like a Hurricane." That would not be the only time in my life a healthy dose of crafty determination would come in handy.

With the bullying behind me and a newfound sense of purpose ahead of me, I set free the fearless and whimsical girl who had been trapped behind a wall of insecurity and self-consciousness and started making plans for the future.

However, the present wasn't quite done with me yet.

3

A TWIST IN THE ROAD

**If you aren't in over your head,
how do you know how tall you are?**
—*T. S. Eliot*

Woody Allen once said, "If you want to make God laugh, tell him about your plans." Well, God must have been laughing his ass off during my senior year of high school. You see, I had it all figured out: a new boyfriend, a new job, and a killer internship at a record label. I was going to have little time for the nonsense with the girls in school, and I was going to be focused on my future career in music. Everything was going to be fun and simple and easy. Not so, as I was about to experience one of those defining moments that tears apart who you are and rebuilds you into who you're supposed to be. Of course, I didn't know that then, but there appeared to be a twist in the road ahead.

My senior year started with a bang. Literally. I was in love with a boy named Pete, and all was right with the world. The first time I laid eyes on him was on a sunny afternoon in the park. Through a smoky haze of hippie stoners dancing around to a bootleg of the Grateful Dead, I noticed this beautiful boy off to the side, playing Hacky Sack. Every time he would leap into the air to catch it, his long hair would flow in the wind like Nicolas Cage's locks in the beginning of the movie *Con Air* . . . almost in slow motion. It was mesmerizing. I was so lost in it. I couldn't take my eyes off him. Just like in *Wayne's World*, I could hear

Gary Wright's song "Dream Weaver" wafting through the atmosphere. I was his and he was going to be mine. All he had to do was say hi. But sadly, he was one of those tragically shy hot guys. No matter. He eventually got the hint and JACKPOT!!

Pete and I were inseparable. We were ridiculous. Like a couple of out-of-control, horny teenagers, we spent every waking minute at his house, trying to have sex. Mostly because that's exactly what we were and it was the only time in our lives we could get away with that excuse. The only hiccup was Pete lived with his mom. So having sex was all about timing or the risk of being caught *ass-up* giving his mom a mental picture of her son to last a lifetime. Not on my watch. Fortunately, his mom was a bartender at a local dive, which meant she was gone from happy hour until whenever the local drunks decided they weren't happy anymore, which usually meant we'd have the place to ourselves from 5 P.M. to about 3 A.M.

So I settled into my daily routine, which was school until 2 P.M., then over to Pete's house for sex, grilled cheese sandwiches with mustard hearts (my specialty), a dose of *Star Trek: The Next Generation* followed by more sex, and then home. The only real intrusions we faced were dealing with his mom on those few occasions when she would come home drunk with her boyfriend, all loopy and frisky, forget we were there, stumble over us in the living room, then start screaming that two homeless people had broken into her house and try to call the cops. That and Pete's adorable dog, Casey, whose fascination with the *horizontal mambo* bordered on the absurd.

Casey was always getting himself in the middle of things he shouldn't. You see, like most pets, he loved watching us have sex. In fact, thanks to Casey, I'll never forget the very first time I had an orgasm. Pete and I were upstairs in his bedroom, deeply focused on performing government-mandated stress tests on his mattress. As my body edged closer and closer to a soul-shattering mega-explosion, so did the level of commotion we were making. Lost in the moment, we had caught Casey's attention and tickled his curiosity. So, unbeknownst to us, up the stairs and into the bedroom he came, slowly nosing his way onto the bed. I should have heard him breathing or seen the light from the hallway, but instead, all I felt, as I was violently climaxing, was a cold, wet nose up my ass!! The shock of it made me tense up and scream so loudly, it made Pete think he was the *"Einstein of orgasms."* He took a victory lap and declared himself the *"Pontiff of poonani."* I never had the heart to tell him what had actually happened . . . until now, I guess.

All things considered, life was good. But just like every great episode of VH1's *Behind the Music*, it was all about to end.

Days turned into weeks and before we knew it, we were having our one-month anniversary, which is like a year for a teenager. It's a big fucking deal. But there was to be no celebration. Pete got the news that his father, who lived in Florida, had been diagnosed with a late-stage cancer, so he immediately left to be with him. His one-week trip turned into three months away, ending in gut-wrenching sadness. It wasn't enough that Pete lost his father but it was left to him to make the impossible decision to pull the plug. What little was left of his childhood innocence was robbed of him that day. He returned to me shattered, covered in tattoos, and a complete stranger. So I held him in my arms as tightly as I could, and we promised each other we'd start again from scratch. So we did. A month or so later, he slowly started to find his smile again, and we both found our way back to our special little routine. But fate had other plans.

It was a year of firsts. My first real boyfriend. My first job in the music business. My first orgasm. (Did you see how I just slipped that in there? Speaking of slipping things in . . .) One afternoon, while Pete and I were watching a Borg named Hugh find his humanity on *Star Trek: The Next Generation* and sexing on his mom's lumpy, plaid couch, he started cringing and told me to get off of him. He was in an insane amount of pain. Turns out, he had a hernia, and when he went in for surgery, the doctors realized he had cancer. (Now there's a real curse word for ya!) In that instant, two major earth-shattering events took place: 1) I was about to get a lesson in humility and bravery that would impact me for years to come, and 2) It turns out, I had a cancer-smelling vagina.

I have to admit I'm a bit hesitant to get into all the intimate details of Pete's battle with cancer. It's a heroic story but it is his story and not mine to tell. Plus, I'm not sure a high school senior is qualified to do anything other than mow your lawn under supervision, let alone reflect on something with such gravity. But it was a crucial part of my life that greatly informed the person that I am today, and not a day goes by where I don't use it as a personal source for inner strength. Today, I have a much deeper understanding of what was happening to me at the time . . . and that's a story I'd love to share.

When someone you love gets very sick it changes you. All the bullshit you thought was so critical suddenly becomes irrelevant. You develop a level of focus you never thought possible without your cousin's Adderall. You stop measuring life by years, months, days, or even hours. It all comes down to seconds and your need to make each one of them count. At least, that's the romantic description of the *clusterfuck-bomb* that was about to explode in my life. I was seventeen years old and the boy I was in love with had just been diagnosed with testicular cancer that had metastasized into seminoma. BALL-FUCKING CATASTROFUCK!!!

"If you think the word 'fuck' is healing, then the
word 'fuck' is gonna heal you."
—*Shailene Woodley*

Up until that point in my life, I had not spent a great deal of time focusing on the balls as I had been distracted by their more handsome and striking companion—another hard-learned life lesson: always mind *the stepchildren*. But that was all about to change as *the backup singers* took center stage in my life like Lisa Lisa stepping aside and allowing Cult Jam to take the spotlight. Whether I liked it or not I was about to become incredibly familiar with the *two veg* that accompany *the meat*. Now, you don't go through an experience like this without adopting a fair amount of "ball humor," and I would be remiss if I didn't take a moment to share with you some of my personal favs: *bollocks, cojones, family jewels, coin purse, giggleberries, nards, plums, yam bag*, and my all-time hero, *deez nutz*. Trust me when I tell you *deez nuts* will save your life some day.

Cancer is often called the C-word. I think it's probably because it's the cunt of all the diseases. But to me there's another C-word that describes everyone who has ever faced this *bitch with a capital C* and that word is courageous. I'm not going to pretend to know the depths of the pain and self-inflicted psychological torture Pete suffered through as he faced his own mortality, but I can show you a glimpse of our amazing time together and its profound impact on my life. Quite simply, he was a boy facing invisibility who chose to fight for his life. I was the girl who had the rare privilege of being his companion on his extraordinary journey. When I look back at my time with Pete, I mostly remember his humor, affection, and above all else, his courage.

Pete's journey didn't start when he received his cancer diagnosis. Nope, his dying plate of a meal was served with an aperitif in the form of losing his father to cancer two months earlier. It's as if life was cleansing his palate in preparation for the hot *turd-on-weck* about to be served. It was devastating to watch him face the loss of his father then try to find some sort of equilibrium in order to move forward only to be upended. It brings tears to my eyes when I look back on how much I didn't know what to do for him, how much I felt inadequate in every moment, and how much I wished I could have calmed his fears. But, ultimately, I came to understand that that was not my purpose. I realized that I didn't need to fill every quiet moment with words, I didn't need to have everything or anything figured out, and that I absolutely shouldn't go down the black hole with him. I was there to be the antidote to the darkness. We all were. His family, his friends, and I—we were all points of light in his night sky to help him find his way home.

It was remarkable witnessing Pete navigate this mindfuck-soulfuck of a body slam, twist in the road. There was a certain poetry to it. There's a darkness that envelops the mind when this slim thread of an existence we call life is threatened. That free fall into oblivion is then followed by a deep calm, which at first feels like surrender but it isn't. It's followed by a sense of acceptance and release that then metamorphosizes into a serene state of grace. That's when the fight begins. I didn't know it at the time, but I was getting a life lesson on how to overcome almost anything. A lesson that I would use over and over again in my life. As Pete disintegrated and reemerged, I learned that the fight only ends when you give up.

The journey ahead would be filled with stomach-knotting, heart-racing, vomit-inducing sob fests, and that was just me. I was completely unprepared for what came next, and yet I was totally ready to stand by his side as he wandered through the dangerous part of the city that was his life now. The next twelve months, at times, felt like the longest of our lives. Each day came with a new set of worries and hurdles and each night ended with the illusion of hope. There was a quiet dignity to how Pete handled it all. He was nothing short of heroic.

Senior year was a bit of a blur, to say the least. With my new internship, job, and taking care of my boyfriend, I turned into a motivated machine. Most kids slack off during their last year of school, but I'd never been busier or had more drive and purpose. Truth be told, there was no time to slow down or hesitate. Pete's life was on the line and the first three months were the most complicated. A week after being diagnosed, Pete had to have a very intricate surgery in which many of the surrounding organs had to be removed and examined to eradicate the spreading cancer. If your brain just did a backflip visualizing what I just described, then I think you'd be relieved to know that neither of us knew exactly the nature of the surgery he was about to have at the time. It really didn't matter. We were both in a state of shock.

After the surgery went to plan, he had chemotherapy and radiation treatments for a few months that were so severe that it required him to stay in the hospital for a week at a time. So each day after school let out, I'd head to either my internship at the record label or to my new job at a pet store. Then, around 7 P.M., I'd get myself over to the hospital to snuggle with Pete on his hospital bed until they kicked me out after midnight. When he wasn't at the hospital, I was at his house until I was sent home. Battling cancer can be an isolating experience, but I was determined to be there every second I could. My heart and my embrace were all I had to offer, and they were his for the taking.

We had some sweet times during the year of hell. I can't remember why, but for some reason they had placed him in the children's ward at the hospital, which was a little bizarre, but it didn't stop us from having fun. It's funny the things you remember, like sneaking meatball subs into the hospital or hanging out the window smoking weed . . . you know, to combat nausea . . . it was for medicinal purposes! Then there were the times when we'd have The Germs blasting on the boom box while he was puking his guts out from the chemo, or when I'd make him my famous grilled cheese sandwiches with mustard squeezed into heart shapes on top. Perhaps the gentlest moments were when he was feeling good for a few hours and we'd lie in each other's arms, watching TV like a normal couple. You take what you can get.

Over the course of that year, I learned to stop looking backward and focus on what was right in front of me. To this day, that's how I deal with problems. I don't dwell on what just happened and/or the things I can't control. I don't wallow in misery. I move forward with great deliberation and force and do not allow sentimentality to get in the way. Not because I'm a hard ass, I'm actually quite the softie, but because I gained a singular perspective about what really matters and how not to confuse real problems with the artificial day-to-day nonsense we exaggerate for ourselves. That was Pete's gift to me.

After a year of treatment, I'm happy to say that Pete survived his bout with the blight. Unfortunately, he and I didn't. SHIT-FUCKER-HELL!!!! Soon after he was cleared, Pete dumped me. I was devastated then, but looking back now, I think, perhaps, I was a constant reminder of the year of hell he wanted to put behind him. Perhaps he wanted to set me free because he was back to square one and rebooting his life. Perhaps we had done what we'd each come to do in each other's lives and it was just time. Either way, it didn't matter. I was a rock for that whole year of hell, but at the moment we broke up, I completely fell apart. I think I needed to. Like I said before, I'm a real softie. Pete and I never lost touch and are still friends to this day. He'll always have a special place in my heart.

There were other disappointments waiting for me as well. I thought the music business was going to be something mystical like the Garden of the Hesperides. But alas, my amazing internship ended up being anything but magical. In fact, it was a total buzzkill. What fresh hell was this?!? Where was the sex? The drugs? The MOTHERFUCKINGROCKANDROLL?!?! I had a lot to learn about paying your dues. It turns out that in the music biz, the top executives are the only ones who get to play and live the glamorous life. Everyone else is just a grunt who gets free tickets to shows that nobody wants to go to. And I was the lowliest of grunts, essentially a telemarketer. About 99 percent of what I did was pick up the phone, call radio stations, and say, "Here's this new single; we want you to put it into rotation, mmmkay?" Some people are just born salesmen and know how to talk the talk. I am not a bullshit artist, or as Mel Brooks would say, a "stand-up philosopher," on any level. Anyone who's done it will tell you a hard sell is uncomfortable as fuck and requires a lot of confidence in yourself and what you're selling. Short of that, you better like the taste of urine because you're pissing in the wind. I didn't know what I was doing, and nobody ever said, "Hey, just call up and make friends with these people! Once they get to know you, they might listen to what you're selling." Because, essentially, that's what networking is all about. I was so nervous that I'd cut right to the chase. I didn't even talk about the fucking weather. "Hi," I'd say quickly. "About this album, you're going to play it, right? No? What's that? I should go kill myself? Okay. Thanks. Bye." I was a pathetic saleswoman. It just wasn't in me.

So when I wasn't making an ass out of myself on the phone, I had the mind-numbing job of putting hundreds of CDs in envelopes and mailing them out. But I didn't care. I was living the dream, man. I mean, just the people I was meeting were inspirational. I was so serious about my future career I would take any opportunity to go to music conventions just to practice the art of networking. I remember this one time I drove down to Rochester with a friend to attend a music conference. We saw tons of band showcases and sat in on lectures about making a demo and how to break into the business. I met a super-famous music engineer named Eddie Kramer, who'd been behind the boards for legendary artists like The Beatles, Led Zeppelin, Jimi Hendrix, Eric Clapton, Joe Cocker, KISS, The Rolling Stones, and Whitesnake. (Yeah! I said Whitesnake!) He even recorded the original legendary Woodstock festival. He was the *man,* and he became kind of a mentor to me. When I was stuck not knowing what the next step toward my dream of working at a major record label was because there was no School of Rock or Music Business 101, he's the one that told me, "Go to college and major in communications." So that's what I did.

I didn't have the typical college experience at SUNY Buffalo State. I lived at home instead of in the dorms. While other students were binge drinking, pledging sororities, and fucking frat boys, I was putting in my time at the bars and studying MTV. Hey, it all sounds like fun and games, but this shit was serious! Seriously badass! I majored in communications, but designed my curriculum around music. I took business and marketing courses along with music theory, piano, and singing to complete my electives. Don't get me wrong, I can hold a tune, but I'm no Suzi Quatro!

I remember one time, as part of my grade, I actually had to get up in front of an auditorium filled with thirty-five or forty music students and teachers and sing an old Italian classic called "Dolce Scherza." I had practiced all semester. I was mentally prepared, but it seemed my body had other plans. I had dressed up in recital attire right down to my best Payless heels. As I stood there on the stage, looking out at all the *real* musicians I went to school with, listening to the opening bars of my song, my ankles began to tremble and wouldn't stop. I felt like a fledgling drag queen wearing her first stilettos. It was so disconcerting. I remember thinking, *What the fuck is happening to me? Am I having a ground-up seizure?* I was completely out of control of my own limbs. As I sang, I commanded my body to stop shaking. *Listen, asshole (and all other parts), this is not the time!* That didn't work at all. I decided that directly after this performance my body and I would need to have a serious Janet Jackson–inspired talk about who was in control.

From then on I made it a point to get up in front of people as often as I could, and when my ankles flinched I would hum that Italian classic to myself while mentally reenacting the hobbling scene from *Misery*. It's how I've managed my nerves going forward. So when my body says, *Nope, I'm not doing this anymore,* my brain starts singing "Dolce Scherza." It's a brilliant coping mechanism and not at all that strange to hum aloud and hobble around in public. IT HELPS, OKAY?!

It was around that time that it occurred to me that if I wanted to manage and promote bands, I should probably get a better understanding of what it is they go through. So I started my own acoustic cover band with my buddy Mike, called Blonde on Blonde. If you didn't look too closely, we kind of resembled Gregg Allman and Edie Brickell and had a reputation for killing it in many friends' living rooms, as well as two local dive bars. I put myself in the line of fire in any way I could: dealing with cocky club owners, exhausted tour managers, confused booking agents, lazy label reps, dramatic radio people, fourth-tier roadies, drunken local yokels, you name it! It proved to be very useful because the road to a successful career in music is paved with a cavalcade of shitballs being thrown at you, so learning how to duck and weave is critical. After a while, I perfected my signature move, which was a combo duck, weave, sachet, jazz hands, and "look over there!"

During my time in college, I added three more music internships to my growing résumé—with a promoter, a radio station, and another label, Rhapsody Music, owned by local icon and "hit maker," Jerry Meyers, who had worked with the likes of Neil Diamond, Dolly Parton, and

Barry Manilow. I was making friends everywhere, which led to my very first on-camera gig interviewing area bands for a public-access TV show. To me, this might as well have been MTV!! But it was an epic night of missteps. First off, they sent me to a show at a club, but I was under twenty-one, and they wouldn't let me in. I snuck in by picking up gear in the loading area out back and walking it in like I was a roadie (think Baby carrying a watermelon into the club in the movie *Dirty Dancing*). Second, I was nervous as a motherfucker and had no idea what I was doing. Third, I made the cardinal sin of calling the band the wrong name—instead of Grain Assault, I called them Grain of Salt—and they made sure to, painfully, correct me live on TV. Horrifying! If you know anything about bands, you know their names are sacrosanct. I might as well have called their mothers whores. It would have been slightly more forgivable. And last, but certainly not least, as soon as the interview started, our lights turned on, and the security recognized me from earlier and kicked me out of the club. My first day in "the showbiz" was an ignominious fucktastrophe!!

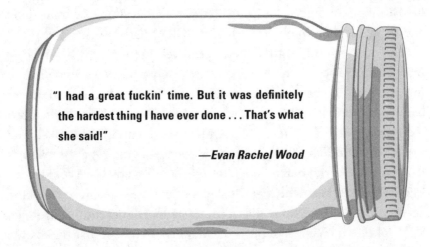

"I had a great fuckin' time. But it was definitely the hardest thing I have ever done . . . That's what she said!"

—*Evan Rachel Wood*

My entire time in college, I dated a really talented and respected guitar player in a local heavy metal band with a decent following. He was as close as you could get to a local rock star in Buffalo. He had perfected the lifestyle. From his music, to his hair, to his *inner asshole* (an absolute necessity if you want to be a *panty-dropper*). I was so in love, and pretty soon my whole life centered on him and the band. I was their promoter, their roadie, their flyer-putter-upper—I was doing everything. I also used the band for any projects I was doing for school. In one class I had to design a mock magazine cover, so I put them on *Rolling Stone*. I came up with my own Lollapalooza-style festival and used them as the headliners. Just so we're clear, I was more Sharon Osbourne than Yoko Ono!

Anyway, my heavy metal boyfriend was my initiation to all things rock 'n' roll. I'd go to school, go to work, and do my internship, then go straight to his house and do him or whatever we had to do for the band. Are you seeing a pattern here? So, no, I wasn't playing beer pong, Saran-wrapping my passed-out roommate to a couch, or setting anything on fire. My biggest concern wasn't drinking on the weekends or drawing dicks on people's faces. I was having a blast, but I was hustling. While I was out I was pressing flesh and making sure people would show up to my boyfriend's gigs because that's what a real promoter would be doing: always working it. That was my idea of fun. In the immortal words of Pharrell and Jay Z, "I'm a hustler, baby. I just want you to know. It ain't where I been, it's where I'm 'bout to go." I'm still like that now when I go out. I always feel better when I have something to do or a reason for being. It didn't take long before I started getting antsy. I wanted more from my life than this city had to offer. I yearned for better opportunities and broader horizons. I was ready to take the necessary steps. The scene in Buffalo was starting to close in around me, and it was starting to feel like it was time for me to get the fuck out of Dodge.

There was one big problem: I was super motivated and working my ass off, but my boyfriend appeared to be working really hard at being a medium-sized fish in a shrinking pond (with the exception of his reign as New York state foosball champion, of course. Long live the king!). There was a certain point where it felt like I couldn't get him to leave the house unless he had a gig or a foosball tournament. He'd sit in front of the TV watching football and get irritated when I'd beg him to do anything other than that. We began to fight constantly. I was ready to help him take his band to the next level, which meant moving out of the city. But it seemed like he didn't want to leave the comfort of the fading glow of his current spotlight. Like the old saying goes, "You can lead a jack-ass to water, but you can't make him do the two-step."

The closer I got to graduation, the more and more I realized I needed way more money if I was planning to shuffle out of Buffalo. The most immediate solution to my problem was questionable, at best, but it ended up becoming an unexpected life lesson. One that would reignite years of angst and self-doubt before putting me on the road to recovery. And it happened, of all places . . . at Hooters. That's right, the restaurant that probably started one day when two guys were sitting around and one of them said, "I really wish there was a place we could go to eat where all of the women have huge knockers that we could stare at but we could pretend we weren't because they also serve food." That's right, the home of objectification and wings (I made that up. Pretty catchy right?)—with probably the single most revealing and unflattering company uniform in the history of uniforms (with the exception of the 2014 Colombian Women's Cycling Team)—turned out to be my turning point.

I really needed a job that paid more than minimum wage, and since I had zero work experience, my options were fairly limited. My brother had a friend who worked at Hooters, and she suggested that I fill out an application. Being a former stripper, working at Hooters was no big deal to her (again, from another one of my favorite rappers, Missy Elliott: "Ain't no shame, ladies do your thang. Just make sure you ahead of the game." Rappers really are the best when it comes to business and acquisitions). Plus, she was a cute rocker chick who had teased-out long brown hair, wore short-shorts, and had her tits out on a daily basis anyway. I was frightened. I had spent my whole life hiding my *balloons* and now I was just supposed to float them out for everyone to see? Not only that, I had never waited a table in my life. She told me not to worry and that I would be perfect. I said, "How does having no experience at something make you perfect for it?" To which she quickly replied, "You have big tits! You could spit on their wings as you put them on the table and you'd still be perfect."

It was a nightmare, but I was in serious need of cash and desperate times call for desperate measures. So I decided to go for it. I didn't sleep at all the night before the interview. It was awful. When I woke up in the morning, I put on a bathing suit and some jean shorts, which was the skimpiest outfit I could find, gave myself a pep talk, and drove down there. The interview was degrading on every fucking level. But I knew I had to act the part to get the job, and by "act the part" I mean show off my *sweater puppies*. Basically, I got the job right when I walked into the office. No shocker, seeing as my *momma's spongecakes* were bigger than EVERYONE ELSE'S in the whole place! I barely had to open my mouth before the dude was like, "Sure! We'll give you a job!"

He then took out a Hooters uniform to talk to me about sizes. Sensing that I had a little bit of leverage in the situation (and by leverage I mean more than *two handfuls* of leverage), I played a little hard-to-get. "Here's the thing—I'm not comfortable wearing that," I said bluntly. You know, the minuscule white tank and orange shorts. The guy looked at me like I was out of my fucking mind, as I sat there in front of him with my *funbags* in his face. You would have thought that I'd just told him we lived on Mars and his penis was actually a coin purse (which is ridiculous because everyone knows that's what your balls are).

"This is the uniform that all of our girls wear," he said.

"I get that. What jobs do you have available where the girls don't wear that?" I asked.

Still stunned, he said, "Ummm . . . Okayyyy? How about we make you our hostess? They wear white tennis shorts and a polo shirt."

"I'll take it!" I replied.

Did I look like Blair O'Neal's awkward little sister? Yes! But it was better than the alternative and I was officially employed.

So there I was: a hostess at Hooters. It was my first successful negotiation. I thanked my lucky stars every day that I was not a waitress working at that place. It was horrifying watching the way people treat the waitresses! For me, working there turned out to be an incredible societal experiment on the power of *paw patties*. I noticed that people judged you immediately on the size of your *milk cans* and how tight your shirt was. What I wasn't prepared for was that the MOST judgmental people were the women. I couldn't believe it. They would come in and just act disgusted toward all of us, like we had made them come into the restaurant and made them stare at our *cha-chas*. They made snide remarks under their breath about "getting a real job" and "having some respect for yourself" and "How the fuck can you even work here?" but still those same women came in every day to eat lunch. I couldn't quite figure it out. The female employees of Hooters are a tough bunch of women just trying to make an honest buck. The way I see it, if you can deal with that place every day, you can deal with fucking anything life throws at you!

The male customers weren't much better, either, and the managers were scumbags. It was as if we were at a *Caligulan grab-ass* tournament run by a group of hormonal teenagers on a power trip. I heard rumors about girls who would get cornered by the bosses in the back room and end up sleeping with them, thinking that's how to get a leg up at the restaurant. (Word to the wise: a leg up gets you further, two legs up gets you fucked!) Luckily, none of that happened to me. By then I had developed a higher tolerance for that sort of harassment, having dealt with my décolletage constantly from such an early age. So when anyone made cruder than normal comments about my *Gerber-servers*, I'd say, "Thank you!" with a smile, and then seat them at the table closest to the *shitter*. Why do I call it the shitter? Because on any average day, those toilets were the victims of *T.S.R. (Toilet Shit Rape.)* What people were doing in there after gobbling up twenty-five Original Hooters Style hot wings and a pitcher of beer was nothing short of a *fecal sexual assault*. You could file charges. It was fucking gross. Trust me when I tell you, you'd rather rub your naked body against a peep show booth's wall on *"all you can pud"* night than use those bathrooms.

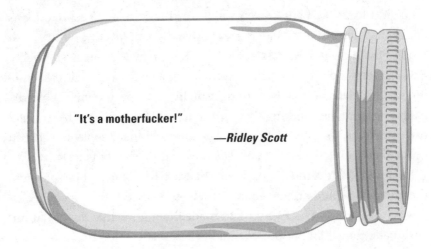

"It's a motherfucker!"

—*Ridley Scott*

But, overall, men were easier to figure out: **Boobs = Good**.

It was the same expression you would see on a dog's face if you held a treat just out of reach in front of its nose. Tongue out and everything, Snapchat-style! That's when I started to figure out the give-and-take that came with my *chesticles*. I had been objectified by men for years, and one day it just clicked. If you are going to objectify me, I am going to manipulate you. Not in a horrible way where you leave your family and sell your house, but in the exact way that the people who had opened Hooters had envisioned. You get to stare and make stupid comments that you think are funny, and I get to make a few extra bucks.

The venom that was spit at us by other women was actually harder for me to come to grips with. But as I looked at the waitresses, they walked around that place with confidence that I could only wish I had. One of the girls said to me:

"If you had a giant belly would they hate you?"
No.
"If you had big, buck teeth would they hate you?"
No.
"If you had a lazy eye would they hate you?"
No.
"Then what do you think the problem really is?"

Whatever hate they were spewing had nothing to do with me and my *coconuts*; it was all them. It was a great lesson to learn from someone named "Cinnamon," who had a winking-cheetah tramp-stamp tattoo. Sages come in all shapes and sizes, I guess.

I was finally feeling free from the burden of my *Danny DeVitos* and was excited to start inviting them to be a part of my life. The more I used them to my "advantage," the less ashamed of them I became. All of the shame I used to feel about people looking at them, I started to turn into power and confidence. I was starting to make peace with my *Chumbawumbas* and it felt good.

I didn't know it then, but there would come a day when me and my *Brad Pitts* would bounce rampant all over Hollywood, breaking all of its rules and leaving a trail of happy celebrities in our wake. I could never have imagined little ol' me, face-to-face with Will Smith, getting into some ridiculous situation involving my *Pointer Sisters*!

Years later I would be invited to interview Will at the junket for his movie *I Am Legend*, and things quickly veered off track. Will's great in interview situations. He totally gets it. The man knows how to play along while giving you exactly what you need to put together a hilarious piece of footage. I've interviewed him several times, but none were ever quite as raucous as this one. My buddies in the room had given him a heads-up that I was coming. So when I walked in, the scene was already set for some craziness. Will knew the seat belts were off on this *anything goes ride!*

Me: I actually heard a rumor, they're installing plastic seat covers on the theater seats . . .

Will: The theater seats . . . yeah, yeah, yeah. *(Nodding.)*

Me: Because people are actually shitting themselves.

Will: Yeah . . . it's not shit. It's . . . you know . . . it's not . . . people's asses are leaking.

Me: Oh . . . we got the cross. *(I try to get comfortable in this awkwardly low chair by crossing my legs and in the process lean forward just enough to accidentally set him up for the* Cleavage Challenge.*)*

Will: Wooooooh! *(Will catches a glimpse and that's all she wrote. He was going to take full advantage of this opportunity to have some fun messing with me and I was happy to play along.)* That's really sexy to me right now! *(He's got a huge smile on his face and is trying to keep it together. He yells:)* You have no idea. What you just did to me.
(The whole room comes alive: cameramen, publicists, studio reps, everyone just gets louder and louder with laughter.)

Me: Woah . . . Woah. *(Turning around in amazement of all the commotion.)*

Will: All right, guys, all right, all right, okay . . . all right. *(Trying to calm the room and himself down.)* . . . So I'm . . . I'm gonna . . .

Me: It's the leaning thing, isn't it? *(So I start fucking with him back as I lean over again, revealing a little more of the* snuggle pups *and playing into the whole craziness.)* I apologize . . . *(Laughing sarcastically.)*

Will: Yeah . . . you're doin' . . . you're doin' it a lot . . . you're doin' it a lot.

Me: Wooooh . . . *(I laugh and then it happens as I lean over again for another sampling of the* dueling banjos.*)* And I'm sorry.

Will: I'm keepin' my legs crossed, keepin' my legs crossed. *(Jokingly implying that there might be some tightness in his pants.)*

Me: *(Laughing. All expectations of an actual Q&A interview are gone, but I know that this exchange is nothing short of hysterical.)*

Will: She'll be here all week, folks, don't forget to try the veal. Ha-ha. *(Laughing.)*

You see, when I finally embraced *Fred and Ethel*, the whole world opened up. By not running from what was obviously a big part of me, I became comfortable in my own skin and, in turn, a lot more of my personality was able to shine. It was incredibly liberating in every aspect of my life. It would have been unfathomable to me, in my early twenties, to be in a room where my *double whammies* were the subject of a fun game and yet, here I was, years later, actually the one instigating it. Will was playing with me, and I was playing with him right back. How much better could it get?!!

But in that moment, way back then, it was one important step in the evolution of me becoming friends with my *bouncing Buddhas*. I had managed to sustain a job at Hooters and not exploit myself. I learned that I can control how people see me by how much I reveal to them. Up to this point, I had been pretty oblivious to the power of my *Picasso cubes*. For the first time, I realized that I can actually get shit done with these things. I thought, *We're going to be stuck together for a while, so let's make the best of it.* And, free drinks. Did I mention free drinks?

Right before my next birthday, the foosball champ and I broke up for the last time. I had had enough and felt that the time was right to make my journey to Mecca—Los Angeles. I left his house crying, picked up the phone, called the airline, and bought a one-way ticket. I had seven hundred dollars saved and a buddy's couch to crash on.

"I'm going to Los Angeles for a month," I told my parents. "If I can find a job, I'm not coming home."

I never came home.

4

GLORY, GLORY, HO-LE-LUYAH!

I don't exactly know what I mean by that,
but I mean it.
—The Catcher in the Rye, *J. D. Salinger*

If you ask me, I'd say the key to succeeding in show business can be narrowed down to two things: perseverance and integrity. More aptly put: the ability to persevere in the complete absence of integrity. Don't get me wrong, show business is a lot of fun, and all of us who have had the privilege of taking a hit of its sweet kush will tell you it's an intoxicating treat. But as with all things intoxicating, it brings out the best and the very worst in people. So be true to yourself, leave your inhibitions and insecurities at the door, and enjoy the ride. It's a doozy!

An old industry pro once told me that if you were to rank the four key components of the entertainment industry in order of the least slimy to the most it would be:

Film.
TV.
Porn.
. . . then Music.

Well, it was safe to say I was starting at the bottom, and apparently, the forecast for the journey ahead was *"creepy with a chance of the bizarre"* that would challenge even a teratophiliac. What was not clear at the time was that in order to find success, I'd not only have to play many games of Dodge the Weasel but I'd also have to help launch a whole new category. No, not a new porn category: a new entertainment category. The only thing standing in the way was my total lack of ambition to be a star. I mean zero fucking interest. I liked getting my hands dirty behind the scenes, I had a potty mouth, I called bands by the wrong name, and I laughed too much. Not exactly broadcast material.

They never saw me coming. Hell, I never saw me coming. Basically, nobody saw anybody coming!

My dream was to have a business card that said, I'LL MAKE YA FAMOUS! stolen from my favorite line in the movie *Young Guns*. But it's hard to make rent, let alone make anyone famous, when you're just getting on your feet. That was me two weeks after landing in LA. This town has a way of sobering you up fast, like a coffee enema. To make matters worse, I lost what little I had when my purse was stolen at the Key Club on Sunset Boulevard. Ironically, it all went down when the same girl who got me the Hooters job back in Buffalo, and had since also moved out to Los Angeles, invited me out dancing with a bunch of her stripper friends.

Again, I should have known better.

"You guys can just leave your bags with the bartender!" she screamed over the music. So of course, like a *fucktard*, I handed my purse with my New York State driver's license, credit cards, and the last of my cash to a complete stranger. I return ten minutes later . . . presto chango . . . "Doug Henning" behind the bar had disappeared along with my purse. I had literally lost everything. I was devastated. But just as things were getting bleak, a male friend of the strippers' came to my rescue and helped me find my purse. He would later become a close friend of mine and eventually help me find my first job in LA and a place to stay. That's the other interesting thing about this town: right after someone smacks you in the back of the head, someone else shows up with an ice pack and helps you get up. Anyway, later in the night, we found my bag downstairs, shoved in the corner of a pee-stained bathroom stall, completely emptied and covered in something only a black light would appreciate.

Needless to say, I had to find a job right away and a new ID. My mom had to snail mail me my birth certificate for a new driver's license, and just like that, I became a California resident. A jobless, penniless, homeless California resident. I crashed on a friend's couch and sent my résumé to every record label I could think of—the majors like Warner Bros., Capitol, Geffen when it was still Geffen, and a bunch of smaller ones. Eddie Kramer, my engineer friend from back home, hooked me up with a few meet-and-greets, and I busted my ass to meet as many people as I could. Here's how these interviews went down: Either the guys I met with tried to talk me into having sex with them or they simply said, "Good luck, kid, wish I could help but I've got my own problems."

A couple of contacts suggested that I start in the mailroom. That's how so many media moguls, like David Geffen, Barry Diller, and Ron Meyer, started their careers. Simon Cowell started at the bottom in the EMI mailroom and became an A&R legend. Jim Toth cut his teeth in the legendary CAA mailroom, and now he's the agent for Scarlett Johansson and Matthew McConaughey, and married to Reese Wither-spoon.

"Cool, how do I do that?" I asked hopefully.

"You gotta fuck somebody in the mailroom, silly."

Okay, nobody actually said that, and it's unlikely Ron Meyer ever had to throw his legs in the air (like he just don't care) to get ahead . . . Simon Cowell, perhaps . . . just kidding, but it was crystal clear that for me that was the path of least resistance. Maybe it's different now, but I doubt it. That's just how it kind of works. I'd say that half the people in the business have positions that they deserve and the other half have positions they've "earned" . . . the hard way. I'm not here to judge who did what to whom and where in order to get to where they are. I prefer to assume that regardless of how anyone got to where they're at, it's a safe bet that they paid a heavy price . . . one way or the other. And unless you've walked a mile in their shoes, what the fuck do you know?!

I know the casting couch seems very seventies-mustache porn, but don't kid yourself into thinking it doesn't exist anymore just because Be-yoncé, Rihanna, Lady Gaga, and Katy Perry have convened a girl-power summit at the top of the charts. It still comes up all the time, at every level. Not too long ago, I had a very prominent agent take me out to din-ner and tell me, "You should probably just have sex with me. It won't get complicated because I'm not going to rep you anyway." As if somehow the pressure was now off of me, and the all-night game of *Alabama Whac-a-Mole* he'd been imagining on the drive over to Cecconi's was a go. There were many, many ways I could have reacted to this, but I've developed a sense of humor about this kind of nonsense and I rebuffed his *self-felating* moment with, "Wow. That's a relief! I hate messy sex." And then proceeded to order shaved white truffles on everything and let him pay the bill. I figured, tonight, it was this *shizzbubble's* turn to get the *prolapsed butthole*. Ladies, remember, no matter what, you must keep your cool. As Patrick Swayze's character Dalton said in *Road House,* "Be nice. Be nice until it's time to not be nice." Trust me, you'll know when.

Truth be told, there is something strangely bizarre about the antiquated rites and rituals of the blatant misogyny that pervades the entertainment industry. It's like a self-perpetuating, self-contained *schlong-based ecosystem* that exists outside of time and space. It's nothing short of Kafkaesque. Now if you haven't read your Franz Kafka like good little boys and girls, don't take my word for it. In a December 1991 interview with *The New York Times,* celebrated literary biographer Frederick R. Karl defined "Kafkaesque" to be "when you enter a surreal world in which all of your control patterns, all your plans, the whole way in which you have configured your own behavior, begins to fall to pieces, when you find yourself against a force that does not lend itself to the way you perceive the world." Or as one of my agents once put it, "It's counterintuitive, baby." Eventually this archaic *cum-bubble* will burst, but until then, here's my advice on how to best handle yourself. Cue Ice Cube . . . "You betta check yo'self, before you wreck yo'self!"

Think of the entertainment industry as a giant "glory hole convention." It's sold out, very crowded, and incredibly *hard* to get into. The members that organize and operate this event insist on a certain degree of anonymity and are very selective about who they allow in. Most people will do just about anything to get in and walk through this *magical kingdom,* while others might find a lucky ticket. Once you're in, be prepared: There are *dicks* everywhere. There are *peckers* covering the floors, the walls, and the ceilings. A parade of *dong* as far as the eyes can see; all of them seeking attention, adulation, and respect. It's competitive, too. Oh, yes. Everyone thinks their own *cock* is bigger and better; with every *dodel* being waved around like a magic wand casting a spell. Some attendees will be mesmerized and others repulsed. Some will partake of the *dong buffet* while others will run for the exit. This is where we as women must separate the wheat from the *shaft.* Don't be distracted, don't despair, and above all else, don't run away. That's what they want you to do. These *pricks* are only as powerful as you allow them to be. Believe it or not, you are still in control of your destiny.

These four easy steps will help you navigate this *penis pavilion*. First, accept the fact that you are attending a glory hole convention and not your grandma's garden party. Second, realize that behind every *schwantz* is an insecure person trying to stand out in a congregation of *willies*. Third, understand that coexistence with these *knobs* is not a defeat and it doesn't mean you have to engage with them. Just exercise a bit of tolerance. Think of them as shitty art on the wall of a fleabag motel that rents by the hour. And lastly, don't be afraid to grow a *dick* yourself because at some point you're going to find out that quite a few of those *todgers* coming out of the walls belong to women. If you take my advice, pretty soon you'll just stop being distracted by the ocean of *wang* and move about your business, enjoying everything else the convention has to offer. What you will eventually figure out is that this glory hole convention known as "the showbiz" is nothing but a meaningless display of a postmodern existential crisis, otherwise known as *Disneyland for dicks*. Once you get past the fact that you're getting manipulated for money, it's an awesome time!

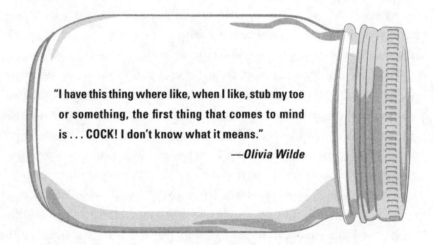

"I have this thing where like, when I like, stub my toe or something, the first thing that comes to mind is . . . COCK! I don't know what it means."
—*Olivia Wilde*

But I digress. Now, back to my story.

On the record label job front, I'd give myself an A+ for effort, but an F for execution. It just wasn't happening. I was starting to feel as useless as a shirt on Matthew McConaughey. But it just so happened that I had made a friend who lived at a *Melrose Place*–looking apartment complex in West LA who kept inviting me to come hang out and meet some of her friends in the biz. I was a bit reticent because, for the uninitiated, usually those types of apartment complexes are the perfect front for "incall" escorts. Not that I have a problem with that, but I wasn't looking for a career giving HJs on the DL. So I was a bit concerned about what "biz" she was trying to hook me up in. However, I set my concerns aside and swung by and discovered that it was legit. It was teeming with young and hungry actors, writers, producers, musicians, and hustlers, so I started hanging out there a lot and meeting all kinds of cool people. It was networking without actually networking. One afternoon, while I was lying out at the pool, I met a girl who said she worked for Hans Zimmer. "You want to work around music, right?" she asked. "We need a receptionist."

Yeah, I did, but I had no clue who Hans Zimmer was. I pretended I did and made a mental note to look him up later on this fabulous new Web site called Google. Turns out, he was and is one of the most prolific Academy Award–winning film composers in Hollywood history. *Rain Man, Driving Miss Daisy, Thelma & Louise, The Lion King, Gladiator, The Simpsons Movie,* The *Dark Knight* Trilogy, *12 Years a Slave, Man of Steel, Interstellar* . . . the list is endless and epic. I had very little knowledge about what music in film was but got schooled the second I walked through his front door. The heavens opened up and every hair on my body got a stiffy. Imagine this huge office-building compound, where every room has the most heavenly, ethereal music wafting out of the doors. Walking down the hallways, it was like a creative mega-hive filled with composers, scoring all of the biggest movies you've ever heard of. After the interview, which I didn't screw up thanks to my Google search, they asked me if I wanted the job. I believe my answer was, "Fuck yes! I want the job."

It was a pivotal moment in my life working for Hans. My understanding of the music world was blown wide open. Turns out, composers are rock stars as well. I was so happy and energized being around all of these creative people 24/7. I got a promotion pretty quickly, running a department that had three music editors. My job was to keep everybody in line, making sure they showed up to their temp scores and dubbing sessions and filling out their cue sheets, a log of all the music used in the movies. This was a whole new world for me, and I was absorbing all of it. I made a lot of lifelong friends there who I'm still in touch with today and who have played crucial roles in this crazy voyage I've been on. Hans was an amazing and inspirational person to work for, and I couldn't have asked for a better mentor in my life. His kindness and generosity toward me all these years has only been eclipsed by his grace. From buying me my first television set to being the first call I receive every time I get a new gig or leave one, he set the bar super high on what being a man of great character is, and I'm incredibly proud to call him my friend.

I was making a decent salary and able to rent my first little studio apartment in Studio City. It had a Murphy bed coming out of the wall, and it was next to a reservoir where police had recently found a human head. It was both functional and fucked up. I was home. After bumming rides for far too long, I decided it was time to buy a car. Back in Buffalo, I'd always gotten two-hundred-buck hand-me-downs from my siblings, like a green Chevy Impala and a little black Fiero I christened "the Batmobile." A clunker wasn't going to cut it here. In Hollywood, it's all about the car you drive. You could be living in a cardboard box under the 101 freeway, but you better have some sweet wheels to pull up to the valet you can't afford.

I noticed that all the cool kids drove vintage muscle cars. So one day, when I spotted a candy-apple-red 1964 ½ Mustang for sale in a parking lot off the 405, I just knew it had to be mine. So what if it was in a go-kart racing lot and had a bumper sticker on it that read: IS YOUR DADDY IN JAIL? 'CAUSE IF I WAS YOUR DADDY, I'D BE IN JAIL? She and I were meant to be together. Like a nine-year-old anxiously coveting her first My Little Pony, I took it for a test drive but never bothered looking under the hood. Which is too bad because if I had, I would have discovered that the car was more of a *Cleveland steamer* than a Ford Mustang. And despite the fact that it was missing spark plugs, I happily plunked down fifteen hundred dollars and drove off the lot believing I had legit street cred.

On the ride home on the 405, in that spot between Santa Monica and the Valley, my beautiful lemon barely made it up the hill. I had to putter along in the right lane like a grandma, while fully functioning automobiles whizzed by, honking and waving the finger out the window at me. Flash forward a year: I'd hemorrhaged about seven thousand dollars trying to keep it running, then sold it for a thousand. I lost my ass on that car. Which reminds me of a great joke I saw on Instagram: "How did the hipster burn his tongue? He sipped his coffee before it was cool." I was in no position, in my current financial situation, to be driving a cool kids cars. After that fiasco, I decided to drive a very sensible black

Nissan Sentra that I bought on the cheap as it came with a unique theft-deterrent system I affectionately called *"the Skunkmaster 2000."* The Sentra was on the top ten list of most stolen cars, but anyone who would try to steal my baby would be engulfed in the soul-hugging stench of cat piss and Febreze: a noxious cocktail that did not buy me any friends in the valet-parking community.

So I had a few setbacks, but I was loving my new life and hoped my brother, Sean, might follow me out to the West Coast. My brother has always been a dreamer, with all these amazing ideas that I thought he would have a better chance of bringing to life out here in LA. So I lured him out for a visit, and even though we rocked out together at a Pantera/Black Sabbath show, I could tell that LA just wasn't for him. He was a country mouse at heart and I was becoming a full-on city mouse. I realize now that Sean was exactly where he needed to be because less than a year later he met the love of his life, Jill, and married her in a fairy-tale wedding. She wrapped her arms around the fireball that is my brother with love and devotion; gave him a sense of purpose and turned his world right-side up. I don't see my brother as much I'd like to and I really miss getting into trouble with him, but each time I see their beautiful daughter (my niece), Piper, I stop wondering about what could've been and feel great about what is. Me, on the other hand, I was 2,534.6 miles away from Buffalo in every way: body, mind, and soul, and it was, exactly, where I needed to be.

After working for Hans for a while, I started to get the itch. I wasn't a composer, so there was only so far I could advance at his company. I got wind that another legendary composer, W. G. Snuffy Walden, was looking for someone to manage his shop, and something inside told me I needed to be there. So off I went. Little did I know how that decision would play a huge role in crafting the rest of my life. Snuffy was another incredible soul and mentor. He was and is arguably one the best composers on TV as well as one of the kindest and most caring people I've ever met. He is a recovering alcoholic and has spent more time than you could imagine sponsoring and helping those in recovery. We bonded pretty quickly, and I learned so much from him about compassion and humanity. Those lessons would prove themselves to be priceless in the future as I dealt with friends who had been crippled by drugs and alcohol. And, as a bonus, he introduced me to his friend "Uncle Steve," aka the legendary Steve Perry from Journey. Woohoo!

It was while I was at Snuffy's that I became friends with an extremely talented musician and all-around *cool cat* named Troy Hardy. He was the son of a luthier, who had moved to LA from the Midwest with his wife, Melissa, with a dream of working in the music industry. He was from western Michigan, I was from western New York, and our relationship was basically two people giving each other shit all day. I sarcastically called him "Boy" to make him feel like less of a man and to put a *pickle* in his ass, and he called me "Girl" to shove that same *pickle* right back. We were the same kind of idiot. Brothers from another mother. Needless to say, we truly enjoyed working together, and it was he who introduced me to the man who would completely change my life.

Troy knew I was growing tired of doing office work when I really wanted to be out there doing what I loved, which was promoting bands. So one day, out of the blue, he came to me with an interesting opportunity. He told me his bandmate and lead singer in their group, The Gingerpigs, was looking to hire someone at his Web start-up called Netgroupie, which was going to be a new music marketing platform. Once I got past the notion that it sounded like a dating site for band sluts, I thought, what the hell, it could be cool. It was the dawn of the digital Wild West, and a lot of interesting things were happening. I was intrigued. The only problem was ideas are like toilets; everyone has them but most of them are full of shit. I told Troy I'd check out one of their live gigs and meet him. I figured the worst that could happen was I'd spend an evening being verbally molested by another showbiz schmuck wafting in the smell of his own *dook.*

It wouldn't have been the first time.

5

IT'S ALL ABOUT THE COCK!

When in doubt, go for the dick joke.
—Robin Williams

Kourosh.

What can I say about the man who was destined to become my best friend and business partner? He's always been a bit mysterious and somewhat enigmatic. When I first met him, he had a ponytail and didn't talk a lot. He's always believed that there is great strength in silence (very Yoda of him). He has these really intense eyes that are both intimidating and yet very kind. There is a strange duality about him. He is creative at heart and business in mind. He is the juxtaposition of mutually independent disciplines in an industry that is typically all crazy or all business. On top of that, he wasn't preoccupied with how big his dick was and how badly he wanted to show it to me. Quite the surprise he was (there's that Yoda thing, again).

Without a doubt, meeting Kourosh Taj was my *butterfly effect* moment. The one single occurrence that changed the course of my life forever. When I showed up that night, at some shitty bar in Santa Monica, I didn't really have any major expectations. Little did I know that this enigmatic Persian guy already had big plans for me, simply based on Troy telling him, "Carrie's a good hang. You should talk to her." Good ol' Troy, always great with the heavy-handed and layered introductions. It was his gift!

Kourosh and I instantly hit it off. Even though he had a debonair British accent and this way about him, he was actually quite humble and a little shy, which was quite endearing. But when he started talking about his Web project, he came alive with a massive jolt of charisma. He had such vision and boldness that it almost bordered on arrogance. But it was incredibly captivating. I've always had a thing for confidence. Besides, once we bonded over our mutual love of *Rocky, Rambo,* and all things Stallone, it was, in my mind, a fait accompli. I mean we spoke for twenty minutes about the impact Sly's trucker-arm-wrestling movie *Over the Top* had on our lives when we were kids and why his movie *Oscar* is an underappreciated gem. It quickly became obvious that we shared the same fucked-up sense of humor. So after chatting a bit, I told him I'd love to talk further about a job at his company.

A week later, we sat down at this awesomely crappy little diner in the Valley, and Kourosh passionately painted me an even bigger picture of what he had planned. At the time, they had raised an initial round of funding from an angel investor, had a staff of about five people, and were an aggregator of music content from a hundred producer/affiliates and another fifty live music venues nationwide. They were building an independent music marketing network, which was music to my ears. But Kourosh had bigger plans. He wanted to create his own channel. He had big ideas and even bigger balls. I have to admit I respect a big ego, but only if you can back it up. There are so many douchebags in Hollywood who talk a big game but don't do jack. Sometimes, this town feels like a never-ending World Series of Talk where a *verbal jerkoff* is the equivalent of a grand slam home run! For some reason, I instinctively knew Kourosh was not full of shit. At that point, I wasn't exactly sure why he wanted me so badly to be a part of this grand scheme, but I could tell he wasn't going to take no for an answer. Like my dad, Kourosh was an entrepreneur, dreamer, thinker, and doer. No risk, no reward was in my blood. I told him I was in.

A lot of people think they know exactly what they want. They become so adamant that it can only be one way that they end up missing out on all of the other amazing things that can happen. In my case, I went where the Santa Ana winds took me as long as it was in the neighborhood of what I loved. It wasn't like one day I wanted to work at a record label and the next day I decided to be a professional snake milker. Although that would be fun, too. What Kourosh was doing with Netgroupie was music related and it was building something from the ground up. He was a pioneer in a new frontier. Laying down creative roots and building a professional family, which were things that mattered to me. Whether it failed or succeeded, at least it would be mine, ours.

Eventually, Kourosh revealed his hand at our next meeting. It turns out he knew from the beginning that he wanted me to be on camera. He started telling me about his exhaustive search for a lead anchor and a face for the network. And how everyone he had met with had had a lot of media training and/or received a degree in broadcast journalism but that none of them felt right. He wanted someone spontaneous and unlike the robotic mannequins who speak with the same cadence that we're used to seeing on entertainment newsmagazine shows. He was determined to find someone *not* classically trained in journalism. Someone who wouldn't know what the rules were so they would be free to break them and just have fun having raw, real conversations with the talent. Someone who could jump right in and engage people during interviews. He was looking for charisma and told me he was convinced that since I had disarmed him in our meetings, I could disarm anyone.

Here I was, thinking we were joining forces so we could build this amazing company together. I had no clue that he had an ulterior motive. He may have been right, but it was completely overwhelming and not at all what I was even remotely interested in. It wasn't what I'd signed up for, and I didn't want to do it. I said "No" on the spot. Then the chase to get me to change my mind began.

I saw Kourosh as a visionary, but I thought he was delusional about me being the face of the network. I was no Mary Hart, and I had zilch for experience. He envisioned me on camera. I saw myself marketing, promoting, and working behind the scenes. He was insistent. "Come and do the interviews for me," he'd plead. I must have said no a hundred times! I simply had no interest in being in the spotlight. So then, in his infinite wisdom or a brilliant display of cajolery, he backed down and offered me a position behind the scenes in affiliate relations.

My first day working at Netgroupie was kind of a disaster. My very first assignment was to continue building relationships with our affiliates so they'd feel comfortable sending us their content. As we developed this national marketing network, we were basically working with some of the best local producers and live venues across the country in an effort to aggregate their original video content in all different genres— hip-hop, country, pop, punk, everything. It all felt oddly familiar. I was networking with and soliciting people, which was the exact thing I'd sucked at when I'd interned at the record labels. "Um, hi, do you want to send us stuff? No? Okay, thanks. Bye!" These kinds of calls are uncomfortable at best, and I was so nervous about doing it. But I had my own office and I was getting paid, so I had no choice but to dive right in. Ultimately, I discovered that our affiliates were really sweet people who were excited to be working with us. There really was no hard sell, just fun conversations.

Already in place at Netgroupie was a small but interesting cast of characters. A couple of standouts were their chairman of the board of directors, Al Cafaro, a music industry icon and former CEO of A&M Records. Kourosh thinks the world of Al and was incredibly honored when he agreed to join the company. He would always tell me that Al was the first person to stand up and be counted and provide legitimacy to his idea. Without him, we would never have gotten off the ground. I found Al to be smart and incredibly charming. He has always been supportive and kind to me, even to this day.

On the opposite end of the spectrum, there was a guy who was related to music industry royalty. I guess he and Kourosh started out as friends, and he was brought into the company as a partner for his connections and to help with fund-raising. As Kourosh would say, "It's not about who you know, it's about who knows you." But things don't always work out the way they're meant to, and you've got to roll with the hand you're dealt. Start-ups are a major fucking 24/7 hustle. You've got to be willing to put yourself on the line and get your hands dirty to get shit done. It ain't no nine-to-five *yak-shaving* exercise! Some people are built for that shit while others are in no way prepared for the fly-by-the-seat-of-your-pants environment we lived in. When it came to how he ran the company, Kourosh was an *"all hands on dick"* kind of guy, and his fund-raising partner came across as more of a *"get your hand off my dick"* kind of guy, so, unfortunately, their relationship soured.

He and I never got along, which was weird because I, generally, got along with everybody. That was my curse! But when I arrived at the company, it seemed like I landed smack dab in the middle of a dick-swinging contest he imagined himself in with Kourosh. I remember him being pretty condescending to me, but then again, I felt he was condescending to everyone. That was his gift. He reminded me of the Walter Kerr zinger "He had delusions of adequacy." He was the living embodiment of James Spader's character Steff in *Pretty in Pink*. He treated us all like peasants. But he had a relationship with the company's angel investor, which he reminded us of on the daily, so I suppose he was a necessary evil. I don't think he ever understood or appreciated what the company was doing and ultimately positioned himself as Kourosh's archnemesis.

On the flip side, I immediately bonded with another coworker named Ken Stroscher. He was a tall blue-eyed blond-haired guy who became Netgroupie's first cameraman, writer, and master editor. He grew up with Kourosh in the same town, and they'd worked together at a mom-and-pop video store, just like Quentin Tarantino. In fact, Ken gave Kourosh his first job. Ken was obsessed with video equipment and was sort of the early, unofficial creator of TiVo. He had a dozen VCRs set up around town to record TV shows like *The X-Files*, and he'd walk around with a bag of VHS tapes and loan them out to everybody. Ken was creative and brilliant but a bit eccentric. I affectionately called him my idiot savant.

I remember a story Kourosh would tell about their old days at the video store. Ken had decided he didn't like to see dicks in his porn, so he *MacGyver*'d all of his video machines together and somehow figured out how to edit all the dicks out, film by film. He ended up with a massive VHS collection of porno. With no dicks! At the video store, Ken and Kourosh watched every movie under the sun together, which, unbeknownst to them at the time, would end up formulating the style of our future company. At the time, neither had any clue that they would start a multimillion-dollar business together. Kourosh was twenty and in a rock band, and Ken moonlighted as a stock boy for a beauty-supply wholesaler. Years later when Kourosh decided to start Netgroupie, he brought in Ken to be his editor and cameraman. He was the obvious choice.

Ken and I had an immediate connection. Unlike Kourosh, he was socially awkward and a total nerd. He had really bad sinuses, making him a major mouth breather, putting him in a special category with the likes of Darth Vader. This one time, I was in the middle of interviewing Jon Voight when he stopped mid-sentence to ask "what that strange noise was coming from the back of the room." Of course, I had to pretend I didn't know what he was talking about while I waited for Kourosh to gracefully make his way over to behind the camera and whisper, from behind clenched teeth, "Ken, close your fucking mouth!" On more than a few occasions, we actually had to stop rolling on an interview because the distraction was just too much. Despite his idiosyncrasies, Ken and I became the best of friends. Like Rob & Big, Scooby and Shaggy–style best friends. We were working our asses off, but we were also making each other laugh, constantly. We did everything together. Ken and I took it upon ourselves to learn how to edit and segment produce, and before long, the three of us kind of evolved into a streamlined production unit. We no longer needed to rely on anyone else, so anything was possible. Whatever we set our minds to, we did.

But editing—and calling affiliates—wasn't to be my destiny. Oh, no. So remember how I said Kourosh could never take no for an answer? Well, I learned that he's also willing to wait as long as it takes for the right opportunity to get exactly what he wants. Inevitably, the company had accomplished all it could with its affiliate program and needed to take the leap into creating new, original content with the bands so it could begin to form its own identity. Of course, the conversation, once again, turned to me being on camera. UGH!!

Don't get me wrong, the whole pirate radio vibe he wanted to create with the company sounded exciting, and I was deeply flattered that he wanted me to do this. I just didn't think I had anything to offer in the way of skills. I had met a few celebrities in my life, like football players my dad introduced me to, but I never knew what to say to them. I never wanted to meet them just to say that I did. If I was going to have an encounter with someone famous, I wanted it to be a hang, not some awkwardly forced fan moment. On the other hand, I didn't want our new company falling on its ass because I wasn't flexible. Luckily, Kourosh is an amazing hype-man and salesman. He got me where my heart is. One day he came to me with an offer I couldn't refuse:

"How'd you like to hang with Lemmy from Motörhead?"

I couldn't believe it. He knew how big a fan I was and had gone after this only to use it as bait. Like the voodoo priest in *Indiana Jones and the Temple of Doom*, he reached into my chest and grabbed my heart. All I could say was, "Fuck, who *wouldn't* want to have a beer with Lemmy? Damn you, Kourosh!" He had found my kryptonite and broken me down. At that point, I knew I had opened the door to being on camera. My final words to Kourosh as I gave in to his "evil plan" were, "I'm agreeing to do this for you. Please don't fuck with me." Meaning—don't lead me down this path to fail. In my soul, I knew he wouldn't. He was true to his word. That was over a decade ago.

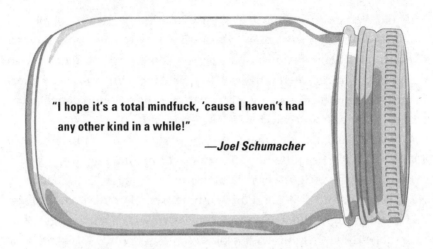

"I hope it's a total mindfuck, 'cause I haven't had any other kind in a while!"

—*Joel Schumacher*

Here's the funny part . . . it never actually happened. We went down to the Cat Club on Sunset, a tiny little club owned by Stray Cats' drummer Slim Jim Phantom, where legendary artists would randomly show up and perform unannounced. Sure enough, Lemmy hit the stage and brought the house down, then proceeded to bail out the back door during our scheduled interview time. Fucking perfect! But Pandora's box had been opened, and Kourosh took full advantage of my weakened state of mind and scheduled twenty more interviews. That's how I started on camera. It was not part of the plan. In fact, it was everything I never wanted. Here's the thing Kourosh always said to me: "You only need one person to believe in you and you can accomplish anything." It was that singular act of faith on his part that I could do this that inspired me to be fearless and move forward. He told me there was nothing to be afraid of, and I believed him. Why the fuck I believed him, I have no idea.

[Cue Wayne's World *ripple transition for flash-forward.]*

Who'da thunk that the girl who said "Hell No!" to being in front of the camera would find herself, just a few years later, on the set of a big Hollywood movie, preparing to shoot her first scene? Warner Bros. Pictures would fly me to Caesars Palace Hotel and Casino in Las Vegas to team up with the film's stars: Bradley Cooper, Ed Helms, Zach Galifianakis, Heather Graham, and director Todd Phillips in a then-unknown movie called *The Hangover*. I couldn't make this shit up if I wanted to! Having embraced our out-of-the-box approach to promoting movies early on, Warner Bros. came to us with an interesting idea to get me and NGTV behind what was going to be a very dirty movie, and it seemed like a wonderful opportunity and a perfect fit. Having become the go-to person in the uncensored universe, they went big with this one by offering me a role in the film along with carte blanche on set to do whatever I wanted behind the scenes for NGTV. And I did.

Nobody had any idea that this film would become a phenomenon. To them it was a fun little film that was so filthy that they weren't sure people would even go see it. Looking back, Bradley, Ed, Zach, and Heather seemed so sweet and unassuming when I arrived on set. They had been on night-shoots all week, so everyone was a bit groggy. But I was able to rile them up with a jolt of sarcasm and my excitement for being deep inside Sin City: the land of bad decisions.

A toothless Ed Helms told me a story about how he, Bradley, and Zach were driving down the strip in a convertible Mercedes for one of the scenes, and while stopped at a traffic light, a couple of pedestrians walked by and started making fun of Zach's beard. Saying "Your beard looks like pubes. Did you glue pubes to your face?" He got a real kick out of making fun of Zach's *bum fluff.* I quickly realized that Ed was the devilish one in the cast. I got the distinct impression that he was THE go-to guy for all the Vegas "specialties," and if I had a hankering for something I could only get in vegas, he knew exactly what to do. "Talk to the concierge," he said. "I think they can get you some hookers and some blow." Take note, it's good to know in case of an emergency. Then he spent some time talking to me about my character arc in the film: "We have a whole C story, where you and I go on a bender in Reno. Which we're shooting later." I have to say that even though the C story ultimately didn't get shot, for budgetary reasons, those two weeks of rehearsal with Ed in Reno were priceless. I kid!

Heather Graham joked with me about the "rules" of shooting a film about a night of drunken debauchery: "Everyone has to be drunk, basically, to work on the film. When you show up at work, they make sure that you're drunk in order to let you come to work." Basically, the whole cast was studying with Stanislavski himself. "It's a method-acting film," she said. "I'm really wasted right now."

Bradley Cooper got in the act with me, exchanging a couple of "fucks" and sharing a "smoky treat" in between takes. We were sharing screen time in a very intense and pivotal moment of the film, which had us both feeling anxious:

Bradley: They pump oxygen, apparently. I don't know if that's an old
wives' tale.

Me: Is that why I'm high right now?

Bradley: No, no . . . that's from the crack you were smoking!

Me: OHHHHH, riiiiight. *(Sweet relief.)*

Zach and I had a bumpy start. He mistook me for a stripper and
tipped me a dollar while he was playing the slots. Once I convinced him
that I was actually in the scene with him, he laughed. "Oh, did you read
for the part of Two Big-Boobs?" Once that was cleared up, he explained to
me why he thought the film would be successful: "Everybody should go
see *The Hangover*," he said, "it's rated G, it's a Pixar film . . . and I know a
lot of people think Hollywood does too many movies about the Holo-
caust but this one I think you're gonna like!"

What's really cool is that that brief time we spent together has forever bonded me with those guys, and every time I see them, it's always
a mini reunion. And I wouldn't have experienced any of that if I had
stuck to my first decision of "Hell No!"

[Cue Wayne's World *ripple transition for flashback.]*

Kourosh, Ken, and I believed in each other . . . and the fact that we
could do anything. Think of us as a *creative threesome*. An *artistic orgy*.
Where the only thing getting fucked was going to be your mind. We set
aside all the naysayers at the company and realized we didn't need
them, or really anyone else for that matter, to reach our goals. We were
The Three Musketeers. We didn't know what the fuck we were doing;
we were making it up as we went along. Come to think of it, I guess we
were more like *The Three Amigos*!

The approach for us in the beginning was that whoever said yes,
we interviewed. Unfortunately for me, that meant a lot of underground
hip-hop artists. The only thing I knew about underground hip-hop was
that I knew absolutely fucking nothing about underground hip-hop.
We also needed to get a lot of talent at one time, and that meant hitting
up a bunch of random music festivals. So I was a little worried. Trust
me, any reporter who has ever done this will tell you that covering a
music festival is nothing short of a *bareback verbal gangbang*. At the end
of the day you just feel sore, filthy, used up, and in need of a vaginal

steam . . . and that's just the guys. I was about to undergo a baptism by fire with the flames being fanned by Kourosh. I remember the first time we had to hit up one of these big festivals, Kourosh reassured me that this was just something to get my feet wet and that it would be a one-time deal. I've since learned that promising someone that it's a "one-time deal" is the businessman's version of *"just the tip."*

Our first big score was getting access to a hip-hop Halloween party at the El Rey Theatre in LA where the show's promoter allowed us to take over the VIP suite on the balcony and do interviews with the talent. We had no idea what we were walking into. To put it mildly, it was wildly chaotic, and the entire venue was just one thick cloud of pot smoke. And it wasn't something that you could wave out of your face, either. It was almost like the pot smoke had replaced the air. We were being *pot-raped.* In other words, a total blast!

We set up our lights and equipment, the show started, and we waited. After each act, Kourosh would run down to the stage, an impossible undertaking since the place was oversold and packed like sardines. He'd grab an artist and pull them through the crowd all the way to the back of the venue and up the stairs. I have no idea what he said to get these guys to follow him. Probably the promise of a six-foot bong and a five-foot blonde. Well, one out of two ain't bad!

Keep in mind, I am not a pot smoker, so inhaling all of that pot smoke got me high pretty fucking quickly. Which, of course, makes for the perfect time for me to conduct my first interview, right? Now, I definitely was not at the point in my career where I was comfortable enough to cuss it up and command a moment with the people whom I was interviewing. Mary Hart never swore and she was, sorta, the person I went into this thinking I was going to be. Well, if I was Mary Hart, then tonight, I was Mary Hart, high as a motherfucker. There's a good chance that the very first question out of my mouth, to the very first person I ever interviewed was, "Where are we right now?" And it all pretty much went downhill from there. Because I'm pretty sure the second question was, "Where do you guys keep the pizza?"

Once the artist got up to us, we had another problem. We didn't anticipate that the house would go dark again almost immediately, and the next band would start playing. It was earsplittingly loud, and when we turned our lights on, it was as if a giant homing beacon was illuminated inside the building. Imagine the Luxor Sky Beam indoors!! It created such a fucking disruption that the entire crowd turned away from the stage to look up to our corner of the balcony to see what the hell was going on. The artists onstage were getting completely distracted. What a fucking mess!! On top of that, my interviews were a joke because it was just me yelling:

> **Musician:** I can't hear anything!
> **Me:** What?
> **Cameraman:** Pull the mic away from your mouth!
> **Me:** You wanna put what in my mouth?

After about ten of these useless interviews, there was a half-hour lull before the main act took the stage. It was *hot as balls* in the balcony, and we were all as high as a kite because, as luck would have it, all the pot smoke had floated up to our corner. Kourosh then left to go grab the headliner before he went on, the only person that we'd ever heard of, and our biggest and best reason for being there. We were new to this and were trying our best to make a good impression and be professional. But when Kourosh finally got the headliner up to the balcony, we were so fucking stoned that we had all completely passed out. Imagine if you will the door opening, those infamous *fuck-ton* lights going on, and six passed-out, drooling bodies lying there, dead to the world, with a couple on top of each other. What a sight! *#Unprofessional*

I think we tried to pull ourselves together as fast as we could, which I'm sure was not as fast as we thought considering we were all fucking *blitzed*. Let's just say we all learned a lot that night about what *not* to do in the future. Too bad none of us remembered!

In the beginning stages of starting a business, you hustle—you do whatever it takes—to make it successful. For us, hustling meant bending the rules a bit.

We had to be creative in order to get into some of the bigger festivals. Hustling our way into these events became Kourosh's new unintentional specialty after sneaking into Cypress Hill's Smokeout Festival and a few of Xzibit's "Alkaholik" parties. You do what you've got to do sometimes to get to the people you need to get to. It was awesome meeting all the celebrities I'd watched and listened to growing up. Every once in a while, one of them would leave quite an impression.

I recall how exciting it was to run into porn legend Ron Jeremy, "The Hedgehog" himself, at one of these parties we were covering at the

Key Club. I was so excited that I asked Kourosh to find a way to wrangle him over to us. So off he went to make my strange wish come true. Kourosh was good like that. A little later, out of nowhere, Ron came up behind me, grabbed me in a full-body embrace, pulled my hair aside, and licked all the way up my neck, then walked away, leaving me in a disheveled stupor. Kourosh and Ken witnessed the whole thing and were dumbfounded waiting for my reaction. I stood there speechless for about twenty seconds and then cried out "GROSS!!! That was AWE-SOME!!!!" It was exactly what I didn't know I wanted my Ron Jeremy experience to be. Some celebrities really know how to deliver a fan encounter. Gene Simmons, whom I'd meet later down the road and spend a great deal of time with, had that in common with Ron Jeremy. He really understood his brand and would give his fans what they expected. Love him or hate him, whenever you'd encounter Gene, he would always deliver exactly what you needed: some fucked-up pseudosexual encounter that left you breathless, a little insulted, and armed with a story to pass down to your grandchildren.

Anyway, we set our sights on the next big thing we wanted to cover: the Bob Marley Festival. A two-day event featuring the who's who of megastars in the world of reggae. Shaggy, who was pretty huge at the time, was headlining, and we wanted to get him badly. Unfortunately, none of the people working the event knew who we were or cared, so we couldn't get press credentials. Then Kourosh came up with an unorthodox but genius plan. We'd been going back and forth with some execs at BET about doing something together, but they weren't completely convinced about our capabilities. "Well, show us what you can get," they had told us. So Kourosh, who saw the challenge as more of an opportunity in disguise, called the festival reps and said, "We're with BET," which was not entirely untrue . . . so to speak . . . if you know what I mean. And lo and behold, the gates to the kingdom that weed built opened wide and welcomed us in. I have to admit, I was a little worried about how we would pull this off at the event, but Kourosh had a plan for that as well. He printed a BET logo on his color printer, slapped it on the back of a clipboard, and voilà! We had credentials, and our disguise was complete. I remember thinking that "there's no fucking way this is going to work!" But I loved that we were crazy enough to go for it any way.

Backstage, it was a cavalcade of artists and their people as well as some truly random celebrities. All the Marleys were there, plus the twenty thousand people in their entourage. I remember walking in, out, and around the dressing rooms as we went from interview to interview. At one point we encountered a group of kids ranging from five to sixteen years old, sitting Indian-style on the floor, shelling cigars, cleaning weed, taking out the stems and seeds, and grinding and rolling blunts like pros. It was as if we were looking at a *joint assembly line*. It was efficient, effortless, and perfect in its execution. It was mind-blowing! Keep in mind this is over a decade before weed was legalized anywhere. Believe me when I tell you that I had never seen so much weed in my entire life. Two things really stuck out from that experience: the baseball bat–sized joint that they were passing around and the sight of Steven Seagal wearing what looked like a muumuu, just strolling around, head and shoulders above everyone else. Good lord, I wish Instagram was around back then.

I couldn't fuckin' believe it! It was incredible. Not a single person there ever questioned us, even though our crew had not one person of color and I, blond-haired and pasty as a vampire, was the host. It was so ridiculous. We had the run of the place, and we interviewed everybody, including the entire Marley family and, of course, Shaggy on his tour bus while he ate dinner after his performance. Shaggy had done a tour in the Gulf War, and he liked talking about his military service. I, of course, love to support our troops, so naturally the conversation turned toward the obvious:

Shaggy: Got any Marine in you?
Me: No.
Shaggy: Would you like some?

As short and incredibly tame as it sounds today, this was a pivotal moment for us back then. Here was a global pop superstar at the top of the charts making a straight up sex joke in an interview with a girl. This is something that just wasn't part of the DNA of TV interviews and press appearances. It got a big laugh on the bus, and it was the first time I thought, *Oh, we can go there with these interviews? Okay!* This relatively benign comment that sounded like a *creeper-joke* from *Uncle Bad-Touch* was a precursor to a whole new world within reach, just a little beyond the horizon. Today, networks clamor to show the latest thong Rihanna's wearing as an entire outfit to an awards show or the latest giant dildo a birthday-suited Miley Cyrus might be strapping on at the latest teenage hoedown. But even this little burp of a joke would never have seen the light of day on BET or anywhere back then, so we never even bothered sharing it with them.

But thanks to their clout, we ruled the day. And we saw one of the greatest family gatherings anyone should NEVER see. By the way, in defense of the guilty and the innocent, the *purple haze* we spent the day walking through was as dense as a nimbus cloud. We were so stoned, who knows if any of this even happened.

So, festival-hopping was going fine and we were making great contacts, but to keep me happy, Kourosh knew he had to get bands that I was interested in. God love him, he booked so many has-been metal bands, even though he really didn't want to. I mean, a lot of the bands we booked at first were pretty low-hanging fruit, and I often would only get an interview with the keyboard player or the bassist, who were at times about as interesting as watching a banana take a nap. I don't wanna name names, but it rhymes with Linkin Park. But our hard work paid off, and soon enough we'd infiltrated one of the biggest festivals of them all—Coachella.

Up until a few years ago, Coachella had a strict no-video-cameras-allowed policy for the press. Back then, you could barely even get photo passes. Behind the scenes, it was super-exclusive and strictly an all-VIP event. It was their way of protecting the purity and integrity of the artistic experience. Which I always interpreted to mean A-listers could make out with someone else's girlfriend in the corner without being scooped, and celebrities could get into catfights without being seen, all the while listening to some awesome live music. It was beyond too cool for school and not very media friendly. So Kourosh came up with yet another ingenious way to get us in (MUAHAHAH!). He said we weren't going to shoot any video; we were just going to take thousands of still photos and create a flip book. Yeah . . . that's the ticket! (In my best Jon Lovitz voice.) It was completely fucking absurd, yet utterly brilliant if you really think about it. They fucking went for it.

Once we got there, our plan was to be super stealthy and keep me hidden. But, like all festivals, it was organized chaos, and with so much going on, nobody was really paying much attention to what we were doing. So we set up our own tent and got everybody to come hang with us, including The Crystal Method, Robbie Williams, and Jack Johnson. We had full-on video cameras shooting for two days, and we never got caught. The artists were fully aware of our little scheme and were more than happy to play along. They fucking loved it! Of course, it didn't hurt that Ken had become the master of subterfuge with the video camera. He had developed a bit of a *Spidey sense* when it came to shooting without being noticed and knew how to keep it on the down low when necessary. He knocked out the red lights in all the cameras so no one could tell when we were rolling except for the artists we were interviewing, and he would casually place them in odd places or hold them in what appeared to be a nonfunctional way. It was another one of those inspired ideas that helped us create magic!

It was trial by fire and the greatest training period for all of us. We were so grateful to anyone who said yes. Events like Street Scene in San Diego ended up being a really great way to network. The promoters ultimately went on to do other events and invited us. We got to interview all kinds of mainstream acts, from Nickelback to The Black Eyed Peas. In the beginning it was insanity, and we were working our asses off from dusk to dawn, weekends, whatever it took. We were working nonstop, and none of us had time for a social life. Kourosh would be like, "C'mon, we have to be in three different places at the same time!" It was very much run and gun! I'd interview people for five hours straight in fifteen-minute pops, and Ken would put it all together. We complemented each other perfectly, and we trusted each other unequivocally.

Those days of struggle and hustle to get in front of bands people cared about were exhausting but amazing times. But there would come a time when we'd have no trouble getting in front of the biggest artists on the planet and doing far, far more outrageous things than anything we could have ever imagined back then. Case in point: Carrie Keagan vs. Justin Timberlake in a classic verbal combat known as the *Game of Bones* or the *Duel of the Dicks*!

The title of this chapter being what it is, I just had to take a minute and jump forward again. This time to my interview with Justin Timberlake in 2008 in support of the Mike Myers movie *The Love Guru*. The movie didn't do so well, but my interviews were some of the best ever. Especially the one with Justin, which was destined to become an instant classic for us. In the film he plays a character called *Le Coq* who is primarily known for his giant *package*, which he always kept on display and in everyone's face during the movie.

Let me just say that there are very few times in your life when you're going to be able to go toe-to-toe, face-to-face, or *tip-to-tip* with a superstar of this caliber and have the unfettered license to talk about *wang* with the cameras rolling. So there was no fucking way I was going to miss out on this *cockfight*! BTW, JT may play innocent but he loves to joke around, and this little verbal *"dick-dodging-duel"* was right up his alley. It would turn out to be one of my all-time favorite exchanges. That day was most definitely all about *"Le Coq"*!

My entire strategy was to immediately deal with the *elephant COCK* in the room. Making sure I made eye contact and a *crotch acknowledgment*, I made the first move . . .

Me: Is IT all in a NAME?
(He catches the crotch nod and responds with a coy, mischievous look on his face.)
Justin: What are you talking about?
Me: Your NAME! *(I lean in with a smile that says I know that you know.)*
Justin: Where are you going with this? *(With a huge grin.)*
Me: Nowhere. *(Sounding all guilty.)* It's *The Love Guru*, man.
Justin: You're a dirty person. *(Giving me a suggestive look.)*
Me: YOU ARE! *(Giving him one right back.)*
(My quick return, even more overtly sexual than his, throws him off and, not able to keep his deadpan stare intact, he breaks and smiles all shy at the camera.)
Me: *Le Coq!* Does IT say it all? Is IT all in the NAME?
Justin: So it's pretty . . . *(Exhales 'cause it's such a burden, turns to camera, and says in a low, sexy voice:)* I think it's pretty self-explanatory.
Me: Uh . . . HUH!
Justin: Somebody could lose an eye!
Me: You have to be careful.
Justin: You do!
Me: And you have skills! *(Raising one eyebrow.)*
Justin: *(Starts laughing then stops to deadpan:)* You don't know me!

Me: Did you get cast . . . I mean . . . *(I start using my hands to draw his attention to his crotch.)* Was this specifically because of you . . . *(using my hands, again to emphasize that this is about his cock)* or, you know, was this just a character . . .

Justin: I'd love to . . . I'd really . . . Tell your friends that . . .

Me: Okay . . . *(I will and I did. I'm a woman of my word; if Justin Timberlake needs me to tell all my friends that he has a huge cock, who am I to argue?)*

Justin: I'd love to believe that.

Me: Mike [Myers] said that it was obviously 'cause . . . you just FIT the part.

Justin: Well, you know . . . it's straight from the horse's mouth.

Me: Hmmm.

Justin: It's a special CHARACTER . . . that I really enjoyed playing. *(Going all Barry White on me . . . smooooooooth.)*

Me: How come, I wonder?

Justin: HOW CUM . . . I wonder?

Me: OH!! I didn't even mean that! Way to go.

Justin: OH MY GOD!

Me: Way to pick that one up so early in the morning. *(I make a gesture with my hands like I'm throwing something up in the air. Yeah, he's my kind of guy.)*

Justin: *(Looks at the camera with a grin.)* I'm QUICK!!

Me: YEAH!!!! *(Giggling that he made a cum joke.)*

Justin: But not that QUICK! *(All serious . . . oh, he's really into this.)*

When it came time to wrap and promote, I thought I'd do JT a solid and get the ladies, who were watching, really ready:

Me: *(To camera:)* You're gonna wanna probably pay extra for this one . . . *(I turn to Justin)* 'cause it does CUM with a HAPPY ENDING! *(I start laughing.)*

Justin: It does! CUM with a HAPPY ENDING. *(Grinning to camera.)*

Me: So serious this film?

Justin: Really serious! TOUCHES on a lot of ISSUES.

Me: Does it TOUCH on a lot of THINGS?

Justin: Yes. It does TOUCH on a lot of THINGS.

Justin: God! This is the most "in the gutter interview" I've ever done!!
(*Cannot stop smiling. Like he got away with something.*)

Me: (*Laughing my ass off!!*)

Justin: I mean if there could be any more innuendos toward the male anatomy . . . there can't!

Me: I don't think there could be. But YOU brought it! It felt like you were giving me all the ammunition I needed!

Justin: (*Very proud of himself.*) I'LL BRING IT!!! (*Slamming his fist down.*)

Me: YEAH!?? Where's IT gonna be???!!!!

And that's it for this latest edition of "Dick-Talk" with Mr. "Dick in a Box." Now back to your originally scheduled programming.

We were building up a business from nothing based on blood, sweat, and tears. It was all trial and error, mostly error. It's not like I had any training for this. Yes, like every woman with a vagina on this planet, I'd watched Oprah and Barbara Walters, and they were great at what they did, but they didn't represent a path I thought I'd go on in a million years. I never modeled myself after anyone, and Kourosh didn't want me to be something I wasn't anyway. In fact, he'd deter me from ever watching or emulating any of that.

If I had to name some of my influences growing up, they would have to be Joan Rivers, George Carlin, and Howard Stern. They made being dirty a fundamental element of their public persona so gracefully that you were able to see past the subversive and focus on its purpose: to communicate with the language of truth, the language of everyday people. It made them instantly more relatable and funnier than the ocean of bland that they were up against. These were my heroes.

It was the same with Tenacious D, Jack Black, and Kyle Gass's comedic rock band. Those talented motherfuckers really got into my head in my twenties and fucked me up good with their uncanny ability to turn profanity into poetry. There was so much swearing in their songs, but it was all smooth and organic. It was beautiful. The D treated foul language with respect. There was never anything ambivalent or ambiguous about the way they used it. They never threw a *shock-bomb* into a crowd only to run away and watch what happened. In fact, it was quite the opposite. They genuflected before its expressive power as if it was high art. They had the power to move you. That's the shit that mattered. That's the shit I connected with. Basically, that was the shit! Oh, and by the way, if you haven't heard their classic DIY/how-to song, "Fuck Her Gently" then you haven't lived.

I needed to find my groove, my voice, my purpose, and my point of view. The answer came from an unlikely source. I'd become friends with a super-talented comedian named Colin Malone, who used to host a buzzy late-night public access show called *Colin's Sleazy Friends*. It was like a filthy *Wayne's World*, and if you were in the know, you knew about this show, and if you didn't know about this show then you didn't know shit. Colin was like Jack Black on crack and funny as fuck. On his show, he would interview porn stars and get them to do incredible things, like go full-frontal and have in-depth conversations about fisting, because, apparently, there were no rules governing public access at midnight. To this day, I couldn't tell you how the fuck that show got on the air except for an improbable but genius loophole about public airwaves. The show went from being *jerk-off material* for fourteen-year-olds to becoming a cult phenomenon. It got so big that stars like Kathy Griffin, Seth Green, Weezer, and Kid Rock, to name a few, would come on and mix it up with the porn stars and his crazy antics. It truly was amazing and groundbreaking TV.

Anyway, flash forward, Colin caused such a splash and made a name for himself that the networks came knockin'. He ultimately scored some sort of deal with Fox and was working on a late-night show. He and I got along great, so he thought it would be fun to try doing some interviews together. So off we went on our little adventure. Next thing I know Colin went ahead and set up an interview with Sully Erna, the lead singer of Godsmack, who were pretty fucking huge at the time. It was all coming together beautifully . . . except in Kourosh's mind, of course.

Kourosh was sort of apoplectic when he heard about it. He was a HUGE fan of Colin's but was very concerned about me getting caught up in some fucked-up, ass-backward, and compromising position, which was, with all due respect, Colin's specialty! He was becoming maniacally defensive when it came to me and didn't want Colin to do anything that might potentially damage my fledgling career. Typically the women in Colin's segments were porn stars who were there to flash a little *under carriage* or hypersexualize the interviews in order to illicit a response from the celebrities. Trust me, it was really fucking funny. He'd get these porn stars to do the raunchiest bits, and Kourosh knew that I could be easily swayed when it came to having fun. If someone told me to "Stand on your head!" it's fairly certain I'd say, "Cool, I knew my keg standing skills would come in handy someday." Kourosh didn't want me to be used in that way and be a sexual pawn in someone else's game. Colin, with his unassuming demeanor and killer instincts, was a master at this, and Kourosh was worried I was going to be fed to the wolves once the cameras started rolling. Little did either of us know that the wolf on set that day was in sheep's clothing, and not at all the person who anyone thought it was going to be.

On the day of the interview, Kourosh was as tightly wound as an Earth Angel hand-crank vibrator set to stun, especially when I walked in wearing tight black leather pants, a baby-T, and stilettos. The level of anxiety in the room was at a Lamaze-breathing level. Kourosh has this unique way of exuding tension from his stare like radioactive waves that you can feel against your skin. As Tenacious D would say, he had "the power to move you." He's an incredibly nice guy, but not one to fuck with. Especially as it related to me. He felt that he'd coerced me into this game and was very protective. Yup, it was like having my very own *dadager.*

Colin was there with his manager as well, and Kourosh invited them both into another room and basically read them the riot act, even though nothing had even happened yet. We could all hear him through the door. "Listen, here are the rules," he said firmly. "Just so we're clear, Carrie is not getting out of her chair. She's not bending over, taking her top off, or pulling down her pants. She's not here to fondle anyone or be fondled. Do not mess with me or I will shut it down." Colin and his manager appeared a bit freaked about Kourosh's attitude, but they assured him that they were shooting for Fox and that Colin's new image was about being more palatable for mainstream TV. Basically, the message from them was that this was going to be clean-cut and funny but not dirty. So there was nothing to be concerned about. Plus, they said Sully was a pretty serious guy and that this was probably going to be more of a straightforward interview.

Let's just say the fear factor in the room was palpable. Usually, when you're doing an interview with a big celebrity, you're worried about making sure you don't piss them off. Not today! It was safe to say that Colin and Co. were more worried about Kourosh and, probably, regretting the whole thing. So we start rolling, and, sure enough, the conversation between the three of us was totally vanilla because "Dad" had just yelled at Colin. Sully, who was pretty shy to begin with, had a rule of his own: He hated talking about his Wiccan religion because he was sick of being the poster boy for witchcraft. With not much left to talk about, the interview was playing out like a total dud and looking more and more like a fucked opportunity for both Colin and myself. Doing his best to keep fishing for something, and nervous about getting dirty and having to deal with the wrath of Kourosh, Colin turned to Sully and simply asked him about his dating life: "What do you look for in a girl?" When he answered with "funny" and "good personality," making him dull as dishwater, Colin turned to me with desperation in his eyes, and feeling like the whole interview was going to shit, he asked:

"Carrie . . . so what do you look for in a guy?"

Without skipping a beat and in a moment of pure instinct, I blurted out:

"IT'S ALL ABOUT THE COCK!"

Kourosh dropped his clipboard. Colin dropped his jaw. His manager glared at Kourosh with an angry look that screamed, "You motherfucker, you set us up!" Of course, we hadn't. Kourosh was in as much of a state of shock as anyone. Colin looked around the room in stunned surprise, not quite sure what to do next. There was nervous laughter. Then Sully looked at me and turned to Colin and said, "What show is this? What network are we on?" And Colin, seizing the opportunity to have a little fun now that I had opened the door, jumped right in:

Colin: This is for Fox.
Sully: What? You can talk like this on Fox?
Colin: Yup. It's owned by Rupert Murdoch and Rupert Murdoch is all about the COCK!

Everyone started laughing and, just like that, we all went from being on the verge of a *boregasm* to *off the nut!* Thinking that since I had crossed the line all bets were off, and I was now cool with being toyed with, Colin decided to make a notorious but predictable move in our impromptu game of *Sex Chess: sexual pawn sacrifice, doggie style.* A smart yet bold professional maneuver with a high-risk/high-yield profile. That's why I've always respected Colin. He was never afraid to roll the dice. So he started talking to Sully about my sexy black leather pants, and of course, Sully played along. He then asked his opinion on the sound leather pants make when they get slapped, thinking that I'd stand up, bend over, and let Sully have at me. Yeah, right! I guess Colin had forgotten that it was women who invented *Sex Chess*. And just as he was getting ready to *stroke his bishop* with glee, I quickly turned the conversation around with a *Zwischenzug* countertactic: Queen to Bishop 6, leaving him vulnerable. And, before he knew it, Colin was bent over, grabbing his ankles in the middle of the room, with rock star Sully Erna smacking dat ass! CHECKMATE!

That smack was so hard and so loud that it almost felt like Sully took a running start because the echo went on for days. I'm sure somewhere in the universe it's still blowing minds. There are *erotic flagellation symposiums* celebrating its art and form. Without a doubt, it was the smack heard around the world. In the end, I quite inadvertently flipped the switch. It wasn't planned. It happened organically when I was just being me. The "me" I didn't know existed until that moment.

"It's all about the cock." In an undeniable stroke of irony, in this male-dominated business, those were the five words that brought me to life.

6

PUTTING THE F-U BACK INTO FUN

Some people never go crazy.
What truly horrible lives they must lead.
—Charles Bukowski

It was an epiphany. A four-letter revelation. A momentary lapse of reason that led me to an inexhaustible and absolute truth. Kind of like how you should never, under any circumstances, take a sleeping pill and a laxative on the same night. You may say, "What's the big deal? You said 'cock.' Women say 'cock' all the time; especially if they're trying to get the guy to cum faster so they can get back to doing their nails." I say one woman's *"Copulating Oblong Cavity Killer"* is another woman's road to Damascus. In an industry where women are expected to do a lot of plotting & planning, ducking & diving, running & gunning, slamming & jamming, moving & shaking, shucking & jiving, and blowing & going, I went from doing to *being* . . .

The second I stopped worrying about my surroundings and over-thinking my words and actions, I became present. The moment I became present I stopped being a victim of the circumstances around me and I started to be in control of them. This was a defining moment, not just for me but for our company. What I would say, what I would do, and how I would do it would forever be inextricably interwoven into its DNA. If I played it right, I'd be Olivia Newton-John in *Grease* (a worldwide smash), and if I didn't, I'd be Michelle Pfeiffer in *Grease 2* (a film most people don't know exists). So from that point forward, I started to really have fun experimenting during interviews. As it turned out, my independent spirt and potty mouth gave us the keys to the kingdom. There was nothing like us at the time, and as we braved forward, it became abundantly clear to me that being a girl at the center of this tornado was a unique privilege. I would have my share of prejudices to overcome in an industry that wasn't terribly accepting of girls being dirty. But I saw it all as an opportunity to change the rules and redefine what girls should and should not do.

Not a day goes by since that fateful moment over a decade ago without me thanking my lucky stars that I found that opportunity surrounded by a creative, daring, and supportive team of incomprehensively filthy-minded people. It was and is an incredibly empowering experience being a woman in control and uncensored. Ask any of the women making waves today, from Amy Schumer to Lena Dunham, and I'm sure they'll tell you the same thing. But Voltaire once wrote: "With great power comes great responsibility," so I needed to make it count and venture forward with purpose. I know what you're thinking, and no, *Spider-Man*'s Uncle Ben did not say that first, it was Voltaire! And yes, by quoting Voltaire instead of *Spider-Man* you might get the emo-chicks you've been Tinder-stalking to actually swipe right. I would, however, suggest changing your profile pic to one where you're not wearing a belly shirt that says MY SPIDEY SENSE ISN'T THE ONLY THING TINGLING while you're pissing on your six-year-old nephew's *Green Goblin* car. Just a suggestion, do what you will. Anyway, now that I had found my voice, and our company had found its reason for being as an uncensored and unfiltered media outlet . . . how would we define it? What would we do with it? What was our point of view . . . ?

The answer was simple. We would search for truth, and our guides would be the best two F-U's there are: FUN and FUNNY. I've always believed that you can talk about the most vile, ridiculous, and disgusting shit as long as it's funny and you're laughing. No Good TV was an exercise in joy and an escape from the ordinary. It was an opportunity for celebrities to be themselves: to just fuck around and laugh. Giving the average person a chance to feel what it's like to hang out with them and have a beer. In some ways, it's a greater truth than any revealing interview that exploits their personal life for publicity. Swearing is the common ground that unites us all. No matter who we are, rich or poor, famous or not, when we're with our friends and we drop our guard and start shooting the shit, we become the most authentic version of ourselves. No pretense, no bullshit, and no fear. That's who we wanted to be and where we wanted to go in the celebrity world. To get there would require time, consistency, trust, and above all else, it had to be super fun for the stars. Because at the end of the day, in one form or another, everybody curses.

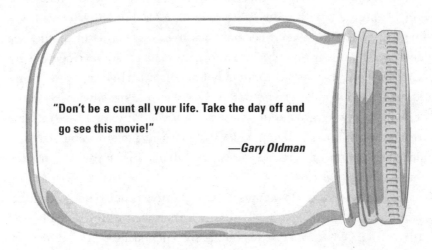

"Don't be a cunt all your life. Take the day off and go see this movie!"

—*Gary Oldman*

I grew up listening to legends like Joan Rivers, Freddie Prinze, Sam Kinison, Roseanne Barr, George Carlin, Margaret Cho, Richard Pryor, Lisa Lampanelli, Denis Leary, and Eddie Murphy, who bled blue and funny. It was clear to us that there was an art to vulgarity, and it was the palette with which we were going to paint. Once we mixed in the funny, the colors became vibrant and dramatic. The trick was to get down and dirty. We figured that if you could get people to talk about anything taboo, make them love it and laugh about it, then you've got something. From that moment forward, our motto, our mantra, our mission, and our raison d'etre became "Putting the F-U back into fun."

Much like the Bashophiliacs who follow Matsuo Bashō, a Japanese Haiku poet, and cannot achieve orgasm without the writing or reciting of his haiku poetry, we would not consider our interviews a success unless the proverbial F-U had been adequately tossed around the room and everyone had had an appropriate amount of the aforementioned fun. There were challenges. I have to admit, it wasn't all roses, but our new format really worked—99 percent of the time. What we were doing was truly revolutionary, and that meant that every once in a while, we'd have a minor misstep. There were times when I'd interview a band and they'd get gun-shy. There were other times when, after a great and rowdy interview, the band's manager or publicist would second-guess whether the world should see them being so unfiltered.

The first time it happened was with the band Queens of the Stone Age. Hard-ass rock guys who had a hard time being dirty. I couldn't tell you why. Maybe it was an image issue. Maybe it was the fact that I was a girl being racy with them. Who really knows, but either way, it was fine. This wasn't for everyone, and back then I was still getting my sea legs. I'm sure it was probably not as organic as it could have been. After our interview, they asked that we not air it, and while we were disappointed, of course we agreed not to. That was and has always been our deal with anyone nice enough to play with us. If it wasn't the fun time we promised, it never happened. Our goal was never to embarrass or make anyone uncomfortable. We wanted them "in" on the joke, not the "butt" of the joke.

It's strange how nowadays artists go out of their way to connect with fans on the rawest level, but back then, being unreachable was still a thing. Old-school PR was on the cusp of getting schooled by new-school PR, and I'd like to think we played our small role in that. Regardless, each rough patch gave us the chance to build trust with the bands and their reps, which would ultimately open doors in the years to come. What I'm most proud of is that after all these years, and thousands of interviews later, the number of people who weren't comfortable with what we did and asked us not to use the interview is minuscule. To me that's an incredible accomplishment, given what we were doing.

Another issue we were discovering was that sometimes musicians/bands who were killer onstage didn't have personalities to match offstage and would give really boring interviews. It's weird how they could be larger than life playing the rock star onstage but completely lost being themselves. It's something that I've found to be common with some actors as well. They are chameleons on camera and a blank slate off. The sad truth is they weren't all going to be fuel-tanker-crash-into-a-gas-station, tell-it-like-it-is, and restore-your-faith-in-rock-'n'-roll sit-downs like the one I had with Poison guitarist C. C. DeVille at the Viper Room. C. C. had stories for days and left no stone unturned. My favorite was his description of all the scars he had on his *nut sack* because he used to love smoking crack naked and would frequently drop his crack pipe in his lap. (Note to self: wear pants if you plan on smoking a *glass dick*.)

I realized that we'd need to figure out how to fill the dead space and make it entertaining, even when it didn't look like it was going to be. Out of pure necessity, my personality really started coming out. I couldn't just rely on the talent to give me a good interview. I was going to have to rely on my energy and preparation to ultimately dictate what was going to happen. The good news was that nothing offended me; I lived for spontaneity and had energy for days. And I fuckin' loved it when an interviewee would think they were going to shock me or one-up me just to see if I could hold my own. My reaction to that was always to quote Roddy Piper's genius line from the movie *They Live*: "Oh yeah, well, I came here to chew bubblegum and kick ass and guess what, I'm all out of gum!" As we figured out more of what we were going to do in the interviews, it was inevitable that we would also discover what we weren't going to do . . . sooner than we expected.

So there we were, creators of this brand-new, uncensored format, making the daring move to take it out into the world and try to execute it in an EXTREMELY tame press environment. Yet, luckily, interview after interview, it was working. We were succeeding and rising up the ranks of the music world and getting away with murder doing these incredible no-holds-barred interviews. What could go wrong? Plenty! This was uncharted territory for everyone involved. There were lessons to be learned, rules to be created, and lines never to be crossed. After all, the word "uncensored" means different things to different people, and not everyone plays by the same rules.

The word "uncensored" is a complicated beast. I've discovered that the way men and women define "uncensored" is as vastly different as the way men and women respond to the mere suggestion of performing *ass to mouth* during sex! Men seem to be open to trying it, while women are more in the camp of "Are you fucking kidding me?! You ASSHOLE!!" It turns out when some guys hear a girl say "uncensored," they immediately think, *Oh, it's porn and you're getting naked. Sweet!* Girls, on the other hand, tend to take a less *rapey* position and assume there's going to be some foul language . . . followed by a request for them to get naked! So when I would show up to do an interview with a band made up of guys and tell them we were *uncensored*, there was a good chance that they immediately thought they had just scored a free pass to the Girls

Gone Wild shower show. As you can imagine, this was going to be tricky at best. Almost as tricky as running into the guy you've been crushing on for six months when you're buying Vagisil . . . almost!

There I was thinking "uncensored" was a path to freedom of speech without realizing that for some people it's actually a silent activator of their dormant misogyny. It was an almost Pavlovian response. Go figure! It became clear to me that it wasn't going to be easy being a girl fronting an uncensored format. It was going to be a ground war, and I was going to have to redefine the term "uncensored" interview by interview. Sort of like how the folks at Starbucks had to reposition their corporate logo to be perceived as a nod to Seattle's nautical heritage, in spite of the fact that it looked virtually identical to the Siren from Greek mythology, who represented obsession, addiction, and death. Talk about a *Freudian fingerbang*! I definitely had my work cut out for me, and just like any good roller coaster, there would be screams, laughter, some harrowing moments, and more than my share of loop-de-loops.

Then came the fateful day we were invited to cover the legendary Vans Warped Tour. New Found Glory, Something Corporate, and Finch were the headliners, and I got to go on their tour bus to interview them. It was a total blast, and like out of a scene from *Almost Famous*, it erupted into an impromptu karaoke party with everyone singing "Africa" by Toto with the whole bus rocking back and forth. The conversation was filthy from moment one. It started with a light discussion about poop choppers and how the low-rent tour buses didn't have them, meaning you had to take a dump in a plastic bag and take it with you. It ended with an insanely X-rated chat about sexual positions, as you'd expect with three huge young bands at the height of their fame and in the most rebellious and raucous state. It was awesome!!

Super funny and dirty, the interview continued rolling with me singing and dancing in the middle of *twelve* guys from *three* bands. Ken was doing his best to navigate the tight space with his camera, and Kourosh was standing in the stairwell at the entrance to the bus without a clear line of sight to me. As our interview proceeded, one of the guys said his favorite move was *the dip.*

"What's the dip?" I asked naively.

"Can I show you?"

"Sure!" I said, thinking he was going to gallantly dip me in a Fred Astaire/Ginger Rogers manner. Let's just say Fred and Ginger would be turning in their graves if they saw what happened next. In that instant, the excitement of the moment overwhelmed me, and I became an idiot. He told me to sit down on the floor so I did. He then told me to lay back and bring my knees up. The next thing I know he's grabbed my ankles, pulling my legs up, and is maneuvering me around, getting ready to mount me. At that moment I started to panic and thought, *Oh, no, oh, shit, here it comes. What the fuck did I get myself into?* My back was on the floor in the middle of the tour bus, I was surrounded by a dozen dudes, both of my legs were spread-eagle in the air, and a strange guy started doing the dip maneuver. Basically reenacting some move I'm sure he'd seen in countless pornos. To his credit, Kourosh tore his way through the *sausage party* before the third dip and got me back on my feet. As much as it sounds like I was caught in the *"ass-to-ass"* scene in *Requiem for a Dream*, it was all quite innocent. They weren't trying to hurt me. There was no *double-dong*. They just didn't know what our boundaries were, and up until that happened, neither did we. Lesson fucking learned!

As my Philosophy of Scatological Behavior professor would say, "It turned out to be a teachable moment." From that day forth, we instituted our own *"Rules of Engagement."* A growing set of guidelines that would help define our format and identity. Our goal was to create something positive and fun, not filthy and fucked up. There's a fine line between hitting up McDonald's for a Big Mac and fries, where they love to see you smile, versus finding yourself at *"CrackDonalds,"* where Big Mac is the guy in the corner handing out *glass dicks* and the last thing you want to do is see anyone smile. We would obey these rules as if they were gospel. **RULE #1:** Carrie's feet never go up in the air.

RULE #2, aka "The Johnson Dilemma," landed like the infamous *rope* on Monica Lewinsky's dress after my interview with a legendary band. The band had seven or eight members who were all going to be in the interview. Just getting them set up in a semi-workable manner for shooting the interview was complicated, so we ended up having a couple of members on each side of me and the remainder behind me. It was a pretty fun and lively interview right from the start. The band had a huge horn section so I decided to get cute and ask them who was the horniest in the band and who was the sax addict (get it?). Well, unbeknownst to me, while I was distracted with this circus of an interview, one of the guys in the back had taken the lid off the *pickle jar,* removed his *flesh* *trombone* from its case, and gently rested it on my shoulder. In other words, he put his dick on me! Yeah . . . that happened.

I guess I must have been in the zone because I didn't even notice his *micro-toy* at first. I mean, can you fuckin' imagine this *shitwaffle*? What nerve! Interestingly enough, when I finally saw it, I didn't freak out. I wasn't going to give this *wank stain* the satisfaction. I just, very casually, moved forward to get it off me. I'm very proud of the fact that I didn't play into this guy's bullshit. It caught all of us by surprise, and within seconds, Kourosh gave me the signal to end the interview, which was only maybe six or seven minutes in. Funnily enough, the abrupt ending caught *penis-boy* in the middle of what can best be described as his *"cumshot vulnerability period"* (that thirty-second window where there is no possibility that you could act fast enough so that a roommate opening the door would not catch you in the act of masturbation) and he didn't have time to put his *schmeckle* away. There he was with his dick in the breeze to the horror of his bandmates. Then came the shit-storm. We were all disgusted with what had taken place, and Kourosh was beside himself and furious with the guy and the band. To their credit, the other members of the band and the entourage were mortified, but we were way beyond apologies. They were all asked to leave, and we banned them from ever being a part of anything we ever did. They went too far, and there are some lines you can never cross.

Thus was born **RULE #2**: No *yogurt slinger* shall be placed on the host at any time. So sayeth the shepherd, so sayeth the flock.

Kourosh and I had long-term goals, and me being perceived as a whore wasn't part of that master plan. It was important that I came across as carefree and fun-loving, that I was one of the guys and I could keep up with anybody. But I was not a blow-up doll. We were creating an environment where I was in control, I made the rules, and I set the boundaries. This was my world and my guests were living in it. There would be more rules to learn along the way and we had plenty more shit to figure out. But we were getting better and more confident as we churned away interview after interview, festival after festival, and month after month. We were having fun, but not one part of this was easy and every single moment was a stretch for us. Luckily, we had the foresight to know that everything was a continually evolving process, and as long as we were always moving forward, growing, and learning, that that would ultimately define our success.

We were amassing interviews and content at a frantic pace. We were building relationships while creating a bit of a name for ourselves. We were going at it so hard that there were days where it felt like we were at all places at all times. We hadn't stopped to think about how it was all supposed to come together or how this was ultimately going to be its own network. It took a strange encounter with unlikely company to push us to our creative limits and compel us to create the big picture. The greater purpose: the uncensored network that would ultimately define us.

Having made some waves in the investment banking community, we were sought out by a major media company with distribution deals with all the big players like DirecTV, Time Warner Cable, DISH, etc. to possibly partner with them on a project. It seemed too good to be true and in some ways it was. You see, this particular company had made their name as a distributor of pay-per-view porn on TV. They didn't produce pornography, but they sure made a mint from selling it. Of course, this was a problem for us because we wanted to have nothing to do with the porn industry. It just wasn't where we saw ourselves. But we were a small company and couldn't afford not to explore every opportunity. So we agreed to meet with them to hear what they had to say.

When you think about meeting with a company in the porn industry, my guess is you're imagining a sunken living room, a circular bed, naked bodies on swings, and a centrally located bucket of "Anal Eaze" lube. Okay, so maybe you didn't imagine the circular bed but you get the point. Not this company. This place was about as porno as an IRS auditor's office. They were all business. They had made a lot of money, had impeccable relationships with the distributors, and they wanted to grow by diversifying their programming and wanted to distribute something other than hardcore XXX. They needed a partner with a big idea and the content to back it up. That's where we came in. Their plan was to use their distribution relationships to launch a new mainstream channel. So they asked us to show them what we were up to and what our concept was.

That was music to our ears, and the second we realized that they wanted to move away from porn, we were raring to go. So Kourosh pitched them the idea we'd been developing of a mainstream entertainment channel geared toward adults. Sort of an E! meets MTV but with the gloves off. The channel would be populated with original uncensored programs, unfiltered interviews with huge bands, and director's cuts of music videos from the biggest artists in the world. Remember, this was before you could go on Vevo and see the unrated version of music videos. It was unlike anything else that had come before, and we had a huge content library to support it.

Sure enough, they loved it! He showed them a few of our interviews and some of those racy music videos, and they said, "Put it all together, and if it works, we'll be your partners." We were beside ourselves with glee, but as the saying goes, be careful what you wish for. They asked us to create a forty-five-minute sizzle reel for a fully fleshed-out twenty-four-hour uncensored entertainment network with our original programming and our own unique branding. We thought: *Great! No problem.* Kourosh had the whole idea floating around in his head, and we could have it all figured out within a couple of months. They gave us fourteen days to put the whole thing together—soup to nuts. Holy mother of God! Shit fucker hell!

The task before us was biblical and nothing short of a miracle would be needed to complete it on time. We were a small company with limited resources and a production capacity that would be best described as having half an ass. But in the end, it took only four friends with dedicated minds, killer instincts, and a penchant for masochism to get the job done. It was fourteen days of 24/7 self-flagellation that would have made a Roman Catholic proud. But there was no stopping us; we were on a mission to change the world, and we didn't care if we almost died in the process. Besides, as Ken would say, "Death is overrated." Yeah, I'm not quite sure what that meant.

We dove in right away and without thinking, which was a good thing because if we had really thought through what we had promised to deliver, the end result would have been more of a ritualistic suicide video than a promo tape. It was safe to say "thought" was definitely the enemy of this project. Anyway, after Kourosh, Ken, and I were done mapping out the arc of the reel, we determined that Ken and I were going to do all the editing and Kourosh was going to conceive, write, and produce. We immediately ran into two problems: 1) we needed a graphics guy on the team to help us package it, and 2) Ken and I didn't really know how to edit! Well, we solved problem one by recruiting our buddy Amul Patel, who was an absolute motherfucker in graphics and visual design. Looking like a sexy Indian

Jeff Goldblum all decked out in techno gear, he had an eye for the sublime and the skills of a hacker wizard king. Problem two could only be solved by good old-fashioned on-the-job training. They say necessity is the mother of invention, and we were about to turn this mother out!!

Without much choice, we ignited an idea factory and churned out product. There was something insanely brilliant about how fast and furiously we'd take the nugget of an idea and bring it to life. Kourosh would come to the table with an idea for a program, a name, and a tagline. We'd all brainstorm, then Ken and I would hit the content to find the footage to support the show and start cutting while he and Amul created the graphics package that we would later integrate. We were up all hours, burning the candle on both ends, and battling the elements.

One of the dumbest things we had to deal with was air-conditioning. We were in a typical high-rise at the time, so the AC in our building would shut off at 6 P.M. We didn't have any windows, so there was no ventilation and it quickly turned into a stenchful steam room. Of course, we had no choice but to work through the night and couldn't shut down 'til 8 A.M. when it came back on. Naked editing wasn't an option, so Kourosh went out and bought two portable air-conditioner units that we affectionately called R2 and D2. The first night we used them, everything was fine for about two hours, then we shorted out the power on our floor. We found the fuse box to reboot, but it became clear that we were running so many machines in order to do all this editing, rendering, and graphics that there would be no way to have AC without constantly shorting out our entire floor. Quite a fucking nightmare. So Ken and I ran out and bought a couple of hundred-foot extension cords. Then Kourosh literally *Spider-Man*'d his way up the building, crawled in the fire exits on the floors above and below, and plugged the units in. It worked! It got us through the nights, and I think we only blew out the other floors a handful of times. Of course, the building never knew why.

The days melted into nights, and the work engulfed us in an overwhelming sense of delirium. There were times when we were so frazzled that Ken and I would take five-minute breaks and literally run out into the street to get fresh air and scream, "We're balancing." We were giving 150 percent of ourselves 100 percent of the time and found ourselves in an "Ecstasy-laced Adderall frenzy." But this lucid dream was not without its intense moments. You see, Kourosh and I work fast and rely on our gut; Ken and Amul loved to re-engineer. Amul, a Picasso in his own right, was the epitome of the struggling artist seeking perfection who overthought everything and questioned the very nature of existence during font selection. Ken was a video Banksy. His work had darkness, humor, subtlety, and depth, but unlike Banksy, he worked at the speed of a snail. We were all after perfection, but our paths were very disparate. Fortunately, Kourosh's brand of insanity came with precision. He knew exactly where we needed to go and made sure our *short bus* got there on time.

We literally finished the promo reel the morning of the presentation. It was a bold statement both incendiary in its vision and exquisite in its execution, at least that's what my mom said. Our baby was beautiful and we were all so proud. Dead to the world and ready to kill ourselves, but damn proud! What we had put together was the dirtiest, foulest, funniest programming you could ever imagine. We mined all of our raunchiest, most uncensored content and jam-packed it into these incredibly well-packaged shows all under a cohesive brand. It was quite the accomplishment for a bunch of misfit neophytes. We had created our own *Last Tango in Paris* except it was called *First Torque-Fest in Fucktown*. And we're talking UNCENSORED!!! The biggest music artists talking shit like you've never imagined, full-frontal bush, swinging dicks, cocksucker and motherfucker cursing off the charts, and hip-hop orgies. You name it, we had it!! We had done it. We had created the network. There was no stopping us now.

It was time to blow their socks off!! Kourosh, who literally hadn't slept in two weeks, splashed water on his face and dashed off to the meeting. Upon showing the reel to the executives, there was no applause, backslapping, or champagne toasts. It was crickets.

"Jesus Christ, we can't show that to DirecTV!" one suit said, exasperated. "They'll throw us out of the building! What the hell, Kourosh?"

"This is what it needs to be!" Kourosh screamed. "There is no compromise; this is who we are! Fuck you guys!" Then he stormed out (cue cape flourish). Kourosh had a flare for the dramatic on par with the Count's passion for numbers on *Sesame Street*.

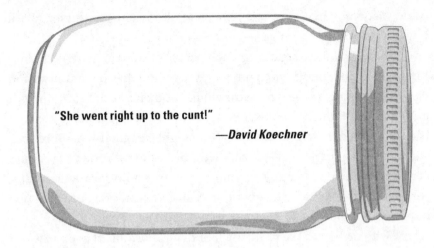

"She went right up to the cunt!"

—*David Koechner*

Our beautiful baby was so sensational it was unsellable. We got so delirious and desensitized during the process of making it that we lost track of how far off the reservation we'd gone. Like a bunch of horny German businessmen in Thailand, we were trying to *fuck* everything. The content was all punch line and no joke, all peak and no valley. We never set anything up and we never once thought, *Oh, we should temper this.* Sitting in a room of our own farts for two weeks had anesthetized our brains, and we just did what made us laugh. And what makes you laugh at 4 A.M. after seventy-two hours of no sleep is probably not fit for human consumption. So after a day of rest, we revisited some of our more questionable choices and agreed that they were definitely questionable. To quote Dinah Washington, "What a difference a day makes. . . ."

Ultimately, we made a couple of iterations to our *pageantry of perversion* and created a more balanced and sellable product. The suits saw the error in their ways, started to acknowledge the enormous potential it had, and made us an offer to become partners. But as we got to know them better, we realized that they weren't the best fit for where we wanted to go. As much as we wanted to do it, sometimes you have to walk away. We believed we had a great idea, and the wrong partner would be the kiss of death. Kind of like how Ilya Salkind ultimately walked away from casting Neil Diamond as *Superman* in favor of Christopher Reeve. Getting into business with a porn distribution company had no future for us. We wanted to expand into the mainstream, and we didn't think they could ever really make the transition, and ultimately the deal fell apart. It was a blessing in disguise.

When we finished the reel, some people at the company, including Kourosh's archnemesis, were not happy with the uncensored direction we were heading. He saw no future in it, but then again, I saw him as a guy who still thought Betamax recorders were going to make a comeback. So while we were working day and night, he quietly convinced his friend and our angel investor that we were heading down the wrong path and to force us out of the company. Our funding was cut off and we were unable to pay the rent or any bills. We came to our office one day and the doors were chained shut. We'd been evicted. We were a whore with no house. We suddenly found ourselves adrift in open water and the sharks were circling.

Desperate but refusing to give up, we called everyone we knew for help. I reached out to one of my closest composer friends, Harry Gregson-Williams, the brilliant mind behind the scores of countless hits including all the *Shrek* movies and 2015's *The Martian*, and quite miraculously, he had a solution. He had just purchased a building near the beach and was renovating it for six months and offered us the space to move into for next to nothing. He saved us. He saved our business. With our nemesis temporarily foiled and a new office literally on the beach, just like that we were alive again and stronger than ever. The three musketeers felt invincible.

The process of courting this company had pushed us to create the vision of our own network, its programming, and the overall aesthetic of rapid-fire editing and graphics. When we came out of it, we were different people and now saw a bigger picture and our place in it. The company was fractured, and we knew we had to find a permanent solution to our internal issues. But one thing was for certain: It was time to say good-bye to Netgroupie. The next phase was at hand.

NGTV was invented that day.

7

PRISON RULES

Never laugh at live dragons.
—The Hobbit, *J. R. R. Tolkien*

What good is an idea if not born of torture? Years of painful sacrifice in pursuit of a vision based on nothing more tangible than your instincts. What good is an idea if not an exercise in self-mutilation and humility? Years of tearing away at your own flesh, mining for the material to create your masterpiece in full view of the critical savagery of a subjective world. What good is an idea if not the harbinger of the future and the catalyst for progress? Years of pushing boundaries in pursuit of a future that you hope to usher in. And yet, in spite of the sadistic and masochistic nature of the entertainment business, such beauty emerges. The idea that is No Good TV was created for the people. And after years of development, we stood on the edge of the precipice that separated us from our destiny, ready to take that final leap of faith. And if you happen to agree with Karl Marx and believe that religion "is the opium of the people," then the idea of No Good TV is, without a doubt, the people's intellectualized, underground porno!

I was born on the Fourth of July. It's probably why I have such a fiercely independent spirit. My mother practically delivered me while watching the fireworks show. So you could say I was born to bang! I'm a dreamer and I like to dream big. My journey, to this day, has never been anything short of extraordinary in its highs, its lows, and everything in between. One of the most important things I've learned is that it's not about what you think you know; it's about knowing what you don't know. It can be the difference between living your dream or dying in someone else's. I have learned a lot and have a closet full of experiences and memories that I take out and wear when I need inspiration. They all have a special place in my heart, but some will live forever.

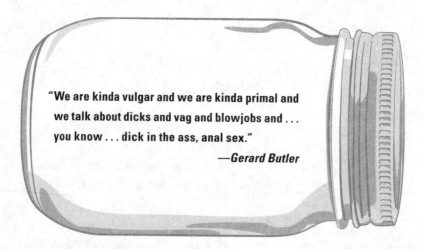

"We are kinda vulgar and we are kinda primal and we talk about dicks and vag and blowjobs and . . . you know . . . dick in the ass, anal sex."

—Gerard Butler

It was the summer of 2007 and everywhere you turned you were bombarded with Nickelback's music video for their hit song "Rockstar." It's the one that features cameos from a multitude of celebrities drowning in self-adulation because there's nothing more rock 'n' roll than a bunch of rich and famous people patting themselves on the back and telling you how awesome they are!!! Now, if you look closely at Gene Simmons's appearances in the video, you'll notice he's wearing a T-shirt that says NGTV.com. There we were, cemented in pop culture history for posterity. In the ultimate game of "How'd they do that?" it was a strange dream to think that only a few years before that, we were on the verge of bankruptcy and surrounded by dissent. How we went from Netgroupie to No Good TV, from bankruptcy to an Internet phenomenon, and from a company of eight to a production powerhouse of a hundred is the stuff of legend. That legend began with my friend Gene Simmons.

We were running on *ribs 'n' dick*, our angel investor had turned on us, the company's board was divided, our big media partnership had disintegrated, and we'd been evicted and locked out of our offices. It appeared like the sun was about to set on our dreams. With our backs against the wall, I threw a *Hail Mary* pass to my buddy Harry, who stepped in with a last-second catch. Suddenly and unbeknownst to the scheming few that surrounded us, we returned from the dead. Then, in the still of night and without telling a soul, we talked the landlord into letting us retrieve our property. Ken, Kourosh, and I moved everything into our new beach pad. Then we went silent to regroup. We could see the new dawn breaking ahead.

Almost a week went by before the board, our investor, or any of our partners realized that everything hadn't gone to shit and somehow, somewhere we had survived. It was odd. We had saved the company and its assets and somehow they were upset by that. Our nemesis had done such a number on our investor that he was upside down and didn't know it. Upon realizing that their coup had failed, the proverbial shit really hit the fan. Lawyers were being called and threats were being made. The level of insanity was at an all-time high. We didn't trust people involved in the coup, so we didn't tell them where we were and what we were doing. Then, in a final declaration of war, our nemesis did the unthinkable. In what can only be described, in hindsight, as an epic blunder, he resigned from the company and from its board. If the investor decided to sue the company, as threatened, to force us out, he needed to distance himself from the litigation. It was a beautiful mess. And as he lunged forth with his coup de grace to finish us off, we received the most unexpected phone call. "Hello. This is Gene Simmons."

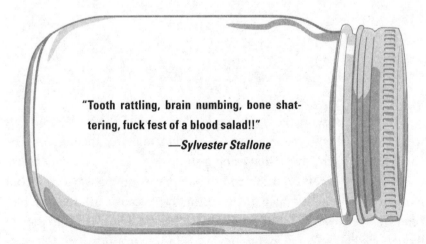

"Tooth rattling, brain numbing, bone shattering, fuck fest of a blood salad!!"
—*Sylvester Stallone*

Two hours later, we were at the demon's lair, and by lair I mean palatial, KISS-themed dungeon, OMG, estate. Gene had received a copy of the sizzle reel we had created from a friend and loved it. He and his partners had become true believers, and somehow he tracked us down. A few days later Gene and co. invested in our company. Gene doesn't like to fuck around when he sees an opportunity. Needless to say, our internal problems faded as quickly, as our previously hostile investor became an ally who wanted to help with the transaction. At which point, our nemesis became a forgotten casualty of war. Our angel investor was bought out at a modest profit; the idiot brigade had marched off a cliff, and we were renewed and re-invigorated. At the closing, I remember Gene serenading me in his best Frank Sinatra: "Fairy tales can come true, it can happen to you" while giving me a twirl. It was a beautiful moment of vindication. Together, we and Gene went on to raise millions of dollars of investment to launch our new digital network: No Good TV.

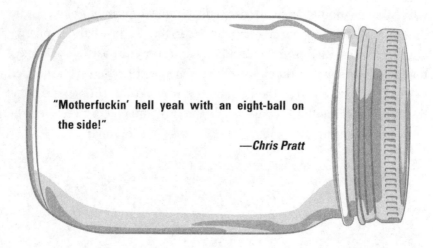

"Motherfuckin' hell yeah with an eight-ball on the side!"

—*Chris Pratt*

Building any business is a game. The rules of the game aren't always clear and your enemies are never quick to reveal themselves. The game begins with a handshake and a smile on your face on the way in, and if you're not careful it can end the same way on the way out . . . but without the smile. We had survived this far because, after all we had been through, we were all out of arrogance, and we knew that even though we had new partners, we were blind, surrounded, and our adversary was far superior in force. The only useful weapons we had at our disposal were humility and character. Trust me when I tell you there is nothing that better illuminates the gray areas where most business is transacted than humility and character. It's like a black light on a motel room bed. It doesn't tell you what you want to know; it tells you what you need to know.

In a business where there are no angels, I have often heard, "Better the devil you know than the devil you don't." But I say, *when venturing into the devil's playground, beware the horny little bastard, for all he wants to do is fork you!* That was our relationship with Gene and co. A little give, a little take, a little real, a little fake. It's what I affectionately call *Prison Rules: Fuck or Get Fucked!* Gene is smart and methodical and will challenge you with all guns blazing. There is no subtlety to him. He's not delicate about your feelings. That's not his game. He's there to poke and prod you to see what you're made of and help you make whatever decision He wants you to make or vomit from the pressure like a little bitch. Sometimes he's wrong, sometimes he's right, but the only way to deal with him is to have the courage of your convictions. It's the only thing he respects. Everything else, he could give two shits about. As he would always say, "I'm too rich to care."

He could be an asshole. In fact, there are a lot of people in this world who think Gene is an asshole. What they may not know is that he really relishes the idea of being one. He loves it. He works hard to earn it and wears it as a badge of honor. It's his calling card. He would often claim to be "the world's biggest asshole." It's a serious point of pride. He identifies with it so much that it became the title of his second solo album. But, in my opinion, there is such a thing as too much asshole, and it was my sit-down with the creators of *South Park*, Trey Parker and Matt Stone, that really put things into perspective for me:

> Sometimes in your life, you're more of a dick and sometimes, you're more of a pussy. Sometimes you're an asshole, just for an afternoon, and, hopefully, you think about it: 'I don't want to be an asshole anymore.' That's our big political statement. People have been asking us, all these reporters and stuff, 'What's your political stand?' And the only real political stand we take is a dick is different than an asshole. We don't think it's a huge stand. That's it. That's the only stand we take. Dicks are different than pussies. But pussies and dicks are both . . . we need them in the world, and they exist in the world. What

we don't need in the world is assholes 'cause they just shit all over everything.

Myself, I don't think you should put all your assholes in one basket. Try to mix it up with some dick and pussy for a more even spread.

In spite of his blunt personality, I always felt that Gene and I had a great relationship. In a funny way, we were two sides of the same asshole. He reveled in being a misogynistic prick, and I was the punk that gave him a lot of shit for it. It was all friendly. It was just our special relationship. No matter what, he was always supportive and protective of me, and we had fun when we were together. But it did all begin with a little bump in the road . . . actually two.

So there we were, partners, ready to commence our new business venture. Now that we were all on the same page, it was time to find out what that page was, exactly. Gene was a big fan of what we had accomplished with my uncensored interviews with musicians. He was even more impressed with the leap that we had taken, going from just doing bands to branching out to A-list movie stars and other celebrities. We had come a long way, but with new partners come new ideas. As part owner and chairman of the board, Gene wielded a lot of power about the direction we'd be going in, and he and his team weren't afraid to use it.

At our first board meeting, I secretly hoped Gene would spit blood or drop tongue, but it was surprisingly very formal. After Gene and his team sat down, the first words out of their mouths were:

"We think Carrie should do the interviews topless."

The room went silent. The pause wasn't just nine-months pregnant; it was octuplets. I remember thinking, *Oh shit. What have we gotten ourselves into?* Without exchanging any words, Kourosh and I looked at each other not knowing exactly how to proceed. I mean, at this point, Gene and his team held all the cards and were far more powerful than we were. Kourosh had always said, "When facing an extreme situation, the only response is escalation." (*Prison rules!*) Then, as if we had come to some silent agreement as to what needed to happen next . . . he took a deep breath and proceeded to escalate the situation.

"If we're doing that, I'm out!" Kourosh said loudly and angrily. "Respectfully, what is wrong with you guys? Did we come all this way to fail out of the gate with one profoundly stupid decision?! This is never going to happen!"

Then began two hours of heated debate over whether we were now going to serve *double Whoppers* during my interviews. I have to say that the most amusing part to me was that at no point did anyone stop to ask me if I would even be open to the idea of sharing screen time with the *Bobbsey Twins*. It was a conversation around me.

Admittedly, the request wasn't that shocking, considering it was coming from Gene Simmons, of all people. The man who loved bragging about banging 4,897 women and professing that KISS pretty much invented sex, drugs, & rock 'n' roll (though Gene himself claims he's never done drugs). But let's be honest, there was no way any A-list celebrities were going to sit down with me if I was naked and my *Super Big Gulps* were in their faces. We hadn't come all this way to now be diminished to porn-site status.

Strangely enough, a few years later, at the junket for *The King's Speech*, one of my so-called "colleagues" from the international press allegedly and unknowingly decided to prove my point. In her interview with Colin Firth, she opened with a quite serious marriage proposal to which he appeared flattered and amused while the room filled with tension and curiosity. She followed with a couple of throwaway questions about the film to throw the room off the scent, which was smart. But then she returned to her original quest and began to convince him of the seriousness of her marriage proposal and her willingness to do whatever it took to prove her worthiness. In that instant, playfulness took a rather salacious turn, and she took her top off and presented him with an organic *boob salad* for tossing. Realizing the soon-to-be Oscar winner was on the verge of a *bewb riot*, within seconds she was descended upon by security and removed from the suite and then the hotel. Many *spank-banks* were filled with mental postcards that day, but just like Dustin Diamond after releasing the porno film *Screeched*, her career was on life support. Like I said, sometimes Gene was wrong.

Hence, **RULE #3** was created. I was never EVER going to go topless. Period. End of story. I give Lena Dunham all the credit in the world. She can play Ping-Pong nude on camera all day/every day with Patrick Wilson, her boobs flopping around like sockeye salmon on a dry dock, and it's hipster art. Sure, she gets her fair share of criticism, but I don't think she's ever been called a ho. If I played Ping-Pong with Patrick Wilson topless, I'd be slut-shamed out of showbiz. Hell, if I weaved baskets with the topless Zulu tribe for the National Geographic Channel, I'd still probably be slut-shamed. *#bigbreastedlivesmatter*

Knowing this, if we didn't stick to my "no topless" rule, we would fail. We weren't weaving baskets. What we were doing was admittedly salacious, so we had to have lines that I wouldn't cross. Listen, if I managed to get a job at Hooters and *not* wear the shiny *crotch creepers*, I could figure a way out of this, too. This time, the stakes were a tad higher. We had to prove to Gene Simmons and our new investors that we could launch NGTV, now a multimillion-dollar company, and succeed on my talent, not my *chi-chis*. I have to give Gene credit because after everyone cooled down and he heard our position on why this would be a nonstarter and would kill all the relationships we had built, he changed his mind and convinced our investors to trust us on this. I think we gained a little of their respect that day, too. Again, thanks to *prison rules*!!

It was a fucking crazy way to start. It was heartbreaking to realize that after everything it had taken for us to come together, we actually could not have been further apart. But going through the fire that day with them taught us a lot. We learned that building a business is very much like a naked steeplechase with all of its obstacles, hurdles, unnecessary nudity, and blind spots. You never know what lies ahead, and you've got to take more than a few leaps of faith. If you don't stay focused, you will wind up "ass-up" in a ditch, naked. We definitely had our hands full with our new partners, but we all wanted the same thing so we kept on keepin' on. We hit the ground running.

When you raise money, there's an expectation to improve everything almost immediately. It's an impossible task but has to be done. Now that we had turned a corner into the big leagues, Kourosh and I sat down and had a serious conversation about upping our game at every level. We had dreamed about this for a long time, and it was all coming to fruition. We talked about new ways to improve the graphic packages and video design, new programming ideas, and building our own studio space. It was all going great until the conversation ever so subtly turned to me. That crafty son of a bitch! It was then that I realized that he had gotten me all softened up with the fun stuff so he could have a conversation with me about *me*.

Show business is a perception game. The way you look and how you handle yourself walking into a room is your first move in the interview. Kourosh and I both agreed that it was important that I look as polished and professional as the A-list celebrities we were going after. If I was going to sit across from Cate Blanchett and invite her to play a game of *Dirty Yahtzee*, it might be easier if I looked more like her than a *Coyote Ugly* bartender laying out shots. A bit of polish, a hint of sass, and a friendly smile are your greatest tools. I had one shot at making the right impression out of the gate. It was kill or be killed, so to speak. (*Prison rules!*) As Kourosh sweetly put it, "It was time for Norma Jean to become Marilyn Monroe," or as I took it, "It was time to polish the turd!" Kourosh had already taken care of the two essentials by hiring a makeup artist and a wardrobe stylist. Every girl's dream come true!

But in true Kourosh fashion, he took it one step further. I now also had a nutritionist and a celebrity trainer, who also worked with superstars like Madonna. I was petrified and intrigued. Even though my dad owned a gym, and I'd spent many days hanging out there after school, I didn't ever work out. I just played on the machines like a jungle gym. Once, in high school, I got the knuckleheaded idea to train to be an aerobics teacher. I took three classes in a row and literally couldn't get out of bed for a week. I was pretty sure I was dying. I vowed from that day forward that I'd never exercise again. So basically, I'd never worked out in my entire life, except for one day really, *really, REALLY* hard.

I put my head down and committed to three months of pure torture in the name of my future. I hit the gym two hours a day, six days a week, doing cardio, boxing, and weapons training, just to keep it interesting. I kept thinking, *If I'm going to do this, I want to come out the other end a fucking superhero!* I hopped on the bandwagon of one of those celebrity-endorsed, overpriced, tasteless, twelve-hundred-calorie-diet meal plans that get delivered to your house every day. After the first week of inedible nutrition, I wished I could just not eat food anymore.

The whole ordeal was a nightmare. At first, it just hurt physically, but then, over time, it was way more mental anguish. Every waking moment was spent thinking about what I wasn't eating and how many calories I needed to burn before my next meal of carrots and celery. In three months I had completely transformed my body. I had lost a bunch of baby fat, gained a bunch of muscle, and was down to nearly 12 percent body fat. I felt like Linda Hamilton from *Terminator 2*.

On the flip side, I was basically starving and I hadn't had a drink in months, but that wasn't even the worst of it. Much to my surprise, I had completely lost my tits. They shrank down four cup sizes, from a DDDD to a C! They looked like pathetic little deflated water balloons. I had been wearing the same sports bra for three months and didn't notice the severe shrinkage. My whole life I always had *bazookas*, but now I had *slingshots*. I panicked every time I looked in the mirror: *Am I going to be like this forever? Do I, of all fucking people, need to get a boob job? What the fuck did I just do?* When I lost them, I felt like I'd lost part of my identity. A woman without a country. A boat without an oar. A hand without a donut . . . mmm, donut . . .

In the middle of my identity crisis, Kourosh left the country to do some investor fund-raising. I was running the company while he was on the other side of the world. I was left to manage an office full of needy creatives, a barrage of board members, and our ultrasensitive industry relationships, all the while being extremely *hangry*! It was more than I could handle. The pressure of needing to be perfect in mind, body, and soul was killing me. I was at the gym slicing and dicing my imaginary enemy with a samurai sword when the weight of everything kicked me right between the eyes. I fell to my knees and started bawling. The messy, ugly kind of crying. My trainer Johnny must have thought I'd broken my arm or something. He came running over to me and let me melt into a puddle of gross all over his sweatshirt. This was all too much. We had only a few months until the launch, and I was a complete mess. I didn't feel like myself anymore. I didn't feel strong; I felt exhausted. I hadn't seen any of my friends in months. I had lost perspective of why I was doing all this. Does my fitting into a size zero really matter to Michael Douglas or Sharon Stone?

I decided Cate Blanchett and the rest of her porcelain-skinned, perfectly toned pals would just have to deal with the booze-soaked, big-breasted broad sitting across from them. Once I made the decision to go back to a less extreme lifestyle, I started to feel like my strong self again. But it took me another three months to get back to a healthy headspace, where I didn't feel guilty for not going to the gym every day or eating a taco instead of a piece of lettuce. Mmm, taco . . .

Slowly, everything started coming back, including my tits. At the end of that six-month period—three of torture, three of healing—the transformation was complete . . . I have a total appreciation for what

Matthew McConaughey went through while preparing for his role in *Dallas Buyers Club*. For me, it was all about having the right priorities. I realized that my body, my clothes, and my hair and makeup were there to service my mind, not the other way around.

Armed with that bit of wisdom, my body and mind transformed permanently into a woman as close to Power Girl as I, personally, could get. I felt like if I could bring myself to that point and live, I could do anything (cue cape flapping in the wind). Denzel Washington gave me a sweet reminder of that during one of our more fun and "animated" encounters. He complimented me on my swanky boots, and when I thanked him, he gave me this knowing gaze and said, "It's not the shoes; it's who's walkin' in 'em!"

Now it was time to face the moment of truth. We had come one hell of a long way. After years of development, untold hardship and sacrifice, financial ruin, a failed hostile takeover bid, a commercial eviction, a midnight run to save the assets, a world tour with Gene Simmons to raise money, tens of millions of dollars of investment, boardroom showdowns, banker brawls, the birth of a very big idea, and more than a million woman- and man-hours, we found ourselves at the very beginning, again. A new beginning. One filled with infinite possibilities and untold adventures. Launch night was upon us and my heart was beating out of my chest!

The stage was set. The players were in their positions. The atmosphere was electric . . . lights, camera . . .

EPILOGUE

On the day the site was to launch, a potent mixture of exhaustion, anticipation, and adrenaline was the elephant in the room. Some last-minute glitches had pushed the launch from 7 P.M. to 11:30 P.M., so naturally, tensions were high. But by 8 P.M., Ken and I and our entire world of employees, friends, and family had converged on the launch party's secret location. Around two hundred and fifty people had crowded into the home of one of our favorite boosters for a fun little shindig to celebrate this incredible milestone. Unbeknownst to anyone in attendance, the legend of the No Good party would be born that night. I should've seen it coming, given the absurd number of lube bottles hidden in every nook and cranny of that house. We all should have seen it coming and . . . as it turns out . . . some of us did . . . see it . . . coming!

The location was stunning!! A gorgeous mansion located high in the Hollywood Hills with a beautiful pool and mega hot tub with a breathtaking view of the city. Something you'd typically only see in a P. Diddy or Kevin Federline music video or in the finest high-end anal gangbang porn. And I'm talking about the good shit like *Everyone I Did Last Summer* and *A Few Hard Men*. That joint was *built for banging, erected for erections, fabricated for fucking.* You get the picture. We had a super-eclectic mix of people there that night: from multiple cultures to multiple fetishes and everything in between. Our host for the evening had invited maybe fifty friends who all seemed to be getting along great with our crew. The scene was a cross between Thursday night's TigerHeat whatever-the-fuck-thing-happens and Saturday night at the Avalon in Hollywood, and you could feel the excitement in the air.

Gene Simmons arrived at 11 P.M. as scheduled, causing a bit of a stir. He was always good about those things. Proud of the company, he kept an office at NGTV and appeared at everything that mattered. And I don't mean the typical celebrity champagne-room appearance. You know, where a celeb shows up and stays for the length of one lap dance, leaving everyone at *half-chub* on the way out. Not Gene—he was a gentleman and would consistently go the *jizztance.* He always made sure that all the *slits, bits, and clits* were attended to and the walls were a muddle of male and female *cumshots* that would make Jackson Pollock proud. And something told me that our party house had seen its fair share of that sort of thing, since it had hosted Gene many times before. Gene mingled as our people were drinking, eating, dancing, and getting a hard-earned release. This night was theirs for the taking.

Kourosh was the last to arrive at the party after the launch was successful. I met him outside, and when we walked back into the house, the at-capacity crowd erupted into the loudest and most glorious "we just won the Super Bowl" cheer!! I remember us spinning around in its splendor, and upon making eye contact with Ken, we raised our fists in defiant celebration, as did he, spurring on an even more thunderous rebuttal. It was the closest I've ever been to knowing what it's like to be *Rocky*!! What a night! Everyone was plenty drunk and then some . . . and they were just getting started. One thing I'll say about my *Nogoodniks,* they knew how to have a good time, but sometimes, when you least expect it, the good time has you.

I followed Gene out the door about an hour later as I had a call time of 5 A.M. for my gig hosting the Oscars' red carpet for the TV Guide Network. Come rain or shine, launch party or not, I was always working. I said my good-byes and headed out. Now, I can't tell you who was involved, what was done, or to whom. Who instigated, who perpetuated, or who got naked and who didn't. I can tell you nobody got hurt, and I can tell you that those people tell me they look back at that party as one of the greatest experiences of their lives. You see, sometime after I left, the evening took an unexpected and storied turn toward the debauched. And all I know for sure is what was left behind for us to discover the next day. The unforgettable aftermath of a balls-out bacchanal that no one could explain.

The cleanup crew was greeted with a wreckage of half-naked bodies passed out in *cuddle piles* spread out around the house, pool, and hot tub. There were used condoms floating in the pool, next to beer cans and trash. And in between the randomly scattered towels, blankets, and cushions lay an unsettling variety of used sex toys, floggers, paddles, inflatable butt-plugs, and restraints. And you couldn't get away from the dozens of half-empty bottles of Uberlube and Boy Butter or squeezed-out tubes of Fresh Balls and Aveda body products adorning every table like a wedding centerpiece. Which was really too bad because at a certain point Astroglide just starts to smell like burned rubber, and that house smelled like the aftermath of a tire fire inside a brothel. Cleanup was a nightmare, and it took forever to pick up all the cigarettes, blunts, packets of Big League Chew, broken handcuffs, and half-used bananas.

What actually did and didn't happen is anyone's guess, but it was one hell of a party. I was just happy that our crew had embraced being No Good and really went for it. And boy, did they go for it! I didn't expect the full *Caligula* on the first time out but it was a great omen of the good times to come. It was the first of many parties that would be attended by a lot of our friends in this town. Don't even get me started on the seventies-porn-themed Christmas party!

In the interest of protecting the guilty, I'll leave it to your imagination to fill in the blanks of what happened at our parties. I will say that those who left early didn't know anything and those who stayed late wouldn't remember.

8

MORE "FUCK YEAH" THAN "FUCK YOU"

> **We are all in the gutter,**
> **but some of us are looking at the stars.**
> *—Oscar Wilde*

Pop quiz, hotshot!!

An entire nation has just witnessed a dangerous, five-hour-long, collision-filled, high-speed car chase through the streets of Los Angeles. Having run out of gas, the carjacker is now trapped in a standoff with an army of SWAT with their weapons drawn. Heading into the third hour of this tense confrontation, the carjacker moves into the backseat of the stolen black Denali, lights up a fat joint, and is playing Xbox while yelling obscenities out the window. Every moment of the entire day is captured in detail by dozens of network TV cameras who have been sitting on a close-up shot of his windshield and dashboard. Then in a shocking move he pulls out his penis and starts masturbating for the cameras as the networks fight the urge to cut away. With the carjacker's *dick-hand* out of commission, the cops seize the opportunity to finally make their move and use armored vehicles to pull the truck apart and arrest the ejaculating felon safely with everything but his dignity intact. Within minutes, numerous press outlets are calling you for a comment!

What do you do? What do you do?

Well, if you're me, you just spent the whole day surrounded by your entire company, drinks in hand, channel surfing all of the TV networks and watching in utter disbelief as these incredible events unfolded with a huge No Good TV logo sitting in full view of every conceivable camera shot. "Project of destiny!" yelled Kourosh, as I rolled my eyes. He was always prone to hyperbole. But somehow, today, he was right on the money!

So I turned to our newest employee, Scott Bachmann, who was sitting next to me, and I said, "Well, Scott. It's your truck. What do you want to do?" Unbeknownst to any of us, earlier in the morning, his top-of-the-line, tricked-out spectacle of a beautiful black Denali had been stolen from our parking lot on a collision course with destiny that no one could have imagined. And sitting on its recently detailed dashboard, and in full view of the world, was none other than a giant No Good TV logo printed on his temporary parking pass. While it tore him to pieces to watch his prized possession get stolen, crashed multiple times, and have its tires blown out and its interior desecrated before being drawn and quartered on its way to being totaled all on live TV, the ridiculousness of the moment wasn't lost on him. So he looked at me and said, "Well, nobody was hurt, so if I'm going to be at the center of a media circus, then let's bring the circus to NGTV!"

Within forty-five minutes, our production crew had set up and lit a shooting space at our bar. Our wardrobe stylists pimped out Scott with some cool threads along with an NGTV cap, an NGTV gold medallion on a chain, and a pair of Dolce & Gabbana sunglasses. His "hip-hop on steroids" style was a perfect match for the farce that had played out on national television all day. Soon thereafter came the onslaught of press to shoot our beautiful studio and interview the man of the hour, who was workin' it almost as hard as James Franco begging for relevance. Yeah . . . Scott was playin' on that "next level visual shit!" (Thank you, Black Eyed Peas.)

When I first met this remarkable guy who, in time, would become a trusted friend, I didn't know what to make of this man who appeared to have stepped right out of the thirteenth century and into our lobby at NGTV. But he turned out to be an amazing executive producer as well as a fuckin' badass editor who really knew how to make an Avid sing. He was a warrior in search of a battle, who fought like a champion, and his experience and passion was a huge part of what made NGTV such a force to be reckoned with. Clearly, he was destined to be a part of our No Good family, and we were lucky to have found him.

This wouldn't be the only time we'd find ourselves front and center in the inexplicable theater of the bizarre as we fought to bring this dream to life. But this sure did set the stage for our brand. We were eight months out from launching, and *this* was our introduction to national media attention. What a fuckin' way to get our name out there and cement our reputation as our date with destiny quickly approached.

Neck-deep in cultural mockery and wearing a wink and a smile, No Good TV officially launched on YouTube on February 21, 2007, with a dozen original series, including *Up Close with Carrie Keagan*, *Down and Dirty*, *Deep Inside*, *Fresh Meat*, *Hustla's Ball*, and *Reel Junkie*. There was a great deal of creative energy at work, and the shows were reflective of the amazing talent assembled at the company. We saw ourselves as an idea factory, and we dreamed big and went for it. We weren't afraid to improvise and run with whatever momentary lapse of reason came before us. And, just like most inspired ideas, one of our most popular series was conceived from just such a moment.

I'd gone to a hotel to interview Alicia Keys, but the room they threw us into was so small that once we brought in all the equipment and set up, I had nowhere to sit. Before we had time to figure out an alternative, Alicia and her people arrived. So out of pure necessity, I suggested we do it in bed. Without really thinking it through and being the cool chick she was, she agreed. We hopped into bed together and made sweet, sweet love. Just kidding, it was only *oral*. And just like that, *In Bed with Carrie* was born.

We had come such a long way by then. When I look back to the very beginning, it's hard to believe how scared shitless I was, at first, with the movie stars. I broke my cherry with Nicolas Cage—he was the first big movie star I interviewed—and I was as lily-livered as Brian Williams in a Black Hawk. My very first press junket was for Nic's directorial debut, *Sonny*, which starred James Franco (post *Freaks and Geeks*, pre sexting teen girls he met in Times Square) as a gigolo who sleeps with all these MILFs. Perfect content for what we were trying to do, but you have no idea what people are really like until you get in the room with them. I found out pretty quickly that Nic's incredibly soft-spoken and pretty shy. I asked a generic question or two and realized it was going to go nowhere. So I took the plunge. No risk, no reward!

Me: So, Nic, are you into the older women or was it just for the movie? *(I say it with a wink.)*

(He bursts out laughing. Phew! That worked.)

Nic: Oh, wow, no . . . *(Blushing.)*

Me: I'm surprised you got the older women to show their breasts because it's not something you see every day.

He laughed again and it was on. After I broke the ice, he could see where I was coming from, and the interview went off without a hitch. That was me dipping my pinky toe into the world of edgy interviews with the A-list. Who knew then that the calm, almost serene, gentle drizzle of suggestiveness would eventually turn into a torrential downpour of filth?

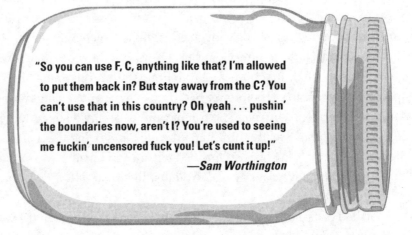

"So you can use F, C, anything like that? I'm allowed to put them back in? But stay away from the C? You can't use that in this country? Oh yeah . . . pushin' the boundaries now, aren't I? You're used to seeing me fuckin' uncensored fuck you! Let's cunt it up!"
—*Sam Worthington*

In the early days, we worked like fiends, going to every single junket, press event, red carpet, or paper bag opening we could get into. But the press junkets, where you could get one-on-one interviews with talent, were, without a doubt, the *money shot*. Short of having your own talk show, this is the nirvana of entertainment journalism. Press junkets are very serious business, with studios often spending enormous amounts of money to create elaborate events in multiple destinations to help launch their movies. Often held in fancy hotels, like the Four Seasons in LA or the Regency in New York, the studio reps usher the movie's stars through dozens of structured and heavily monitored interviews with journalists from a variety of different outlets.

You're expected to behave a certain way, ask the usual questions, not ask personal questions, and basically adhere to a certain degree of decorum. They've been doing it the same way for as long as anyone cares to remember. Probably longer. If you've ever seen the film *America's Sweethearts* starring Billy Crystal and Catherine Zeta-Jones, it'll give you an idea of what I'm talking about. It is an immovable object that stands at the very center of the promotions process. It's limited in its accessibility and almost machinelike in its precision. There's a lot of money at stake, and the people behind it are used to doing things in a certain very safe and very predictable fashion. Like any old-school tradition, change is met with great consternation. Usually being delivered in the form of your ass being handed to you in dramatic fashion. So you can imagine what a shock to the system it must have been when this purveyor of the potty mouth persuasion entered the picture. It should have been a recipe for disaster. It shoulda!

In an amusing way, a press junket is a lot like a sex-toy factory. Imagine the queue of press people as a long assembly line and every journalist as a *Pocket Rocket* slowly moving down the conveyor belt into a variety of interview rooms. Think of the interview rooms as the place where product testing and quality control occurs. In each room the *pocket-rocket*s are turned on and tested on the talent, all under the watchful eye of the studio and personal publicists, who act as the quality assurance team. If the interview was satisfactory and nobody stepped out of line, meaning the *Pocket Rocket* created just the right tingling sensation for the talent, then it's approved, packaged, and sent out into the world for public consumption. However, if the *Pocket Rocket* doesn't get the talent in the mood, the interview tapes are confiscated and the *Pocket Rocket* dispensed with.

Junket after junket, week after week, year after year, it had been a *Pocket Rockets–only* club. Now, don't get me wrong, *Pocket Rockets* are awesome. They are proficient, super fun, and get the job done. But unless you were a *Pocket Rocket*, there was no place for you at a press junket. So when I showed up on the conveyor belt, no one knew exactly what I was, but they knew I was no *Pocket Rocket*. And when I got into the room and revealed myself as a *ribbed rabbit vibrator with an anal tickler* . . . somebody should have called security. But they didn't. Perhaps they were just a little . . . let's say . . . overstimulated. Whatever it was, by the time it was over, reaching for a deep drag of a cigarette was more important than questioning what had just happened.

There was nothing like No Good TV at the time, and I wouldn't have been surprised if there was some apprehension about what we were doing. Given what E! had done a couple of years back with their show *Celebrities Uncensored,* it would not have been crazy for reps to think we might be trying to ambush their celebrity clients. But E!'s show was based on paparazzi footage and *gotcha* journalism, which was the furthest thing from what we were doing. It was never our goal to ambush anyone. Our motto was more *"Fuck yeah!"* than *"Fuck you!"* We wanted the celebs to be in on the joke, not the butt of the joke. You'll recall that I was bullied as a kid, so the last thing I wanted to do was make anyone feel bushwhacked. Our goal was to create a friendly, party atmosphere that would lead to candid moments with the stars. It was unheard of at the time, so it made us different.

That simple motto would enable me to create an atmosphere where big celebrities would push all kinds of boundaries, and sometimes, lead the charge. Like when I met up with Gerard Butler to interview him for *P.S. I Love You.* He and I had crossed paths a few times before, and he really enjoyed the insanity of my interviews. So it was no surprise that, on that occasion, he took the lead, and I played along with what ended up being a ridiculously sexually charged interview. (Emphasis on ridiculous. When he saw me walk into the room, he started pretend-tweaking his nipples in preparation for the interview, and I knew it was on! We definitely pushed a few boundaries that day!)

Gerard: I was playing with my nipples. *(Acting out rubbing his nipples with his fingers.)*

Me: That was the move I showed you, like the week before . . . right . . . that was the one.

Gerard: Ohh . . . you did that really well.

Me: Thanks, man! I tried.

Gerard: Not as good as . . . the other things you did.

Me: Well, yeah . . . right . . . thanks! Now, there's this thing you guys do [in the movie] . . . this look that you supposedly have that can get girls to kiss you . . . is that true?

Gerard: You ready?

Me: Uh-huh.

Gerard: *(Proceeds to cross his eyes and slowly nod his head left to right.)* How's that?

Me: *(I pretend to completely lose myself in a state of bliss and fall forward from weakness with my hand on his knee and scream:)* OH MY GOD!

Gerard: You're not kissing me; you're grabbing my leg.

Me: *(So I get up and go in for a passionate kiss—at least that's what it looked like on camera—then return to my seat.)* I can't even tell you how fuckin' hot that was!

Gerard: *(Giving me an overtly sexy look.)* You are!

Me: *(Giving him an overtly sexy look back.)* No, you are! *(Then I aggressively and loudly shake and sigh in a sexual manner . . . a little bit like the diner scene in* When Harry Met Sally *but more like 20 percent orgasm . . . you can never go full orgasm . . . it's not professional.)*

Gerard: I just came! *(To camera with a playful grin on his face.)* I did!

Me: *(Laughing in disbelief.)*

Gerard: And again . . . wooooh! *(Loudly, with big eyes and a smile.)* . . . And again!

Me: Weeeeeeee! *(Loudly.)*

Gerard: Multiple!!!!!

Me: This is where the happy endings just keep cumming!!! *(Both laughing.)*

I mean, come on, when in the hell has something like this ever happened in a junket interview—or in any interview! After which Gerard and his reps thank me while laughing uncontrollably. This was special.

It didn't stop there; this motto created a world where even the most serious and revered celebrities would unwind. I don't know what other journalists' experiences have been like with Denzel Washington, but from what I've seen he's a pretty no nonsense guy who takes his craft seriously and does not suffer fools gladly. He's also surrounded by tough reps who are not there to fuck around. Now, the Denzel I know, from our several encounters over the years, is playful, funny, edgy, witty, and loves to laugh! Some of our exchanges are legendary (see Chapter 12: *The Lap Dance*). He's not a potty mouth in the typical sense, but he knows a thing or two and—man, oh man—does he know how to work an innuendo.

When I interviewed him at the junket for *The Taking of Pelham 123*, Denzel was jokingly explaining to me how, even though there was nothing but nonstop cursing in the film, he, personally, didn't like to curse. But in true Denzel fashion, he then proceeded to teach me something far worse . . . you see, one way or another we all curse.

Denzel: I don't have to stoop to that level. I'm an artist!! I'm . . . I'm an AC-TOR!! (*Moving his hands like a conductor and doing his best flagrant Marlon Brando impression.*)

Me: You have the voice. That's all you need.

Denzel: That's what it is?

Me: Yes. And he [John Travolta in the movie] said, you know, because of your smooth voice you'd be actually a *bitch* in prison!

Then there was a very, very pregnant pause. Let's face it, I had just, indirectly, called Denzel a *bitch* . . . hmm . . . Now I was in for a game of Who Blinks First. He looked at me with those intense Denzel eyes that either end in someone getting killed or being made love to. I stayed right there with him, eye-to-eye, keeping a subtle, friendly smile on my face. If he sensed weakness in me, I'd be dead. He kept rubbing his chin . . . and then he broke and took a left turn . . . 'cause why . . . 'cause he's Denzel *"Motherfucking"* Washington . . . that's why!

Denzel: They used to call it a *Maytag*. You ever hearda that?

Me: No.

Denzel: Be a *Maytag*!

Me: Why? What does that mean?

Denzel: Aahhhhh. (*With a wry smile on his face.*) You'll find out!

Me: (*I turn to my friend who was running the room and ask:*) Tony, what does that mean?

Denzel: Go to No Good TV! *Maytag*! (*Laughing.*)

Me: (*Tony's waving me off like he doesn't want to touch this.*) He's [Tony] staying out of it! (*Laughing.*)

Denzel: *Maytag.* Wash the clothes! . . . *Maytag.* Cook the food! Hahaha, haaaaa!! *(Laughing loudly . . . just lovin' it.)*

Me: Lead dog! *(Pointing into the camera.)*

Denzel: Das right! Nah . . . *Maytag* is sore. Sore behind! *Maytag* on the top bunk! *Maytag!*

Me: We're in trouble!

Denzel: *(Big smile on his face.)* Not talking about the dishwasher! But he does wash the dishes!! *(WIDE GRIN!)*

He is, without a doubt, one of the most intelligent and fun celebrities I have ever had the pleasure of playing with, and he wasn't done. Before it was over he decided to promote the film with the newest word on my naughty list, "Go see the movie or you might end up being a *MAYTAG!*" Damn!

Witnessing Denzel and other A-listers embrace what I was doing was an incredible feeling. Watching them let go, run with the moment, then laugh and enjoy this guilty pleasure called No Good TV made me realize that what we had created was a bit like a roller coaster. Here's Mark Wahlberg and Will Ferrell taking a few loop-de-loops:

Mark: Get the dick out of your butt and go see the movie!

Will: Please . . . please just get the dick out of your butt!

Mark: After two hours, you can put it right back in.

Will: You don't even have to see the movie. Just get the dick out of your butt!

Mark: Yeah!

Me: Or just for like a minute while you're driving.

Will: Yeah, yeah . . . just long enough.

Me: To get to the theater.

Will: Just long enough to see the movie. Once you see the movie you can put the dick back in your butt.

Mark: If you go early in the day or late enough at night, you can put it on the seat.

Will: Go see the movie then you can put the dick back in your butt!

Mark: You could be the other guy.

At some point, even the coolest and most reserved *cats* are compelled to put their hands up and cuss for joy. Fuck yeah! Like when

Robert Downey, Jr., felt compelled to share a very special story about how he fucked with director and co-star Ben Stiller on the set of their hit comedy classic *Tropic Thunder.*

> All I was trying to do was to make either Ben feel disgusted or make him feel like I'd said the strangest thing he's heard all day: *"I'm like the little boy who's playing with his dick when he's nervous. You should come over to my village for dinner. I would serve you rotten donkey vagina. A slithering hot broken donkey vagina."* A rotting donkey vagina. God I still love that line. I'm glad it has somewhere to live.

Now, my entry into this world wasn't without a failed stage dive or two, which I'll get to in later chapters, but an institution that should have rejected me accepted me with open arms. Like a *dirty Tron*, I was a rogue program in a finite system, making changes, stirring up trouble, and getting away with it. I credit that to not really knowing what the hell I was doing or how I was expected to behave. If I had, I probably would have been too afraid to challenge the media industrial complex known as the press junket.

This magical realm is governed by mystical beings called studio reps but is populated by junketeers, who are truly magical creatures. There is no more rare or privileged soul in the world than the junketeer, and to become one with them is a rare blessing that should never be taken for granted. For the most part, they are an extremely friendly group of people stuck in a strange but celebratory never-ending hamster wheel. Week in, week out, flying around the country and sometimes the world, staying in amazing hotels, eating great food, and having the same conversations over and over again with the same celebrities. It is the classic *Groundhog Day* experience and a great gig if you can get it.

Some have been doing it for years, some for decades, and some of the reporters have been doing these since the Stone Age. There are those that take it super seriously and consider each interview to be a celebration of the gospel. There are others who are just enjoying the ride and getting their shit done. And of course, there are always a few who are only interested in the buffet and the swag. Altogether, they are an incredible cast of characters who make up this crazy subculture at the junkets that would make for a great Christopher Guest movie. I consider myself lucky to call many of them my good friends and to have joined their happy crew. They have never been anything but kind and accepting of me. Nobody knows how to party like the junketeers. Nobody!

These two factions, publicists and journalists, are the cornerstones of a quintessential symbiotic relationship that governs entertainment promotions. Everything in entertainment, no matter if it's related to television, music, movies, or what have you, is a bit of a circle jerk. Everybody's *JO'ing* each other for something. I'm sure you've heard the expression that it's more business than show, but in reality, it's more about *show me your business*. In politics, one hand washes the other, but in entertainment it's more of a *rub'n'tug*. And entertainment PR is the constant tug between journalists and publicists. Journalists who want to get one off and publicists who ultimately decide who *cums* . . . and who goes.

Most entertainment news shows tend to place celebrities on a pedestal and surround them with a buffer zone that makes them unattainable. Our goal was the complete opposite. We wanted to give the audience a connection to the stars built on a bridge of relatability. We wanted to hang with them, not on them. For me, this always presented the challenge of walking a fine line between being fun & friendly, flirty & filthy, all while maintaining my respectability. After all, I didn't want to be just another faceless, sycophantic journalist to the talent I was interviewing. While I was being R-rated, the goal for me and my writers was to do it with humor, intelligence, and precision. More Howard Stern than Stuttering John.

We continually challenged ourselves to write smart comedy. So on those occasions where everything came together, it was bawdy but clever. I knew if I wanted to stand out, the key was to define who I was and stay true to it. Be different, be consistent, and be fearless. That way I wouldn't run the risk of getting sucked into the *butt-kissing bonanza* that a press junket can become. There would be no future for me in that. Trust me when I tell you all lips feel the same against a celebrity's ass. It comforts them for a moment, and then they are on to the next pucker!

Coming out of the anarchy of the press and promotions in the music world, I was always quite taken with the whole pomp and circumstance of the movie press junket. Like the hushed, proper vibe and total reverence for the talent. And the generous and respectful way the press was treated. All of which was in stark contrast to my prior experiences with bands. In the music world, the schedule was *whenever* and the interview was a *clusterfuck*. We had fun, but we wasted so much time waiting around and were often treated like rats fighting over the last crumb. I can't even begin to tell you how we killed days waiting for talent to show up. That was our norm. So when the band sucked, it was such a colossal waste, but when they were good, it was magical.

I once waited for six hours for The Black Eyed Peas to show up for a scheduled interview. But unlike some artists who'll show up super late and play the "aloof" card, these guys were very considerate. Will.i.am, Taboo, and apl.de.ap were super apologetic and overly kind about the whole thing. It says a lot about someone when they don't need to be nice to you but they are anyway. So right away, I didn't even care about the wait. Just about ten minutes into the interview, a fuse box blew out, killing the power in the entire facility, which included the dressing room we were in. We lost all of our lights and were left with just our cameras rolling on battery packs.

So there we were, sitting in the dark with the band, not knowing what the fuck to do. We waited for a few minutes, hoping it would come back on, but it wasn't happening. There are plenty of artists who would have called it a night and nobody would've blamed them, but not these guys. Will and the boys felt so bad about making us wait, and they wanted to keep going. "You got flashlights? Get 'em out; let's keep rolling." So try to get your heads around this scene: one of the biggest bands in the world snuggled up closely with me, like we were in a bomb shelter, while Kourosh held one weak-ass flashlight over us and Ken rolled blindly with his camera because nobody could see a fucking thing in the room. I had a hand mic I would move around, and they would take turns holding the other flashlight under their chins when they spoke. If you didn't know better, you'd think we were telling ghost stories around a campfire. Half the interview was just all of us acting like idiots and laughing our asses off. Clearly, they were getting a kick out of this whole *shit-show*, as were their people, who were also standing around in the dark. When I run into the guys every now and then, like when Taboo appeared on *In Bed With*, we reminisce about what it was like to be there on the *darkest* day in the history of The Black Eyed Peas!

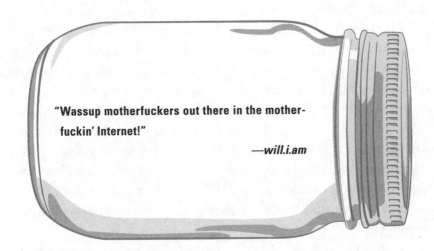

"Wassup motherfuckers out there in the mother-fuckin' Internet!"

—*will.i.am*

I would've waited twenty hours for them, but then not every interview was The Black Eyed Peas. Half the time, it was some band I'd never heard of getting a little ahead of themselves and acting like a bunch of *prima donna wild banshee assholes* before their first record had come out. Back then we'd hang out with them on their bus or backstage. I even did an interview in a bathroom once! Occasionally the interviews were really interesting, some were just us fucking off, and some were simply introverted musicians who didn't know how to do anything other than play their instruments. It was a little bit of a crapshoot. We would usually get about thirty minutes with them, which was just enough time to rile them up and get a few stories. So the overall conditions were crap, but you had plenty of time with the talent to mine for gold.

The movie promotions were a whole other beast. I have to admit though, at first, the junkets were a bit scary. The studios treated you well and everything ran on schedule, but once you're in the room you've got exactly four minutes for your interview. WHAT??!!?? What the fuck was I going to do in four fucking minutes? Believe me when I tell you, those four minutes fly by so fast, I swear if you fart, you'll miss it. To make matters worse, it was timed on a stopwatch, with twelve to fifteen people watching every word coming out of your mouth like a hawk. It was intimidating to say the least. Sometimes the talent's publicist will sit right in your line of vision or right behind you, purposefully making it really uncomfortable. On one particular occasion, it got even weirder.

I remember at a junket many years ago for a big summer tent-pole movie, where the high-profile lead actor was embroiled in a very public relationship with an equally if not more famous actress/singer, and things, allegedly, got a little out of hand. Security was off the charts in the hotel and everyone was on high alert. Then she showed up in a crowd of chaos in what can be best described as the Tasmanian devil landing in a Ping-Pong factory. Yep, there were so many balls flying everywhere, you'd think you were in a Tijuana strip club on Horchata night. Anyway, she proceeded to walk into the interview room and sit behind the journalists and make faces at her boyfriend during their interviews.

From that point on, no one was getting usable interviews, and an already complicated situation turned into theater of the absurd. I suppose there's an element of fun to playing Pickle in the Middle, but when you're the pickle, it's a mindfuck-and-a-half to get through. You just have to shut out all the noise and distractions and get about your business. Out of the gate you've got to be charming, graceful, funny, intriguing, and brilliant. You basically have to find the sweet spot within the first sixty seconds and bring it out over the next three minutes. This shit ain't easy. Just imagine sitting across from your favorite star and having to become their BFF in one minute. It takes a cool head and killer instincts; otherwise you walk out with nothing.

So picture this intense, pressure-filled vibe when I first strolled in with my *norks* and *potty mouth*. It was a *knock for six* on every level. We really had to earn our way into the world, and we earned it by being up front that we were uncensored and, more than anything, entertaining. Who wouldn't find Andy Samberg discussing merkins and mustache rides fun? Well, he did it while promoting *Hot Rod*.

Me: All right, how fucking HOT is *Hot Rod*?
Andy: Woo! *Hot Rod* is like the hottest fucking shit ever made.
Me: Is it the first time in history where Hollywood has actually stolen the porn title before the porn?

Andy: Well . . . *A River Runs Through It? White Squall? Big?*

Me: Umm . . . you got me. *The Big Easy*, also?

Andy: That's just about someone who bones a lot. But that has a really small ween.

Me: Were there any weens hurt in this movie? I mean, you are a stuntman in this movie . . .

Andy: Well, there were a couple times where I sat down on my own nards, I'm not gonna lie to you. Where I got on the bike too fast and crushed a nut. Which is also a really good name for an album . . . Crushed a Nut.

Me: Ooh, yeah. Definitely. You're gonna put that out?

Andy: We're gonna put that out together, right?

Me: Yes! Wait! But I need to be on the cover, looking like this . . . *(I pull out a fake mustache, similar to Andy's in* Hot Rod.*)* Just like you . . . I will be giving out mustache rides to anyone interested.

Andy: *(Pretends to take out a cell phone.)* There are so many butch lesbians who just went beep-boop-beep-beep-boop-bump.

Me: Weirdly enough, mine's not real but I know yours was.

Andy: Nope!

Me: Yes, it was!

Andy: Nope, nope!

Me: I was actually going to bring my own merkin.

Andy: You were going to bring in your merkin and have me wear it on my chin like a Seattle rocker goatee?

Great idea! I love a high-concept marketing idea! For the original *Anchorman*, Will Ferrell promised our audience that if they saw the movie he'd lick their balls. Oh! Speaking of *balls*, his costars Steve Carell and Paul Rudd, fairly unknown at that point, did one of the most fun tag-team interviews I've ever seen. My first sit-down with them was quite literally a *sausage-fest*. They were so taken with the idea that they could be uncensored that they just let loose! Paul unleashed a couple of guttural burps, Steve talked about *vurping*, and the pair took turns screaming, "I LIKE BIG CAT COCK!"

Paul: You're watching the Big Cat Cock Network.

Steve: Coooooooooock. I'm Paul Rudd. Go see *Anchorman*. Cooooooock.

Paul: COCK. Cock.

Me: So did you guys have fun working on the movie?

Steve: Cooooock.

Paul: Co-co-coooooooooock.

Steve: Will Ferrell is hysterical in this movie. The swimming pool scene?

Me: Totally in his underwear.

Steve: Seen the package on that guy?

Me: Huge!

Steve: Coooooock.

Me: Paul, you liked it. You like that scene too much.

Paul: Guilty as charged.

Steve: Now you can say fuck and shit and cock.

Paul: Yeah, say it! Fucking say it!

Me: Do it! Do it!

Steve, Paul, Me: Fuck! Shit! Cock! Fuck! Do it! Cock!

Paul: Balls!

Steve: You cocksuckers better see *Anchorman*!

Paul: Hey, all you cocksuckers, go check out *Anchorman*!

Steve: COCK.

Paul: FUCK YOU.

My interviews got the celebs cursing and laughing so much, the studio reps started scheduling me in prime spots to get the talent going. My favorite was right after lunch when the talent would normally be in a food coma, and I'd go in like a shot of adrenaline. Or they'd have me scheduled at the end the day so that the junket would end with a bang, literally. In fact, much to my delight, many celebs welcomed the relief of being able to be *No Good* after a day of being restrained. For some the reprieve couldn't have come soon enough as was the case with the hilarious Cedric the Entertainer at the *Street Kings* junket. He was on fire and had the room rolling with laughter:

"Shit, I couldn't wait for this interview. (*Loudly.*) WOW!! This is a fuckin' relief. (*Even louder.*) WOOO!!! (*Screaming with joyous relief.*) FUCK!!!!! YEAH!!!! FUCK YOU!! FUCK OFF!! FUCKIN' AROUND!!! HOOOO!!! Thank you so much! All the same fuckin' questions. Everyone was asking the same (*Doing an im-*

pression of a reporter.) 'So, Cedric, how's . . .' (*Yells.*) FUCK
YOU!!! Man, it was a fuckin' movie, that's what it was!! With
fuckin' actors in it. Wow! (*Looks at me.*) Thank you, ma'am.
Wow! I thought I was gonna lose it for a second there."

On occasion, I have also been used as a ringer. My favorite memory was at the junket for the Oscar-winning biopic *Walk the Line*, where
I was brought in to try and liven up the talent in an attempt to save the
day. Rumor had it that the star of the film, Joaquin Phoenix, had allegedly taken some sort of "mind trip" to keep the day interesting and
appeared to be *astral planing* during the interviews. The whole thing
was running way behind. Nobody knew what to do, so they thought
the best way to combat *crazy* was to send in *crazier*. Apparently, that
was me.

A frantic junket producer approached me and filled me in on what
she described as a "complicated" interview room and how I might be
able to help uncomplicate things.

"We know you're not supposed to go in for another two hours, but
we're going to put you in right now."

"All right. What do you want me to do?"

"We don't care!"

I went in all guns blazing and he just continued keeping busy
trying to win the Guinness World Record for not blinking. Was he
floating in another dimension, was he in the early stages of prepping
for his infamous documentary *I'm Still Here,* or was he just being difficult because he hates doing press? Well, it turned out that none of
that was correct. There were no drugs, no hate, just someone in pain.
Poor thing. Joaquin definitely ranks high on the *"interesting"* scale,
but he's also a nice guy, so I did a little digging to find out what had
happened that day. Apparently, early in the day, a journalist had decided to bring up his brother River Phoenix's death in his interview,
which threw him off and trainwrecked the day for everyone, including me.

Every celebrity has topics they don't want to go into, especially during a lighthearted movie promotion, but some press can't resist the
temptation to poke the bear. Kind of like that British journalist from UK's
Channel 4 News who poked Robert Downey Jr. into walking out of the
interview during the *Avengers: Age of Ultron* press day. In this situation,

Joaquin was very sensitive to a very personal tragedy and lost it. No doubt he was actually in another dimension, just not for the reasons anyone thought.

While the junketeers tried to have fun with the celebs, the celebs would also find ways to have some fun with the junketeers. Sometimes bored celebrities at junkets fuck with the press and play a game we call "secret word" where, before you walk into the room, they pick a word they try to subtly work into your interview. Macaulay Culkin did this to me with the word "guacamole." It's a private joke with everyone but you, and you know it the instant it happens. Everyone starts giggling, and everything gets thrown off. It happens a lot. Having said that, there were certain occasions on which this game was played when the planets would align in my favor and the chosen word would be a dirty one. On those glorious days, I felt like I was getting soaked by a gushing geyser of obscenities from a broken fire hydrant on the hottest day in summer.

In the beginning, we had a little pushback from a handful of publicists who were trying to figure us out. I remember one very powerful female flack, from one of the biggest agencies in Hollywood at the time with A-list clients, who did not like us at all. In fact, we got a call from her people—I love that the PR rep even had her own people—tearing into us, saying that she believed junkets were an "inappropriate place for this kind of behavior. It's unprofessional and distasteful." Which was a scary call to get because you never know how these things domino and turn into a shit-storm and then before you know it, you're FUBAR *(Fucked Up Beyond All Recognition)*. It's a small town.

So we handled it in the only way we knew how. We were straightforward, honest, and polite. Kourosh and I always had a big thing about being super polite. It was our belief that what we did on camera required us to hold ourselves to a higher professional standard. You can't fuck around with people on camera and then motherfuck them behind the scenes. That's what the tabloids did. That was not us. I would always jokingly say we were good people who say bad words. So we told her that we certainly didn't mean to offend anyone, that we were just having fun. That it's just language and it plays to a certain audience. We were interested in building a relationship, and if anything crossed the line we'd take it out for her. Our mea culpa worked, and she ended up becoming one of the biggest supporters of NGTV and me. What she and other flacks realized over time was that we were getting positive feedback from the celebs, and it was a big part of the reason they kept asking us back. At the end of the day, it was just a bunch of words, the intent was to make people laugh, and it was always in context. I'm sure it also didn't hurt that my interviews were dominating YouTube.

Even though the reps weren't sure what we were up to in the beginning, luckily they gave us the chance to show them what it was. It was a huge accomplishment for us. Another top male publicist, who repped virtually every top comedian, took a big chance on us, and the result was as life-changing as when I met Kourosh. He repped British actor Sacha Baron Cohen, aka Borat, the fictitious, blissfully ignorant reporter from Kazakhstan. When I got approved to interview Sacha, I was ecstatic, but little did I know that this interview would be the beginning of a chain reaction that would send me and NGTV into the stratosphere.

The one-on-one with Sacha was to promote the movie *Borat: Cultural Learnings of America for Make Benefit Glorious Nation of Kazakhstan*. We had to submit questions ahead of time because he'd be in full-on Borat character and wanted to be prepared. He was doing a few dozen interviews and, obviously, wanted to make sure everyone got great stuff. Sacha is a genius and an absolute pro and probably didn't want to wing it. We were a bit perplexed about what to ask on paper. Normally, my interviews were very off-the-cuff, but in this case we needed to make an exception. For the three people who don't know this, the character of Borat was totally sexist and pervy, so I walked into the interview dressed to impress the man of the hour wearing a super-low-cut, tight leopard-print shirt. His eyes bugged out and his jaw dropped like Stanley Ipkiss in *The Mask*, and I knew it was "game on." He threw the prepared questions out the window and went way the fuck off-script. So I did, too.

Borat: Uh-yees . . . a-very na-ice a-whoa-whoa-woo! A-VERY na-ice.

Me: Thank you! I very much enjoyed your documentary. Can we talk a little bit about the cock that you bring with you?

Borat: A-yes, a-maybe we talk in uh twenty minutes. I have a journalist is coming to talk with me . . . and then we can . . . uh . . . take away de cameras, we will uh . . .

Me: Can we keep the cameras? Because that might be more fun.

Borat: A naughty-naughty! A-whoa-whoa-woo!

Me: Maybe I can stay and just hang out and watch you do your interview. I'll just come over here then.

I stood up, walked over to Borat, sat on his left knee, and slid my arms around his neck. I could tell Sacha was unsure what was happening but stayed in character.

Borat: I am uh-semi-turgid . . .

   Me: I don't think that's semi . . .

Borat: Whoa whoa . . . uh I think I make ejaculate.

   Me: Does anybody have a towel?

Borat: No problem, I will be able to come turgid again . . . give me just three hours, no problem.

   Me: Three hours I have to wait? Well, I don't know if I can wait three hours.

Borat: Whoa-whoa-woo. Uh tell me . . . very a-naice . . . a-how much?

   Me: Oh, I'm free!

Borat: I would-uh pay-uh, fifteen dollars, no problem, for you.

   Me: Fifteen dollars? That's more than I get paid doing this! Wow, you're rich!

Borat: You are very pretty. You remind me of my sister.

   Me: She's number four prostitute in Kazakhstan?

Borat: She is now number six prostitute of Kazakhstan ever since the tour of de Pussycat Dolls in my country. They became number one to number five.

   Me: Hey would you do me a favor? Would you say hello to No Good Television?

Borat: Uh-my name uh-Borat, hello uh-No Good ah-Television . . . naughty-naughty, yes . . . ah-bye bye . . . . I am fully turgid again.

Up to this point, my interviews were getting maybe thirty thousand views. The *Borat* interview went viral—ultimately doing close to ten million views—a huge number even by today's standards, but in 2007 it was unheard of. It was validation that if I just kept doing what I was doing and kept my shirt on, we might have something special. It was the first domino to fall. People were starting to catch on. From that point onward every interview we released online got millions of views.

The next thing I knew, I was on the cover of *The Hollywood Reporter* sitting on Borat's lap being touted as the new secret weapon in film marketing. WOW! I have to admit that that was one of the most amazing fucking things to ever happen to me. I was one of the first online personalities ever to be on the cover of an industry trade magazine. This was long before the current age of the YouTube star, and I was really honored to be taken that seriously so early in the digital game. The only way I can describe the whole experience is it felt like I had been shot out of a confetti cannon into the stratosphere, transitioning into an orbital space dive and landing only after completing a *triple lindy.*

It seemed that, overnight, I had developed a tiny bit of clout in Hollywood, and I got a ton of supportive messages from the most powerful publicists and movie studio reps, congratulating me. What was so touching and humbling was that so many of them had become my friends and had been rooting for me to succeed. Let's face it, if it wasn't for them taking a risk and giving me a chance to go in there and do my thing, none of this would have happened. I owe a great deal to all of them to this day. It's a bit of a thankless job being a studio, agency, or personal publicist, but they are the engine of this business. They are a pretty amazing group of people who constantly innovate and get shit done: all under the radar. My hat's off to them.

All of a sudden, our phones were ringing off the hook, and people wanted to interview *me.* I was featured in *USA Today* and pictured sitting with Seth Rogen and Evan Goldberg on the set of *Superbad.* I ended up on the front page of the *Los Angeles Times* calendar section, where they ran a huge article on me being the alternative to Charlie Rose with a photo of me in bed with the stars of *Reno 911,* Tom Lennon and Robert Ben Garant. I got a call from *The Tonight Show*! Syndicated entertainment newsmagazine show *Extra* made a deal with us to feature mini episodes of NGTV at the end of their shows. In the press release announcing it, the executive producer of *Extra* called me "Barbara Walters on acid and Red Bull." I had never dreamed of being in the same sentence as Barbara Walters, but I suppose if it was going to happen, it was only natural that it would include a hallucinogenic drug. Anyway, after that, our access was wide open, and it started an A-list train that, gratefully, hasn't stopped to this day.

We also started getting invited to do exclusive set visits for what would ultimately become some of the biggest comedies. Back then, there was nowhere to put this kind of content. There was no Funny Or

Die or anything else like it. So we got these exclusive opportunities, interviews, clips, and Red Band trailers and became *the* place to launch raunchy comedies. Before Michael Cera and Jonah Hill became household names, I got to hang out all day with them on the set of *Superbad*—or as it's known in Israel, *Super Horny*. Jonah and I went way back to the very beginning of his career, which made this set visit extra special. . . .

It took place at a very interesting moment in time. Unbeknownst to any of us, the birth of our brand and the reemergence of the hard-R-rated comedy were about to intersect in a profoundly impactful way. Hot off their success with *Knocked Up*, Judd Apatow and Seth Rogen reunited for this movie. It was Seth and Evan Goldberg's first script, which was loosely based on their lives, to be made into a film. Jonah and Michael were starting to get some buzz, but Christopher Mintz-Plasse and Emma Stone were complete unknowns. It had a relatively small budget of twenty million dollars, and while everyone involved hoped it would do okay, I don't think the studio was sure it would cause much of a stir. It was so dirty that I don't think they knew exactly how to market it, and so they were doing their best to think outside of the box.

I guess that's where we came in—the dirty network with a huge male audience. They pretty much gave us the run of the set and access to interview everyone with no limitations. Hell, they even gave me a cameo in the movie. The whole experience was SuperAWESOME! When it was all said and done, we launched a channel dedicated to the film, garnering millions of views for my interviews, and spearheaded the promotion for the film, which ultimately became a massive hit and a defining moment for our brand. We were so proud to have played a small part in its success.

That day began at 6 A.M. in the Valley. I remember Jonah was a little under the weather, but when he saw us, he perked up and gave us his all. Seth and Evan didn't know what to make of me, but our filthy format was second nature to them, so they were hilarious. I ended up making a bit of an impression on them, which I'll get to a little later. That day was also the start of a beautiful relationship between me and Judd Apatow. A kinship built on a bridge of obscenity. The set visit made for some unforgettable exchanges with the cast. I mean, can you imagine Mary Hart having this conversation?

Me: What's up, you guys! I am on the set of *Superbad* with the number one and number two cocksuckers on the set. What's happening, you guys?

Jonah: Who's the number one cocksucker?

Me: I don't know, but you guys can decide amongst yourselves who's going to be number one and number two.

Michael: If it's based on who sucks more cock . . .

Me: Then you win?

Michael: How do you rank these things?

Jonah: Ummm . . . I'd say by the amount of penis you put into your mouth. That would be the ranking system. I can't speak on behalf of Michael, but for myself, I . . . I . . . I . . .

Michael: He's number one in his own eyes.

Jonah: I'm number one in my own eyes. Yeah. I mean, look, I don't want to be rude but . . .

Me: I'm getting top billing in the cocksucking, okay! *(To Michael:)* Do you know that we've been stalking him [Jonah]? Have you heard the stories?

Michael: No.

Me: I think we've gone to like seventeen of your films now where we've been on the set.

Jonah: A few. Probably like four.

Me: Uh . . . huh.

Jonah: My first interview was with you.

Me: In *Grandma's Boy* you had all boob all the time. He was sucking on a girl's boobie the entire movie.

Jonah: No, for a little bit of the movie.

Me: It was pretty damn good.

Jonah: I'd like to think I've advanced a lot since that time . . . uh . . . in my technique of . . . sucking boob.

Me: Who was responsible for the flow of hookers and blow on this set?

Jonah: Ummm . . .

Michael: The producers, I guess. I mean, who do you, who does that? I don't know who does what really. I assume it all just kinda shows up.

Jonah: Yeah. It just shows up. It just comes together.

Michael having spilled the beans on the producers, I decided to find out firsthand if that was the case. That led me to a life lesson from producer Judd Apatow that day about how movie sets work in general:

Me: Who was responsible for the flow of hookers and blow on this set?

Judd: Well, that is something that naturally happens around all movie sets. A movie is like a little city. So whether or not you're doing a movie like *The Departed* or you're doing *Flags of Our Fathers* or *Superbad*, as soon as you start shooting somewhere, cocaine and dealers and hookers will come around and service the crew. That's just part of the business. You don't hear much about it. That's just how the business works.

Me: So it's like, would you like a line of blow with your eggs? Is that how it works at catering?

Judd: Just there's this guy that'll sidle up next to you. You'll see. You go to any movie. Go to a Meryl Streep movie. Got to a Meg Ryan movie. Go to the set. There's hookers and blow everywhere. It's part of the business and people understand it. They let it go. But it's fine.

Me: It's not considered cheating then if it's on the set?

Judd: No. Of course not. That's . . . that's the ultimate rule of show business.

Shooting the cameo was great fun. They put me in the party scene where the girl *periods* on Jonah's leg. Periods is a verb, right? Then it was back to my filthy interview with them. Having discussed the central issue of hookers and blow, I moved on to the socio-political quandary of the *ham sandwich dilemma*. Which is this: Let's say you're in an orgy, and you're going down on a girl. Suddenly, it feels like you're getting the greatest blowjob ever. You look down and see a four-hundred-pound sweaty dude jerking you off with a ham sandwich. The dilemma is: Do you let him finish? Do you blow your load or hit the road?

Michael: Why did I come to this orgy with this four-hundred-pound guy who always pulls this ham sandwich thing? Why did I get myself into this situation?

Jonah: I say does he know that I'm Jewish and I don't like pork products.

Michael: But what does this have to do with being hungry?

Jonah: Couldn't it have been a turkey sandwich?

Me: It could have been a turkey sandwich. What if it was tuna salad?

Michael: It's not kosher.

Jonah: I'd say no to the whole thing.

Michael: Then this would be the tuna salad dilemma.

Jonah: I gotta be honest, the whole thing is not for me.

Michael: Why are you having an orgy with a four-hundred-pound guy?

Me: You don't know the four-hundred-pound guy is there. You just look down and there he is.

Jonah: Here's what I would do. If I walked into an orgy I would walk around and see like, hey, are there any four-hundred-pound guys walking around with a ham sandwich?

Michael: Exactly.

Jonah: And I would look in every crevice and room, and if there were none in there, I would go on, and if there was, I'd be like, not my kind of orgy.

Me: So I've actually just informed you both on how to get out of a bad orgy situation.

Jonah: Proper etiquette. Right.

Me: Yes. So now you're going to be looking for the ham sandwich . . .

Jonah: I'm going to even go in the fridge and see if they have ham, bread, and mayonnaise.

Michael: You're awful!

Me: 'Cause if someone's making the ham sandwich, you're done!

Michael: That's not traditionally what ham sandwiches are used for. Is that what you're saying?

Jonah: Ummm . . . ayyyy . . . ummmm . . .

Michael: Yeah, 'cause normally people just eat them. You don't normally . . . (*Makes jerking off with a ham sandwich hand gesture.*)

Jonah: Woah! You're blowing my mind.

Apparently any time on set ended up being a bit more memorable for Seth Rogen than I could have ever imagined. If you listen to the DVD commentary, when I flash across the screen dancing in the movie, Seth says, "Remember that girl? She's fucking bat-shit crazy!" Which of course is a huge honor coming from the Dalai Lama of bat-shit crazy!

9

WHEN I'M GOOD, I'M GOOD
WHEN I'M NO GOOD, I'M BETTER

Though this be madness,
yet, there is method in it.
—Hamlet, *William Shakespeare*

Our name was never meant to just be a clever entrée into a realm of mischief and mayhem. In a business where every *Dipshit McGee* has the next big idea, it was our battle cry against mediocrity. It's as much about who we are as it is about what we do. Being *"No Good"* is a state of mind. It's all about attitude. It's about closing your eyes, opening your mind, and letting go. Think of it as smoking an *existential wonder-joint*.

Those two words have always represented a creative culture, a point of view, and a sense of purpose. A vow to constantly evolve while always staying true to yourself. I know it sounds like heady shit for our brand of lunacy, but I forged my identity on these ideals and discovered I was better for it because there is a huge difference between being *"No Good"* and *not good*. You may think it's ironic that a business built on blasphemy would have such ethics and standards, but like I've been saying all along, this was no ordinary *donkey show*. It was an extraordinary one!

Our little company that we affectionately called "the little NG that could" was blazing through the entertainment landscape like a *hotshot*. We were growing faster than any of us ever anticipated, and it was time to find a bigger playpen to house the soon-to-be one hundred members of our team. After an exhaustive search of every office building, warehouse, and outhouse in Los Angeles, we stumbled onto a beautiful twenty-four-thousand-square-foot, three-story office space smack dab in the middle of Beverly Hills. We quickly set about invading the space and converting it into the nightclub/state-of-the-art production facility/Thai whorehouse we needed. Wall-to-wall fur, a twenty-foot fully stocked bar, and every toy a creative mind could dream of filled our playground of the imagination. As comedian Bob Saget succinctly put it, "I feel like I'm inside a hooker's vagina right now" when he waltzed into NGTV.

From the outside, it purposefully looked like an empty building, but on the inside it was a twenty-four-hour party palace where anything could happen and often did. The only way to describe the vibe would be *The Wolf of Wall Street* meets *Animal House*. During the day, everybody wore white lab coats around the office and called each other doctor because we were creating programming we likened to media rocket science. After all, we were all members of the *Surgical Media Strike Team*, a phrase coined by Kourosh and myself. At night, the lab coats came off and the real fun began. Everything from an *ABC party* to *human Jenga*. Let's just say we had a twenty-foot-tall chandelier in the middle of the space, and it really knew how to swing!

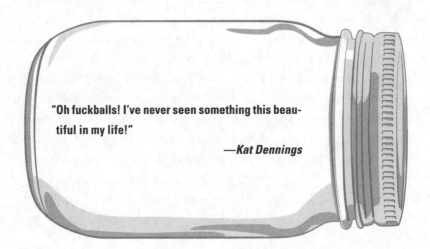

"Oh fuckballs! I've never seen something this beautiful in my life!"

—*Kat Dennings*

We built a full-fledged, legit, and operational television studio complete with two shooting stages, an audio mixing suite, green screen, 3D graphics department, screening room, and an eighties arcade. But the center of our universe was our bar, which we lovingly named the Shark Tank. It was our place to congregate, brainstorm, and celebrate. The complex was designed to give us everything we'd ever need so we never had to leave. A soup-to-nuts solution for the creative mind . . . heavy on the *nuts*! The environment at No Good TV was what you might call lax. The bar was always open, and we took hour-long breaks every four hours to play Halo. There was never any judgment, and you were free to indulge. As long as you met your deadlines, we didn't care.

Without a doubt, the key ingredient to No Good was always our people. They were second to none. A group of twisted badass motherfucking genius mad men and women!! Talented, fearless, and exceptionally skilled at partying! They are the ones who delivered the unforgettable experience you'll be telling your grandkids about once you determine if they'll forgive you or not. Like a collection of characters out of a Scorsese movie or, better yet, *This Is Spinal Tap,* they helped you get down with your bad self, and they were flawless in their execution.

Just like two fingers of Macallan 18 served on one large rock by master of ceremonies and my partner in crime, Shark *"Is this gorilla thong too much?"* Firestone, the atmosphere at No Good TV was always just right. No matter when you walked in, whether it was for a job interview with our kick-ass head of production Kenneth *"My Spidey sense is tingling"* Stroscher and our exceptionally talented creative director Ismael *"Anything is possible, but . . ."* Obregon, or for a creative rap sesh with our brilliant marketing maharishi Ron *"Can I get a witness?"* Hebshie, or for that highly sought-after 9 A.M. Clamato Chelada service on the rooftop lounge by our inordinately hot makeup prodigy Nicole *"What's wrong with girls showering together?"* Armijo and the Michelangelo of hair, Matthew *"Don't worry, I won't be late"* Motherhead, where you could have your portrait drawn by world-renowned artist Mari Inukai while discussing Piaget's theory of cognitive development with her Mensa-candidate daughter, Sena, oh yeah, the joint was hopping!!

The music was louder than it should be in an office thanks to wunderkind audio engineer Avi *"Steak and a blowjob"* Kipper and guitarphenom and mega-composer Gabriel *"Elevator Party"* Moses and the lights were dimmer than legally required to actually work thanks to cinematography maestro Chris *"Can I get a little more bounce off the 2K?"* Burns and his lighting commandos, Jamar *"It's all right, I brought my own sheets"* Franklin and Justin *"Why would he?"* Woiwode.

There would always be more than a few people at the bar to keep you company, like the uber-talented 3D animators, CG artists, and compositors Adam *"Windex will fix that laser disc player"* Ghering, Colin *"I don't want to talk about my dad"* Cromwell, Joi *"to the World"* Klinmalai, Amanda *"Would you like to hug my pillow"* Lee, Maria *"Hello Kitty"* Fleischman, Ariel *"I'll have the surf 'n' turf for dinner and another one to go!"* Sinson, N!K *"The Dick"* (not because of a character flaw), and Ken *"Avatar was good but I think I can do better"* Dackermann.

And that lingering feeling you couldn't shake that two people were fucking somewhere close by and could probably use a third was thanks to the twenty cubic miles of purple and red fur quaffed to perfection by in-house renaissance man Jon *"I've never created artificial intelligence but gimme the weekend"* Gaiser (aka McGaiser) and his wife, talented licensed architect Audrey *"You want me to put fur on what?"* McEwan. By the way, that wasn't just a feeling but an actual state of being thanks to the mood visualist and virtuoso art director Amul *"Can I get a wingman?"* Patel. You should have gone with your gut! Many did. The DO NOT ENTER sign created by our shrewdly skilled social media manager Emily *"I give tittie twisters when I'm drunk"* Carroll was just a suggestion.

You would swear that we were throwing full-blown parties every day thanks to our incredibly crafty associate producer and troublemaker Tania *"I think it's totaled!"* Hamidi under the watchful eye of her sister, our brilliant head of finance and emergency consultant Natasha *"Are we Persianing this?"* Hamidi. Every business pitch with gifted executive producer, philosopher, and resident *"Braveheart"* Scott Bachmann; interview taping with our incomparable production manager Nicole *"We don't have a coke bowl!"* Elliott; or confab with our tour-de-force assistant editor Dan *"Everyday should be your birthday!"* Thompson and exceptional segment producer/editor Jesse *"Now that's a knife"* Kane, ended in a key party!

It was like a nightclub on the edge of forever. Except here you were surrounded by stunning women who didn't treat you like shit or only hung with you for your drugs, like our lethally gorgeous production team made up of Devorah Reyna, Carissa Blades, and Nan Savage. You couldn't tell what time it was thanks to all the hydrating you were doing all night with our signature *spa water*, a reenergizing and refreshing beverage made from vodka with a splash of water served with an orange slice courtesy of our magnificent fashion stylists Quentin *"I don't mind a dirty boy, 'cause I can get 'em clean!"* Owens, who brought the recipe, and Niki *"In pursuit of sexy"* Schwan, who brought the attitude. And you never wanted to leave and always spent way too much time in the thera-peutic meditation lounges thanks to the diabolical genius of head writer and senior producer Beth *"It's all about the bio-availability"* Spruill and her partner in *"It's a grey area in federal crime"* mischief and exceptional 3D artist Michael *"It's about the implication"* Ore.

We also had our own Captain Jack Sparrow roaming the halls and giving away free *booty* to everyone (it's not what you think . . . or is it?) thanks to our invaluable production coordinator, Jack Tavitian. And just to throw you off balance, walking around, making sure everyone was busy being . . . busy, was our talented five-year-old chairman emeritus, who appeared in some of our fucked-up videos as Nickles McFidget, Super Agent. Because if you're shooting a scene with hook-ers, blow, weed, and booze, why wouldn't you want a kid in it? And to top things off, we even had a couple of Russian OGs in charge of VIP security and keeping an eye on you, the beautiful twins Mila and Gera Marinova; what else would you expect at NG? To the men, women, and children of the *Surgical Media Strike Team,* I salute you!

The vibe was freewheeling seventies, anything goes. Movie stars, rock stars, TV stars, porn stars, at least one billionaire, and our celeb "regulars," like NBC's *Chuck* star Zachary Levi, stopped by like it was their corner bar. "Chicks with guns and alcohol! That's NGTV. You don't get this on CNN, son!" Zach would exclaim in one of his many appear-ances. On one occasion, we were giving a huge presentation to the heads of Showtime with our superagent Ari Emmanuel (whom Ari Gold in *Entourage* is based on) while my dear friend and star of Showtime's *Mas-ters of Sex* Michael Sheen just sat at the bar enjoying a glass of Merlot. It was surreal . . . but that was just a normal Thursday.

We had several signature cocktails, including one called *The Asshole,* a lethal combo of Bacardi 151, Old Grand-Dad, and Cuervo. An-other deceivingly delicious adult beverage that we concocted using liquor that we imported from another state (because it wasn't legally sold in California) we called *Fist* because it was stronger than punch! Our guests loved them and asked for them by name. Some of your fa-vorite celebrities have been *Fisted* at No Good TV, including *Star Trek's* Zachary Quinto; *Glee's* Jane Lynch; *Shark Tank's* Mark Cuban; *Battlestar*

Galactica's Tricia Helfer; *Two Broke Girls'* Beth Behrs; *Newsroom's* Emily Mortimer; Taboo from The Black Eyed Peas; Margaret Cho; Bob Saget; Tom Green; author Jackie Collins; Larry the Cable Guy; director Guy Ritchie; Stephen Dorff; Marvel's *Avengers'* Aaron Taylor-Johnson; *Superbad's* Christopher Mintz-Plasse; rockers Bret Michaels, Sebastian Bach, and my hero, Mike Patton from Faith No More; David S. Goyer; sci-fi legend and *Star Trek: The Next Generation's* executive producer Brannon Braga; Cobra Starship; hip-hop stars Akon, Ray J, and Luther Campbell; *The Good Wife's* Matt Czuchry; the Broken Lizard crew; and *Community's* Danny Pudi, to name a few.

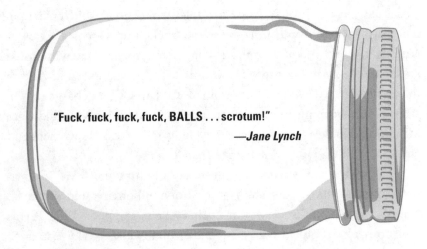

"Fuck, fuck, fuck, fuck, BALLS . . . scrotum!"

—*Jane Lynch*

Paris Hilton happily got *Fisted* twice while comfortably, yet obliviously, sitting on one of the many cock-shaped pillows we had lying around the studio. Which was mild compared to what else was going on at NGTV. The stars that showed up came to know that they were totally safe inside our walls. They could party their asses off and none of it would ever end up in the tabloids. What happened at No Good TV stayed at No Good TV. Our parties were off the chain, and everyone who was anyone in the business tried to find their way to our den of iniquity nestled amongst the unsuspecting mom-and-pop retail stores on Santa Monica Boulevard. Discretion is a key distinction between being *No Good* and being *not good*.

Being the face of No Good TV has always been a singular experience. The things I've had the chance to do and the places I've been to are unparalleled and have redefined my view of the world. In those days, I was living inside the eye of the hurricane. I was aware of our success and how we were blowing up but I was working harder than the seams on Lenny Kravitz's leather pants. I never really had time to sleep, let alone stop and smell the roses. When I wasn't interviewing stars at the Shark Tank, we had junkets every other day—indie films during the week and the big tent-pole films on the weekends. And because the studios had really started to embrace us, I started traveling all over the world, shooting segments, which were fun, but the rapid-fire schedule could sometimes be taxing.

It's not like we'd fly to some exotic location, fuck off for a week, and call it work. Some of these jaunts were hilariously short. I remember when 20th Century Fox flew me to Cairo and then to Rome over the span of three days to interview the cast of the movie *Jumper*. Do you have any idea how far Africa is from the U.S.? I shot my dirty interviews, literally, sitting a few feet away from the Sphinx on the Giza Plateau in Egypt, then immediately boarded a bus, then a plane, took a four-hour flight, then another bus, and "magically" jumped to Italy, where we were standing smack dab in the center of the Coliseum for the sum total of fifteen minutes, then boarded a bus, then a plane . . . you see where I'm going with this. In the two hours between the Coliseum and my flight, I ended up fucking around in the streets of Rome with Hayden Christensen, Jamie Bell, and director Doug Liman, who just happened to have a camera in his hands. With the help of a little jetlag and alcohol, we created our own mini homage to *Roman Holiday* but with fewer Vespas and more wine. A once-in-a-lifetime opportunity, to say the least, but man, it was a whirlwind.

It wasn't out of the ordinary for me to fly very long distances for very short periods of time. There was this one time I jetted off to London for, and I shit you not, a two-minute interview with Jeremy Irons and jetted right back. I spent more time in the makeup chair than I did interviewing him. But hey, that's just the way it goes. It was a major live-and-learn era for me, and it took me a while to master the art of juggling work and play.

The first time we ever attended the Cannes Film Festival in France was in 2008, and it was one for the books. Our reputation for knowing how to get a party started caught the attention of Rebel Media, a media conglomerate in Europe, who really wanted to make an impression on the in-crowd at the festival. And what better way to get noticed than by throwing an "anything goes" VIP-only yacht party? At a length of 238 feet, thirty-three staterooms, a thirty-one-member crew, and room for up to 150 party guests, the world-class *RM Elegant* was transformed into the NO GOOD MEGA YACHT!

It was nothing short of a spectacular dreamlike wonderland filled to capacity with celebs and the like, where we partied like rock stars and never *pardoned our French*. A few hours later, I was walking the famous red carpet on the steps at the Palais des Festivals for the world premiere of *Indiana Jones and the Kingdom of the Crystal Skull*. And when the sun came up, I found myself seated across from Harrison Ford, Shia LaBeouf, Cate Blanchett, Karen Allen, and Steven Spielberg at the junket for the film.

There we were, this fledgling Internet TV network, creating a stir on the Riviera, and it was unforgettable. One night at a party in the hills, I got separated from my crew and got lost. There I was, wandering the streets in the middle of the night, in a gown, holding my heels, looking for my ride. Pretty much the last thing you want to have happen to you in Cannes during the festival, where the only difference between a call girl and a movie starlet is the call girl is getting paid to be there. I looked like the bat-signal for Eurotrash!

Having made it out of the south of France's version of *sexual Frogger* alive, I thought the worst was behind me. I couldn't have been more wrong and more right! I remember making the critical mistake of wearing bedroom-only underwear under my dress—a thong with rhinestones. And after partying nonstop for two days (in the same dress, walk-of-shame style), my ass-crack was carved up like a jack-o'-lantern, and I could barely walk. All I can say is thank God that, on the flight back, the champagne was flowing like a river and sent me into a euphoric state of bliss because they sure as hell weren't handing out donut pillows. Being *No Good* is about living, not just a little, but a lot! You never know how long something's going to last, and the last thing you want to do is live in the world of woulda, coulda, shoulda. Fuck that!

It's good to be *No Good*.

10

BETWEEN SASQUATCH'S NUTSACK
AND HOBSON'S CHOICE

We are what we pretend to be,
so we must be careful about what we pretend to be.
—Mother Night, *Kurt Vonnegut*

Nothing says you've made it in show business quite like the moment you receive an email from your manager telling you that a picture of your rear-end is being featured on the front page of guessdatass.com. Apparently, nowadays, once people can recognize you purely by your *dumper*, you become elevated to a new elite class of super-stardom known as the Cele-Butt-Ocracy. Where your *bung hole* becomes a beacon of hope for current and future generations of young women searching for their place in the world. And here you were thinking that the Kardashians' only contribution to the world was the monetization of vapidity and an emoji for *baby dick*. Nope! It turns out that wearing your own ass as a hat spoke to an entire generation of assholes in search of *gaping* role models. This new *keister-driven* social media art known as a *belfie* (butt-selfie) has enticed legions of public figures to enter into a mindless race for anal distinction, having mistaken the photograph of a fart box to be a symbol of empowerment and purpose, thereby ushering in new era of pop culture existentialism by rewriting the assertion of the great, French philosopher, René Descartes with the defiant declaration "We shart; therefore we are."

Guilty of getting caught up in this frenzy myself, I revealed a hint of crack on social media on one occasion, and I couldn't help but ask myself, *What the fuck am I doing*? Then I remember seeing a photoshoot of a famous popstar, whom I adore and who's been a good role model for young girls, sitting naked on the edge of a bathtub with her butt cheeks spread apart just enough to suggest a hint of hole without showing it, and I thought to myself, *What the fuck is she doing*? Or when I saw a well-known and respected comedienne suddenly start posting naked ass shots, all I thought was, *What the fuckin' fuck is she doing*? In fact, when I think about the sheer number of people who are, at this very moment, contorting themselves to get their very best ass-shot with just the right reflection of hole to post on social media, I have to ask, *What the fuck are you doing? Hell, what the fuck are any of us doing*?

And just so we're clear, I'm not trying to shame or cajole anyone from doing anything. Far from it, and I'm certainly in no position to judge. But I can't help but wonder how the hint of sphincter became the aspirational photo? Somebody needs to explain that to me, goddamn it!!! It feels like we missed a step in there somewhere. We women used to be so protective and concerned about being objectified by the media and the press and the hoo and haa! Hell, I remember fighting so hard throughout my career to keep my top on, no cooter shots, no leather cheerio suggestion and no bonch flashes. Now, we're the ones dishing out naked photos of every conceivable angle of our clits and bits like we're making it rain in the champagne room at a fuckin' strip club. I'm not fuckin' shy and I could give a fuck, but am I the only one wondering how, now that we girls are in control of the pics, we seem to be steadily heading toward Grundle city!? What the fuck are we doing? And why the fuck are we doing it? We all seem to be happily running with the herd and trying our best to keep up. But who exactly the fuck is leading the herd? And if it's who I suspect it is, then really . . . girls . . . **WHAT THE FUCK** are we doing?

I bring all this up because there's a great deal of pressure today to do all kinds of crazy shit on social media or wherever to be noticed, get people's attention or keep people's attention. But that shit is FOREVER!!! And this whole fucking business comes down to the choices you make. And it looks a lot like the multiple choice is rigged in favor of camel toe and gooch! Who you present yourself to the world as, and how you move forward in this business, is something you'll have to live with for your entire career. And if you compromise early and often enough, you may very well play yourself out fast. So even when you don't think anyone's watching or gives a shit, don't compromise; because at some point they will be watching and will give a shit.

The harshest part of it all is that the path to success is pretty much a *shit-show* of compromises and impossible choices. With opportunities so few and far between, often, saying no to something is really hard because it can mean not working for a long time. The only advice is: be true to yourself and make the choice that you can live with. It can be a controversial choice like taking on a role in an off-Broadway play where your character walks on stage naked and proceeds to take an actual 5 minute shit to establish the mood of the times. (It's a seedy apartment on the lower east side of New York City, in the 1970s, where the toilet is in the center of the room and, therefore, metaphorically the center of his existence, and taking a shit is what he's doing to his life. But you'll have to sit through another two hours before putting that together.) Hey man, it's art, and as long it's the best choice for you and you can live with it, fuck it! Roll the dice. How do I know the past has a dangerous way of coming back to haunt you? I know this firsthand because it happened to me.

My choice to not go topless in my interviews could have ended my career before it started, but that was the chance I willing to take because it wasn't true to me and I instinctively knew that it would be a recipe for disaster. But that wasn't the last of such dilemmas I'd have to face. With success came new opportunities, and with them came new challenges. My friend, the late, great novelist Jackie Collins, once told me "There's a rite of passage for women, actresses; they have to either play a hooker or a stripper. It's a rite of passage for women in Hollywood." She had a knack for being right all the time, and little did I know that I would come face-to-face with this situation myself. Thankfully, I was prepared.

Despite all the fun I was having, I did take my job very seriously. NGTV was getting me in the room to do all of these amazing interviews, and on top of that, all of these exciting new opportunities were pouring in for me personally, too. I got hired for a bunch of hosting gigs, a lot for VH1, like their *Critics' Choice Awards*, *Rock Honors*, *Mark Burnett's Rock 'n' Roll Fantasy Camp,* and *One-Hit Wonders*. The TV Guide Network also started hiring me to do their pre-shows and red carpet coverage for events like the Academy Awards, the Screen Actors Guild Awards, the Emmys, and the Golden Globes. Ironically, my first offer to host their Golden Globes pre-show was also the year of the writers' strike, so, literally, nobody showed up. But the show must go on, so there I was, trying desperately to fill five hours of programming with my own kind of song and dance. I call that "Nailing it for nobody!" I was all over the television dial, making new friends and fans while gaining a lot of experience. When I think about it now, half the opportunities I was being offered would never have materialized if I'd been doing my interviews topless, as Gene Simmons suggested. Though some of the other half of the opportunities I was offered were in some way related to my *blouse bunnies*. One of the coolest things to come my way was being offered a small role on Comedy Central's *Reno 911!* It all started when I was invited to cover the junket for the film version *Reno 911!: Miami*. The cast had decided to do all their press interviews in character and on the set. I, unlike most of the reporters who had to do real interviews with fictional characters, decided to embrace the spirt of it and push the situation to its limits. The cast didn't know what hit them, and I just figured the worst that could happen was I'd get escorted off the set, but I couldn't have anticipated what would happen when it was over.

First off, this was a dream scenario for me. I love improv. Anytime there's no real script and fucking off is the order of the day, count me in! These guys were the masters, and I was a kid in a candy store. I was familiar with their whole shtick from watching the television series, so I knew what kind of fun lay ahead. All I needed was for them to give me an opening, and apparently, they were in a very giving mood.

Me: I was wondering, ya know, if you guys could show me the proper technique for frisking, ya know, a suspect.

Kerri: I thought for sure you were gonna say blowjob, and I am so relieved because I don't have a clue!

Ben: We fell for this before. We got two cameras here. I ain't gonna fall for this again.

Mary: Well I don't mind.

Tom: We always have a lady officer do it . . . ah present.

Carlos: I would just stay clear of this region right here. (*Motioning towards my chest area.*)

Tom: (*Grabbing his hand away from my chest.*) No, no, no we're good.

Ben: See we have cameras around us all the time so we learn. You ask us that and pretty soon we got law suits pending . . .

Cedric: Someone's pregnant . . .

Me: Has that happened?

Cedric: Ah . . .

Ben: No comment.

Cedric: No!

And just like that, at every turn, a fucked-up conversation would turn into something borderline illegal.

When the day was all said and done, I had quite the collection of un-expected confessions from the Reno PD. Like how you can tell a lot about a cop from the size of his gun and the flavor of his mustache. Apparently, mustache rides are legal if bartered for with a cop in exchange for tickets to Disneyland. Do with that what you will. Also, with their unforeseen admissions, we established these additions to the Miranda warning that I think the red states are probably going to adopt first: You have the right to wear a candy G-string. You have the right to choke a chicken. You have the right to flick your bean. You have the right to jerk off in private. You have the right to showcase your camel toe. And you have the right to make a three-foot nightstick disappear. It all ended with Tom Lennon blurting out, "Oh my good God almighty!!" In my mind, the single greatest com-pliment is when the talent's mind is so blown that they involuntarily in-voke the lord's name because there's just nothing left to say! Remember, boys and girls, I'm a trained professional, don't try this at home.

After I was done with all the frisking and double entendres, creators Thomas Lennon and Robert Ben Garant approached me with the most amazing offer. They asked me if I'd come play a character named Frosty on their TV show. I said, "Fuck, yeah!" followed by a quick "Oh fuck!" I'd never acted in my life, except for a starring turn in my junior high's holi-day production of *Mrs. Claus to the Rescue*, which opened to tepid reviews. The good news was that *Reno 911!* was mostly improvised, so if they liked how I ad-libbed today at the junket, I might be okay.

When I showed up on set, I was shown to my very own trailer with my name on the door. OH. MY. GOD. It was really happening! I started making myself at home when I heard a knock on the door. It was a girl from production, and I could immediately tell by the look on her face that she gave no *fucks* about me or my complete euphoria for being cast in the show. I was just one more person that needed to be attended to and she'd never see me again.

"Are you Carrie?" she said without looking up from her clip-board.

"Yeah!" I squeaked with anticipation.

"You're the stripper," she replied, dry as a bone. (*Of course, I was. Jackie Collins strikes, again!*)

"Here." She handed me two hangers with black bits of fabric dangling from them.

"What's this?" I inquired innocently.

"Your costume," she insisted, and walked away.

Clinging to the hangers now in my hand was the most minuscule black fur bikini I had ever seen—it was basically *Sasquatch's nutsack* on a string!

I held it up in a state of disbelief. One cup of my bra had three times as much fabric as this entire "outfit." You'd be amazed at how often *Sasquatch's nutsack* is the measuring tool with which wardrobe is selected for women. It's ubiquitous in the entertainment industry. Make a mental note before you go into any fitting and you'll be prepared.

Listen, I'm no prude. And I think, by now, I've established that. But I still have my own hang-ups. Up until this point, I'd never been asked to expose anything other than my vulgar sense of humor. And now, what choice did I have? So I tried it on, nervously. My thoughts went straight back to that fitting room with my mom and the hideous blue flowered bra. I started to sweat as the voices of the girls in school tormenting me echoed in my head . . . followed by the line from the movie *Carrie*, "They're all gonna laugh at you!" Is this what I've become? A blonde with big boobs who gets typecast as the stripper? Did I just make a huge mistake? Fortunately, by some miracle of gravity and the art of nautical knotting, the two pieces of dental floss that represented my wardrobe that day held my *hottentots* together just sufficiently enough to not get me arrested (pun intended).

But I was still, basically, naked. I started to panic on my way to freaking out. *What did I just agree to?* I thought to myself. I felt so exposed, like Elizabeth Berkley must have felt at the wardrobe fitting for *Showgirls* when she discovered that the only body part her outfit would be covering was her *butthole*. Except that I didn't even have that luxury. Suddenly the idea of begging for a Twinkle Tush, a jewel designed to class up your cat's *chocolate starfish*, didn't seem like such a bad idea. So I put my clothes back on, walked over to the wardrobe trailer, and knocked on the door. The same girl opened it.

"Hi." I said sheepishly. "Is there any way I could maybe, ya know, I don't know, possibly wear anything with this? Like a leopard print micro mini? Or a vinyl trench coat or anything?" I was attempting to be reasonable given the character.

She let out a lengthy sigh, just brimming with impatience. Then checked her list.

"Carrie, right?" she asked, again not looking up from her clipboard.

(I'd just met her like ten minutes ago.)

"Yes, I'm Carrie," I replied, trying to not sound frustrated.

"You're playing a stripper." This time she looked at me dead in the face. "You are aware of that?"

(Suddenly and quite subconsciously, I began to frantically defend myself.)

"I know. I know, buuuuuut I was thinking, ya know, maybe my character is on her way to night school; right after her shift . . . right? And it's a chilly night. Or, she's on her period and needs the full brief fur panties this week instead?! That could work! Right??" Hoping I could break through her cold demeanor.

She just stood there, stone faced, for what felt like an eternity before disappearing into the trailer.

(OH GOD. I thought. What did I just do? Is she calling security? Did I just get myself fired for being difficult?)

Then, maybe two minutes later, she reappeared, and I could see she was holding something in her hand.

"Here!"

(She handed me a pair of black fishnet stockings.)

"Are we good now?"

That wasn't exactly what I was hoping for, but I wasn't about to argue. I went straight back to my trailer to suit up. I stood there staring at myself in the mirror for quite some time, feeling very uneasy. Then I remembered Demi Moore in *Striptease*. She was sexy and tough and clever. Demi didn't get caught up in being typecast as a stripper. In fact, GI Jane, where she shaves her head and becomes a war hero, was released the very next year. I immediately launched into a *full-on* angry "Dr. Bailey from *Grey's Anatomy*–level" hype speech to the tune of "We don't have to take our clothes off" by Jermaine Stewart to myself about how I can be whatever I want to be regardless of my body! I am in control of how people see me! My image is mine alone to control. No dumbblonde rep for me thank you!

Filming my four episode arc as Frosty was an incredible opportunity, and I made long-lasting friendships with the cast. Yes, I was wearing next to nothing, but I didn't feed into any stereotype with my improvising. I focused on THE part and not *my parts*, if you catch my drift. This was an interesting corner me and my body had just been dropped off on. It can be a slippery slope between sordid and sexy and a fine line between edgy and predictable. I didn't want to be predictable, or sordid, for that matter! I mean, there's chest cleavage, butt cleavage, toe cleavage and, even, Wicked Weasel cleavage, and if you look closely enough, it's just a line each person draws for themselves. So how do you decide which line you won't cross? I stopped where I couldn't get an A-lister to look me in the eye!

Which is why when *Playboy* approached me during this hot streak, I faced a true crisis of conscience and the biggest challenge yet. This was a fork-in-the-road moment that would define me and dictate the direction of my career.

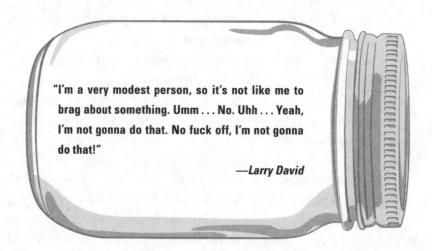

"I'm a very modest person, so it's not like me to brag about something. Umm . . . No. Uhh . . . Yeah, I'm not gonna do that. No fuck off, I'm not gonna do that!"

—*Larry David*

I was in my office one afternoon after the *Los Angeles Times* story came out with the photo of me wearing my signature silk PJs while taping an episode of *In Bed with Carrie*. My phone rang. "Hi, I'm from *Playboy* magazine," a friendly voice, who I'll call Veronica, greeted me on the other end of the line. "We've been following you in the press and we just saw your story in the *Los Angeles Times*, and I think you're *Playboy* material. We'd love to offer you a spread in the magazine and potentially the cover."

Suddenly time stood still as I left my body and started dancing around the building, belting out the "Hallelujah" chorus at the top of my lungs. All of the parkour training I'd never had immediately kicked in, and I found myself running, climbing, swinging, mantling, vaulting, jumping, and rolling off of every wall and punching every ceiling. It was a magnificent volley of pure joy in the form of emotional cartwheels. I saw myself taking my place in the annals of *Playboy* history, and I imagined I was leading a parade filled with the decades of playmates that had come before me, all dancing in unison to Survivor's "Eye of the Tiger" from *Rocky III* as I fake punched my way down Times Square. My entire life lit up like a festival of lights, twisting and twirling like the Scramble ride at an amusement park. It was as if everything in my life was leading me to this moment; the rush of anticipation was palpable!

After a lengthy pause during which I was collecting myself and trying to close my stunned and gaping mouth to the soundtrack of Veronica repeating, "Are you still there? Hello! Did I lose you?," I very calmly said, "While I am so deeply flattered, I'm sure you understand that I absolutely couldn't possibly accept. It's just not the right fit for me, but I can't thank you enough for calling."

I hung up in a state of disbelief and started laughing hysterically. It was totally surreal. It's that one moment that many, if not all, girls dream of their whole lives. I'm not saying that every girl wants to be in *Playboy*, but I'm willing to bet that pretty much every girl would love to be asked. Plus, they wanted to give me all kinds of money to be in their magazine! It was a mind-blowing moment, to say the least, and apparently it wasn't over yet.

Veronica called me back the next day, and we talked for a while longer. The more she spoke about the family atmosphere at *Playboy* and the camaraderie between the girls, the more interested I became. There is something very intoxicating about being appreciated and sought after. So I started softening up to the idea. She had me *ass over teakettle* with excitement over the prospect of doing a really high-end photo shoot with herself as the photographer and all the expertise that Playboy had to offer. I was loving every minute of the chase.

But here was the rub. (Not that kind of rub, you perv!) After we hung up the phone and I had stopped trying to re-create a leap to a mid-air still-shot screaming "YES," the reality of the situation started to sink in. Oh God! Did *Playboy* expect me to be topless? Duh! Or bottomless? Duh! Or completely *bare-ass nekkid*? DUH! The excitement of the moment had me so focused on having been asked that I had completely ignored considering the reality and consequences of actually going through with it. Issues that had somehow seemed irrelevant until after I hung up. So before I let myself go too far down the road towards this *buck-naked buffet,* I decided to get on the phone, again, with Veronica, knowing full well that this next call would be the end of this adventure. I explained to her that while I was beyond flattered, posing completely naked wasn't in the cards for me. I was shocked when she explained to me that that wasn't going to be a problem. WHAA?? They were completely fine with me doing more of a *Maxim*-type shoot, and we'd figure out exactly how much skin would be shown. I hung up the phone, feeling relieved and even more excited.

"It's super fuckin' cool. It's super fuckin' funny. And it is a cock-knocker of a movie!"

—*Jessica Biel*

Fortunately, I had a publicist at this point, so I asked her to step in and do the hard part—negotiating the nudity. I told her, "Straight up, I do not want to get naked!" I said, "I'll show some side boob, some ass cheek, maybe a hint of crack, but that's it. There will be no photos of me bending over a table with a *peek-a-boo* backward glance that whispers, 'Oh no, you can't see my butthole, can you?' or me playing a *spread eagle* psychoanalyst on a leather chaise with a 'tell me about your father' gaze, and there was no way I am going to be on all fours with my ass two feet above my head casually thumbing thru *The Wall Street Journal* because that's how I like to read at home." I continued, "If they're not okay with that, I don't need to do any of this." I knew a little bit about the ins and outs of shooting for *Playboy* from the time I'd interviewed Playmate of the Year Kara Monaco at the Shark Tank, and she said that waxing was a personal preference, left up to each individual girl:

"You can go full seventies bush if you wanted to?" I asked.

"They wouldn't care," Kara explained. "They like it. I call it the fur bikini."

Hmm, my mind started wandering to merkins. *I could have one in every color!*

My publicist relayed the terms of my disrobement to Veronica, then called me back, exasperated. "These are the strangest calls I've ever made. I mean, we're talking about what percentage of an areola we're allowed to show. Or how many inches of an ass crack! And I don't even want to tell you how many times I've had to firmly state 'no lips, no side lips, no hint of lips, NO FUCKING LIPS!' I feel like I'm negotiating your deal to do a porno film or an episode of *Californication*!"

I replied, "Welcome to Hollywood."

During the course of the next few weeks, negotiations inched forward without much drama, and Veronica had me feeling really good about the shoot. I was so excited that I arranged for my mom, who lived in Buffalo, and my sister Katie, who lived in Florida, to fly out for the occasion. They were so proud . . . actually, I'm not entirely sure if proud was the word they used, but they were very excited for me. And relieved that it wasn't a coming out party for my *Pikachu*! Either way, they sure as shit weren't going to miss it.

It was a particularly sweet bonding moment for me and my sister. Growing up, we really hadn't been that close. Like most sisters, we love-hated each other. You know, we made the requisite cameo appearance at birthdays, heartbreaks, and parental humiliations (for ammunition or blackmail). But for the most part, it was an uneasy peace with the occasional wardrobe skirmish thrown in for good measure. (Look! It was a cute cashmere sweater, and I could have sworn I got all the candle wax out.) Then, sadly and before I knew it, she met her prince charming, David, and moved away.

Not that I blamed her for moving; David was a good-looking action-hero-brave super-cop who could easily have been Evel Knievel's stunt double! (David, don't let this go to your head and feel free to *dip your balls in it*!) And in case that wasn't enough, she had two perfect kids in addition to becoming a stepmom to David's beautiful and whip-smart daughter Alexis. First came Kira, who I'm sure will be running a billion-dollar corporation someday, and then came Rhys, who's probably just a couple of years shy of winning the Olympic gold medal in gymnastics. Yeah, Katie found her bliss.

Fortunately, as we got older, we forgot why we didn't used to get along and rediscovered one another, which was the most wonderful and unexpected gift. The fact that she was going to take time out of her crazy schedule as a working mom to come out to be with me was just beyond amazing. Especially since it was also going to be her first time away from Kira, so I knew it wasn't an easy decision for her. And that made it all mean so much more.

Anyway, next up was the wardrobe fitting where my stylist, Niki, and Veronica would create the visual feast that was to be my spread. I arrived with great anticipation for the lingerie and bathing suits I was going to wear. But as soon as we got into it, a few red flags started going up. Niki, who was working under the impression that this was supposed to be a more-sexy-than-naked shoot, was handing me articles of cloth-ing to try on. All the while, Veronica and her people were poo-pooing Niki's ideas and basically handing me minuscule bits of sheer cloth say-ing, "You can just drape this in front of you!" A friendship bracelet would have provided more coverage!

What the fuck was going on? Clearly, Veronica and I were not on the same page. I was growing fearful of the entire endeavor. I left the fit-ting feeling very uneasy and wanting to bail. This was not what we had agreed to. I frantically called Veronica and expressed my complete dis-comfort with the situation. At this point, we were weeks into this pro-cess, lawyers had been carefully negotiating the contract, the shoot was set, my family had bought their tickets, and I was emotionally pregnant with the idea of this shoot. I did not know what to do, and just when I was about to lose my shit . . . Veronica made a masterful maneuver.

DUN-DUN-DUNNNNNNNN (that's the universal sound effect for holy shit) . . . *I got THE invite.*

Hef—*Playboy* founder Hugh Hefner for anyone living on a desert island for the last fifty years—invited me over for Sunday dinner and a movie at the legendary Playboy Mansion. Whaaaa? Veronica talked up how much Hef wanted to meet me and how excited he was about the photo shoot. Of course, I ate it all up because wow . . . it was fucking Hugh Hefner. The man is a legend, and with a hit show on television at the time, his myth and mystique was at an all-time high. So I started to forget about the wardrobe fiasco for a moment and got caught up in the thought of being the guest of honor at the Playboy Mansion. It wasn't as if I had spent my entire life aspiring to reach this moment; if anything it was the opposite. But come the fuck on! This was a motherfucking cool-as-fuck, bucket-list moment! Both the *balls* and the *jizz*!! So I told Kourosh I was going to Sunday dinner, but I wasn't going alone.

"Not a problem!" he said without skipping a beat. As if *that* was going to be a hard sell.

Leading up to the big day, I was really excited, but also somewhat anxious. I was flattered, thinking, *Ooh they're wooing me to be in the magazine!* On the other hand, what if Hef, himself, confronted me about taking my clothes off? How would I turn him turn down without insulting him? But Veronica, who was an old hand at this, calmed my fears by laying another doozy on me. She told me not to worry about the fitting, that everything with the shoot would be the way I wanted it, and that Hef always met the women he was thinking of putting on the cover. HUH?? In my mind, life hit the brakes hard and screeched to a dramatic halt (with glass-breaking and cat-screaming in tow), and I thought, *Say what?! Cover? Moi?* I've got to tell you . . . if that wasn't the smoothest move ever, I don't know what is. In one sentence she had me go from "There's no fucking way I'm getting naked for the fucking magazine" to "Well, I mean, nudity is the ultimate expression of art. Am I right?" In this town, negotiating is a lot like swimming for a shark: If you stop, you die.

That day, I decided to dress sexy-adjacent, opting for blue jeans and a tank top. I decided I'd be most comfortable going as me, the girl next door, but with full hair and makeup, of course—I was meeting Hef. Be yourself first, last, and always; great words to live by. Unless, of course, you're the guy behind the Craigslist casual encounters ad looking for a *Big Beautiful Man (BBM)* to come over, get naked, and stomp all over your son's vintage model train set, pretending to be a growling horny Godzilla, while you sit in the corner in a "full" diaper, eating shrimp and pleasuring yourself. You, sir, can feel free to stop being yourself.

I'm not sure what I expected as I was walking into the mansion, but I was kind of stunned. Apparently the clock had stopped at 10236 Charing Cross Road sometime in the mid-1970s. Everything from the carpets, to the drapes, to the furniture looked frozen in time. Like most things, reality often pales in comparison to the mythology, but I could not help but still be mesmerized by my surroundings. Hef hadn't made his grand entrance yet, so Veronica and her husband gave us a tour of the mansion, the petting zoo, the famous grotto, the private dens, and the game house where I spent time in a hidden circular room surrounded by mirrors and big cushions. Let's just say, the floor had a lot of bounce, if you know what I mean. It was quite something. Aside from playing with the monkeys at the zoo, my favorite part of the tour was the extensive history lesson that came with each location we were walking through. And by history lesson I mean who fucked who, where, and when. No detail was left unsaid, and no *jizz-stain* was left unanalyzed. It reminded me of the time Ken took us on his "Bullets and Blowjobs" tour of Hollywood. Which was basically a lighthearted look at LA with an emphasis on death and sex. Something he had cooked up for his family who was visiting from Germany for the first time. Ken was a fucking genius!!

As we wandered through the mansion, I swear, if you listened closely, you could still hear the echoes of all the countless orgasms wafting through its hallowed halls. In some ways the mansion is one giant glorified *fuck palace* held together like a house of cards by the countless celebrity *cumshots* that have graffitied its walls. Yet, I have to admit, there's a timeless beauty and elegance to the house that can only have come into existence through the cultural and historical revolution that was witnessed within it. You could feel the history all around you, but unfortunately, you could taste it, too. It was on your skin. It was in your hair. It coated the back of your throat!

After the tour, we were invited into the dining room, where people had gathered. There was a big round table in the middle that could fit maybe thirty people, but there were only, maybe, a half a dozen of us there, which was pretty cool. Hef and Holly were still MIA, but Kendra and Bridget were there along with his pal, Oscar winning actor Martin Landau, who I was told was a regular. The eighty-year-old icon and star of the original *Mission: Impossible* TV series and the sci-fi classic *Space: 1999*, hung out and ate with us. I have to admit that was definitely a high point because that dude dated Marilyn Monroe and was friends with James Dean back in the day. The food service was very elegant and proper, and the vibe was really chill. Experiencing the mansion in that way was truly unique and special to me because no one was putting on a show for anyone. We were all just hanging. The experience felt quite real and tangible; I almost felt like one of the regulars.

After dinner, it was finally time for me to meet Hef. There's a big two-sided stairwell that comes down from the second floor into the main landing. It looks like something glorious from one of the mansions in *Gone with the Wind*. It was only appropriate that Hef would make his grand entrance coming down those stairs. I was made to wait at the bottom to one side so that I could witness the floating arrival of their resident deity. He was quite something to behold in his trademark burgundy smoking jacket and silk pajamas. Not since witnessing Gene Simmons in action, up close, had I seen a man recognize that he was more of a brand than a person. He was delightful and every bit aware of his iconic presence. Like the upholstery, he was a lot older and frailer than I thought he'd be. But he was incredibly nice and charming.

I must admit, I was genuinely caught off guard when he knew who I was and why I was there. I honestly thought that meeting young girls at the mansion was perfunctory for him at this point. I was wrong. He took a little time to talk with me about how they had discovered me and showered me with gentle praise and kindness. He told me a couple of stories about the house, and we talked about the zoo and the grotto. I remember joking with him about there being more animals in the grotto than in the zoo. Afterwards, he invited us all into the screening room to watch one of his favorite classic films. The screening room had a huge fireplace, floor-to-ceiling wood paneling (and I'm talking early seventies not late seventies—the good shit!), an ornamental ceiling, and an old grand piano with pictures of ghosts from a time gone by and a life well lived. The few of us there nestled comfortably on old fabric couches that had been *fucked* into the comfort zone, waiting for the film to start. Hef then told a couple of stories after which we sank into the movie. And when it was over, he gracefully disappeared from whence he came.

Over the course of my time there, I had played over in my head a million times what I'd say to Hef if my magazine spread came up.

Ultimately deciding that I was going to politely agree to consider everything he'd say. No point in being rude. After all, his life had been dedicated to disrobing women, and no one should be criticized for loving their job. But to his credit, Hef never even brought it up. Was he a total gentleman? Or a master chess player who knew, from the countless other women around him with daddy issues, that disappointing him would be the worst kind of guilt? Well, I didn't have daddy issues, so as cool as meeting Hef was, I still wasn't going to take my *kit* off. Before leaving, I asked if I could see Hef to thank him for his hospitality and for a most memorable night. I was told that he had retired for the evening but that there was a box at the top of the infamous staircase with a slot in it and that I could leave a note for him there and slide it in. Apparently, it was a tradition for guests to leave thank-you notes or phone numbers for the aging lothario. I wrote him a sweet thank-you note, made the trek up those wondrous stairs, dropped it in the box, took one last look around, and left with a smile.

Photoshoot week had arrived, and Veronica and I had, finally, figured out the boundaries we all could live with. Then two days before the shoot, as my mom and sister boarded their planes to LA, it all went to shit! Without any warning, Veronica suddenly changed her tune. She denied everything she had said about a *Maxim*-style shoot and told us point-blank that this was *Playboy* and if I didn't sign the agreement for full nudity, there would be no shoot. Period. And there it was, my Hobson's Choice. I couldn't believe what I was hearing. This woman, whom I had grown to trust and feel empowered by, was no better than a common street hustler. I was devastated and, frankly, a little embarrassed that I didn't see this coming. I suppose it was naive of me to think that a *non-nude* shoot was even possible at *Playboy*, but I was very straightforward with them from day one. What the hell kind of business were they running? It felt like I was *ass-up* on the wrong end of a sixties stag shoot.

I couldn't even comprehend what was happening, and how I was now being threatened by some sort of schoolyard bully. I couldn't believe it. I didn't like being lied to and fucked with. This dream scenario had turned into a fucking nightmare. The only difference was that I had been dealing with bullies all my life, and I wasn't about to be forced into anything. Nothing was worth debasing myself for. And as much as I was excited about doing the shoot, it was always going to be on my terms. Fuck this and fuck them.

The project falling apart had left me so disappointed. Especially as my mom and sister arrived in LA only to discover that the shit had hit the fan and there was likely not going to be a shoot. It was all a giant buzzkill. But it ended up being a real blessing to have them with me during what turned out to be an emotionally draining time. To be perfectly honest, I think my mom was a bit relieved. She was leery of this whole thing from the very beginning. I guess she saw through them even though I couldn't. My sister actually did a lot to cheer me up. After giving me the requisite amount of time to sulk, alone and without judgment, she showed up with a bottle of my favorite pinot and three glasses. I was about to tell her that I wasn't in the mood, but my eye caught the giant wheel of Brie under her arm. At that point, I knew that whatever disappointment and self-pity I had committed to would have to wait. A wheel of Brie trumps pretty much everything. Growing up, my sister always had a knack for laying on the cheese when it counted. My mom's and Kate's words and comfort meant the world to me. It was just what I needed right when I needed it.

The next morning I woke up feeling PISSED OFF (and a smidge lactose intolerant)!! I knew who I was, I knew what I was willing to do and what was out of the question. I wasn't about to compromise my dignity. If building No Good TV had taught me anything, it was that. I was *No Good* and damn proud of it, and nobody could take that away from me. I was so angry I refused to budge. She could take her Hobson's Choice and shove it up her ass!!

"I don't want to do it," I said firmly to my publicist. "No way this chick is going to bully me and make me second-guess myself. Fuck that. We're done!"

And just as soon as I called it quits, I got an urgent call from a senior editor at *Playboy* asking WTF had just happened. Oddly enough, this was the first time we had actually spoken to someone from *Playboy*. All business prior to this had been conducted with Veronica. Turns out, Veronica was a bit of a hustler and totally misrepresenting us both to each other. It seemed that the whole time she was promising me that I wouldn't have to do anything nude, she was assuring *Playboy* that I had agreed to give up the *full Monty*! I guess she figured she would have the leverage to coerce me into doing it right before the shoot. Later on I would be told that she was losing favor with Hef and that this had the makings of some desperate attempt at winning him back. She had gotten word that *Playboy* was interested in me and decided to be the one to bring me in like a "Prize Turkey." Not sure it quite worked out the way she had hoped.

Much to my relief, the editor was astounded and completely shocked to hear the sequence of events. She was in an utter state of disbelief, but fortunately my team had held on to and sent over all the correspondence between us and Veronica to support our position. She was beyond apologetic, embarrassed, and mortified at what had happened. I can only imagine that playing the old bait and switch is bad for business, and it's the last thing you want out there. I was glad that *Playboy* had not been involved in the deception, but I kind of got the feeling that this wasn't the first time a girl got hustled by a photographer in this town.

After apologizing profusely, the editor, wanting to make up for this whole mess, found a way to give this saga a happy ending. She offered me the tamer "Babe of the Month" pictorial, which meant no nakedness.

"Yes!" I said, so happy. "That's all I ever wanted to begin with!"

They ended up bringing in a wonderful photographer whom they use quite often named Brie Childers, who was very good at making an uncomfortable situation way less weird. "Just relax and try to feel sexy," Brie said. "Umm . . . You're gonna have to show me what to do," I responded.

To make things even more interesting, this pink-haired punk chick happened to be nine months pregnant. So there she was during our photo shoot, literally rolling around on the floor, showing me how to pose like a pinup girl, all belly-with-baby. She had me roaring with laughter.

I imitated her moves, and for the first time in this whole mess, felt safe and sexy. After starting out so dodgy, in the end my pictorial turned out to be the perfect collaboration, and I owe it all to Brie, that kindhearted little mama. I loved the photos, and I loved the interview.

I stuck to my guns, and now I'm able to say I was in *Playboy* on my own terms, without compromising my rules.

Flash forward almost five years, and I'd just been hired to become the host of my very first national broadcast television talk show and VH1's first morning show. I had just arrived in New York and was getting settled in. The excitement and pressure was palpable. I remember getting a call to come in for a meeting with the heads of the network, the executive producers of the show, and the head of publicity, the agenda being the public rollout and introduction of me and the show. So there I was listening to the plan, and suddenly I was confronted by one of the honchos, who was pissed.

"Why are we just finding out you did a naked photo spread in *Playboy*? This is of grave concern to us as this is a morning show geared towards families, and we don't want any tawdry rumors out of the gate about our host, and what else should we be worried about? What other skeletons do you have in your closet?" Needless to say, my heart was beating out of my chest because I really didn't know where this was going. But it presented me with one of the most gratifying moments of that whole experience, as I addressed the room and let them know that whoever did their research was wrong and that I never did a naked photoshoot for *Playboy* or anywhere else, and that there were no skeletons in my closet. I had done right by me, and the rest is history.

As women in this business, it seems that we're always going to be stuck between a rock and a hard place or between Sasquatch's nutsack and Hobson's Choice. It's always going to be the way of things until we decide it's not anymore. But that will require less herd mentality and more real empowerment, not this over-the-counter horseshit we're being sold by social media's elites who are willing to showcase their *wrinkle star galactica* in exchange for your "Likes."

There's no denying the powerful effects of this *selfie-objectification* movement that has engulfed all areas of entertainment, utilizing social media as its weapon of choice. It's been a highly contagious phenomenon, primarily driven by women, under the guise of taking back control of their self-expression while seeing it as a tool for empowerment. I also understand that it's a way to get attention and to get your message heard, but at what level of absurdity do we stop? Is it a naked supermodel delivering hope to the downtrodden with a hashtag written on a sign covering her ass? Being charitable for show doesn't help. I would like to point out that back before there was Internet, if someone came up and pressed their naked ass against your car window with a Post-it message attached to it, you'd be mortified, and the last thing you'd be thinking is *Oh, thank God, I got that message!* Today, it makes all the sense in the world. Oh how times have changed.

Somehow we've convinced ourselves that objectification by our own hand is perfectly fine. Only at the hands of others is it bad. But the truth is self-objectification is more lethal by your own hand because there's nothing to limit you. There's no one to draw any lines. And the *belfie* is just the tip of the iceberg when examining the sheer number of ways we're contributing to being sexualized, scrutinized, and analyzed nowadays. You see, whether you've taken a *selfie, felfie, delfie, helfie, welfie, drelfie, purrfie, shelfie, bedsie, dronie, freebie, groupie,* or the donkey *shot supreme known as, the belfie,* you, too, are part of this crusade to return objectification back into the rightful hands of its subjects. Who are then free to continue objectifying . . . themselves! Huh?

All this talk about how we need to deemphasize our body parts and focus on what is inside seems to pale in comparison to the influx of sexualized images of body parts being uploaded every day in every possible way. We complained about our magazines Photoshopping images, so now we use other tools to do the same. It's hilarious! We're now the ones doing what's been done to us for decades. Except now have no one else to blame.

If you truly think about it, you'll realize that this is not empowerment. Empowerment has nothing to do with the way you look and has everything to with how you feel and who you are. It has nothing to do with how you physically compare with others. It has nothing to do with your appearance. Because you are not your appearance.

So when you look at the images on the various social media accounts of countless celebrities, keep in mind that this is not a representation of who they actually are, just who they're pretending to be. It's actually a representation of the most shallow version of themselves. And if that's all they're putting out there, then maybe they have become who they're pretending to be. And if their entire social media profiles are just a collection of body parts, especially their *dumper,* then you're not even looking at a person; you're just looking at an ASS!

When I'm not sure what to do, Kourosh always says to me: "Let Carrie be Carrie!" It helps me focus on what's important. So I'm going to pass it on to you for when you find yourself distracted by all the noise and the funk and you're not sure what to do: "Let you be you!"

11

FUCK MICKEY MOUSE!

> One day I will find the right words,
> and they will be simple.
> —The Dharma Bums, *Jack Kerouac*

Each time you walk into a room for an interview with a celebrity, the game board changes like an ever-evolving maze. Much like a snowflake, no two rooms are the same. There are a lot of variables at work on any given day, most of which you're not even aware of, with multiple concealed agendas converging right before your eyes. It genuinely feels like you're inside M. C. Escher's *Relativity* lithograph. To borrow a famous quote from *Forrest Gump*, "Interviews are like a box of chocolates. You never know what you're gonna get." The celebrities and their handlers are firmly in control, and if you don't have your wits about you, you can become nothing more than a marionette who is there for their amusement.

From the timer who places you in your finite box to the publicist's soul-grabbing eye contact to the studio's ever-present expectation that you're not going to *shit the bed* to the celebrities' sudden emotional whims. At that moment, you, your planning, and your preparation are suddenly lying on a colonic table, waiting for a wheatgrass enema (apparently you can drink it and blow it up your ass). Some days they clean your clock, but most days you walk out with your dignity intact. Unless, of course, it's a box of sugar-free chocolates, and anyone who's had the misfortune of being on the wrong side of sugar-free chocolates knows that, one way or another, it's going to be painful and sooner rather than later you'll be *painting the walls*. (More on that in Chapter 15: *A Kick in the Cunt*.) It can be frightening, exhilarating, or both.

I love the mystery of where it's going to go in the room. I was lucky to have a format that allowed me to go with the flow, and I didn't have to ask certain typical things or fulfill some mandated quota of inappropriate personal questions that were nobody's business. Like, "Michael Jackson has just passed away. How does that make you feel?" or "Ben Affleck is getting a divorce from Jennifer Garner. Do you have any comments about his alleged infidelity?" Being free not to have to follow that kind of tabloid questioning model made for some memorable and usually unexpected interactions. Moments that redefined being "uncensored" as something customizable to suit each individual's boundaries. There were relationships with celebrities that spanned years and had the emotional arc of *The Notebook*. And then there were the times when I came face-to-face with complicated icons who turned the tables on me and blew my mind. Sometimes you just have to be willing to take that leap of faith and see where the day takes you.

"This fuckin' movie is incredible! And there's a couple of real fucks in it . . . and then some motherfuckers!"

—*Demi Moore*

I interview the biggest stars on the planet, and sometimes it's hard to remain calm. I try to make it look easy-breezy Covergirl, but to be honest, there have been a few times I looked *cool as a cucumber* on camera while desperately holding back my inner Chris Farley. Sometimes I find myself in these surreal situations with AAA-list celebrities that so many people would chop off their left nut to be in, and I can't help but *nerd* the fuck out.

The first time that happened to me was at an interview with one of my heroes, Rob Zombie. Yes, technically, Rob Zombie is everything I'm obsessed with stuffed into one long-haired, bearded, "more human than human" being—a head banger and a horror movie director. This guy knows his way around boobs and blood, and that makes my head explode. So when I got to meet him at the *House of 1000 Corpses* junket, I turned into a tongue-tied idiot. I couldn't get a sentence out. Just nothing. I would start out asking a solid, well-informed, legit question only to then burst into Anderson Cooper–like fits of giggling. Rob would just look at me, calmly waiting for my giggle-fit to end. He's a pretty reserved guy, which can be intimidating. But if you can engage him in an in-depth geek-out convo about comic books, horror films, or music, he'll gab until the day is done. Of course, I didn't know that yet, so he put up with me nervously giggling my way through this interview.

I brought the tapes back to the office, and my editor, upon watching them, was like, "What the hell happened to you?" He had never seen me lose my cool like that before.

Fuck if I know. Some people just have that effect on you, and it's out of your control. Take George Clooney. Stop anyone on the street—man, woman, child, mime—and they'll swoon at the mention of George Clooney. Likewise, in the junket world, he's the Holy Grail interview, the end-all and be-all, a god. Clooney was one of those *white elephants* for NGTV. Years went by and we couldn't book him. I spent so many junkets sitting out in the hall, watching people come out of the room with him with this postcoital glow on their faces. Every woman, one by one, was like, "Oh my God, George Clooney!" and basically had an orgasm right there in the hallway. Every man, one by one, was like, "I want to be George Clooney!" And basically had an orgasm right there in the hallway. I should've been handing out Kleenex and cigarettes.

Now, I appreciate George Clooney as a fine physical specimen, too, but he never gave me the sweats the way someone like Jason Momoa did. I always imagined that George Clooney had an aroma of fresh laundry, vanilla birthday cake, and a light spritz of Tom Ford cologne, where I was more into whiskey breath and aged leather. So I never quite got why everyone was so gaga over this guy. I made it through *The Facts of Life*, *Ocean's Eleven*, even the Caesar haircut, never going into a state of *musth.* Say what? That's the term for the periodic state of heightened sexual activity and aggression in adult male elephants, characterized by the discharge of secretions from glands near the eyes and the continuous dribbling of urine. Don't say I never taught you anything, and don't complain about how you're not quite sure how to use this information to get laid.

Everyone going cuckoo for Cocoa Puffs over George really confused me. How dare I even say that about the two-time winner of *People*'s "Sexiest Man Alive"—who the hell do I think I am? Well, I guess it's possible that being left out made me a little bitter. But my bitterness also motivated me. I made it my mission in life to get him, and I refused to give up.

Getting Clooney would be easier said than done. There were two major challenges: How do we book him? Even if we did book him, would he curse?

For any outlet, landing an interview with an A-lister is a tall order. With NGTV's uncensored format, landing a star that huge was extremely difficult in our early days. The irony of it was that when it was all said and done, many of them were surprisingly game. Brad Pitt, Justin Timberlake, Bradley Cooper, and Johnny Depp, to name a few, totally dug the format and appreciated its humor. At the end of the day, these guys were so big that they weren't afraid to let their guards down and have fun. They had nothing to prove and nothing to lose. If anything, this was a way to connect to their fans on a more intimate level. Cursing is the language of the masses, and we are the Rosetta Stone.

There are definitely those A-listers, like Beyoncé, who protect their images as Sasha Fiercely as Fort Knox. Please don't Tweet mean things about me being a Beyoncé-hater, such as "Carrie Keagan looks like Meg Ryan, if Meg Ryan was a crack addict!" I love Queen Bey. I've done the "Single Ladies" dance in a leotard like every other estrogen-infused woman and gay man in the world. She's super nice, but I think she subscribes to that old-school unattainable superstar ethos. Let's face it, J. D. Salinger was more open about himself than Beyoncé.

Matt Damon, on the other hand, is always down to play. His usual response to me reminding him we're uncensored is, "Thank fucking God!" He's just about the most normal megastar you're ever going to run into. My guess is that he, like quite a few other major players, never bothered attending the special ceremony that takes place when an actor

or actress ascends to becoming an A-lister, where they are presented the
"Sceptre of Poot." A private ritual, similar to becoming a "made man" in
the Mafia, where the ascendee has a rather long stick inserted into their
ass as a "welcome basket" of sorts.

One of my favorite encounters with him was at the junket for *The
Departed.* I let you *"nibble the tip"* of this story in the introduction, but I
figured I'd let you get your hands around the whole *braciola*! It was a big
important film being lined up for awards, so I had to finesse the filth. So
naturally, we dove deep into Jack Nicholson's junk. That's where Matt
blew me away with his flawless impersonations of Martin Scorsese and
Jack Nicholson to give me this revealing and fun story. If you've seen
the movie, you know what we're talking about, but if you haven't, this is
going to make you want to see it more.

> **Me:** Okay, so we have to talk. You might be the only man alive to ac-
> tually have seen Jack's junk.
>
> **Matt:** Well, I, uh, wouldn't call that Jack's junk . . . If that was Jack's
> junk he would've been a bigger porn star than he was a, you
> know . . . movie star.
>
> **Me:** I was hoping . . .
>
> **Matt:** Yeah.
>
> **Me:** I was wondering . . . because everyone was wondering . . . Did it
> look like the right color even?
>
> **Matt:** No, it wasn't. Were people actually wondering if that was his?
>
> **Me:** There were a few black men in the junket circuit that were like . . .
> *(My face contorts as if mimicking the face of someone who felt they were
> being lied to . . . I put my fingers to my lips.)* HOLD ON A MINUTE!
> Now we're all curious . . .
>
> **Matt:** Yeah, yeah, no, no . . . you know Jack . . . It was my first day
> working with him, and I got this call from Scorsese . . . he
> goes . . . *(Perfectly mimicking Martin Scorsese's fast-talking, slightly
> high-pitched voice—celebrity imitations being one of Matt Damon's
> more popular skills.)* "Hello. Hi, Matt. Hi. Marty. The director. Uh,
> listen . . ." And he always would do that . . . He would introduce
> himself as the director, you know, "Marty, the director." And he
> said, "Well, I don't know if you know other Martys." And I was
> like, "Yeah, no, I know who you are . . ." But he was like, "Listen.
> Uh . . . Interesting story. Uh . . . Things with Jack are going very

well, very well. Uh . . . Good changes. Good stuff. He's brought a lot. He's really focused on the job. He's got an interesting idea for tomorrow . . ." *(He pauses.)* "The movie theater. So. I'm just gonna come out and say it . . ." *(Long pause.)* "Jack wants to wear a dildo." *(Damon breaks the Martin Scorsese character and laughs along with me as I'm all but doubled over in my chair.)* And I was like, "All right, man . . . all right . . ."

Me: And you went, do I have to look at it?

Matt: No, I mean, I was like, "I'll see in the morning, man." I mean, what was I to say, you know? And he [Jack Nicholson] gets in there and he's like . . . *(Doing a spot-on Jack Nicholson imperson-ation.)* "I just thought the whole thing would make a whole lot more sense if I turned around and had a big black cock in your face."

It was such a perfect moment that I could have walked out and been quite satisfied, but Matt wasn't done trying to win the Perfect In-terview Award. When we got to our curse-word tradition, he decided that this interview was being brought to you by the "letter" Boston and the "number" fuck.

Matt: Well, my favorite curse word, being from Boston, I mean, is defi-nitely FUCK. It's so flexible. And in Boston we use it, you know, you can say . . . Fuck you. Fuck him. Fuck me. Fuck that guy. But you can also use it as a bridge, like, we'll say . . . um, if you're thinking of something . . . *(He elongates the word.)* Fuckiiiiiiiiiiin' oh I know what I wanted to tell you . . . uh . . . We're all filthy mouthed there . . . so I'll say *(in a heavy Boston accent)* THE DAPAWTED is fawkin' aw'some!!

Back to Clooney, who falls somewhere between Salinger and Kim Kardashian on the self-promotion meter. The key to getting him was trust. Could he and his people trust me unequivocally not to make him look bad? When we first started out, there was an outlet that made my job a little harder. They'd ask inappropriate questions in a "Gotcha!" sort of way that was making fun of the stars. They would attempt to create chaos, but they didn't know how to manage it effectively the way us pro-fessional idiots knew how to do it. So even though other A-listers had learned over time that they could trust us, I don't blame Clooney for avoiding us. He may have a reputation as the ultimate on-set prankster, but he's also an Oscar winner as an actor and producer. On the personal side, he recently married an international human rights lawyer named Amal who wears long white gloves un-ironically. The last time I wore long white gloves un-ironically I cleaned the toilet. So not only was he going to be reluctant to sit down with us, it's highly unlikely he'd bust out "cumguzzling pussy fart."

Thing is, he didn't have to. I put no pressure on celebs to be dirty, and I'm totally direct and up front. The minute they sit down, I tell them NGTV is uncensored, and they should feel free to curse or take it as far as they want. I let them decide where the line is. And it works because they feel like they're in control, which usually makes them comfortable.

Michael Douglas is as old-school Hollywood as they come. He's one of the few celebrities that stand up to greet every journalist when they enter the room. Some won't look at you until the camera starts rolling. Some will make sure they have something in their hands, like a cup and saucer of tea, so they don't have to touch you. But Michael, he is nothing but class. He understood he needed to reach a younger audience and wanted to have fun with the cool kids, so he happily played along with me at *The Sentinel* junket. Legends are no shrieking violets, but the furthest he would go was saying "ass," and you could tell that was a stretch for him. That was perfectly fine and perfectly awesome. Everyone has their own level of dirty. Now, Michael's been through a lot these last few years, and these days he's a bit more freewheeling with his expressiveness. There is nothing like a life-or-death situation to loosen your inhibitions and expand your vocabulary. These days he freely talks and jokes about oral sex and having a big dick, but back then, "ass" was his "fuck" and he gave that "ass" up like a pro!

It's kind of the same with *Star Wars* creator George Lucas. For the *Star Wars: Episode III—Revenge of the Sith* junket, I was invited up to the Skywalker Ranch in Marin County, California, and even got to spend the night on those hallowed grounds! I anticipated my trip into the world of the Jedi in much the same way I did my first time seeing Skid Row perform live. I could feel its force inside me! That totally came out wrong . . . but it came nonetheless, didn't it?

I imagined it would be something close to landing on the planet of Coruscant in a Lamda-class Imperial shuttle. (*Oh my!*) Having my senses overwhelmed by the hundreds of *Star Wars* characters populating the walkways just going about their space business. *(Oh . . . God!)* Watching my childhood come to life as I bore witness to countless demonstrations ranging from parkouring through a Dagobah bog with Yoda on my back *(OH!!!!)* to spelunking into the Sarlacc pit looking for Boba Fett *(OH . . . YES!)* to Lightsaber Dueling 101 with Jedi Master Luminara Unduli *(YES! YES!)* to Wookiee Warfare Strategy on Kashyyyk with Chewbacca *(YES! YES! YES!)* to a flight simulation ride aboard the *Millennium Falcon (Dear lord, have mercy!)*. I just wanted to grab the "Han Solo frozen in carbonite" headboard in my room with both hands and scream, "I love you . . . I know," as I burst into a *Death Star*-explosion–level orgasm. And I'm talking about the *Return of the Jedi*-special-edition *Death Star* explosion, with the light ring and everything. At least that's what I had imagined.

The reality was a smidge different. It was more like visiting a bed-and-breakfast at a large ranch in Maine. Less Neverland, more *The Truman Show* with its hundreds of closed-circuit cameras watching your every move. It's really beautiful, but the Jedi magic is well hidden within the minds of the people working there and not so much in its décor. It's a bucolic world of quiet reflection at a pond called Lake Ewok where there's an X-wing fighter on display and bike rides through the meadow with the cows. Don't get me wrong, it's a special place, and you feel it all around you, but it's not what you might expect. At the time, George lived on the property in a big house, and I remember stealing plenty of time on his front steps. That was cool.

That night we watched a screening of the movie in "the Stag," the property's three-hundred-seat, toe-curling, head-spinning, mind-bending, bed-wetting, jizz-yourself-into-oblivion masterpiece of a movie theater. And the next day I got to interview George and the cast of the film. George, who is very cool, is also very PG, like a big teddy bear. To be honest, I was nervous about making a good impression and not offending him in any way because I am a total *Star Wars* geek and this was fucking George Lucas. The mastermind behind the fantasy classic *Willow* and the only guy with balls big enough to bring Marvel's *Howard the Duck* to life. So there I was, trying to find an angle for the interview that would satisfy NGTV's needs while not turning the idyllic Skywalker Ranch into ground zero for a septic tank explosion. But then the immortal words of Yoda flooded into my brain: "Do or do not. There is no try." Fuck it, I was going to kill it with George Lucas—my way.

Then it struck me like a *Force blast*! George had created entire languages in the *Star Wars* universe with their own built-in curse words because that's how important they are. And as luck would have it, aside from my familiarity with the complete works of William Shakespeare in the original Klingon, I am, also, well versed in Huttese. Being one of the primary languages spoken on Tatooine, I knew from my years of studying it at the University of Kashyyyk that if I reached into its depths, I would find the key. And I was right. The answer lay in *"bantha poodoo,"* which is the intergalactic equivalent of guano. Not only is it a rare substance that the Galactic Empire used to power the *Death Star* but it's also a curse word meaning "shit." It was the perfect entry point that ended up creating a rare, amusing, and relaxed interview. It turns out even George Lucas enjoys cursing as long as it's in the context of the *Star Wars* universe. Now that I had found a way to break the ice, I couldn't help but wonder if I could politely nudge George into a dick joke. Now that would be a Jedi mind trick!

Me: I heard a rumor . . . that Hayden [Christensen] actually said he would only agree to do the third episode if his lightsaber got to be bigger than Ewan's [McGregor].

George: *(He takes a moment, smiles, and sucks air through his teeth.)* They fought over it.

Me: They did, did they?

George: They did. Yeah, to see who had the bigger lightsaber.

Me: Who won, do you know? *(I say it softly, not quite sure if George hears me.)*

George: They were very, very good. *(George's thoughts start catching up to his speech. Having now heard my question.)* Well, I actually made them the same length . . . They, they saw themselves— each one—having a bigger lightsaber, but the reality is that they're actually the same size. But you know what? It really doesn't make any difference, does it? *(He asks as if suddenly not talking about lightsabers anymore . . . everyone in the room senses this and begins to laugh . . . George throws his head back and laughs, too.)*

Me: *(With a big smile of accomplishment on my face.)* It's all in how they use it, I guess.

George: *(Nodding in agreement.)* It is! It's all in how they use it.

It was official. I was a now a Jedi Master from the *Order of the Sch-meckle.* What started out as a potential *"Poodoo Show"* turned into an endearing connection with a legend. It was epic. George must have enjoyed himself, too. He did me a huge solid in the form of what turned out to be an incredibly lengthy network ID for No Good TV. He very simply said, "You're watching NGTV," only he said it a number of times and in a number of ways. Not everybody did IDs, definitely nobody of George's magnitude, so when Kourosh saw it for the first time, he almost cried like a little girl.

At the end of the press day, all the junketeers had gathered in the hospitality area for a drink, and easily one of the greatest moments of my life occurred. George Lucas, gracious as he is, casually walked into the room to thank all the press people for coming up and supporting the film. Then, as he was about to leave, he noticed me and stopped, walked over, and in front of this room full of people turned to me and said, "We all agreed that you were our favorite interview today!" I shakily said thank you and tried to keep my shit together, but inside my heart exploded like the *Death Star,* and ten thousand celebratory Ewoks raised their voices in unison chanting the chorus to "Yub Nub" while the night sky filled with fireworks. My work was done there. I am geek. Hear me roar!

George Clooney wouldn't have necessarily known this, but I tend to tailor the filthiness of my interviews to jibe with the star's comfort level. Sorry I used "jive" in a sentence; I just finished watching *Airplane!* "Ain't no thang!" So, if George Lucas only wanted to go as far as to talk about *bantha poop,* then it's *bantha poop* all day, son! I always tailor it to the humor or tone of the movie they're promoting. If it's a really serious film like *Selma,* the uncensored conversation comes by way of the message of the film. I don't push the envelope unless the star wants to. However, if it's a raunchy comedy, I let the dick jokes fly! I play to the room.

Case in point, for some reason, No Good TV was asked to cover *Shrek the Third,* a PG-rated, animated, family film. The studio had always been great to us, so I wasn't going to turn down the invite. If they wanted our support, they had it. But I was somewhat perplexed about how to cover it and did ask myself, more than a few times, *Why am I even show-ing up to this?* But I'm a glass-half-full-of-whiskey girl so I decided, *Hell yeah, I'm going to make this work.* I just had to figure out how to do it without getting kicked out of the junket. In every interview, there's a line you shouldn't cross, and it's just a matter of finding that line here. Strangely enough, the answer came to me when I was doing a little research on old nursery rhymes, which we ended up integrating into our piece for that all important context. It's shocking just how suggestive some of them were just from reading the first line. You be the judge . . .

"Wee Willie Winkie runs through the town. Upstairs, downstairs in his nightgown . . ." I'm not quite sure what's going on here but someone needs to call the cops.

"Old mother Hubbard went to the cupboard to fetch her poor dog a bone . . ." All I hear is Andrew Dice Clay and Rover takin' over, so moving on!

"Rub-a-dub-dub three men in a tub . . ." Deplorable and potentially messy.

"I love little pussy . . ." WHAT??

"Where are all the little boys?" Oh, come on! That's not even subtle.

"She'll be comin' 'round the mountain when she comes . . . when she comes . . ." Rather progressive subject matter for a child's rhyme.

"Little Miss Muff . . . et . . ." Really? That's the only name we could call her? Really?

"Little Boy Blue, come blow . . ." I'm not even going to finish this one out of respect.

"Dance to your daddy . . ." I just hope they weren't shooting any video.

"Diddle, diddle, dumpling . . ." Too much diddling in this for my comfort.

"Ride a cock horse . . ." That's just plainly obscene and grammatically incorrect as it appears the last two words are in the wrong order.

All I can say is that they sounded very different to me when I was a kid. Today, they are no longer nursery *rhymes;* they are nursery *crimes.*

Clearly there were plenty of precedents in the world of children's literature to help me find my way through this junket. However depraved things may have been historically, I was going to take the high road. To that end, I came up with simple and innocent themes for the movie's stars, Mike Myers, Cameron Diaz, Justin Timberlake, Eddie Murphy, and Antonio Banderas, that we could all agree on and talk about. By far, my favorite of the day was with Mike Myers. He's regarded as being a tough interview and an all-around pretty serious guy. Some of the funniest actors in the world are completely the opposite off-camera. I definitely had my apprehensions that day, and I sure as hell didn't want to fuck up a chance to play *verbal catch* with *Austin Powers*. But I liked the angle we had for the interviews, and I was feeling feisty! I figured that if I took a leap of faith, he would meet me halfway, and just maybe, my story piece would have a *happy ending*:

Me: To start, let's just clear up something. So the Frog King croaks?

Mike Myers: Yes.

Me: And leaves the Frog King Kingdom?

Mike: Yes.

Me: And you have a Frog King problem?

Mike: Why are you shouting at me? That's my question. What did I do? And let me start off by saying 'I'm sorry!'

Me: You know . . .

Mike: *(Shouting.)* I have no depth perception.

Me: What? What was that? *(Leaning in and shouting.)*

Mike: I'm sorry. Are you close? YES. The Frog King dies. They don't want me to be the king. I don't feel that ogres can be a king, so I set off on a journey to find an alternative, and I do so in the form of King Arthur, played by Justin Timberlake.

Me: Dun, dun, daahh!! The best part of this movie . . .

Mike: Mmmm.

Me: The ogre shows a little more of himself this time than the last few.

Mike: Ogre bottom! You know what? I've actually showed my bottom in everything that I've done.

Me: Why is that?

Mike: Because it's insured by Lloyd's of London for ten million dollars is why.

Me: Really?!

Mike: No!

Me: Ooo!!!! Can I give you a little? *(Gesturing a slap.)*

Mike: You literally want to smack my bottom?

Me: I did! Now that it's worth ten million dollars, I'm in!

Mike: No, actually part of the insurance is that you cannot smack my bottom.

Me: Oh! Are they okay that it already has a crack in it?

Mike: Jamumumbarumbum! Bop! How come I feel like I'm on the set of *Hee Haw* right now? "Jamumumbarumbum! And now The Good Old Boys!" *(Makes an open-mouth smile to the camera then proceeds to play the* Hee Haw *theme on air-banjo, emphasizing the word, "Shrek.")*

Me: What cracks you up the most in the film?

Mike: My favorite is the Frog King. How long it takes for him to die makes me laugh a great deal.

Me: You are a sick man.

Mike: You don't even know the beginning of it. Help me, man!

Me: Were you willing to give him mouth-to-mouth if it came to that?

Mike: Oh, lord!

Me: Now I've always heard that Far Far Away is awesome because everybody gets a happy ending?

Mike: Oh my God!! Yes. I think you make your own happy ending.

Me: I usually have to pay for mine!

Mike: Oh, lord! Oh, no! This has turned a very dirty corner. And I want to tell you that I have nothing to do with it. Hi, I'm Mike Myers! Go see *Shrek the Third* or "Potty Mouth" will come and shout at ya!
(We both laugh.)

Mike: Okay, let's recap now. My bottom is insured?

Me: Definitely!

Mike: There's a crack in it?

Me: Totally!

Mike: And you're asking me if I want to open-mouth-kiss a frog?

Me: And if there's happy endings in Far Far Away?

Mike: *(To camera:)* Good night, everybody! Hi, I'm Mike Myers. *(He, again, plays the* Hee Haw *theme on air-banjo with the room laughing.)*

The *Shrek* interviews were, in a way, a great accomplishment for me because I conducted a genuine No Good TV interview without anyone ever actually using a traditional curse word. Granted, there were more innuendos flying around the room than poison darts in the opening scene of *Raiders of the Lost Ark*! Still, it made me super proud, and it proved something very important: Being *No Good* didn't require swearing . . . it's the whole state-of-mind thing.

Ultimately, you don't have to be a super-dirty human being or swear every other word to be *No Good*. But I will say this: There's a mentality that goes with swearing that says about a person, "I do not take myself too seriously," which I think is critical. When an Oscar-winning actor/director like Kevin Costner admits his favorite curse word is "dick," or showbiz legend and afterlife aficionado Shirley MacLaine drops multiple F-bombs, with wild abandon and ease, while promoting her spiritual book *Sage-ing While Age-ing*, it's like a breath of fresh air.

Shirley: You should fucking get this book because it's really fucking interesting. It won't teach you anything about fucking, but it will teach you about love. Love as opposed to fucking, and I think it's a fucking good idea. So fuck. Do it!

In the immortal words of Shirley, Yoda, and Nike: Just do it already, Clooney!

I know the suspense is killing you so I'll stop the torture.

We finally got George for the movie *Leatherheads*.

But it had almost nothing to do with us. Universal, the studio behind it, decided that our audience, mostly young college-age guys, was the perfect target audience for the film about a college football hero in the 1920s.

Fine, whatever you say, we'll take it!

I wanted to be *on fleek* for George, so I prepared like an OCD maniac for this interview. I'm using *"on fleek"* ironically, unlike Amal Clooney's long white gloves. I pray so hard that by the time this book comes out *"on fleek"* is as extinct as dusky seaside sparrows, Jamaican giant galliwasps, "amazeballs," "meh," and "totes." Anyhoo (ugh, I can't stop), I don't just walk into interviews blindly and wing it. You'd be surprised how many interviewers do. Literally, standing in the hall five minutes before, going, "What should I ask Nicole Kidman?" Before I meet anyone, I don't care if it's George Clooney or Kirk Cameron (well maybe not Kirk Cameron), I've researched them to the point of a possible restraining order (I'm pretty sure I'm not allowed to be within five hundred feet of *Game of Thrones* star Jason Momoa for another six months; I need to check with my lawyer). I've also seen the movie and taken notes. Even though NGTV is funny and chill, I get made fun of for being one of the only people who walks into a screening with a notepad, clipboard, and pen like Julie McCoy on *The Love Boat*. Writing *dick jokes* is a serious business, don'tcha know!

After I do all my research, I come up with a solid icebreaker as the best opening question. Before they get to me, these stars have been asked a lot of the same questions over and over until they're numb, like, "Tell me about your character." I hate that question and I'll never ask it. "What inspired you?" I don't care! It's like daggers in my eyes. I want to be different, original, and memorable, so I spend a shitload of time on my opener because it will set the tone for the whole thing. When I did Samuel L. Jackson for *Snakes on a Plane*, my first question wasn't, "What was it like to work with all of those snakes?" Zzzzzzzzzz. Instead, I went with "Does the size of the snake matter?" and his answer was priceless:

Samuel: So I've heard, but no, not in this one because we have some snakes that are about this big . . . *(he holds his hands roughly six inches apart)* that do a lot of damage.

Who doesn't love a good dick double entendre? I know I do!

Penis size was probably not the best direction to go with Clooney, though he's not averse to *dick jokes*. According to Roseanne Barr, he allegedly put a picture of his manhood wearing Groucho Marx glasses on the set's refrigerator and reportedly once slapped a SMALL PENIS ON-BOARD bumper sticker on his BFF Brad Pitt's car. But I didn't want to blow it—get it?—with George in the first few seconds, so I decided to focus on the movie instead. I was so psyched that we finally got the interview, yet nervous to finally come face-to-face with the man that causes so many to get *"Cloners"* aka *Clooney boners*. Not because I thought I'd go weak in the knees and become a babbling fool as soon as I saw him, like I did with Rob Zombie. It was more because it was nerve-wracking just walking into the unknown. That room is a huge question mark. You have no idea what happened right before you got there, if the interviewer before you pissed them off, if they took their meds that day or got an angry text from a secret gay lover, if their shrink's on vacation, if they have explosive diarrhea from eating Indian food for lunch or haven't eaten carbs in five days . . . there are so many factors out of your control.

Jeremy Renner was a classic example of how the unknown can spin you sideways. The first time I interviewed Jeremy, for the movie *Dahmer* at the Toronto Film Festival, we bonded over our mutual love of keepin' it real, in the form of a no-cussword-left-behind cluster bombing. It was the start of a long and interesting relationship. My overall take on Jeremy is that he's a salt-of-the-earth guy who oozes talent and abhors industry bullshit. He wasn't handed his A-list status overnight so he doesn't take it for granted. He had to earn it over time, and in the process, he developed a deep appreciation for everything he's gained. There's a groundedness to him that is very endearing.

He's very similar in that way to another remarkably grounded actor/director, Ben Affleck. Now there's a guy who was unceremoniously stripped of his VIP status at the *"Blockbuster Bathhouse,"* then found himself dragged naked through the streets of *Gigli* en route to a showbiz prison *shanking* called "straight to DVD," only to turn it around and make those *soul assassins* his bitch. Never once *turning asshole.* Ben has always been one of the most gracious guys in the biz. Like his buddy Matt Damon, he's from Boston, so cursing is like an oxygen bar; he pulls up to the counter and lines up shots.

He was always welcoming, always funny, and genuinely *No Good!* Never shy when it came to cussin' up a storm, his head-spinning, crazy good impressions are legendary. And his over-the-top impression of Colin Farrell from back when they were shooting *Daredevil* might just be, hands down, one of his funniest moments we ever caught on tape:

Ben: A Colin Farrell impersonation is just basically like this . . .
(He drops his head and raises his arms, to emulate Colin Farrell's wild personality. Then turns on a super thick, almost Lucky Charms, Irish accent.)
"Oh, heey, how are ya? Fuuuck, I'm fuckin' greeeat."
(He's now practically out of his chair and looking around the room, crazily.)
"I tell ya what, have you seen that fuckin' girl? I fucked 'er! I did . . . she's DY-NA-MITE n' I fucked 'er! Dynamite gal . . . ya? That one?"
(He points in the other direction.)
"Did you see *Playboy* ninety-nine, mate? I fucked HER! I did, and it was fuckin' great . . . Do you want a pint? Let's go have a fuckin' pint and fuck girls. I can't! I can't fuckin' believe it. I mean

they hire me in this fuckin' business to be a fuckin' actor, and they're paying fuckin' millions, AND fuckin' girls!"
(Ben turns off the "Colin" switch with a giant grin on his face.)

And there he is! That's why Colin Farrell's the coolest guy to hang out with in the world.

Then, of course, there was the junket for *The Town*, where we had a funny exchange about his costar, my buddy Jeremy Renner, when it was time to throw down and promote the film. A tradition of ours he was very familiar with:

Ben: *(Thinking stressfully to himself, aloud:)* What's my favorite curse word? Well, I know what Renner's would be . . .

Me: His was basic.

Ben: *(Getting excited.)* What did he say? . . . *(Whispering:)* "Cunt?"

Me: FUCK! *(I'm disappointed, having now realized that "cunt" was on the table.)* Oh no! He didn't! That must be his favorite one though, huh?

Ben: It is! He must've been too shy . . . um . . . favorite curse word? You know what? Renner's real favorite curse word was the one thing he did that he improvised all the time, and I cut out. I cut this out of the movie in like *forty* different scenes! He'd say *(in a Boston accent)* "Fuck you, you cocksuck!"
(I erupt into laughter as Ben shakes his is head, remembering his disapproval on set.)

Ben: *(With his director hat on.)* And I'd be like . . . *(Shaking his head.)* "No one's a cocksuck, let's not . . ." *(Smiling.)* "Great, let's do that again? Maybe without the cocksuck? Great. Great, thanks."

Me: Nice! *(Laughing so hard 'cause I could just visualize this ridiculous exchange on set.)*

Ben: There you go, my least favorite curse word.

To this day, it's always a pleasure to get in the ring with Ben. It seems that no matter how far he rises, he appreciates the people who were there to pick him up when he fell.

Back to Jeremy . . . Our paths crossed many times over the years, always with hugs and high fives, until one day he showed up to a junket a totally different Jeremy. He didn't want to play. He acted like he didn't really know me and was very uncomfortable. The whole thing was very odd, and it seemed that our great connection was *kaput*! I came back to Kourosh and said, "I don't know what happened, but Jeremy's not that guy anymore. He's either gotten too famous and affected or he just plain hates me." After that I was always apprehensive to interview him because it was so obvious that he wasn't having fun with us, so I'd have to cool my jets and just get through it. I was never going to force the format down his throat. What we do is not *pussy darts*, where you're trying to nail someone with pointed questions coming from an unexpected place. That's TMZ. What we do is more like ballroom dancing. It's as graceful as it is sexy, and it only really works when both people are working together and on the same page.

Then one day some time later, the most surprising thing happened. I went to interview Jeremy in New York for *American Hustle*, and I just figured that it would be the same polite-but-removed exchange. But when I walked into that room something had changed, and much to my delight, he was back to the original familiar and friendly Jeremy.

"Oh my God! How are you?" he said so enthusiastically, like we were old chums again. "How have you been?"

I was quite overcome with the joy of having my buddy back. And of course, we went right back to having great chemistry and cursing up a storm. I was really happy. In the hustle and bustle of the junket, we didn't have too much time to reminisce, but our exchange at the top of the interview did shed a little light on what may have happened. As he got comfortable in his chair, we started to banter about the seventies before the interview started, and the conversation automatically took a left turn into the gutter:

Jeremy: Then there's the seventies' camel toe.
   Me: But it sort of added to the mystique of everything, didn't it?
Jeremy: Yeah. Wait . . . why do you bring this out in me every time?
   Me: I didn't mean to . . . we just literally . . . it was an innocent conversation.
Jeremy: But you always take it to camel toe!
   Me: But I didn't. You did!
Jeremy: I know but . . . it's 'cause of you. *(Laughing.)*

Me: And by the way, on you it would have been moose knuckle
        not camel toe!

Jeremy: That's right!

Yay! My boy was back. After that we started following each other
on Twitter, which is the modern-day equivalent of the friendship pin,
and from there we became actual friends. Sometime later, I got the
chance to talk to him about our little *kerfuffle* and asked him what had
happened. I said, "You know, for a long time I thought you hated me. It's
funny that we're talking like this now."

"No, I never hated you," he replied. "You just always made me so
comfortable I forgot where I was and said things I shouldn't be saying
on camera."

It literally made me breathe a huge sigh of relief. It was kind of a
bittersweet thing, but I was very flattered because that really was the
whole point: getting a celebrity to be themselves. In this industry, that
very concept is so odd that it made him second-guess it. But thankfully,
he trusted me and knew we had his back.

I have to admit that I felt really badly for him when he got all that
grief in the media for calling the fictional character of Black Widow a
"slut" during the *Avengers: Age of Ultron* junket. I hoped that wasn't my
bad influence! But I also secretly hoped it was my bad influence. Anyone with any common sense knows that the whole thing was a joke.
They were asked a silly question and they gave a silly answer. I think it
was a little unfair for the media to string him and Chris Evans up for a
clearly meaningless remark. But the blowback was proof that we still
live in a world where celebrities can't really let their hair down even for
an instant. Fucking around has consequences. Their interview wasn't
going to change the course of the world's socio-political agenda, but it
sure was covered like it would. In the end, they had to issue apologies
and express remorse and regret. It was ridiculous. There was not one
thing about that entire situation that was anything but ridiculous.

It's funny because that interview would have been no big deal,
status quo, had it been done with me on No Good TV. In fact, celebrities
have joked about much, much worse with me for years and haven't
courted the wrath of the political correctness police. In my mind, it all
comes down to context. On No Good TV, crazy, dirty, irreverent, nonsensical comments all make sense, and you're safe. Elsewhere, it can be

a minefield. In some fucked-up way, we just might be one of the only true free-speech forums out there. Which, of course, makes me proud.

Okay, back to Clooney. As soon as I walked into the room with him, I was immediately put at ease. First, he stood up to say hello. Like I said, only the good ones, the gentlemen, stand up, like Will Smith and Michael Douglas. It's fucking classy. Then, I experienced Clooney's *panty-dropping* charisma the minute he opened his mouth. He's really unassuming but definitely controls the room. He's attractive. He's personable. He's welcoming. He's like melting butter on a good piece of steak.

After chitchatting about what he had for lunch—no Indian, thank God—we got right into it.

> **Me:** So, I just need to tell you that I'm with No Good Television and our outlet is uncensored, so if you feel like going there, I heard you got a potty mouth.
>
> **George:** FUCKING A!

In an instant, with one hearty expletive, he literally turned into the coolest man I'd ever met. I had a massive *Cloner*! He was one of us, and I finally got it. Like every other earthling, I fell in love. "Oh my God! You're George Clooney!" And then I had THE Clooney orgasm. I kid, I kid. I did not. Not until later that night in the privacy of my own bedroom with a *selfie stick* I renamed Gorgeous George.

When George said, "Fucking A," everyone in the room erupted into laughter, of course, because that's what people do when George talks. He could say, "shoehorn" and have everyone rolling on the floor. But he was genuinely funny. He looked off camera, playfully shocked that he'd been outed as a curser. Then it only got better.

> **George:** Now I'm just gonna talk like it's a G-rated show. *(He looks squarely into the camera, polished and smooth.)* Well, it's so nice to be here.
>
> **Me:** Golly gee, George!
>
> **George:** Poop.
>
> **Me:** I did find it interesting that in *Leatherheads*, the first swear word we got was from, like, a ten-year-old kid. Well done!

George: Thank you, we have him smoking, drinking, and cussing, and chasing women.

Me: And bar fights, too!

George: And fighting. What's important to us is that we help the children of America.

Me: You are a good man.

George: That's right, kids, smoke at home.

Me: And make sure you use the *F–bomb* with Mom and Dad as much as you can!

George: *(Momentarily perplexed.)* F-bomb? I thought you can say it if you wanted to? *(He's antagonizing me.)*

Me: *(Playing along.)* Oh, well, you could say *fuck*. Say *fuck* to your mom and dad as much as possible! No Good TV has no rules.

George: *(He looks directly into the camera with eyes wide and an open mouth like a child on Christmas morning.)* I just like hearing her say that! *(With a BIG smile.)*

Me: Sometimes it just feels good! *(Laughing.)*

George: It's better that way, okay.

Me: So, you actually manage to sleep with Renée Zellweger on the first night [in the movie]. How did you manage to do that?

George: Yeah, you gotta get her really drunk in the train!

Me: Well, you know, when people are watching and hoping . . . *(Implying the audience wants to see him get nasty.)*

George: And bouncing you around. *(He puts his hands up and makes a cranking motion.)*

Me: Yeah!

George: You really don't have to work that hard!

Me: Normally, I get paid extra for that. *(Implying that I could sacrifice myself for art's sake.)*

George: Yeah. *(He pauses, taking in what I just said . . . then he looks up to the ceiling . . . assuming it could get gymnastic . . . and considers how to respond.)* But it'd break the ceiling, the mirror on the ceiling . . .

Me: That would be bad.

George: Very dangerous.

Me: Okay, so what is with the rules? Rules tend to just ruin everything, do they not?

George: They seem to, and yes. I think that's true. Do you agree?

Me: *(Exhilarated.)* YES!!

George: *(He looks straight into the camera and winks.)* That's right!

Me: That's why I don't have any rules.

George: I have no rules.

Me: No Good TV has NO RULES!

George: *(Inquisitively.)* You have no rules on No Good TV?

Me: None! You can do anything you want . . .

George: *Really?*

Me: Yep!

George: So, wait, where are you?

Me: *(Whispering.) Everywhere.*

George: That's what I hear. Yeah. But we're talking about the show. *(Wake the kids, phone the neighbors—did he just flirt with me? It didn't trip me up because I'm a professional.)*

Me: Ohhh! We go out everywhere. Actually, everybody can get it, especially, like, preschoolers. We're big with the preschoolers.

George: Gotta be very big and preschool . . . you know . . . *finish your cereal, and say FUCK!*

Me: It really goes over well.

George: *(Laughing.)* It does . . . I bet!

Me: You know . . . Cap'n Crunch and . . .

George: Here's the problem. *(He puts his hands up, demonstratively.)* You're the first interview I've done after lunch, right? So now you set the bar—the dirty-word bar—here. *(He holds both hands out, like the top of a bar at eye level.)* So the next guy comes in from, you know . . .

Me: CNN?

George: The Disney Channel . . .

Me: Right!!

George: He's . . . I mean . . . literally, he's fucked!! I mean there's no way around that. He's gonna be like, *"Hey, you know Mickey Mouse . . ."* and I'm gonna be like, *FUCK MICKEY MOUSE!*

Fuck.

Mickey.

Mouse.

It was a "drop the mic" moment. For years we couldn't get George Timothy Clooney, and now he gave me one of the best quotes in the history of NGTV. The best part about "Fuck Mickey Mouse!" was that it was pretty scandalous coming from a man that has been in/produced a bunch of Disney movies. Yo, Disney got served, muthafucka! And what if George wanted to run for president of the United States of America one day? I can just imagine Fox News running "Fuck Mickey Mouse!" on a loop for a week straight with an angry panel, including the Parents Television Council, Elisabeth Hasselbeck, and Megyn Kelly, saying he hates children. But, of course, none of that did or will ever happen because George was fucking around and having a fucking blast in the safe confines of the No Good TV sanitarium. Where we never hurt with hypocrisy. We only heal with humor.

And that was the beauty of it. When an A-lister like George Clooney is allowed to be totally spontaneous and uninhibited, the result is unexpected, magical, and most importantly, relatable. I've done my job. And I deserve a drink . . . or ten. My *selfie stick* is waiting.

12

THE LAP DANCE

Failure is unimportant.
It takes courage to make a fool of yourself.
—Charlie Chaplin

Dutch Scratching.

If you know what it is then you're probably making a breathy but resounding "OHHH" noise accompanied with a purposeful grimace. If you don't know what it is, let's just say it was a great motivator for me. More on that in a minute. Why do I bring it up? Well, it's really quite simple. Now, I'm no different from anyone who gives a shit about what they're doing every day with their lives. Everything I've ever done has been about reinvention and trying to be different because what the fuck else is there? My colorful repertoire was slowly but surely altering the landscape of the junket world, and it was only a matter of time before my inability to sit still would also make its presence known.

So let's get physical. No, you did not just reference Olivia Newton-John again! Oh, but I did. Have you ever fantasized about running your fingers through Jared Leto's silky hair? Rubbing your cheek on Jon Hamm's Fred Flintstone-like five o'clock shadow? (I'm pretty sure that's not what you want to rub your cheek on but I'm trying to keep it classy!) Cupping Kim Kardashian's Internet-breaking ass in your hand? Actually you'd need two hands. Or hands as big as Uma Thurman's.

Well, I'm sorry, but you can't. Touching a celeb is a big no-no. They're like rare jewels behind a fragile glass case, and if you dare get too close, there's an excellent chance you'll get tackled by four former Israeli Mossad agents and have your neck snapped in half. With all the crazy-ass stalkers out there (shout-out to my **#Keagals**), it makes sense. That's why, since I have a certain amount of access to our favorite stars, I feel a personal responsibility to touch them for you, so you can live vicariously through me. I know. I'm so selfless. You're welcome.

Nowadays, physical interaction with celebrities is such the norm on chat shows that if you tune into Fallon and see that it's just two people talking, your first instinct is to think that something's terribly wrong. Your second is to start screaming, "Oh, lord, why hast thou forsaken me?" But back in the day when I started doing interviews, nobody got out of the chair. And to be perfectly honest, at junkets today, it's still a bit of an oddity. It's as if our asses are made of iron and the chairs are super magnets. Granted, junket interview setups aren't exactly designed for a game of Twister, but I still wanted to find every way I could to change things up. And where there's a will, there's a way.

Now, before you give me an award for my philanthropy, there's a small problem with this idea. It was kind of forbidden for me to do it, too. It's not written in the junket bylaws in hieroglyphics on a cave wall in Egypt or anything; it's just very much implied. Publicists already get their panties in a bunch about smaller things, like having green M&M's or scented candles in the green room. So imagine the hysteria if their clients are manhandled without prior warning, releases being signed, Xanax being popped. You get the picture?

"My dick's in everyone's ass in this fuckin' movie!"
— *Aubrey Plaza*

Now, I grew up watching Harold Lloyd, Laurel and Hardy, Charlie Chaplin, Lucille Ball, Peter Sellers, French and Saunders, John Cleese . . . the list goes on. I live in their shadow and dream of one day having a fraction of their skill and talent. They are the *dog's bollocks*! I love physical comedy. Sometimes it's subtle, sometimes it's extensive, but it is always entertaining. I like getting in there and getting my hands dirty. It can be risky, and more often than not, you fall flat on your face, but when it works, it's a thing of beauty.

I was never going to be able to stay in that chair. It was only a matter of time. Junket after junket, I would stay seated, grit my teeth, and keep it together. But eventually, staying in that seat started to feel like what? Being *Dutch Scratched*. See, I brought it back. I knew that getting out of the seat had the potential to backfire and put everything we'd accomplished in jeopardy, but once I get a *pickle up my ass* about something, I've got to get it out of my system! Remember the scene in *Casino Royale* where Daniel Craig as James Bond is sitting naked in a bottomless chair being viciously tortured by having his balls smacked with a knotted rope? Well, welcome to the wonderful world of *Dutch Scratching*! I know it sounds extreme, but that's what it felt like to watch opportunity after opportunity pass me by during the interviews. Just like James Bond, my *interview balls* were being compromised, and I really needed to get out of that motherfucking chair!

As you've probably gathered so far, I've never been big on following rules. When I've bent them a bit, knowingly or not, that's when the best stuff happens. When I get my *back-gina* out of the chair and move around, it changes the dynamics of everything, and what you end up with is pure unadulterated comedy.

Or sheer panic. Sheer panic is what happened on one such occasion when I dared make illegal contact with rapper Nelly during the junket for *The Longest Yard*. See how I created that football metaphor there? Grammy Award–winning rappers rarely show up to these things, so it was a breath of fresh air to have him in a room. Nelly was huge at the time, after his singles "Ride Wit Me" and "Hot in Herre" blew up. It all started with a misunderstanding that tested the strength of our relationship with Paramount Pictures, who released the film. But ultimately, it served to build a lasting trust with the cool folks over there that would someday be tested again when the shoe was on the other foot.

It had been an amazing day of funny and dirty interviews with

Adam Sandler, Chris Rock, and the rest of the cast. My final interview was with Nelly, and from the moment I walked into the interview room, sparks flew. We're talking Walter White in an underground meth lab kind of chemistry. I'll say this until the day I die: Pound for pound, hip-hop artists give the best interviews. They like to have fun, fuck around, and get crazy. They're not just selling songs with their music; they're selling a lifestyle. So they intrinsically understand that attitude, charisma, and spontaneity are the necessary ingredients of creating a fucking crazy moment on camera. Take it from me, nothing travels faster or sells better. Right on cue, Nelly looked up at me and smiled like the cat that ate the canary.

Me: Just so you know, we're completely uncensored, so we get to have some fun, okay? Are you ready!?

Nelly: I am so ready!

I don't know what came over me, but I popped out of my chair, went over to him, and climbed onto his lap. His eyes opened wide with wonderment and joy, then laser-beamed onto my *umlauts*, which were now right in his face.

Me: So is this the greatest ass-kicking fiesta in football history?

Nelly: I really think this movie is the best football movie ever made.

Me: I thought it was going to be about football. It's not a football movie; this is a balls movie, right?

Nelly: You didn't like it?

Me: This is definitely a chick flick! There are more guys in wet shirts running around the football field. What guy is going to want to see this movie?

Nelly: Um, you have a point.

Me: You get out there and you're doing your thing. You look very sexy doing your thing.

Nelly: I'm trying. Thank you.

Me: This is my thing. *(I point to my cleavage, but I didn't need to because he hasn't taken his peepers off my pom-poms yet.)* What does a cheeseburger taste like when it's been in somebody's pants for a couple hours?

(I hear somebody off camera moan, "Oh my lord!" really loudly.)

Me: That's in the movie!

(I always take notes at screenings, remember . . .)

Nelly: She's absolutely right but I have no idea. Unfortunately I got some of the cheeseburgers that came off the top.

(I make an "Mmmmm" sound.)

Me: Before the headcheese!

Nelly: Before he had to hide them and divide them! You know what I'm talking about!

Me: No special sauce on those.

Nelly: No, no special sauce on mine, you know what I'm saying?

Me: Now, most movies that have these water montages, they usually have the girls during the car wash and they get all soapy. You have a bunch of guys jumping in a water puddle and rubbing all over each other.

Nelly: I'm just a running back in this film; I did not put it together. You know what I'm saying? *(He laughs, grabs my waist, and pulls me closer to him.)*

Me: We have a little tradition; we want you to promote *The Longest Yard*, NGTV style.

Nelly: Oh, okay. This is the best fucking movie you are ever going to see in your fucking life. All right? So, all you shitheads, get out of the bed, carry your fucking asses down to the theater, spend every goddamn dime you got in your pocket, and you buy all the fucking popcorn that's in the damn studio that's allowed, and I want you to sit down and enjoy this shit, because it's the best movie that you bitches can ever see. All right? Take your ass down—it's *The Longest* fucking *Yard* . . . Peace!

I spent the entire interview on Nelly's lap, and it was a touchdown with a two-point conversion. It could not have gone any better. I grabbed my tapes, said good-bye to all my friends, and left the junket with a sense of accomplishment. I had crossed the line and lived to tell the tale. But when I got back to the office, Kourosh looked like someone had just walked over his grave and was on the verge of wigging out.

"What the hell happened?" he asked me in a low voice with an overwhelming sense of dread and terror in his eyes.

Utterly confused and with my heart firmly in my stomach, I said,

"I have no idea what you're talking about. What's wrong? What happened?"

He responded with a question. "Did you give Nelly a lap dance?"

Apparently, in between me skipping out of the junket and arriving at the office, Kourosh had gotten a furious phone call from his contact at the studio who was incredibly upset. She was someone who had believed in us and who we both adored and respected, so the very last thing we wanted was to create a problem for her, in turn creating an ugly situation with Paramount. This was horrible. She'd said to Kourosh, "I'm in a state of shock. Carrie gave Nelly a sexually explicit lap dance during the interview and his manager, publicist, and her bosses at the studio are beyond themselves angry and Nelly is pissed! What was she thinking? This is very serious." She told Kourosh that we may be banned from attending any more junkets. HOLY SHIT! WHAT THE FUCK!

The whole thing made no sense. I knew Adam and was buddies with the Happy Madison people, so if something had gone wrong, they would have said something. In my defense, Kourosh had politely maintained that this didn't sound like me and seemed improbable and asked if there was any possibility that this was an error. But the studio rep stood firm. He said he'd call her back once he'd connected with me.

Back up there just a second. "A lap dance?" I said. "Are you kidding? That doesn't make any sense." I told him, "That is not what happened. During the interview the room was laughing it up, and when I left, Nelly gave me a huge hug." I continued, "There was plenty of time in between the end of my interview and when I left for someone, anyone, to approach me and lodge a complaint or a concern, but no one did." Plus, anyone who knows me knows I can't dance. I'm worse than Elaine Benes on *Seinfeld*. People assume based on how I look that I like to dance. I hate to dance. I know I'm not good at it, so I just don't, and if I did, it wouldn't be at a junket.

And I don't shake my *titties* for *anyone*. Put them in a face, why not. But shake my ass? No, sir.

"Are you sure?" Kourosh asked me.

"Yes, I'm sure!"

Next thing we did was grab the tapes and watch them. Sure enough, there was no lap dance. Just Nelly loving me sitting on his lap and having a blast doing the interview with people laughing throughout. Now we really had a mystery on our hands. What was going on? Were we being set up? Was someone out to get us? None of it made sense. So after several tense phone calls back and forth, Kourosh swore up and down the cross to our friend at Paramount that nothing had happened and that if she'd please watch the tape, she'd have the proof to clear us.

We messengered the tape over to her office. A few tense, stomach-wrenching hours later, she called us back. This time her tone was quite different. I would describe it as relief. You see, she was the one who'd vouched for us, so if we turned out to be fuck-ups, her ass was on the line. That was the worst part because no one deserves that, and we prided ourselves on doing right by our friends at the studios. Anyway, it turns out that it was all a poor choice of words and a stupid misunderstanding with a junior publicist who had just started working at the studio. She didn't know our outlet, saw me sit on Nelly's lap, and without staying to see what happened next started a wildfire of innuendo with the studio that almost burned us to the ground.

Looking to impress her boss, she described my lap *sit* as a lap *dance*, and by the time the story got back to *their* office, I'd bumped and grinded on Nelly so hard we could have shot a sequel to Ludacris's video for "Pussy Poppin'"! No one, including our rep, was physically present during the interview, so nobody had actually seen it for real. The vicious rumor had spread everywhere as fact. Fortunately, our rep made sure to play the tape for all the higher-ups and cleared us. In the end I was happy to hear that apparently my interviews with the cast were a huge hit, and Nelly loved me the most! His team had nothing but nice things to say. The whole thing was a crazy aberration. It was embarrassing for a few hours, but by the time it was done, we were tighter than ever with the studio and had proven ourselves to be a legit crew. Plus we got a sweet apology, which is always nice.

After my name was cleared, I felt emboldened and went on a bit of a *Lap-A-Palooza* that was unprecedented in the junket world. I climbed aboard Usher, Paul Giamatti, and Sacha Baron Cohen and got some of my favorite sound bites because of it. I found sitting on someone's lap to be especially helpful for the celebs who could be a little gun-shy about press in general. *Star Wars* prequel star Hayden Christensen was being his normal timid self, but when I told him, "I'm interested in coming over to the dark side" and sidled up on him, it changed the interview completely.

Then, of course, there was cinematic legend Dustin Hoffman, who is actually quite charming and funny and may not be so far off from his *randy* Bernie Focker character in real life. He's fun to tangle with and definitely enjoyed the occasional *interview mambo*. He's been doing this a long time, and I think, if anything, he loves the change of pace—especially if it's served with a side of *cheek*.

To meet Dustin Hoffman is to love Dustin Hoffman. He is astonishingly unaffected, pleasant, and captivating in spite of a body of work that would make lesser actors scream vitriolic arrogance from the hilltops. He's got funny stories to tell for days and endless opinions on a variety of subjects ranging from lactating to diarrhea. When I sat down with him for *I Heart Huckabees*, our conversation naturally turned to lactation and the plight of the modern man, about which he had this bit of wisdom to share that I'm sure will keep you up at night:

> Why do men have nipples? Because breasts, you know, in utero, are created before the gender is differentiated, and so we do have milk glands. It's not as good as women, but men have been known to lactate, usually out of sympathy. I know that you guys that are out there watching this . . . you know . . . check it out! Hang out with a pregnant woman sometime, and you'll be very surprised with a little leakage!

When you sit down to interview him, you have to be careful what your first question is because it will probably be your last. He loves to tell stories, and you'll love to listen. It could well be a tactic he uses to control the interview (which some celebrities use to stay on message), but my guess is he's just an old-school raconteur. He'll easily go off on some tangent and tell you some fascinating story that will swallow your four minutes whole like an elephant eating an apple! You really need a plan of attack when you interview him because if you don't have one, he'll kidnap you with his charm offensive and you'll walk away with a four-minute sound bite on why Warren Beatty thinks mulching leaves is better than raking them. Yes, you can always tell your editor it's an exclusive Warren Beatty story, and yes, your editor will let you know exactly where you can file it!

I learned early in the game you've got to distract Mr. Hoffman and get what you need out onto the table right away. Because he will grab that ball and run it into the end zone for a touchdown. So getting physical was always the move and trust me, he seemed to get a kick out of it, even if sometimes his people didn't. But hey, it's hard out there for a pimp! I remember on one occasion I did my thing. I asked him about a holy shit moment that really impacted his career. He responded with a long captivating story about how famous boxer Sugar Ray Leonard won some of his greatest fights with a certain degree of, shall we say, *haste* due to a constant battle with his bowels. Essentially, every time he entered the ring, he would get major butterflies in his stomach and suffered from massive cramps and the onset of potentially severe diarrhea. The fear of humiliation at the hands of Montezuma's revenge was the motivational force for Sugar Ray's ferocious performance in the ring. He needed to get in the ring, knock his opponent out, and get the fuck out of the ring before the *mudslide* hit! Pretty wild! Apparently, Sugar Ray's battle with his nerves had encouraged Dustin to use his own butterflies toward honing his craft! How much of this story was true and how much was fiction I'll never know, but talk about a holy shit moment.

Speaking of fiction, there was the time I interviewed Dustin at the *Stranger than Fiction* junket. He was feeling quite sassy that day, and I was happy to oblige. I walk in, we say hi, and I take my seat on the Hoffman *throne.* The guys in the room knew to start rolling the cameras once my ass was in place. We immediately launched into chitchatting, which, admittedly, is dangerous territory. He started commenting on my clothes, and I feared I was about to get an earful about the socio-political impact of denim on 1940s Americana, but that's not where he was going. *Operation Distract Dustin* had deployed perfectly, his dirty sense of humor kicked in, and he just started riffing on what I was wearing and how guys reacted to me and dating. And then came a couple of dirty jokes that brought the room to tears. It was awesome. He was on fire. I was a giggling fool just enjoying being in the presence of what was undoubtedly a singular moment that I was never going to forget and my audience was going to LOVE! But it was not to be. Even though Dustin seemed to be having a blast behind the scenes his publicist looked like she was about to have an aneurism! She completely lost it on me. "STOP! STOP ROLLING!" she screamed. "Go over there and be a professional."

I'm not going to lie, it was a bit jarring, but it was also a bizarrely cute moment as both Dustin and I sheepishly looked at each other as if we'd been caught passing notes in class. Adorable! It was an odd move for the publicist, too, since it was her client who had initiated the conversation and was doing 90 percent of the talking, but she wasn't going to confront him. What was most intriguing to me was that she didn't bring the interview to a halt; she just wanted to change the flow, like an NBA coach calling a time-out to kill the opposing team's momentum. So I took two steps and sat down in the chair, and we continued the interview as if nothing had happened. In my mind I was thinking, *Holy shit, I just got the interview of a lifetime with Dustin Hoffman. Just keep it together, get out of the room, grab the tapes, and leave.* Unfortunately, his publicist got the last laugh. When I got back to the office, ranting and raving about the interview, we all gathered around to watch the tape. It was wiped clean until the three-minute mark. Without telling me, they had erased the *money shot.* All evidence of this charming, funny, brilliant, and edgy stream-of-consciousness comedic routine from a legend was destroyed. Shit!

I'm sure she had her reasons, but in my mind, she overreacted, and sadly, something special was lost forever. Nobody was getting hurt, and no one was offended. It was just a sublimely funny improvisation. The worst thing in life is when people apply their vague sense of morality to others under the guise of protecting them. So, fine, I hadn't made getting out of the chair completely acceptable yet. I still had some work to do.

I've always found immeasurable joy in interviewing the elder statesmen of showbiz; as living legends with impressive bodies of work, they bring a certain honesty and boldness to a conversation that their contemporaries simply cannot. But the main reason I'm always drawn to them is because they are amazing company to keep. Charming, charismatic, and confident in their own skin, they never try too hard; is they don't have to. Instead, they exude an effortless grace that takes a lifetime to perfect and is unparalleled in its appeal and magnetism. Therefore, we always get along swimmingly. One of my favorite old dudes is Donald Sutherland, star of classics like *M*A*S*H, The Dirty Dozen,* and *Invasion of the Body Snatchers,* but you might know him best for playing evil President Coriolanus Snow in *The Hunger Games* movies and, of course, for being Kiefer's dad. Those eyebrows aren't the only thing mischievous about Donald; once, he actually sought me out in the hallway during a junket just to tell me this dirty joke he knew I'd love:

One day two sperm were swimming vigorously, and one sperm asks the other: "How much farther do we have until we reach the egg?" The other sperm replies: "I dunno, but I think we just passed the tonsils!!"

Before Robin Thicke twerked his way into the Horny Hall of Fame, his father, Alan, star of the classic eighties TV show *Growing Pains* and the newer boastfully named reality show *Unusually Thicke*, was known as quite the ladies' man. He still had serious game when I interviewed him for the movie *The Goods*.

  Me: Okay, um, how fucking good is this movie?
Alan: You know, I think it's effin' good. See, they won't let me swear on camera. I'm the straight authoritarian nurturing dad in this film, as I am in life, of course.
  Me: Wait, do I get to call you Daddy then?
Alan: You could!

  (I take this as an invitation to jump out of my chair and sit right on his lap. So I do. He isn't mad at me.)

Alan: You could sit on my knee; I'd spank you right now . . . and um . . . oh, she smells SO much better than [costar] Ed Helms.
  Me: Do you like his outfit? Very tight pants.
Alan: You know, I don't notice those things. I don't even go there. I noticed that you're almost naked.
  Me: I knew I was coming to you, so I had to do something. I was bringing the goods!

  (I switch the conversation to boners, but that has nothing to do with me sitting on Alan's keys [at least I think it was his keys]. It was a scene in the movie.)

  Me: Everyone seemed to have boner pants.
Alan: Well, I think James Brolin is the only one seen with that in the movie.
  Me: He did bring them. Yes, he did.
Alan: Well, you know, you see a boner and everyone wants one, I guess.
  Me: So it wasn't CGI then, huh?
Alan: Oh no, no, that was the real thing.
  Me: Impressive.
Alan: I can't say it's the real thing. I just met the man.
  Me: I think you should find a very large pair of *boner pants* and sport them around Hollywood, and we'll see what happens from there. We might change your image.
Alan: We'll market that!

Me: I love you. I think this may be the first and only time they actually had a scene where it was raining dildos. I've never seen that before.

Alan: It's so hard to push the envelope nowadays. And the cloudburst of sex toys was a pretty original vision.

Me: It'll be remembered like "Singing in the Rain."

Alan: Like "Dildos in the Rain," yes.

I realize that, to the untrained eye, I make this look easy. Trust me when I tell you, it's anything but. There's a fine art to *lap hunting* that requires a certain *je ne sais quoi* and a hunter's instinct. Because you most certainly cannot go from lap to lap to lap all willy nilly. Somebody could get hurt or worse. Plus, there is a fine line between being a *lap hunter* and a *lap jockey*. Professional *lap hunters*, like myself, we do it for the love of the game, our families, and world peace. *Lap Jockeys*, on the other hand, are in it for meth. They have no respect for the sport. In much the same way as professional birding does, *lap hunting* has certain seasonal opportunities, considered low-hanging fruit (unrelated to their testicle yaw), that the accomplished *lunter* can't ignore. The most prestigious of these is known as the "Claus Pause." That's when Santa himself takes a break during his busy season, goes incognito in search of Christmas spirit. Now, it just so happens that jolly old St. Nick took a "Pause" to visit the junket for *Elf,* where I spotted Santa, I mean "Ed Asner," and asked if he would do me the honor.

Now, for those of you who've never heard of Ed Asner, either because you were born after the invention of Taylor Swift or never watch TV Land, the man is a legitimate icon. He's won seven Emmys, the most for a male actor in the history of television, for *The Mary Tyler Moore Show*; *Lou Grant*; *Roots*; and *Rich Man, Poor Man*. So, for me to ask this serious, accomplished man to sit on his lap was slightly inappropriate, especially because *Elf* was a cute family movie, not even remotely dirty.

But in that moment, I was feeling naughty, not nice.

"Can I sit on your knee? Will you play Santa?"

"Sure, come on over!"

I sat on Santa's, I mean Ed's, lap for the entire interview. We had a really sweet exchange and just bonded on camera. I loved Christmas, he was Santa, I was naughty . . . he thought that was nice. It was just like a scene out of *Miracle on 34th Street* if *Miracle on 34th Street* was on Showtime After Hours! Anyway, toward the end of the interview, he slipped his arm around my waist and nuzzled his nose into my neck. Just like Santa Claus would do. Wait . . . What?

"Mmmm, you smell good," he said.

I said, "Thank you, Santa," with a smile from ear to ear.

Then he leaned in even closer and whispered into my ear, "I bet you taste good, too."

My eyes went wide and my jaw dropped! WHOA!! I almost died of laughter. I loved that he was fucking around with me like that. I love a good dirty innuendo more than anyone. Ed was awesome!

Here's my closing argument: There are real, recent scientific studies that prove that sitting will kill you. That sounds overly dramatic here, but it's a metaphor. Will I get diabetes, hypertension, or heart disease if I stay in my seat? No, but my interviews would be the equivalent of lying on my couch in a pizza-stained robe, scratching my *nads*. The greatest things in life happen when you get off your butt, reach out, and touch someone. But not in a way that would put you on a national registry.

It's not even about literally sitting on top of someone. Sometimes it's as simple as a high five. Or, at the *RocknRolla* junket, I boogied with Idris Elba, and we had an Uma Thurman/John Travolta moment. For *All About Steve*, Sandra Bullock was sweet enough to get out of *her* chair and pretend to moon the camera for me. Top that, Barbara Walters!

Hands down, one of the greatest examples of how getting off your ass can be a game changer was the junket for Queen Latifah and Jimmy Fallon's movie *Taxi*. The setup for the interviews was made to look like Jimmy and Queen were sitting in the backseat of a taxi with the interviewer (me) across from them. Well, that just didn't feel right for me. I knew I needed to be in the backseat with them. After all, who wouldn't want to share a cab with those two? So I stepped out of what was expected and into an amazing moment.

The interview hit the ground running. Out of the gate we hit the topic of the almighty *va-jeen*. I mean what else would we be talking about? And the three of us cruised into *make-out city*! It went like this:

As soon as the cameras started rolling, Jimmy decided to bust out a fresh jam on the spot entitled "Her Box" for Queen Latifah, with full acoustic percussion courtesy of their hollow seat, in rhythmic unison:

Jimmy: I put my feet on her box . . . I do my beat on her box . . . I put my sheet on her box.

Queen: He walks the street on my box.

Jimmy: I hang a wreath on your box.

Me: That's a very pretty box.

Jimmy: Yeah.

Queen: It's true.

Me: And very talented, too.

Jimmy: It's the first time she's heard it.

Queen: It's a very lovely box!

(At the first intermission of the song, I told them we were uncensored, and if they wanted to, they "could fuckin' go off!")

Queen: You stole our cusses, man.

Me: No! Do it, do it up!

Queen: 'Cause I'm gonna say fuckin' then you said fuckin' go off and I'm like, awww fuck!!

Jimmy: Yeah, she stole my shit!

Me: Fuck!

Queen: Fuck!

Jimmy: Shit!

Me: Guys! You're fuckin' awesome!!

Jimmy: AAAAHHHHHHHH!!!!!

Me: Wait, are you guys technically in the backseat of this cab?

Jimmy: Yeah . . . well, see, we wanted the illusion of that.

(I get up and get into the backseat of the cab with them and make myself comfortable as I'm prone to do! I lean back on Jimmy and put both my legs up in Queen's lap. That's how I roll.)

Queen: Sit, sit.

Jimmy: Nice. *(As he helps me get comfortable.)*

Queen: Ohhhh you got. *(My legs lift and she grabs them and places them on her lap.)*

Me: Ohhh . . . I totally wanted to be in the backseat of the cab.

Jimmy: *(Puts his arm around me.)* What's up!!

Queen: You had your feet on my box for a second!!

(Then Jimmy takes that cue and starts in on the next verse of "Her Box.")

Jimmy: You had your feet on her box.

Me: Can I touch it? I just want to touch it *[her box]*.

Queen: *(Starts clapping.)* OHHHHH.

Jimmy: I found the beat on her box.

Me: I'm touching her box!!

Jimmy: I found a sheet on her box.

(I start dancing in the backseat.)

Jimmy: She put her hand on your box.

Queen: *(Snapping her fingers.)* Uhhhhhmmmmm.

Jimmy: She want her man on her box.

(Queen starts clapping and the three of us groove to the beat with Jimmy.)

Jimmy: There's a band on your box.

Me: There's a band on her box?

Jimmy: Yeah.

(Queen lifts my leg up high and starts to play a guitar solo on it.)

Queen: Leleleleliiiing. BOX!

Me: That's so cool!

(Jimmy beat boxes and Queen continues playing guitar with my leg while I dance between them.)

Me: You guys didn't have any fun making this movie, did you?

Queen: Shit was the most boring thing I've ever done in my life! It was just horrible . . . .

(At that moment, Jimmy turns into me, grabs me by the back of the neck, and goes into a really loud, full-on fake make-out session with heavy moans for what felt like forever. All while Queen Latifah looks on. Then Queen Latifah begins a countdown . . . .)

Queen: Countdown . . . in . . . five . . . four . . . three . . . two . . . one . . . Interview.

(Then Jimmy and I release each other and return to the interview all disheveled.)

Me: Hey . . . Wow . . . Yeah . . . Uh-huh!

Queen: I guess my box is out of this?

Me: No . . . I'll make out with you, too.

(I reach over and embrace Queen and start kissing her neck while Jimmy looks on and laughs.)

Queen: Oh God! Yeah, that's my spot. All right. Get off me, woman! Now give me back that boot!

We ended up pretend making out at the *Fever Pitch* junket as well. After that, anytime I would interview Jimmy, it was "our thing" to pretend to make out.

Denzel Washington, as I've mentioned before, is one seriously cool customer. But at the *Man on Fire* junket, he was just that . . . on fucking fire and ready to play! So right from the get-go, we both made an unspoken promise to each other to burn that mutha down! I poured the gasoline, he lit the match, and a team of studio reps, publicists, and innocent bystanders gleefully watched that mother-fucker burn!

Me: We are uncensored. That just means you can be a little feisty if you're feeling it.

Denzel: Okay, okay, then take your clothes off. Do the whole thing na-ked! You better start asking questions. You're getting yourself in trouble, or me!

I have to admit, he caught me totally off-guard. I did not see that coming, and I'm pretty sure that I was just standing there looking at him with a silly grin two sizes too big for my face. But I wasn't smiling out of nervousness; I was smiling because I realized I could go with plan B! Plan A was good, but plan B was just plain stoopid!!!

Me: I want to know what a concubine is and how do I become yours? *(It was from a blink-and-you-missed-it moment in the film . . . but I was about to make it the only thing he'll ever remember from it!)*

Denzel: Dial 1-800-LAWYER. Do you feel like giving away half? Dial 1-800-LAWYER, when you meet young women like this. THINK HALF. You're married. Half. *(He pretends to cut off his own hand.)* Because that's what it's gonna be. 1-800-LAWYER, you're broke! You're busted! You're finished.

Me: You're awesome!

Denzel: You know, you're bad. What should we do about that? *(He points at me like a schoolteacher.)* What should we do about that? I think you need to be spanked.

Me: Ohhh! *(With a devilish grin.)*

Denzel: I didn't say by me! Because 1-800-LAWYER.

At this point, the interview was blockbuster, but it got even better. Want to know why? Because I got out of my fucking chair. There was a scene in the movie where Denzel's character teaches a very young Dakota Fanning how to burp, so how could I not ask for a live demonstration? Thinking he would recite the alphabet in one long bass note like most guys, he regressed into something way more childish.

Denzel: Well, if you'll help me . . . you gotta, like, burp me or something.
(I pop up from my seat and walk over to Denzel, who is now sucking his thumb and crying like a baby.)

Denzel: Waah! Waah!

Me: Put your head on my shoulder, honey, okay, okay. *(I pat him a few times, but he is laughing so hard he starts coughing and wheezing.)*

Denzel: I can't do that. I used to really know how to do it. Like, uh, make a belch. Can you do it?

Me: Yes.

Denzel: Go ahead.

Me: *(I rip one from deep in my diaphragm like a boss. I could tell he was impressed and feeling a little competitive.)*

As they started to wrap me up in the room, I decided to ask him for an ID. A-listers seldom did these "mini commercials" unless they really dug the outlet, but now that we had figured out how to split the assets, I just had to know: *Is this was a momentary lapse of reason . . . or true like?*

Me: Would you mind doing an ID for me? Do you do those?

Denzel: Only if you come over here and do it with me.
(I stand behind Denzel, lean on his shoulder, and put my hand up his back like a puppet. As I talk, he moves his mouth silently like a ventriloquist's dummy.)

Me: This is Denzel Washington and you know he's watching NGTV, 'cause that's just No damn Good Television!

Denzel then sealed the deal by buttoning up the ID with a bit of artistic flourish in the form of an expertly cultivated burp from his own private stock. A fitting end to one of my favorite interviews of all time—publicists still rave about our vaudeville act to this day. And I managed not to get dog-piled, tazed, or dragged away by security.

Studios started to really take to this new brand of interview, especially when it fit with the marketing strategy of the film. So much so that they started requesting us to integrate episodes of my other popular series, *In Bed with*, which was taking the whole getting physical to an entirely new level. Let's be clear, I wasn't getting all nasty and grinding the talent. It was still an upstanding interview show, just lying down. But when you're in bed wearing silk pajamas and a plush robe, lying on satin pillows and sheets, surrounded by a pink fur backboard and lit candles while holding the cheapest champagne a four-star hotel can provide, it naturally lends itself to more intimately funny encounters.

Without a doubt, one of the most memorable episodes we made was when we were invited to shoot an *In Bed With* with the cast of the hard-R-rated comedy *Sex Drive*. It was a filthy, filthy movie and perfect for our audience. When we shot these episodes, we were always mindful of the studio folks and publicists because we knew this show was firmly in the gray area and one misinterpreted action could have disastrous consequences. There was always a bit of walking on pins and needles, but that was par for the course. Anyway, we had finished setting up in the suite at the hotel for the shoot, and moments before they were going to bring in the talent, I was summoned by the head of marketing for the studio. Not a junior publicist but the big cheese. It's very unusual to have a senior exec request a chat right before taping, so I assumed they had changed their minds, or something was very wrong. So me and my pink pajamas, ready for disappointment, scurried over to the exec's private room for a quick "How's your father?"

It was there that I was presented with the very last thing I ever expected to hear from a movie studio exec (and I thought I was ahead of the curve). Much to my relief, it turned out that she was a huge fan of our site and format and was the one who'd specifically requested the *In Bed With* setup. So far, so good. Then came the jaw-dropping request that had brought us together:

"I would really appreciate it if you would go further than you normally would in your interviews today," she said.

All I could think of was . . . *huh?* I'm sure my head tilted like a dog's, too. That was a first. I have to admit, I was a bit wary.

She went on, "I really want you to push the boundaries with these guys. I want you to take them to the edge and be as filthy as possible. Just got for it!"

"Absolutely!" I replied. "Whatever you want; as long as you don't call security, I'm down to play."

Not to look a gift horse in the mouth, but I had to ask what this was all about. Apparently, these guys had made this super-dirty film and were boasting about how they had pushed the boundaries of all the execs. This was a little payback. She wanted to have a bit of fun at their expense now, to show them how it's really done, and I was their weapon of choice. As I walked away to fulfill my mission, she repeated:

"Just make this the dirtiest *In Bed With* you've ever done, okay? I want to see how far you can go."

"Done and done!" I confirmed. She didn't need to threaten me with a good time.

"I want you to take them to their breaking point," she ended gleefully.

The interview was indeed one of raunchiest I've ever done, centered on "big black cocks" and oral sex.

First up to join me in bed were costars Seth Green (*Buffy the Vampire Slayer, Family Guy, Robot Chicken*) and Clark Duke (*The Office, Hot Tub Time Machine, Kick-Ass*). Holding a flute of champagne, they each slid into either side of the bed, with me snugly in the middle. We proceeded to talk about group sex, sex toys, motor-boating, being the fluffer on *The Tonight Show,* as well as Seth spreading his seed everywhere he goes, but just before it was over . . . we took it to another level with the *sticky dragon*:

    Me: We need to discuss this film on the boner scale.

  Seth: How?

    Me: How would you rate this?

Clark: This movie gives boners, boners.

    Me: Whoa!

  Seth: It's true.

    Me: Is that probably the highest rating you can give it?

Clark: *(Demonstrates with his hands how a boner gets a boner.)* I'm sorta a Steve McQueen type, you know. The rules just don't apply.

    Me: *(To Seth:)* Doesn't that make him sexier?

  Seth: There are none more sexy than Clark Duke unless you're talking about James Marsden.

    Me: Ummm.

Clark: That's true.

Seth: As far as men go, 'cause with women, you're right at the peak.
Clark: Yeah.
Me: Oooh. Oh God, you just want to fuckin' punch him . . .
Seth: Oh . . . I just wanted to fuck him.
Me: In the greatest way possible.
Clark: I'll just say I want to punch and fuck him.
Me: At the same time?
Clark: Yeah.
(We all laugh.)
Seth: No, no, he's got a very specific sequence where he likes the fucking and then the punching, like right upon the orgasm.
Me: When does the donut come in?
Seth: Me and Clark both with a stack of half a dozen if that's what you mean.
Clark: Thanks, buddy!
Seth: Anytime, buddy! I got your back, man.
Me: *(To camera:)* You guys need to go. Thanks for coming. I hope we didn't keep you up. Motherfuckers, it's *Sex Drive*! And I gotta go. Go away!
(Laughter.)
Clark: Please go see *Sex Drive*.
Seth: *(Gets up from his position and goes to the bottom of the bed and grabs my ankles.)* We really oughta spend a few more minutes going to see *Sex Drive*. *(He lifts my left leg up and pulls me down into position then simulates going down on me.)* Excuse me, guys!

It broke my rule because my legs were up in the air, but it was the craziest end to an interview ever! But I have to admit, I was mortified when the whole thing was *going down*, and not for the reason you're guessing right now. My mind was spinning, thinking:

A. *This is amazing!* Not because he was so good at it (he was faking it and faking it good) but because it was on camera.

B. *Oh fuck. This is on camera!*

C. *I'm sweating my ass off and I'm wearing satin, on satin sheets, under hot lights. Please, please, please don't have any sweat stains or other embarrassing wet spots anywhere!* I was petrified that when he got down there he was going to find something to rival Fergie's infamous pee stain from when she wet herself while performing.

Fortunately, I was in fighting form. That bit of *fake oral* did, however, end up being a wonderful icebreaker every time I would run into Seth and his then-girlfriend and future wife, Clare Grant. Fortunately, I knew Clare before she met Seth because she was a veteran of the NGTV parties, so it was always a big laugh. They are great couple and she's one cool chick, and I'm not just saying that because her husband once went down on me on camera. I swear!

We had quite the crowd watching on the monitors in the other rooms, and it was time to take it even further, so the fun continued with costars Amanda Crew, who was a frequent guest at No Good TV and super fun. (She recently appeared in the film *Age of Adaline* and currently stars in the HBO series *Silicon Valley*.) and NGTV virgin Josh Zuckerman. Josh has gone on to star in *Desperate Housewives* and the reboot of *90210*. Again, it all started with me in the middle of the bed on my knees screaming "AMANDA" with my arms out. Amanda comes running in and throws herself into my arms, and we fly backward into the bed and start making out as I grab her ass. Oh yeah! I know her! We covered a lot of ground that day. It started with Amanda and I feeling each other's *chimichongas* before diving into a little *oral sex etiquette*, but soon thereafter, we settled on a subject we both held very dear: dicks and the age-old discussion of whether two men making sweet, sweet love to a woman in the same orifice is gay or not:

Amanda: I do love penises.

    Me: Who doesn't? Cheers to that. Let's just toast that moment right there.

Amanda: We love the cock!

    Me: We love the cock!

Amanda: Love the cock!

    Me: Love the Cock. Josh, do you love the cock?

    Josh: I'm putting down my champagne!
        (Laughter.)

Amanda: Okay. But let me talk about this penis.

    Me: Yes. Yes.

Amanda: We shot, for the DVD extra features, some naked people in front of a green screen, and so we ended up having this barbecue the night before at John's house—one of the writers. And he's like, you can see some of the models that we chose.

You can go on, anyone can go on this Web site. You don't
have to pay for this site. You can see naked people. You can
see naked girls. And it says what they'll do, like, you know,
um, "cream pie," which is like when a lot of guys . . .

Josh: Oh my God.

Amanda: . . . finish inside of them!

Josh: You gotta be kidding me.

Amanda: Or there's another term for it, but it's like when they take two
penises in at the same time, which we were debating like . . .
is that gay? YES. Their penises are touching each other's.

Me: Not gay. I'm gonna say not gay. Not gay? *(To Josh.)*

Josh: Wait, I'm confused about the whole procedure.

Me: Double penetration. Not gay.

Amanda: It is gay!!

Josh: Wait. Double pene . . . *(Looking confused.)*

Amanda: Your cock is touching another guy's cock. How is that not gay?

Me: You touch one dick. Does not make you gay!

Josh: Well, see . . . if two dicks are touching . . .

Amanda: I disagree.

Me: Two dicks on top of yours might be gay. One dick, not gay!

Amanda: I don't know.

Me: 'Cause you're still fucking a girl.

Josh: *(To me:)* I agree with you.

Amanda: But I think it's almost impossible to get two penises in the
vagina. Not impossible but almost impossible for it to, at
least, feel good. Anyways, back to this LA Direct Models.

Me: You're still young.

Amanda: I know. Right?

Josh: Oh my.

Me: There's time.

Before we were done that day, we had an in-depth discussion on
big black cocks, hooked cocks, banana cocks, as well as *glory holes.* Needless
to say, the studio exec, reps, and publicists got their money's worth.
Everybody laughed their asses off, we shot some funny fuckin' interviews,
and no one got hurt. I would say that was mission accomplished!

There was a time when the stars were practically surrounded by an
invisible fence, and if you crossed the line, you'd get zapped and scolded

like a dog. "Bad, Carrie, no!" But over time, everyone got used to me breaking on through to the other side. True, we had a few bumps and bruises along the way, but hey, who else was going to risk life and limb to push the somatic boundaries of entertainment journalism? To quote an old Vulcan proverb as stated by Captain Spock in *Star Trek VI: The Undiscovered Country,* "Only Nixon could go to China."

Which brings me full circle to the time I interviewed the wild-boyz from *Jackass 3D* at a Paramount Pictures junket. Of course, we were still working with our friend from the Nelly fiasco, but we had come a long way, and there were really no surprises on the horizon. At least that's what everyone told themselves. It doesn't take a genius to figure out that there is no better match made in the movie-verse than *Jackass* and No Good TV. It was inevitable that our two brands would intersect, but I don't think anyone connected all the dots correctly, and what proceeded to happen has gone down in the annals of junket-lore.

It was a filthy, funny, fucked-up movie. I laughed myself into a fit and was on the verge of peeing in my pants at the screening. If you like shit being thrown through the air and people drinking each other's sweat, then *Jackass* is your *Godfather.* On the day of the cast interviews, the more I thought about it, the more it didn't make sense to me to just sit there like a turd in the pool asking questions. They're stuntmen. I'm certifiable. So we had to get physical, but what do you do to outdo a bunch of guys who'll *shart* on each other's necks for a beer? So I wasn't going to be able to outdo them; I just needed to surprise them. That I could do. As I waited in the hospitality suite, I noticed that to promote the movie they were giving away stickers in the shape of cocks. Then it hit me like a dildo to the forehead. I came up with a fun and interactive game to play with them called Pin the Johnson on the Jackass. Word to the wise, *dick games* are like *dick jokes;* they never get old, and they always work. If the *dick joke* is the North Star of comedy, think of my dick game as the Big Dipper I was going to use to find it.

First it was time to warm them up with a little *dick talk:*

Me: Okay. So I'm figuring out that the 3-D stands for the flying dick, the swinging dick, and the pissing dick? Is that what the 3-D stands for?

Ryan Dunn: Yep, you got it.

Ehren McGhehey: That's what you wanted.

Johnny Knoxville: Thank you for the definition.

Me: Now you know.

Bam Margera: You summed it up pretty well.

Me: It's all dick all the time in this film.

Ryan: You are welcome.

Johnny: Thank you. Thank you.

Me: And thank YOU. Well done.

Jeff Tremaine: Really, there's a lot of sexiness.

Preston Lacy: Not to mention the gay overtones.

Johnny: Got my tooth knocked out by the dildo bazooka.

Me: You did not!

Johnny: Yeah.

Me: For real? You took a dick in the face.

Johnny: Yeah. Well . . . in the movie, too.

Jeff: A lot of people think *Jackass* is just for the boys, and it's not.

Me: There were more dicks in this movie than I think, like, any other film ever. Even more than a porno!

Johnny: I know.

Bam: And if it wasn't a real dick then it was a fake dick.

Me: It made me happy on the inside.

Everyone: OHHHHHH!

Me: Chris . . . always has to put in his . . . two dicks . . . or whatever . . . in somewhere.

Bam: He had some bragging points though; why not show it?

Jeff: He had a woodpecker attack. He had a rat trap. Loving kitty cat.

Chris Pontius: No, that backfired!

Me: He could probably do the *infamous booyah* on himself. Get the balls and the dick all in the same hole.

Johnny: Put his nuts in his butt?

Me: Yeah.

Bam: You'd have to have, like, a soft-on.

Johnny: Yeah.

Me: True.

Me: Maybe the next one, *4-D* or whatever you're going to be doing, I think it should probably be all dick all the time!

The plan was working. The interviews were going great. Everybody was eating it up. Talking about *dicks* and pinning *dicks* on various body parts was as much fun as watching a dog get surprised by his own farts over and over. And you know how crazy they can get! Anyway, my last room had a bunch of the *Jackass* crew grouped together, so I had a feeling the Molotov cocktail was just waiting for me to light the wick. I walked in, sat down, and proceeded to break the ice with a little dirty banter, and then I went in for the kill. I brought up the game, and we all started to play. Then, without skipping a beat, Chris Pontius, famous for dancing around in a G-string, stood up, unzipped his pants, reached in, and whipped out his *single-barrel pump-action yogurt rifle*. (You could hear the gasps in the room.)

For the uninitiated, let's just say he's packing a *meter-long King Kong dong*, and that's when it's flaccid. (I'm guessing he's more of a *shower* than a *grower.*) He then started to put on a show by doing the helicopter, or should I say the *heli-cock-ter,* with his *meat tassel*. I could tell that this whole thing was his attempt to take control and shock me into some silly *giggle-fit* or fearful scream. But this was my interview and my game. Truth be told, I was tickled pink. I can only imagine that the smile on my face must have resembled that of a hungry hobo staring down a *Pink's nine-inch stretch chili dog*. So, much to his shock, once his *steamin' semen truck* slowed down into a stationary position, I proceeded to pin a *johnson* sticker on his *deep-V diver*. They took the dick out, and I took the *dick back*!! A hot hand, cool delivery, and more game than they knew what to do with!! To the winner go the spoils! BOOYAH! MUTHA-FUCKAAAAAAAAH!!!!

When I walked out of the room, I was fucking thrilled. I could tell the room was in a state of shock because what had just happened had never happened before, and I don't mean that in a good way. I suddenly got rushed by all the junket employees and studio people in a state of panic. I couldn't adequately describe the fear and genuine concern on all their faces, especially our rep's. But they weren't there to yell at me . . . this time, they were comforting me. That's how much the tables had turned.

"Are you okay!?" they asked gingerly, arms around me like I'd just been rescued from a well. I could have been angry, I suppose, from their perspective, I could have sued Paramount Pictures for truckloads of money, retired to a Caribbean island, and opened my bar, because it was harassment on every level. I mean, let's face it: This is a major studio holding a proper press event. It's one thing for the press to step out of line and be admonished, but how often does the talent engage the press in a sexually explicit way with the cameras rolling? I assure you in the movie marketing handbook, there is plenty on what to do when an actor launches his *heat-seeking moisture missile* on set, but nothing on what to do when he starts *laying pipe* for the press. This was clearly not a good look.

"Yes, why?" I answered, genuinely puzzled. "That was the greatest thing ever!" I was living in my *No Good* bubble, and it didn't even occur to me while it was happening that it was controversial, or possibly legally actionable. Hey, if you put a *baloney pony* in front of me, I don't run screaming. I put a sticker on it! And just like a few years back, when we proved our mettle to the studio by how we handled Nelly, on this day, with the shoe firmly on the other foot, we did it again with how we handled this, further reinforcing our relationship with them. Nothing wrong had happened back with Nelly years before, and nothing wrong had happened today. It was all part of our *No Good* world.

Recorded in the annals of *No Good History* as the *Pontius schwing*, this *piss-weasel* incident was definitely a first—and, as far as I know, a last—in the junket world. I guess there are some lines that shouldn't be crossed. Then again, rules are made to be broken. Without the rebels and pioneers, we wouldn't have thrown tea into Boston Harbor. We wouldn't wear white after Labor Day. And, without *Dutch Scratching*, I wouldn't have felt the joy of unwrapping *Santa's package*.

Is that the kind of world we want to live in? I think not.

13

AMERICA vs. THE FOREIGN CUNT

**There are no bad words.
Bad thoughts. Bad intentions, and wooooords.**
—George Carlin

Before you ask . . . No, this is not an analysis of Donald Trump's book on foreign policy. And, yes, unfortunately, it bears the same title.

Now, I love a good "fuck" as much as the next girl, and lord knows, I've given as good as I've gotten, but if you've studied your Roman lyric poetry like I have, then you know that amongst the *profanum vulgus*, "fuck" is a child's word, and if I was to become an adult, I was going to need to conquer the "cunt." What I could not have anticipated was the epic journey that lay ahead of me, rife with historical triviality and cultural hypocrisy. A decade-long quest that would begin with me, dead center, in the eye of a hurricane of establishment horseshit. Then, have me crawl my way through a septic tank of contradictions and misconceptions, most of which were opinions held firmly as fact by a group of Darwin Award nominees. And finally, see me rise above the fray, triumphant, only to sit upon what can best be described as a *porcelain throne*. But I had a date with destiny. After all, was it not Corinthians 13:11 that taught us, "When I was a child, I spoke as a child, I felt as a child, I thought as a child. Now that I have become a woman I must set aside childish things"? My path was set; I was loaded for bear, and the *"Great Cunt Hunt"* was upon me.

Of all the curse words ever created, *cunt* is, without a doubt, the most controversial. Feminist scholar Germaine Greer said it best when she described it as "one of the few remaining words in the English language with a genuine power to shock." And it's hard to argue with that. Here in the United States, it's the ultimate verbal kill switch. Imagine you're throwing the party of the century at a spectacular mansion in the Hills and it's attended by every A-lister, sports superstar, and supermodel there is. In one corner Jay Z, Kanye, and Queen Bey are trying out some new material on the crowd, in another corner the Victoria's Secret Angels are playing Twister, and in the pool George Clooney, Matt Damon, Brad Pitt, and Ben Affleck are about to get a game of volleyball going. It's around midnight, the joint is packed, and it is slammin'! Then, the front doors swing open, and in struts O. J. Simpson, Gary Glitter, Phil Spector, and Bill Cosby. They are lookin' fly and ready to get turnt up! So how fast do you think your party shuts down and clears out? You guessed it: faster than Jared Fogle when he finds out the hooker's of legal age! That, my friends, is called the *"cunt effect."*

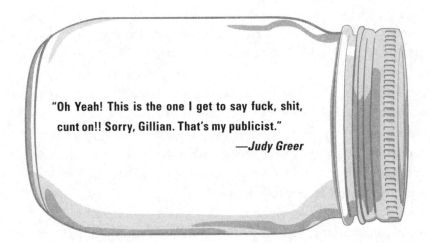

"Oh Yeah! This is the one I get to say fuck, shit, cunt on!! Sorry, Gillian. That's my publicist."
—*Judy Greer*

Now, in spite of all that, "cunt" still happens to be one of my all-time favorite curse words. I still remember how fierce it sounded the first time I heard it used by a woman. The guy I was dating in college brought me home to meet his mother, whose name was Connie. Wanting to make small talk, I told her my mom was also named Connie and asked if her name was short for Constance, to which she replied, "No. It's short for Cunt-Chetta!" That's all I needed to hear. Sign me up for the *cunt show.*

Fact is, if you follow me on Twitter then you know that it was I who originated its use as a collective noun when I tweeted: "As go a 'Murder of Crows,' so go a 'Cunt of Hipsters.'" (You're Welcome.)

It truly is the perfect word. In one syllable it accomplishes as much, emotionally and viscerally, as most of our greatest poetry and prose. It is uniquely feminine yet unabashedly formidable. It represents all that is wrong and all that is right with human interaction and communication. It is a word that means many things to many people, encompassing every emotion from love to hate. Therefore, it has been the subject of a deep philosophical divide between the U.S. and the rest of the world. Which has, in turn, made it the single best example of why the persecution of words over intent is a ridiculous waste of time. On a more personal note, it stands as the root cause of the most complicated and rewarding struggle in my career. As well as being the mightiest weapon in my arsenal to combat what I like to call "lingual bigotry."

While adjectives like "notorious," "lethal," and "powerful" have typically been used to describe it, there are strong arguments to be made that it might, quite possibly, be one of the most influential, impactful, and incredibly important words in history. Now, I wouldn't blame you for having a hard time believing that "cunt" is anything other than disposable and vulgar. Plus, you're still hurt that your mom called you one after she found out she'd spent forty-seven-thousand dollars a year for you to attend Skidmore College only to discover you were majoring in "the Sociology of Miley Cyrus." In all honesty, it wasn't your finest moment, and in her defense, she was just making an observation. But would you believe me if I told you that the very freedom of speech that you and I now take for granted in literature has the word "cunt" to thank? It certainly does.

> "You can forgive a young cunt anything. A young cunt doesn't
> have to have brains. They're better without brains. But an old
> cunt, even if she's brilliant, even if she's the most charming
> woman in the world, nothing makes any difference . . ."

With these audacious and scintillating expressions and many more, in 1934, a forty-three-year-old American writer took Paris and the rest of the literary world by storm with the release of a novel he originally intended to title *Crazy Cock*. However, Henry Miller's extraordinarily graphic and sexually explicit book better known as *Tropic of Cancer* erupted with the force of a supervolcano across the U.S. literary community. It was promptly banned for breaking obscenity laws and remained so for the next thirty years. It wasn't until a reprinting in 1961 that led to sixty obscenity lawsuits across twenty-one states, all leading up to a Supreme Court decision in 1964, that the book was finally declared not obscene. When all was said and done, it was Mr. Miller's multitude of "cunts" that influenced the very literary reform and freedom of speech we Americans hold so dear and declare with pride to the rest of the world. So forgive your mom, and be sure to let your inner "cunt" out. We've earned it.

In spite of its historical significance, the word "cunt" is greatly misunderstood. Without question, the issue of vulgarity has always been at the very core of the cunt debate that has existed for hundreds of years. But what most people don't realize is that it hasn't always had a vulgar connotation, and even today, outside of the U.S., it's commonly used in very familial and friendly ways. In England it's basically a synonym to the word "asshole," and in Australia it has almost replaced the word "mate," proving that vulgarity is truly in the eye of the beholder and not an objective determination. This has undoubtedly added to the endless confusion over why Americans still struggle with its very utterance and why it's perceived so negatively.

The answer may lie in the fact that the word "cunt" stems from feminine symbolism in a male-dominated culture that has spanned thousands of years. Germaine Greer made this very interesting argument: "For hundreds of years, men identified female sexual energy as a dangerous force. And unlike other words for female genitals, this one sounds powerful. It demands to be taken seriously." Sounds to me like cunt might be a secret mystical weapon for women that we should be paying closer attention to instead of being offended by. I mean, who is it that's been telling us that we should be offended all this time?

Let's face it, much of the information available on the origins and first use of the word "cunt" tend to follow the path of *The Oxford English Dictionary*, which traces its use to describe the vulva to AD 1230. In fact, the word was part of a street name in London called Gropecuntlane, which was the name of any street equivalent to a red-light district. Not to be confused with Shavecuntewelle in Kent or Cuntewellewang in Lincolnshire. Not going to lie to you, part of me wishes that I was born on that street just so I could have said it when I was growing up and not gotten into trouble.

To see the look on my friends' moms' faces when I said, "You can drop me off at 69 Gropecunt Lane, please," would have been amazing.

Clearly, this path leads us down the road to a vulgar word for the vagina, which is what most people regard as its source. It's a negative definition that's been fortified in people's minds for hundreds of years through literature, art, and speech. But in stark contrast, if you read Inga Muscio's book *Cunt: A Declaration of Independence*, she traces cunt back much, much further in time and states that it originally stemmed from words that were either titles of respect for women, priestesses, and witches, or derivative of the names of goddesses. So it seems entirely reasonable to reach the conclusion that all that's negative about the word is very much a male construct. In fact, in Germaine Greer's feminist manifesto, "Vaginal Revolution," where she's asking women to reclaim the word "cunt," she states, "the only other terms (women) may deploy have been deformed by centuries of sadistic male use. 'You cunt, gash, slit, crack, slot . . .' Women have no names of their own for what is most surely their own."

I realize that this may be more information about cunt than you ever wanted to know, but it's important to understand that it's just an incredibly versatile word that's been infinitely manipulated. And it appears that every thousand years or so, this particular word becomes the domain of a different sex. So whether you subscribe to Francis Grose's *A Classical Dictionary of the Vulgar Tongue*, which defines cunt as "a nasty name for a nasty thing," or you heed Inga Muscio's call to every woman to be the "Cuntlovin' Ruler of Her Sexual Universe," at the end of the day it's just a word with many definitions that we each can take ownership of and enjoy. I'm talking to you, ladies, and you, America. It's time to make peace with the "foreign cunt!"

From the controversial wonderment of its discovery in 1492 to the horror and exaltation of its quest and subsequent Declaration of Independence in 1776. Through the brutality of its sacrosanct Civil War from 1861 to 1865 and the abolition of its greatest shame, slavery, with the Thirteenth Amendment in 1864. From its meteoric rise as an industrial world power to its hard-earned victory for women's suffrage in 1920. Through its perseverance during the bloody devastation of two world wars and the moral bankruptcy of its darkest days during the McCarthy era. From the decimation of hope that was the Kennedy assassination to its crisis of conscience during the Vietnam War. Through the national betrayal

that was the Nixon presidency and the jubilant resurgence of peace sig-
naled by the end of the Cold War. From the endless crises in the Middle
East to the unforgivable terror at home on 9/11. The people of this great
nation of ours, the United States of America, have survived, overcome,
conquered, overpowered, defeated, overwhelmed, made peace with, or
risen above incomprehensible struggles against impossible odds. Yet,
despite our inexorable ability to heal wounds so deep it boggles the
imagination and our interminable dedication to freedom, growth, and
progress, to this day we are still trying to come to terms with the word
"cunt." Who hurt you, America? Who hurt you?

America's relationship with the word "cunt" seems deeply rooted
in fear and hatred almost bordering on some sort of psychosis. Clearly
resulting from a traumatic incident from when it was younger. It truly is
one of those great mysteries. It's right up there with why is it perfectly
legal in the U.S. for underage kids to smoke cigarettes but it's illegal for
them to purchase them, or what it would be like to live in a world without hypothetical questions. Real heady stuff. If I had to guess what was
at the core of America's intense hatred toward the "foreign cunt," I would
say that it probably involved an open road, two motor vehicles, and a
disagreement over dick size.

Now, I may have gotten a few of the details wrong, but I think you
can understand the gist of how a standoff can start for no good reason
and continue indefinitely for no better one. This is why America's war
against the "foreign cunt" always reminded me of the "War of the
Golden Stool." Which was a pointless conflict that took place in 1900
between the Ashanti Empire in Africa and Great Britain. It was so triv-
ial that the symbolism in the name of the war is more profound than
the war itself. Let's face it: All wars should have a metaphor for feces in
the title because they're always caused by some stupid shit anyway.
After all, why is it that a word that is pretty much regarded as harmless
and friendly all over the world is still seen as a threat in a cultural war
that is entering its 523rd year?

I believe that people tend to get too hung up on words instead of
only being concerned with the intent behind them. This ideal has been
a central theme throughout my entire career because I love freedom of
speech, I love cursing, and I hate being told what is allowed in polite
society and what isn't. Fuck that! Furthermore, cursing, in and of itself,
is not racist, sexist, classist, or any other "ist." It belongs to all of us. Plus,

it's really fucking fun. I have dedicated my professional life to this great cause. And it has been my great pleasure to specialize in the defense and rehabilitation of curse words that have been wrongly persecuted.

So when the "foreign cunt" was first referred to me as a potential client, like most people I was hesitant. I thought, *What would people think of me representing a cunt? How would my association with this cunt affect my business and reputation?* So I decided to get to know the "foreign cunt" and to try to understand why it was that America thought it was such an unacceptable cunt. Eventually, after a great deal of soul-searching, I came to the conclusion that there was goodness and decency in this cunt's heritage. And that centuries of poor treatment at the hands of Americans had left this cunt without a sense of purpose or identity, forced to fend for itself in the harsh and unforgiving surroundings of pulp fiction, stag films, and pseudo-feminist manifestos. Gone was the joy and the laughter that all cunts were entitled to in the old country. It was then that I decided that it was my duty to bring back this cunt's *vertical smile* for present and future generations. What started out as a simple quest for justice soon turned into a crusade for the "foreign cunt."

Without a doubt, the word "cunt" has had quite a mainstream resurgence these days. And with each passing year, people have become more and more comfortable with it. Plus, various commercial industries have adopted it into their nomenclature, where its global applications have proven to be indispensable. Case in point, it's hard to imagine how land surveyors and NASA scientists would describe a small distance without the *exacting precision* of "cunt hair." And it's highly doubtful that doctors could correctly diagnose patients suffering from a life-threatening squinting affliction without the *essential accuracy* of "cunt-eyed." It's unimaginable where modern seafaring would be today without the *critical* rope splice able seamen use to join two lines in the rigging of ships known as the "cunt-splice." And it's unthinkable just how *vulnerable* our armed forces would be without the invaginated flat soft-cover crash helmet with the technical designation "cunt cap." And the list goes on. But in spite of its ubiquitous presence in trade and commerce, a majority of people still consider it to be the most scandalous word you can use in casual conversation.

So, as you can imagine, if we go back ten years or so to when it all started, its shock value exponentially increases in the opposite direction. In the mystical realm of the celebrity interview, cunt is a rare and powerful creature whose appearance has always been regarded as more mythical than actual, much like the unicorn. So there I was, doing what I do, cussing it up with the celebrities and slowly but surely nudging the door open wider and wider. The *big C* had started to show up here and there in interviews, which was exciting, but for the most part in a context that hadn't been making waves and definitely not at a big studio. At least, not yet.

But that all changed when I came face-to-face with its awesome power when I was asked to cover a major studio movie starring well-known teen starlet Mandy Moore. Strangely enough, it wasn't anything she did or anything I did that set the wheels in motion on a ten-year crusade that redefined the acceptance of the word "cunt" in an interview. The first domino to fall on the road to jubilation was my interview with a then-unknown actor named Matthew Goode. That's where I discovered that in a celebrity interview, the mere mention of "cunt" had the same effect as an electromagnetic pulse (EMP). It shuts everything down for miles!

Mandy Moore was apparently so over being wholesome, and in need of a little more edge in her image, that she agreed to sit down with me to promote the Warner Bros. rom-com *Chasing Liberty*. Warner Bros. was one of the first major studios to take NGTV seriously and invite us to their junkets. It was a rare opportunity, and we did not want to fuck it up in any way. But finding the right balance between our format and their comfort zone was a bit of a process. Fortunately, they've always been incredibly cool and progressive-minded, which they continue to be to this day. I've always been very grateful for all our friends there who've stood by us. But in the early days, we gave them a scare, and in return, they gave us a heart attack.

When the invite first arrived, I thought to myself, *How cool!* It felt great to be seen as a journalist who could increase your cool factor. Besides, "fuck"ing in my interviews was becoming so ubiquitous, even the most virginal stars were ripping off their chastity belts and dropping F-bombs. Now, Mandy wasn't the type to smoke salvia or make a sex tape, so this was her big moment to rebel. But she was still hesitant. So we started easy and drifted into slightly deeper waters as she got more comfortable. When I asked her about a brief butt shot in the movie, she was quick to tell me she had a body double.

"I'm a modest girl," she explained. "And it was so funny the other day, some girl was like, 'So I thought I saw part of your boob in the movie.' I was like, 'I don't think so.' And she's like, 'No, I did.' And I'm like, 'Okay . . . I'm not going to show my butt, but yet I'm going to show my boob? That doesn't make sense, lady.' "

Finally, when the time came for her to curse to plug the film, it wasn't a sure thing. She looked nervously off camera to her reps for approval.

"Go for it," they mouthed silently, though I could tell inside they were all screaming, "JUST FUCKING SAY IT ALREADY."

So Mandy pulled up her big-girl panties. "I'M GOING FOR IT!" she said. "I apologize to Mom and Dad and stuff, but I fucking love this movie! Go see it! I feel so good!"

I waited for some sort of alarm to go off. It didn't, and then the room erupted in laughter. SAFE! Mandy seemed quite pleased with herself, and she had that look of the cat that ate the canary. Come to think of it, I probably did, too. I mean, if anything was going to go wrong, it was going to be in that room with her . . . Right?

Believe it or not, at the time, Mandy Moore saying "fuck" was quite an achievement and enormously satisfying. This was still early on in my career and there was always the chance of inadvertently crossing the line, and with a straitlaced star like Mandy Moore, it could've gone either way. But for the most part, I wasn't really getting into trouble with the studios for the word "fuck." They mostly let it go because the celebrities seemed to like me and my anything-goes style of interview.

I have to admit that the fucks flew so frequently that I worried for a split second that perhaps "fuck" had jumped the shark. But then I would think, *Nah. Fuck is eternal, like the Olympic flame.*

After Mandy was done, I had one more interview left for the day with Matthew Goode, her adorable English costar. There was no pressure there. He was a noob, and I couldn't imagine anyone giving a *rat's ass* what went on in that interview. This was a few years before he would go on to become a household name, appearing in big movies like *Watchmen* and hit TV shows like *The Good Wife* and *Downton Abbey*.

I remember casually walking into the room and meeting Matthew, who seemed like a typical nice British boy with a hint of a naughty schoolboy twinkle in his eye. Brits are, typically, great interviews. Contrary to their stuffy stereotype, they're actually quite liberal with their expressions and funny. As we said our brief hellos, I remember thinking, *This is going to be great.* He was charming, he was cheeky, and we were going to be lifelong friends. So like I do in all of my interviews, I told him we were uncensored at the very beginning, and we were off. The interview was pretty basic; it wasn't overly dirty but very suggestive. He dropped a few "fucks," we had a few laughs, and at the very end when I asked him to plug the movie, he didn't hem and haw like Mandy. He was a son of England. His heritage and pride were at stake. This was his first big Hollywood movie and his first big Hollywood junket, so he went for broke and effortlessly dropped THE BIG ONE:

"All right, ya *cunts*, go see the movie!"

I literally felt time stop and all the oxygen leave the room. At the same time, I was ecstatic; I gave Matthew a high five. There might have been some sort of an end zone dance, I'm not sure. I had popped my big studio cherry! It was my first "cunt" at a Warner Bros. junket in the history of NGTV! Of all the "cunts" that I have ever known, his was the most impactful.

Getting anything in the realm of the cunt was always magical. I remember getting handed a slew of them, wrapped in a bouquet of loveliness, from the entire cast of *The Lord of the Rings* at one of the premieres. Not exactly the place I would have considered the "nexus of cunt." But leave it to some of the finest actors of our time to make a meal out of the "filet mignon" of curse words. It turns out that during the holidays they put up a Christmas tree in one of the Winnebago trailers on set. Having nothing to decorate it with, they got creative and used the only ornament they had in vast supply: tampons. And thus the *Cunt-e-Bago* was born. Knowing there was nowhere else where this heartwarming holiday tale could be told but NGTV, each of the stars lent their voices to the chorus of "*Cunt-e-Bago*," like it was a reimagining of the "The Twelve Days of Christmas" but with more cunts. So along with providing these actors with lifelong memories, Peter Jackson and J. R. R. Tolkien had also put the cunt back in Christmas. But as awesome as that was, it was a red carpet victory, which doesn't hold a candle to the awesome difficulty of a *junket cunt*.

It was true that superstar Cher graced me with, "I'm a bitch with a capital C," in an interview at a Fox junket, but she never actually said the word! So as brilliant as it was, it was a bit of a cheat. Especially if you're a purist like me. This one, however, I heard with my own ears in a one-on-one interview at a junket: Matthew said "cunt!" It was an affirmation of everything we were doing. I was genuinely thrilled that celebrities were starting to feel comfortable enough that they were talking to me like they talked to their friends. Both Mandy and Matthew had talked to me like there weren't any cameras in the room, which had always been my goal. The fact that it was happening had me leaving the room on cloud fucking nine!

When I hit the hallway, I saw a team of people walking quickly toward me. Obviously, they were there to congratulate me on a job well done. Obviously, they were coming to tell me how happy they were that I was a woman in a predominantly male business, breaking down walls and doing things that nobody else was doing. I was overjoyed, but it quickly became quite clear that I didn't know what the fuck I was talking about. Because by the time I got to the tape-check room, Matthew's *C-U-Next-Tuesday* had started World War III.

"Carrie, we have a huge problem" were the words that greeted me from the guy running the junket as I entered the suite.

"Oh shit, are my tapes not working?" I responded, completely unaware that Rome was burning and I was the one who had, inadvertently, left the turkey deep fryer unattended and therefore responsible.

"No, they're asking me to erase your tapes," he replied, with little emotion.

My heart stopped. "Why? What's going on?"

"I'm not in charge; all I can tell you is they're telling me to erase it. I shouldn't even be telling you this." (*It was at that exact moment that I experience the faint odor of the proverbial shit that was about to fly past my ear and straight into the fan ahead. This was gonna get messy.*)

The Warner Bros. rep stormed in and came up to me in a fury, with veins popping out of her forehead, ready to tear me to pieces.

"What happened in there?" she said in her sharp pantsuit.

"What happened?" I responded. "You saw what happened. Amazing happened! I had a great interview with Matthew and we totally connected and it was super fun and—"

She cut me off. "He said 'cunt'!"

"Yeah . . . but . . ." was all I got out before she continued. "He said 'CUNT.' The star of our movie said 'cunt' in an interview. Do you think that's going to get people to go see it?"

In my mind, I thought, *Fuck yeah, it's going to get people to go see it. People who probably wouldn't have given this film a second look might think Matthew's cool and worth a look.* But it didn't matter what I thought. Cunt was apparently Dutch for "game over," which is what it felt like for me at that point.

"We can't let you show that. We're going to have to erase these tapes, you know that, right?" My body sank in. Then she delivered the final body blow by intimating that we may no longer be invited to future junkets. UGH!

I didn't understand her anger. They invited us. They knew we were uncensored. We didn't do anything outside of what we normally do. Plus, it was clearly spoken in jest, much like every other curse word in my interviews, ever, and I think that is the critical distinction here. There was nothing negative about what he said. Not only did he mean it in a super-friendly way but he said it in an even friendlier way. But, alas, no! An *oral nuke* had been detonated, and the power of clear thought had been demolished. Apparently, it was the first time anyone there had experienced a celebrity "cunt," and nobody knew what to do.

So the studio went to DEFCON 1, and my C-bomb was declared a *"verbo-nuclear device"* with the combined destructive force of both *Fat Man* and *Little Boy*. I can't even begin to tell you how overwhelming that moment was. In the span of five minutes, I had gone from being "too cool for school" to pleading for my professional life in front of a firing squad. It felt like having an orgasm that gives you a stroke!

"Please don't erase the tape," I begged. "I promise not to use it in our video edit."

She was skeptical and still irate.

"You have to trust me," I added. "I would never do anything to jeopardize our relationship." And it was true. Anytime anyone—past or future—asked us not to run something, we stuck to our word and didn't. Even when *Thor* star Chris Hemsworth shouted with abandon on camera, "Dear God, I have a hammer in my pants!" It was such a beautiful sound bite, maybe one of the best ever. His publicist had concerns about how it might be perceived given it was his first major film, and so, out of consideration, we didn't use it in the video edit for the film.

To their credit, and as much as they were angry, Warner Bros. didn't end up erasing Matthew's tape, and I wasn't banned from their junkets. But it was a traumatizing, heated battle that could have destroyed my career. It wasn't Matthew's fault. The poor guy couldn't have known that his little *cunt* would cause such a big row. In England cunt is thrown around like confetti. It's not malicious—it's actually a sort of jolly term of endearment between friends. And it's been infused in their pop culture for centuries. Chaucer used it liberally in *The Canterbury Tales*; Shakespeare made cunt references in *Twelfth Night* and *Hamlet*. Sex Pistol Sid Vicious dropped it in his version of "My Way." There are dozens of cunts uttered in the movie *Trainspotting*.

But in America, cunt was still considered the scariest, most evil curse word of all, and if used at all, it was controversial. The first time it was said in a movie—Jack Nicholson called Ann-Margret a "cunt bitch" in *Carnal Knowledge*—people saw it as a sign of the beginning of the end of civilized society by heathen hippies. Since that watershed moment, "cunt" had been slowly making its way into the mainstream to varying degrees of outrage. Jodie Foster was told, "I can smell your cunt" in *The Silence of the Lambs*. Tom Cruise demanded, "Tame the cunt!" in *Magnolia*. Samantha called Carrie the C-word on *Sex and the City*.

I remember getting an interesting perspective when I interviewed my friend, groundbreaking British filmmaker Edgar Wright, for his film *The World's End*. Edgar, who rose to fame with his comedy/horror classic *Shaun of the Dead*, and I go back a bit. To give you a little background, we first met when he and his buddies, Simon Pegg and Nick Frost, were doing press for *Hot Fuzz*, their follow-up to *Shaun*. It was there where we all met to shoot an *In Bed With*. They were all new to the whole major studio thing and trying to get their sea legs. Then the next thing they know, they're lying in bed with me, talking dirty like they're in a pub back home. Needless to say, I made an impression. There's a casual vulgar nature to the dialogue in his films that makes them very accessible, and his characters feel real and relatable. I think my approach to interviews follows a similar path, just in a different medium, and I think that's what sparked our friendship. That and our mutual love of the eighties British sitcom *The Young Ones*. If you ever get your hands on the special edition of *Hot Fuzz* on DVD, be sure to watch one of the extras called "The Fuzzball Rally," and you'll see some footage of that fateful day I bedded Edgar for the first time! I think they all liked me in the sack because virtually every time they did press after that movie, it included a stop in my bedroom. All except for this time, 'cause they didn't come to LA.

So on this occasion, our cuss therapy session ended up more insightful than usual. Edgar, who never shied away from profanity in his films, was getting an unusual amount of shit from the MPAA (Motion Picture Association of America) for this one. It turns out that much like the "fuck" rule, which allows only one mention of the F-word in a PG-13-rated movie, his film was testing the limitations placed on the C-bomb in R-rated movies to amusing effect:

Edgar: Rated R for pervasive language including sexual references; that's all it says! There's, like, violence in the movie, there's exploding heads, references to drugs, and all the MPAA wants to talk about is . . .

Me: Violent sex . . .

Edgar: . . . because we say the word cunt three times.

Me: Nice! (*I high-five Edgar.*)

Edgar: I haven't sworn at all today. I've been saving it all for you!

Me: I'm not buying that at all.

Edgar: I'll just have a sudden, like, explosion of expletives.

Me: I know that cunt has come out of your mouth at least once in the last twenty-four hours.

Edgar: (*Bursts out laughing.*) It's true! . . . You read the letter from the censors? I can't use the C-word to . . .

Me: Well, you can't call me a cunt, but you can call Simon a cunt.

Edgar: You can call me a cunt, but I cannot call you the C-word.

Me: What if I am aggressive about it? You fucking cunt!!! (*I playfully nudged to see if I could break him.*)

Edgar: (*Desperately trying not to say it.*) Yeah, but I'm not gonna say it . . .

Me: So then it's okay?

Edgar: Umm, it's not okay, but, like, so, I can't say it to a lady though . . .

Me: You *cunt* say it to a lady?

Edgar: I can't . . . I cunt . . . I can't say it to a lady.

When I interviewed Matthew, we were in a pretty puritanical moment in time. It was right around the same time as "Nipplegate"—remember at the Super Bowl half-time show, Justin Timberlake pulled down Janet Jackson's black bustier and exposed her right boob for nine-sixteenths of a second, then blamed it on a "wardrobe malfunction"? A million people filed complaints with the FCC, and CBS was fined five hundred and fifty thousand dollars, the largest sum in history at the time.

So even though I believe my "cunt flap" with Matthew was just bad timing, it was inevitable. It was an absolutely necessary event in the evolution of my brand as a progressive journalist and NGTV's brand as a groundbreaking uncensored network. In time, the *cunting* spread across all the studios until none were cunt-free. In fact, it acted as a fire starter of sorts because once the cunt was out of the bag, everything else was possible. I think over the course of the next few years we accomplished more in our mission to take away the negative stigma that surrounded cursing and replace it with fun, humor, and perspective with the ever-present cunt. If anything, the word "cunt" acted like a machete, aggressively chopping away at preconceived notions of what was acceptable language in interviews. We were clearing away mountains and valleys covered in the dense mental foliage of self-censorship in the artistic community. In retrospect, Mathew's "cunt" was without a doubt a transformative watershed moment.

What had initially served as a shock to the system ultimately woke a lot of people up as to what was coming. But it also demonstrated just how powerful being uncensored was as a platform and how quick celebrities would be to embrace it. It also showed that we, NGTV, were responsible and trustworthy administrators of its broadcast. To me profanity is the language of the masses and something all people have in common. The degree to which we are all profane and the manner in which we present it varies. But it is the people's church. Only, in this church, everybody worships in their own way, but we all do worship. And at the end of the day, it turns out that a majority of celebrities are just like you and me and enjoy a good "cunt" every now and then. Like Neil Patrick Harris who, when it came time to promote his movie, brought in the C-unit: "Go see *A Very Harold and Kumar 3D Christmas*, you fucking cunt!"

And, of course, there was Dane Cook, who threw down a great personal story about how a cunt once got between him and his girlfriend:

Me: What was it? Dun dun dun dun dun dumb cunt?
Dane: Dun dun dun dun dun big . . . C-word . . . I don't say that word offstage. I have five sisters.

Me: Oh really.

Dane: The character says it!

Me: You have lines? *(Implying lines he won't cross.)*

Dane: No, I have class. I got into an argument with a girlfriend once and the furthest I went was—I said in the middle of the argument, "You're being the C-word!" I didn't call her the C-word. I said she's being the C-word.

Me: You totally pussed out.

Dane: Then she goes, "That's the same!" Then I go, "Fine, you're a cunt."

So it didn't scare me away from pushing the envelope and getting more "cunts" on camera. In fact, I was empowered. After that, whenever we booked a Brit or an Australian, we made bets on how many "cunts" we'd get that day. But it wasn't just the guys, either. Randomly, girls would take the plunge, like Kirsten Dunst when she was promoting *Spider-Man 3.*

"I can't use my favorite one," she said to me.

"Yeah, you can," I said. I knew where this was going.

She tossed out the "cunt."

Not to be outdone and wanting to keep tradition alive, Andrew Garfield, the latest actor to don the blue and red, closed his eyes and thought of England when it came time to promote his blockbuster. "It's kind of inappropriate, but don't be a cunt and come and see *The Amazing Spider-Man!*"

Don't get me wrong, as emboldened as I was, hearing a celeb toss out the "cunt" was always a scary thing. You just never knew how the publicists were going to react. It was a verbal high-flying trapeze act, without a net. And at any moment I could go plummeting into the crowd. It was not for the fainthearted. But it got easier and easier over time because everybody was getting used to how crazy my interviews would get. Plus, they were laughing hysterically through the silliness, so the bad words stopped feeling like piercing bullets and began feeling like soft pillows. And who doesn't like a good pillow fight?

I think it's crazy that we let words have so much power over us. As a woman, the word "cunt" doesn't bother me any more than any other word because, you know what, some people are cunts. Which could be a compliment or an insult. Either way, it's the truth. We all know a few cunts, and if they aren't cunts all of the time, there are times when they definitely act *cunty*. I think we need to stop giving the words themselves so much power and start focusing on intent. Intent is the real mother-fucker in this equation. Somebody could call me a "cunt," and if I know that they aren't meaning to be hurtful, it's really no big deal.

On the other hand, I've had someone call me "chilly" once, and I knew his intent was to be hurtful. His intent was to call me a "frigid bitch" just because I didn't want to put out in the back of his car, in the parking lot at a bar, as an adult. That got me angry because I knew the intent, and I am far, far, far from "chilly." To be clear, I'm not above a little roll around in the backseat of a car. I just didn't want to do that with you, "Travis!" Holy shit! I love writing this. I mean, obviously, he knows his name isn't Travis, but he knows I'm talking about him, and that makes me feel pretty fucking good. So, again, it's purely about intent.

So, obviously, this issue doesn't just apply to the word "cunt." One story that will undoubtedly challenge your comfort zone as it has mine is about one of my closest friends, Kendrick, who's African-American, and his best friend/brother, Adam, who's white. Just like most BFFs they share a shorthand in their conversations and have nicknames for one another that they've used for over twenty years. When I first started hanging out with them seven years ago, I got a real shock to the system. We were out at some noisy bar one night, and I heard Adam call out to get Kendrick's attention by yelling, "Hey, tar baby!" Well, my jaw dropped, my vision narrowed to almost blacking out, and I waited for the rest of bar to suddenly go silent while the ensuing melee broke out. And nothing happened. No one at the table blinked, and Kendrick had already walked over to Adam and was smiling and laughing. Eventually, I learned that it was a term of endearment for them, and that the problem was mine. Now, I'm not saying there isn't a problem with using that term and I sure as shit have no desire to do so, but it's a great lesson in how words are just words. As fucked up as it sounded, to them it was a private expression of love, and my interpretation was just me inserting my judgement where it didn't belong.

I remember having another funny "misinterpreted" moment when we had Bijou Phillips, Lauren German, and Vera Jordanova in the studio to tape an interview in support of their movie *Hostel: Part II*. I started the interview with my usual ecstatic, energetic, and over-the-top intro:

"What's up, boys and girls, I have three sexy bitches right here! We got Vera, Lauren, and Bijou. All stars of the fucking awesome new movie *Hostel: Part II!*"

Bijou and Vera totally dove right into the energy, but Lauren's face looked like someone had stolen her candy, and I couldn't tell if it was me or unrelated personal crap so I continued. I worked my way into a key question:

"So, ladies, what's more important in a horror movie, the tits or the balls?"

The girls jumped all over that one, and a slew of balls-over-tits and tits-over-balls comments started flying. The debate ended with Bijou settling the issue:

"I think that there are balls, but the ruler of the movie is breasts. But not in a naked-tittie way, but in a, like, power-to-the-bosoms way."

To which I replied, " 'Cause you guys are strong bitches?!"

Bijou emphatically said, "RIIIIGHT!!!" as I pulled a power-fist move.

But again, Lauren looked like someone had peed in her coffee. But there was no time to focus on that 'cause Vera started to get my attention by purposefully clearing her throat loudly, to which I replied:

"Oh, I'm sorry . . . that would be you? Vera, you're the strong bitch?" To which she nodded enthusiastically with a big smile, and I continued, "Are you like a super bitch in this movie?" After which I raised my glass, and we toasted to her *super bitch-ness.*

At this point, I noticed that Lauren had gone way past the "does anyone else smell that?" look to the death knell of the "did you fuck my boyfriend?" look, straight at me. Clearly, there was something amiss, but Bijou and Vera were lovin' every minute of it, and Lauren wasn't havin' any of it. And I could feel that both of them were getting the same vibe I was. We weren't live, so I decided to ask Lauren if she was okay. She hesitated for a second and then she came out with it: "I don't like being called a bitch. I don't like that word. It bothers me." Well, I did not see that coming, and apparently neither did Bijou or Vera.

So I explained that I was using it in a celebratory way and meant no ill will, but I don't think she cared much for how I intended it. She saw the word in one way and that was that. Which was a shame because my intention is all that should have really mattered. But before the buzz was slaughtered, Bijou jumped in and made a funny joke. I took her cue and moved away from the B-word and continued having fun with the interview in a way everyone was comfortable with. I respected Lauren's feelings, but it was a lot of wasted energy on her part. I was celebrating her. I was celebrating the girl power of the movie. It should have been a 100 percent positive experience.

No question the word "bitch" is a divisive word with women. In my mind, it's a second cousin to "cunt." But where cunt strolls into a room in nothing but a pair of crotchless panties, six-inch stilettos, and a cattle prod, demanding your attention, bitch arrives in faded blue jeans, a cute baby-T, and knee-high boots and isn't so obvious about what she wants. But the head tilt coupled with the "where were you last night?" stare definitely gives you the feeling something's on her mind. Anyway, at the end of the day, I just think people need to lighten the fuck up. If you didn't take yourself so seriously, those words wouldn't give you an emotional conniption. You know why it doesn't bother me if someone calls me a "bitch" or a "cunt"? Because sticks and stones, that why! It's that simple. Life's too short.

Now back to more cunt.

One of my favorite *cunting trips* to this day was when I went in to interview Mila Kunis for the movie *The Book of Eli*. Now that was a good time. Mila's really funny, always gives a great interview, and is firmly in the top ten of all-around cool chicks. But that day she was about to turn into the *bomb diggity smack wack attack* of cool chicks! Now, unbeknownst to me, the infamous secret word game I've told you about was in full effect, but thanks to a friend of mine who was running the room, the word chosen for my interview was the ever-popular, under-appreciated yet versatile "cunt." Mila, appreciating that we were uncensored, decided to truly embrace the moment and proceeded to have a field day, *cunting* it up.

I had no idea what was going on but was obviously delighted when Mila went on a Shakespearean *cunt-a-logue*, painting the room with her masterful prose filled with wall-to-wall "cunts." The room was uproarious with laughter during the interview, and I was catching C-bombs like a kid under an exploding piñata at a *quinceañera*. I think there might have been only one sentence that didn't have a "cunt" in it. So there we were, two little *cunts, cunting* it up for cunts' sake. Mila was pitching the verbal equivalent of a no-hitter in baseball and there wasn't a dry eye in the house. It was moments like these that made me realize that what we were doing was as much fun as it was cathartic for the talent.

It was so insanely awesome that even her publicist was rolling on the floor, laughing. Which, when it happens, and it's happened a lot, is a tremendous source of personal pride for me. Because getting a personal publicist to laugh while a major client takes an obscenity submachine gun and lights up a press interview is about as common as people admitting that they use the Today Sponge as their go-to for birth control. I mean, they're out there, but let's face it, even they have no desire to explain why they're using 1985's hottest contraceptive. Anyway, when it was over, Mila gave me a huge hug and a big thank-you, but her rep was immediately all over my ass like cake and whipped cream after a night of *sploshing*.

"I'm not gonna give you that tape," she said.

"Are you kidding me?"

"You want to do it again?"

"No, I want my tape."

"Sorry, I can't do that."

"You know me. Just tell me what you don't want in there."

"Okay, fine. Just use the least *cunty* two minutes."

Boom! Suddenly, cunt was kinda cool. And it started being infused in our daily lives. On TV, Tina Fey did an entire episode of *30 Rock* about the C-word. Jane Fonda threw down "cunt" on a live *Today* show segment discussing *The Vagina Monologues* (though a mortified Meredith Vieira issued an apology immediately after the commercial break). In her interview with me for her latest movie, *What's Your Number?*, Anna Faris renamed it "What's Your Cunty Number?" before giggling and apologizing to her mother: "Sorry . . . Hi, Mommy!" Goopy Gwyneth Paltrow called her grandmother "a real cunt" on *Chelsea Lately*. In music, Iggy Azalea started calling her fans her "kuntz." Nicki Minaj's personal motto became "I'm a bad bitch, I'm a cunt," taken from her song "Roman's Revenge." Rihanna wore a necklace that spelled out "cunt" to a chapel in Brazil. A sexually charged micro-genre of queer rap called Kunt emerged. And One Direction's Niall Horan publicly called a group of his diehard fans a "shower of cunts" at the airport in Dublin. Not to be confused with a "shower of cunt" (singular), which is a whole other matter altogether.

Of course, there's always the cunt you thought you had but somehow slipped away. I rememeber mine like it was a short film, George Clooney starring in *The Cunt that Wasn't There*. So there I was at the end of my interview with him, and it was time to throw down in support of his film, and he was thinking of what to say . . . that's where we pick up the action:

George: *(Scratching his head. Looking like he wants to make it count.)* Okay. *(Then quickly with precision:)* If you go see the fucking movie . . . *(Pauses.)* Then . . . *(Pauses again.)* Uh, they will get? I can do it! *(He looks at me with a little mischief in his eye.)* . . . I was gonna say something worse . . .

    (Holy shit! Am I about to get the Clooney C-bomb? I thought to myself: Be cool.*)*

George: Even worse than you could possibly imagine!

    Me: Not possible! I've heard it all. *(Trying to reassure him.)*

George: And then I backed off. *(Realizing that I probably won't be shocked.)* You probably have! Actually . . .

    Me: *(Shit!)* I may have said a lot of . . . things . . . actually! *(Almost.)*

George: Innocent little flower over here. *(To the room, laughing.)*

We'll never know exactly what he was going to say, but my money is on the immortal "cunt." You be the judge, but experience tells me that nobody hems and haws with the kind of anticipation gamblers have at a craps table unless they're getting ready to tangle with the *devil's pussy*! One day! Even the thought that he could have gone there makes him even cooler!

Anyway, in movies, mainstream chick flicks like *Bridesmaids* and *Gone Girl* jumped on the cunt wagon. *Twilight*'s Kristen Stewart, not exactly known for her cheery demeanor, called herself a "miserable cunt" in *Marie Claire UK*. Denis Leary took cunt to a whole other level when he continued his father's legacy by introducing our audience to an expression he invented during my interview with him for *The Amazing Spider-Man*: "And I think it was invented by my dad, I'm pretty sure, when I was a kid. That's how I remember this motherfucking-cock-sucking-cunt-son-of-a-bitch. *Amazing* motherfucking *Spider-Man*!"

Oh and let's not leave out the kids. In *Kick-Ass*, eleven-year-old Chloë Moretz called a group of adults "you cunts." In fact, in the talk show pilot we shot for EPIX, I invited her costars Aaron Taylor-Johnson, Christopher Mintz-Plasse, and Clark Duke to a no-holds-barred and very bawdy discussion about the importance of the "cunt" in modern cinema. They all concluded that they didn't understand why it was still such a big deal in America but agreed that as long as it's said with a British accent, then everyone should be fine with it.

So many "cunts," in so little time!

Until one day, it happened organically. "Cunt" was the new "fuck."

I know this for sure because almost ten years later, exactly, I had a junket with Warner Bros., the same studio responsible for the Matthew Goode *cunt-tastrophy*. This time I was interviewing Liam Neeson for *Unknown*. He was always nice when I talked to him about *The A-Team* or *Taken*, though some days could be more serious and quiet than others. I was the last interview of the day, and it was also only a few months after his wife, Natasha Richardson, had died tragically in a skiing accident. So I was a little worried about how to vibe it.

Despite my hesitation, Liam had a gleam in his eye when I walked in, and I could tell he wanted to play a bit. We talked about kicking ass, making out in the backseat, and sex in the shower. When we reached the end of the interview and it was time to promote the film No Good TV–style, the last thing in the world anyone expected, happened:

Liam: I don't think you want to hear it. I'm from the north of Ireland.
  Me: Oh, are you going to throw the cunt out? Is that what you're gonna do? *(The whole room is laughing.)* I have heard now.
Liam: You fucking cunt! *(Really leaning into it.)*
  Me: *(Laughing with the whole room and clapping.)*
Liam: You know that word?
  Me: A few times. Yeah.
Liam: That's the bad one in America.
  Me: It is.
Liam: Yup.
  Me: But you guys have now infiltrated America, so I heard it a few times. Thank you.
Liam: Cunt. Cunt. Cunt. Cunt. Cunt. Cunt. Cunt. Cunt. Cunt. Cunt.

When it was over, the Warner Bros. reps ran out of the room high-fiving and walkie-talkie-ing each other as if a NASA rocket had successfully landed on Uranus. It was so jubilant, we should have shot fireworks out of a cannon that spelled CUNT and had a marching band play "Cherry Pie" by Warrant.

"Liam said cunt! Liam said cunt!" they cried in amazement. "Liam said cunt *ten* times!" Then I heard it on the studio walkie-talkies like some sort of critical announcement: "Liam said cunt!"

"Amazing, Carrie!"

"Groundbreaking stuff!"

"Nobody does it like you do!"

W-T-C! *(What the Cunt!)* I love that they were so excited and giddy. I mean, who doesn't want to be the hero of the moment? But the irony was not lost on me or Kourosh, who just happened to be there that day waiting in the hospitality suite. And apparently, the euphoria had reached the suite well before I got there. We both just smirked at each other in unison. It was the same me, doing the same thing I'd always done. Except now I was a professional superspy of obscenity with a license to "cunt."

Times had definitely changed. Nothing seems to be as exciting as it sounds anymore. That's probably why everyone is already having anal sex in ninth grade. I mean, let's face it, even the Mormons are *soaking.* I remember when I first started, studios were nervous when I pushed the envelope, and now they ask me to go there and help lick it! Nobody was doing that before me, and I'm pretty sure nobody's doing it now. The *cunt trade* is a highly specialized field. You really have to know your *cunt,* and you absolutely cannot be one. Now, I don't want to toot my own horn, but you try pushing a *cunt* up a steep and slippery slope for ten fucking years! So . . . TOOT-FUCKIN'-TOOT!!

By the way, that was, officially, the first time I've ever *blown* myself.

I'm not doing anything differently now that I wasn't doing then; it's just that my career trajectory has changed the reactions I get from the same words I've been using the entire time. If my greatest accomplishment in life is getting people to rid themselves of their hang-ups on swear words, or just words in general, I would consider that a huge success. That and having all the Muppets over to my place for a sleepover.

So my *crusade for the cunt* had come full circle. A decade earlier, I was the *genital wart* of the junket world for drawing out one measly C-word. Now, I was a hero. An innovator, a *vaginal virtuoso*, a *mastermind of the muff*! Silly me for underestimating the power of the cunt. Let's turn my mistakes into a teachable moment. For the *pussy* always prevails, my friends!

Always.

14

THE SILENT FUCK

**Never use a big word
when a little filthy one will do.**
—Johnny Carson

If you really think about it, and I have, life is essentially a random collection of experiences, advice, and memories. If you're smart enough to learn from your experiences and humble enough to allow good advice to inform your choices, maybe, just maybe, you won't end up drowning in memories of sucking dick for meth in a blind alley behind the neighborhood Supercuts. And if by some misfortune that's exactly what you're doing right now, I have two things to say to you. First, wow . . . (golf clap) . . . fellatio and reading a book at the same time . . . I'm impressed. You are indeed a Renaissance man or woman and really need to put those multitasking talents to work elsewhere. Secondly, and more importantly, trust me when I tell you it's never too late to put the dick down and make a change. The beautiful thing about memories is that every single day is an opportunity to make new ones . . . better ones. We all come from somewhere, good, bad, or ugly, but all that really matters is where we're going. The rest? Who gives a fuck! The journey's the thing (stepping off soapbox).

Now that I've got that out of the way, I want to talk to you about a great piece of advice I picked up along the way to here called "the 7 P's." It's a huge part of who I am and how I go about my professional life, if you can call it that. Those of you who have served in the U.S. Marine Corps or the British Army, you already know what the fuck I'm talking about, and my hat's off to you. For those of you that haven't, as Gene Simmons would always say in that rich deep voice of his, "This is my gift to you." "Proper planning and preparation prevents piss-poor performance." Now, say that ten times fast!!

It's an amazing mantra, but just like everything in life, it's not about the knowledge; it's about the application. That's where experience comes and creates balance. The road to balance will always have more than its fair share of funny teachable moments, and for me, none was more poignant than when I came face-to-face with the phantom menace known as *the silent fuck*. (And before all of you original trilogy fans start a shit-storm, let me just say that it is possible to not dig a film but still think it had a great title.)

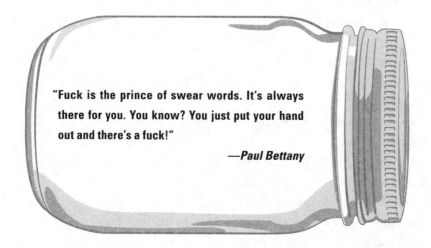

"Fuck is the prince of swear words. It's always there for you. You know? You just put your hand out and there's a fuck!"

—*Paul Bettany*

As I've mentioned, I'm pretty anal about getting ready for interviews. But is there such a thing as being too prepared? Sometimes you're so worried about how things will turn out that you forget to be present in the moment at all. I know a lot of you are thinking, *That sounds like every single one of my birthday parties until I was twenty-eight years old.* Mine, too.

Let's face it: Anything you anticipate for a while is in danger of not living up to your daily imagination. Shit, every time I buy a lottery ticket, I've spent that money before I leave the fucking parking lot. (If you're curious, 50 percent to charity, travel for a year straight, start Keagan Irish

Whiskey, and then get back to work.) Friends of mine who get married always say, "I wish I had sat back and enjoyed the moment," all of the time. It's natural, but in the workplace, in can be dangerous. In my line of work, where the entire interview is based on me being present, it can be a disaster.

I did that during what I thought was the most important interview of my life. It was at a time in my career when I was really starting to feel good about what I was doing and how I was doing it. I was actually being asked to interview people—as opposed to Kourosh and me hustling our way into functions. More importantly, the people I was interviewing were also asking for me. Things were going very well until Kourosh called me into his office one day.

"I've got a big one," he said. Get your minds out of the gutter, please. Or don't—what do I care at this point!

Kourosh is never one to get too excited about an interview, so I knew this had to be good.

"Let me guess!" I exclaimed.

I love this game. Always have, always will. It drives people crazy, but I will keep guessing until I get it right or you tell me to shut the fuck up.

"Uh . . . Ozzy Osbourne? No, wait, Bon Jovi? Is it Bon Jovi? Please tell me it's Bon Jovi!"

"No, it's not fucking Bon Jovi!" he said. "I got you an interview with Colin Farrell!"

Shut. The. Front. Door.

Colin "fucking" Farrell? He breaks rules, I break rules. He likes to have a good time, I like to have a good time. He swears in every interview, I swear in every interview. We're perfect for each other! We're going to be best friends. This was going to be THE BEST interview anyone had ever done in the history of interviews! I'd interviewed big stars before, but for most of them, it took a little time to get them out of their shells, and by the time they were out, the interview was over. Colin Farrell has never been in his shell. Colin Farrell takes a shot, throws up the bird, and pisses on shells. When he was born, he didn't cry; he slapped the nurse, lit a cigarette, and said, "Where's the fucking party?" He was perfect.

Let's return to the days of yesteryear for a second, shall we? At this time, not only was Colin Farrell the "it" guy in Hollywood, the star of fucking *S.W.A.T.*, but he was also Hollywood's bad boy. He was talking about having anal sex with Britney Spears and swearing on national TV, but people loved it. For whatever reason they embraced him, incredibly sexy warts and all. If people who were trying to control him in interviews couldn't get him to stop swearing, my interview with him was going to be like if Tony Montana was talking with Quentin Tarantino. Unstoppable. FYI, they frown on cocaine at these functions.

I knew since the interview was going to be perfect that everything else had to be perfect, too, and that started with me. It was almost like getting ready for prom. I had always wanted to have a prom do-over, and I was finally getting that chance. Hold on one second, please. Just imagining taking Colin Farrell to prom and . . . I'm back.

In my mind, my quest for perfection was a three-step process:

Step One: Get a crisp, new, tight, white, button-down shirt. I wanted to look professional but still sexy and the button-down was perfect for that. It didn't show any skin so I wasn't screaming desperate, but it was still tight enough around the girls where it was whispering, "Oh, these old things?"

Step Two: I had to get my "hairs did." The heavy metal part of me wanted to go back to total Tawny Kitaen sprawled on the hood of a car from the Whitesnake music video, but I thought I'd be sending the wrong message. Side note: It was actually the right message, but not the socially acceptable one. I decided on something in between bridesmaid and businesswoman. Something that said, "I'm here to interview you, but there's a chance I'm not wearing any underwear."

Step Three: Get a Mystic Tan. I am Irish. Need I say more? Let's just say, for most of my people, getting a "suntan" is when our burn finally fades from a dark red to a light pink. I wanted a little color to offset my new white shirt, so I thought I would get a spray tan. The only thing I knew about spray tans was what I learned from the cast of *Jersey Shore*, and those colors varied from dark brown to a fucking pumpkin.

I was sure that these three things, coupled with my interview style, were going to make us lifelong friends. Yes, I was putting in a lot of work here, but so we're clear: I wasn't trying to throw myself at him (minus the whole prom hallucination). I just needed him to realize that every interview from now until the end of time was boring, except of course, the ones he did with me. That's actually my goal with every interview.

In order to get step one out of the way I had to go to the mall, and I hate the fucking mall. Why not shop online, you ask? Great question. The answer is *melons. Mega-melons.* To be more specific, the *quarts of love* that are attached to my body. See, the clothing companies fuck with us women in a big, bad way. A medium in one brand is a small in another. "Oh, honey, that's a large, but it runs small, so it's like a medium." So, let's just call it a fucking medium! Anyway, I make my way into Macy's, I grab a rack of questionably appropriate white button-down shirts, and I head into the dressing room. I just want to make this as quick and painless as possible. After trying on about six shirts that ran the gamut from muumuu to "schoolgirl top for a stripper costume," I hear a knock on the dressing room door.

"Excuse me, please?" I hear a woman say with a heavy Armenian accent.

"Yes?"

"How are things in there?" she asks.

"Fine, I guess."

"Can you open door? I might be able to help."

The last thing I wanted to do was to have some pushy saleswoman tell me what shirt I "needed" to get, but I wasn't having any luck finding one myself so I thought, *Why not?* and opened the door.

Standing in front of me was a short woman, probably about sixty years old, and she had THE BIGGEST *cannonballs* I had ever seen. "I notice you walking around and I figure I can help," she says. "You know, with those." And she poked my right *babaloo* with her index finger.

Whaaaaaaaaaaaaaaat?

"I'm sorry?" I said, a little shocked.

"Honey, don't be shy. We are in the same club," she said as she shook her *mogambos* back and forth. "They are good for the men but not so great for us, am I right? Come." Then she grabbed my hand and walked me back out to the clothes. I had never felt such immediate kinship. With my new BFF in tow, it took me less than ten minutes to find the right white shirt, professional but still sexy, and I was gone.

Step one . . . success.

Next up, taming the *rat's nest*. Back in the pre-stylist days I was a little challenged in the *hair-ea* (that's hair area). If this was like my grown-up prom, I had to do something a little special.

Today, I seriously would never even think about letting someone else touch my hair, but back then? I was one step up from Fantastic Sams.

I remember sitting down in the chair with all of my notes for the interview, showing the woman a picture of what I wanted my hair to look like, drifting off in my work, and then being jolted back into reality by a sharp pain and the ever-so-wonderfully aromatic smell of burning flesh.

"My bad," the stylist said, wrinkling her nose and shrugging her shoulders as she was removing the curling iron from the top of my ear. "Must have gone too low."

I'm sorry, what the fuck did you just say? My bad. My fucking bad?! DON'T YOU KNOW I'M GOING TO PROM WITH COLIN FARRELL?! You just scarred me before the most important moment of my life, and all you can say is, "My bad"? Can we all agree that, from now on, "my bad" should be reserved for things a little more casual, like taking someone's parking spot or farting while doing a sit-up? It definitely should not be used when you alter somebody's life! I looked in the mirror and there was a GIANT red mark on my ear. Fuuuuuuuuuuuuuuuuck! I guess we're not going to prom after all, just straight to my own personal hell. Straighten this mop out so it covers the bloodred hematoma forming on the top quarter of my ear, please.

Step two . . . not great.

Which brings us to the cherry on top of my *shit sundae*: Mystic Tan. The day before the interview I went to get a spray tan.

So believe it or not, fake-n-bake's never really been my thing. I know I live in Hollywood and everyone does it out here, but not me. I've always loved being a pasty, Irish-pale creature of the shadows. I don't know why I thought it was a good idea to change it up for this interview, but I had convinced myself that it had to be done. Since I was an uneducated, pasty noob, I asked my friend where I should go, and she recommended a spot where she promised, "They won't turn you orange like the Landlady from *Kingpin*." Sounds perfect.

There are a few things someone should tell you when you spray tan for the first time. They could start with, "Hey, probably not a great idea to wear super-tight clothes because when you put them back on afterward you're going to rub off a bunch of the tan." Not only that, but putting on sticky, tight jeans might be in my top five of most hated feelings. Another thing someone might want to tell you is that when you are getting a spray tan . . . close your mouth. And then, if you don't close your mouth and happen to ingest a gallon of whatever the fuck they are spraying you with, DO NOT open your eyes to see what is going on. So to wrap up, dress comfortably and stand like a coordinated human being who can function with eyes and mouth closed at the same time without falling over. I guess some of us just aren't made for Mystic.

Regardless of my clearly graceful experience, I walked out of there head held high with a fresh orange paint job. I had the confidence of a superhero in spray-tan armor. No one could stop me now.

The day of the interview was a blur. I don't remember a thing leading up to when we arrived at the junket. I do remember waiting to go into the room to interview Colin when the magnitude of the situation hit me. Wait, what if I can't get him to swear? What if this is supposed to be my wheelhouse and I can't deliver? All of a sudden, this was turning from the perfect interview into the beginning of the end of my career. Fuck a duck! My mind was racing, and I was thinking about how I was going to have to move back in with my parents and that I guess I could open a pet shop in Buffalo because I've always like pets and then . . . I started to sweat. A lot. FAN-FUCKIN-TASTIC!

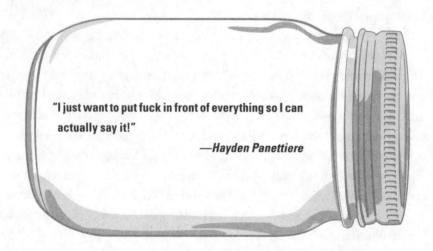

"I just want to put fuck in front of everything so I can actually say it!"

—*Hayden Panettiere*

That's when my director came over and told me that he could see orange stains on my brand-new fancy white shirt. No way! I looked down and I could see my skin secret starting to make its own horrifically timed debut. There was no way my Armenian BFF could have seen this coming. I looked to see if there were stains anywhere else, and sure enough there was some major damage in the pit area. Mental note: *Do not give Colin a high five.* The next thing I thought about? Honestly? *This shirt was tight enough to where if my* mammaroonies *started sweating it might look like I was lactating chocolate milk.*

"Five minutes," I heard.

I was panicked. An interview that, in my mind, could make my company and me a household name was happening in five minutes, and I have spots developing that would worry a caretaker at a leprosy colony.

"Three minutes."

The next thing I knew, the interview was over, and I was on my way to pick up my tapes. To be completely honest, I don't remember a thing. It was a complete blur. I remember sitting in front of Colin and someone saying, "Okay, your time is up," and I walked out. I remember walking down the hallway, a sweaty orange mess, thinking, *How could I have fucked that up so badly? That was the worst interview I have ever done.* I've had blackouts before, but those were the fun kind. This was *not* one of those.

To this day I don't remember what happened in the room, but I vividly remember talking to myself, saying, *He never swore. Not once.* On the way back to the office, all I could think about was how I was going to tell the people at my company that we're through. If I couldn't make the potty mouth of Hollywood swear, I needed to quit and sell my company for two chickens and a goat. I came back to the office, threw the tapes on Kourosh's desk, walked into my office, and looked at flights to Buffalo. I was planning on starting a nice bender, picking up thirty boxes of Triple Double Oreo cookies, and heading straight to the airport. Just the Triple Double Oreo cookies and me. I was leaving all of my clothes, my furniture, everything, and I was moving home. An hour later Kourosh came into my office. "What's your problem?" he said.

"What's my problem? That was the worst interview," I said.

He said he'd watched the tape, and then he asked what I thought had happened.

"What happened? What happened? He didn't swear!"

"Carrie, he said fuck about twelve times in four minutes."

What? How could I not have heard that? Because I wasn't present, that's how. I was so busy sweating and worrying about the future, I didn't allow myself to be in the room.

Here is what actually happened: Colin sat in a chair, drinking a beer.

Colin: How are you doing, man?

Me: Good.

Colin: Good, good.

Me: Fun movie.

Colin: Good.

Me: Tell everybody how much this movie completely kicks ass.

Colin: This movie completely . . . *(He grabs both arms of the chair and moves around.)* I can't **fucking** say that; it sounds terrible, like promotion . . . *(He reaches for a pack of cigarettes.)* Did you enjoy it, did you?

Me: I did.

Colin: Oh, cool, man. That's good. *(He takes out a cigarette and puts it in his mouth.)*

Me: It was rockin'.

Colin: Good, man, it should be, that is what it was built for, to entertain, loud. Loud and bright and colorful, guns and fire and explosions and **shit.**

Me: Was there anything fun that you remember? Anything weird? I heard there was a car chase on the bridge while you were shooting?

Colin: Oh, yeah, there was. We were on the bridge doing the last scene with the plane there and all that **shit** there in the limousine on the radios came through because the bridge had to be closed off, the Sixth Street bridge, so the guys that were at the top of the bridge were at the barricades and anybody that tried to get on the bridge, they were like, they can't, we're shooting a movie there, and the next thing this **fucking** car came wheeling around through the barricade, we didn't see it because of the long bridge, but the guy's walkie-talkie said somebody just broke through and there were eight cop cars behind him, there's a chase going on, and the helicopter appeared and we waited, waited, we waited, and you see this sedan coming up around the corner on the bridge and there was a crew of about fourteen and they were **fucking** like "get back, get out of the way" because we didn't know if the car would fit between the nose of the plane because the plane was sideways on the bridge, period, between the nose of the plane and the wall it would look like a small gap. It was going to be interesting, and behind the car there was a cop car's **fucking** lights glaring, and the two dudes in the car were just **fucking** chilling straight through, they made it through with six inches on either side, cop cars followed him. They got them about an hour later. But that was good; that was a start before the camera even rolled. The night was all then **hell** after that.

Me: You got to work with Sam.

Colin: Yeah, it was great to work with Sam—that was primarily the reason why I wanted to do the film. You know, to get to play with him you know.

Me: You got to play with him, huh?

Colin: Yeah, I thought you would pick up on that. Being uncensored and crazy and all.

Me: Tell me about SWAT training. Sam said you were the best.

Colin: AHHH! Did he? How much do I owe him now? Couple nice things, **fucking, shit.** I wasn't the best, but it was a fun five days of shooting rifles and shotguns, machine guns and handguns, and all sorts of **fucking** guns.

Me: Excellent! Now this is going to be the best part. I need a sentence to promote *S.W.A.T.*, No Good TV–style?!

Colin: No.

Me: NO? Get out of here! Colin Farrell won't swear for me.

Colin: Not for anyone.

Me: Can you do an ID?

Colin: Sure, what do you want?

Me: Say your name and you're watching NGTV.

Colin: Hey, I'm Collin Farrell and you're watching NGTV.

Me: *(Whispering.)* Perfect.

Colin: *(Whispering.)* Okay.

Me: *(Whispering.)* Now say fuck . . .

Colin: *(Looks around with his eyes without moving his head.)* Is the camera off? Turn that **shit** off. *(Laughs.)* **FUCK YOU**! Get the **fuck** out of here!

He said "fuck" a zillion times, but because I wasn't present, all I could remember was that he didn't say it the one time I asked him to. I learned a lot of things from this experience. I learned to try not to build things up on my end so much because when I do, and the time comes,

I forget to be in the moment. Also, when you build something up that much, it can never live up to your expectations. I had built this up so much that somehow this interview was going to solve world hunger, when at the end of the day, it was just an interview. A good interview, but just an interview. But because I had made it into something that it was never going to be, I was already disappointed in the middle of the interview.

Lastly, the most important lesson of all was that one interview wasn't more important than another. Sure, some interviews were better than others, but not more important. At the end of the day, I learned that the most vital thing in the interview room is me. I'm not saying that I'm better than anyone; I'm saying that for my company to be successful, it was critical that I be fully engaged in the interview. Because when I do my job well, we get good interviews. When I was present and part of the conversation, we were doing things nobody was doing. In an odd way, even though in my head after I had already given away all of my clothing and worldly belongings and bought a plane ticket home . . . I now was more confident in what I was doing than I had ever been before.

Oh, I also learned that when men see what looks to be hot chocolate coming out of your *ay carumbas*, they will take the elevator all the way to the lobby even if they're not going there.

FIND THE FUCKING WORD GAME

```
C W K B M C M F E F B B E I L U G P G J X A D J G J R S K U K R E T U
S O N T K U H I U T X G D H L H G N E N G T J A X A E R G S O S P K O
H R C R I M J O B C A U Z W E E H C I C Q T Z C R Q E R N S P S G W J
S C W K W M D I X K K E O T L E M A C H K X F K E Z E R K O U X P W A
P Y I I Q O E A K C U F M U B V M J D S Q L R S O Q H N R Y F M W X P
U M S T B N C I D E A Q X L D U I K V R S K E S B R A O E B R F D Q V
S H Z U A Z G K C D Z R N L P A X F L K A F O F X N I P J C M D G S G
G D T H A K M R E B O U Z S N Y W G S G D T Z F Y K I S A N G E Y C R
W A N K R K B E F Y T G K H F D J K Q Z D U I J X W X R V J G W B O J
U A W F D P R M L K D C N I I A U O C R D I F Y S O T E L C R P I M A
Q J W H Q F E G K D U Y N T E H J R S I E V Q S W C Z V V D F A P I L
B P A I P L I E G F K F N N U O E G F M D M A R C N W I S E V U L Q Q
Z J R O P V P U Y Z O B C V W K E Q F R I V T O Y B G D X J D C L U X
V H M J C S U T I B P H W Y C T H Y O S I L C Q B P Q F C T V O S T C
Z C C V S L T Q V H E A E U C O C K S U C K E R V U N F D X U X C R T
M W B U C I N B C S N B F B M N M E A T F L A P S Y Y U I Q D F I L G
F J H C T Z N U T G A R I Z C K M P B I R O Y O M S T M M Z X O C A E
U S P H I P U I I R E O E T B S Y Y D S M W B V L H Z D F X F I I V V
N N R E F Q C M P H J D K X S V O Y H G W O H R L K L Z N Z Q N V W B
Y A U Q Z L O U T K R E L Z Z U G M U C J U G E E S S U Z R F Z V H P
Q T R M E F A O N X I Y M B F X H U T W J V P H H H A I K Q F D J T W
K C E S V I M L S J H I T N U C M Y O B P C E C P T J O G E U M R M K
I H M M O S T X L F J I H J V K G L J S J M G N I V K T E F F N X C B
L U L B L T X H J O Y G N E D Y B C U Z S C C U O W I O U E U R S F W
P T Y L S F Z S B Q L X P M M O H M J Q P L W M A B I C E V W R H N D
A B Y R C U Y K M P C G C I J E U M A A H A B T B V K U T Z J B W Q Q
C P B Y P C A D K F Z N D J M F N C C F T E Q E I T Q H E C E V S T H
O E K G B K P R P R G E S U O Q P U H R Y X J P A C S W C C L P D L U
U X O J Q E X A L N Y D R H T J W C G E M H Y R S I C T Q V O H H D J
Y S S U P R P T S T V N I T R K V C H L B X D A I I H W M O H I O S C
Z J F Y Q Z T S H P W B O S R F M F U O P A Q C J N Y A G E S F O G O
I T N N H I J A I J X A K Q I W E V T U A R G G L B Z E G B S R R R I
D I P S H I T B T K E E T A D Z E I L I L M G P Z D S I X O A J X R S
N N U W Y A J B P K I H A H N M B A L L S M W F G T V D F Z W C I U C
```

ASSHOLE	COCK	FUCKTARD	QUEEF
ASSWIPE	COCKJOCKEY	GODDAMMIT	RIMJOB
BALLS	COCKSUCKER	HELL	SHIT
BASTARD	CUM	JACKASS	SNATCH
BITCH	CUMGUZZLER	JERKOFF	SPOOGE
BLOWJOB	CUNT	JIZZ	TITS
BONER	DICKWAD	MEATFLAPS	TITTYFUCK
BULLSHIT	DIPSHIT	MOTHERFUCKER	TWAT
BUMFUCK	DOUCHEBAG	MUFFDIVER	WANK
CAMELTOE	FELCHING	PECKER	
CARPETMUNCHER	FISTFUCKER	POONANY	
CHESTICLES	FUCK	PUSSY	

15

A KICK IN THE CUNT

> Two things are infinite:
> the universe and human stupidity;
> and I'm not sure about the universe.
> —*Albert Einstein*

Never underestimate the value of a good kick in the cunt. It has the potential to be a defining moment in your life. There's something quite liberating about its unexpected immersive agony. In fact, I would go so far as to say that should you ever find yourself in the crosshairs of a *twat kick* or a *nut thump* . . . don't run, don't hide . . . accede, and I promise you . . . you shall ascend.

Believe it or not, each one of these excruciating moments is, actually, an opportunity to take a shortcut and move forward on the metaphysical game board of life. Sort of like landing on the chance or community chest space on a Monopoly board . . . except with more immediate danger for your *crotch!* I know what you're thinking . . . next I'll be telling you to use labradorite crystals to awaken your magical powers and open your crown chakra. I get it. But the truth is that I'm not going to tell you not to do that because first of all, who couldn't use the gift of serendipity and synchronicity in their life? And second, because this happens to NOT be an exercise in mysticism. It's just a simple fact of life. Pain is power. Pain is knowledge. Pain is strength. Sometimes it comes at great cost and from the last person you expect, but the pain of a good kick in the cunt from a personal hero is the greatest teacher of all.

I have learned that life—living, working, loving, and fucking—is pretty much like the movie *Fight Club*. To stay in the game, you have to fight, you have to take the beating, and you can't talk about it to anyone outside of the club. It's okay though. There is a light at the end of the tunnel and it isn't always a train. Trust me when I tell you that you are tougher than you think. You just have to want it. I've never heard it better stated than by one of my heroes who has gone on to become a friend, Sylvester Stallone, in the movie *Rocky Balboa*: "It ain't about how hard you hit, it's about how hard you can get hit and keep moving forward. How much you can take and keep moving forward." The entertainment business is a bit of a topsy-turvy world. Down is up, up is down, and real world rules don't apply. I learned that the hard way and early in the game.

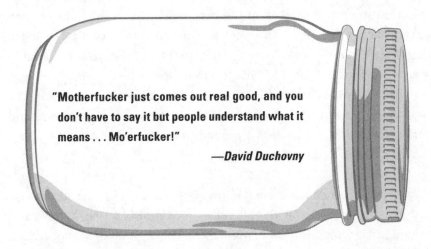

"Motherfucker just comes out real good, and you don't have to say it but people understand what it means . . . Mo'erfucker!"

—David Duchovny

I'm like most people. I'm a fan first. I get all caught up in those uber-talented men and women who create magical wondrous things that dazzle and entertain us for a living: actors, musicians, authors, and artists. The only difference between me and you is that I've gotten to meet a lot of these objects of our obsession, so much of the mystery is gone. I suppose the well-known notion that you should never meet your heroes is actually sound advice, because to be perfectly honest, some of these motherfuckers will rape you of your childhood memories and don't deserve a *shart* of your attention. On one occasion in particular, my heart was broken and my career sideswiped by someone that I had worshipped for years. But in the end, I learned a very valuable lesson.

My hero has fallen, and this is my story (*tung tung—Law & Order–*style).

Anticipation is 10 percent excitation, 10 percent expectation, and 80 percent perspiration. Have you ever built something up in your head so much that when it finally happens, there's no way it can possibly live up to the hype? So when the moment arrives—and doves don't burst out from behind your head and a rainbow doesn't shine out of your ass—the disappointment is so soul crushing, you just want to quit life and move into a thatch hut on the island of Takuu?

Let me tell you about the first time a celebrity hero crashed and burned in my eyes. I was almost six years old, and I was in awe of this magician I had seen at my friend's birthday party. He was so charming and captivating. I just *knew* he was performing *REAL* magic! He knew all of our names at the end of the party and told us we were the best group of boys and girls he had ever performed in front of. That sealed it. Right after that I wanted to be a magician. I wanted to travel around to parties and make boys and girls feel as happy as he had made me feel. He was a true blessing and I wanted to know more about him! After he was done performing, I saw him walk around the side of the house, and since I had tons of questions I wanted to ask him, I grabbed two juice boxes and followed right behind him.

Bad idea.

When I turned the corner, I came face-to-face with an unholy trinity usually reserved for the attendees of a multiday music festival. I found Justin Credible (*that was his magician name*) with his pants around his ankles, squatting on the side of the house, smoking a cigarette, and taking a dump. My hero was shitting on my friend's lawn in the middle of the day. He was definitely not getting a juice box! It was a tough lesson to learn but one that actually helped me a lot in the future. In fact, strangely enough, it would serve as the perfect precursor to lessons that I would learn time and time again in my future adventures in Hollywood. Nobody is who you build them up to be in your head.

Nobody.

It's impossible for that to happen because in your head they don't have flaws. In your head, they're not craving a cigarette so badly that they have to smoke one while dropping a deuce outside in the open at noon on a Sunday. I suppose if it was some form of *scatavism*, I could understand. But you would never imagine your heroes being human because then they couldn't be your heroes anymore, could they?

After that unfortunate Justin Credible incident, I didn't get sucked into the whole hero thing again until I was flipping through the channels one night. It was then that I stumbled upon a beautiful man with a captivating smile and an impish sense of humor. The show was *Moonlighting* and the man was Bruce Willis. *Holy shitolee!!* This guy was a home-fucking-run! I loved everything about him. His boyish charm drew me in so quickly I couldn't believe it. And then . . . the Seagram's wine cooler commercials. He can sing, too? I was smitten. Yes, for those of you too young to remember, Bruce Willis used to skip around, dance, and sing about wine coolers on the idiot box.

Growing up, if you had asked me, "Carrie, who is the perfect man?" I would have said Bruce Willis. The *Die Hard* star was my man crush Monday, Tuesday, Wednesday, Thursday, Friday, Saturday, Sunday, yesterday, holiday, every day. Basically, every word in the English language that ends in day. He seemed like a guy you could pop open a beer with and have a chill yet intelligent conversation about his blues album, *The Return of Bruno*. The wry humor, the smile, and yup, that full head of luscious brown hair all tickled my fancy. And the way he danced around on the porch, singing into his wine cooler bottle where a secret microphone had apparently been hidden . . . Wowsers!

> *"Seagram's, golden wine coolers*
> *Seagram's, golden wine coolers . . . "*

Fuck you if that doesn't get your panties dropping. Have you watched reruns of the show religiously? Have you studied his commercials obsessively? No? Then come back to me when you know what the fuck you're talking about! This guy was the TFP! (*Total Fucking Package!*)

Do you want to know why I thought he was the TFP? Because I liked everything he did. Everything! Let's just say, if I were forced at gunpoint by a German terrorist in a high-rise tower in LA to summarize my obsession with Bruce, and John McClane was *not* available to save me, I could do that in two simple words: *Hudson Hawk.*

I will give everyone a second to stop laughing before I keep going.

Known to almost all as one of the worst movies in the history of cinema—
"unspeakably awful," according to *Rolling Stone* magazine—*Hudson Hawk,* to me, was a comedic masterpiece, and perhaps the most under-rated film of the twentieth century. It has everything you want in an action film: comedy, singing, and slow, thought-provoking drama. I could have watched Bruce's standard-singing burglar every single day. I think I did for at least one year of my life. Not my problem that it was ahead of its time!

So imagine my delight when I found out that I was going to be in-terviewing Bruce "fucking" Willis for his movie *Tears of the Sun.* I nearly fell off my chair! And you can bet your ass I was going to be ready. In-side and out. Not that kind of inside—that sounds dirty. Almost imme-diately, I started fantasizing, like Walter Mitty, about all the brilliant questions I'd ask. I was going to dazzle him with my layered knowledge of his film and TV work. Then I'd surprise him by going old-school and cleverly bringing two wine coolers as our refreshments of choice. I'd then wow him with quotes from *Moonlighting* that even he wouldn't re-member. I was just so excited to meet the funniest, coolest, and most charming guy on the planet. I imagined I'd open by bringing up *Hudson Hawk,* he'd throw his head back, clasp his hands together, laugh heart-ily, and exclaim, "That's your favorite movie? You're a fuckin' whack job! I love it!"

Together, we'd sing the movie's signature song, "Side by Side," in perfect harmony. After we were done taping, Bruce would lean for-ward, grab my knee, and whisper, "You really get me like nobody else ever has. Wanna hang out after the junket's over and talk more about how awesome I am?" There was nothing that was going to ruin the greatest day of my life and the first day of my lifelong relationship with the "Captain Awesome" Mr. Walter Bruce Willis!

When the big day came, all signs pointed to doves and rainbows. I drove to the Ritz-Carlton in Pasadena on a gorgeous day with sunny blue skies. I made a special mix of standards for the ride and was sing-ing and smiling from ear to ear. At the hotel, as I waited my turn to meet Bruce, I had butterflies in my stomach, but they weren't the throw-up-and-have-diarrhea-simultaneously kind; they were the excited-and-I-think-I-might-pass-out kind.

As I prepared to head into Bruce's shooting suite, I overheard some-one in the hallway say the action film, a somewhat serious true story about a Navy SEAL's rescue mission in civil war–torn Nigeria, had been filmed in Hawaii. As I've mentioned before, just because a movie is somber doesn't mean the junket has to be. In fact, the actors, who lived in a dark place making the movie, sometimes look forward to lightening up during the press tour.

I called an audible at the last second. *Hudson Hawk* was out, and a very witty new opener related to Hawaii was in. Now, I've taken a million multiple-choice tests like every other Adderall-addicted student in America. Of course I've heard the adage, "Always go with your first choice."

I did not go with my first choice.

When I walked into the room, there Bruce was, in all his Brucieness. Tall, hairless, and handsome. He was everything I'd imagined, hoped, and dreamed. He was talking to a publicist, so I didn't get to do the customary handshake or have any pre-taping chitchat. I sat down in the chair across from him.

The room was a little cold and still, but I shook it off. Our chairs were unusually and awkwardly low, but I looked past that, too. When I glanced at his face for the first time, I thought I'd see the adorable smirk of David Addison from *Moonlighting*, but the vibe was more, say, Grumpy Cat. I shook it off.

I heard the cameraman say, "Speed," my cue to start.

OMG here we go!

"How are you?" I beamed.

Bruce smiled.

Okay, good start!

"All right, let's talk about this movie. It was shot in Hawaii—that's cool!"

"Yes, it was," he replied.

Perfect! My joke's setup is complete—now go in for the win!

"So did you get lei'd a lot?" I asked with a wink and a gun expression.

Bruce did not blink.

Bruce did not take his eyes off of me.

Bruce did not move.

Within two seconds, I knew I had made a terrible, terrible mistake. My face flushed like it was on fire.

Bruce did not say a word for what felt like a full seventeen years. We kept staring at each other.

A lone cameraman giggled to fill the void.

Then Bruce got up, his eyes still burning a hole right through me, turned, and walked out.

Oh, fuck. What did I just do????

Another excruciating three minutes passed. *Where is he? Is he coming back?* The embarrassment and humiliation was unbearable. *He didn't actually think I really asked him if he got laid l-a-i-d, did he? Everyone knows that joke, right? My DAD told me that joke! Everyone loves a dad joke! Maybe he has to pee? Indian food for lunch? Take a call? Please, God.* The room didn't move. The crew didn't move. I turned around, pleading with my eyes for someone to save me and put the oxygen back into the room.

I got nothing but dead air.

A publicist came in with a look on her face that fell somewhere between concern and shame.

"So, yeah, Carrie . . . this is over; you can come outside."

She did not smile. My heart sank to my toes.

Oh fuck oh fuck oh fuck oh fuck!!

I was having my first-ever panic attack.

She escorted me out of the room by my elbow, like one of those crazy delusional people everyone pities on an *American Idol* audition.

"I'm really sorry but you're not going to be finishing that interview, and you won't be getting those tapes," she said sweetly to me in the hallway. All I could feel was the rippling, crippling, and crushing implosion of my mind, body, and soul that could only come from the death of a dream delivered by the hand of someone I held dearest. My lifelong hero, the coolest guy in every room, and the man that could do no wrong, had just reduced me to a puddle of humiliation, self-doubt, and paranoia in less than twenty seconds and without saying a single word to me. I waited like a scolded five-year-old for her to excuse me from the rest of this junket and every other junket until the end of time. But she didn't. "Would you like to do the other rooms?" she asked.

I was practically catatonic. I wanted to burst into tears and run out of there sobbing, but I couldn't move. My dad has a nickname, Tony the Tiger, because anytime anyone asks him, "Hey, Tom, how you doing?" even if he's feeling shitty, he says, "I'm gr-r-reat!" I remember him telling me once, when I asked if he was really *always* great, "Nobody really wants to know if you're having a bad day." He always put up a positive front no matter what, and that has stuck with me in trying times.

"Gr-r-reat!" I must have told the publicist. I think. I'm not all that sure what the fuck came out of my mouth, but I apparently agreed to finish the other rooms. *Thanks for nothing, Dad!* Somehow, I did three more interviews with Bruce's costars, even though I'd just been kicked in the gut with steel-toed boots and could barely breathe. I do not remember a single one of them, or the ride home, for that matter. I just kept replaying that one sentence in my mind over and over again.

    Me: So you get lei'd a lot?
Bruce: *(Blank stare.)*
    Me: So you get lei'd a lot?
Bruce: *(Look of death.)*
    Me: So you get lei'd a lot?
           (My head explodes as he smiles at the scattered pieces dripping down the wall.)

I think it's safe to say I wasn't singing "Side by Side" out the car window on the way home.

I may have come away with all my limbs attached, but I was a thoroughly broken person after that day. I couldn't get past the humiliation of my complete misfire or the fact that I had somehow misjudged a moment so badly that it resulted in insulting my hero. Until that day I had prided myself on knowing how to read a room. And to top it off, the universe didn't show me any sympathy. I had to continue like it was business as usual, booking four or five junkets a week, as if nothing had happened. I had to walk into what now felt like a volatile situation and face the biggest celebrities in the world, knowing what I know now. That I suck!

If you watched the interviews I did right after Bruce, like Chris Rock in *Head of State* or Adam Sandler for *Anger Management*, I appeared fine on the outside, but inside I was a total mess. I would go into an interview paralyzed with fear. Like a baseball player who gets beaned in the head by a pitch and doesn't want to step foot in the batter's box again. My insecurity and self-doubt were causing me to turn in on myself. I'd walk into the office every day and be bombarded on all sides by *me*. The person I blamed for putting me in this shitty place. The person I hated for not being good enough. All the edit bays had my face on them. Ugh! All I could hear was my voice over and over, echoing throughout the building. *SHUT HER UP!* I couldn't get away from myself.

My brief encounter with Bruce Willis had completely shattered my confidence.

The Japanese say you have three faces. The first face, you show to the world. The second face, you show to your close friends and your family. The third face, you never show anyone. It is the truest reflection of who you are.

In the celebrity world, it's slightly different. The first face is the one that matters the most to them. It's the face they show to the world. The second face is reserved only for people who can help them get ahead in business and their family members. But by far the most interesting and disturbing is who gets to see their third face, the face that even psychotic serial killers elect to hide. That face is actually their day-to-day working face. The face everyone they work with or interact with professionally gets to see. I know: it's *nucking futs!!* Now, you may ask why a celebrity would choose to display the face most people in the world elect to hide? Well, the simple answer is, because they can. Everyone around them either works for them or needs something from them, and therefore will tolerate pretty much any kind of behavior. The sky's the limit. You've all heard the stories. Some are legendary. Most are true.

It's easy to lose yourself in an environment where morality is regarded as more of a mild suggestion than a requirement. There are some who are able to keep it together and maintain their sense of decency, but unfortunately, there are many who can't. They ultimately lose all connection with faces one and two, becoming entirely absorbed by face three. We've all seen it. Stars we love and admire who turn out to be intolerable douchebag divas. I've always felt that to survive celebrity intact, you can't keep your faces separated and be so calculated. You never know if you might wake up one morning and find yourself in a career-ending, couch-jumping spiral or in a J. Lo music video with your third face on display by accident. I think you need to bring all three of your faces together and take the best and worst of you and find a middle ground and try to be that person to everyone as best you can. You may find this shocking, but I believe the key to that is developing a sense of humor and humility by coming to terms with the *profane* side of yourself.

I believe profanity is paramount, profanity is important, profanity is truth, and profanity is reality. It is, in many ways, that which defines us all. I'm not talking about your run-of-the-mill cursing here. That's just one kind and it happens to be my favorite. No, I'm talking about the vulgarity, the blasphemy, and the sacrilege that fills all of our lives and completes the picture of who we really are and not who we pretend to be. I think it's critical to be in touch with the *profane* side of oneself and to acknowledge that every day our greatest challenge is to maintain inner balance. After all, the measure of who we are is built from the good and the bad, the yin and the yang. You've got to let the light and the dark mix; otherwise your life is a lie. That's why I never trust anyone who says they don't swear. I call bullshit!

Celebrity is intangible from its inception yet profound in its impact. The lucky few who are given the gift of harnessing its power have two roads they can take. They can use it to inspire new generations of people, demand social justice, create political change, or simply put a smile on the faces of their fans by making them feel special and appreciated when they run into them. Or they can piss in the face of humility, degrade the professionals they rely on for their careers, take a shit on the hearts and souls of their fans, and make sure that their riders are filled with insecure, self-aggrandizing horseshit like all-white rooms, no eye contact, and rose petals refilling the toilet after every bowel movement. All this so that some poor bastard making minimum wage might get fired because the rose petals weren't Brazilian long stems. Unfortunately, road number two has had a massive traffic jam for decades.

Whether any of us admit it or not, we are all heavily influenced by our perception of the famous even though we rarely get to actually know anything real about them. I know I am. In some ways, they are our society's living gods. There's a level of worship and accolade given to them that is rarely justified, and for the most part, with much help from reality TV, fame tends to shine its whitewashing spotlight on the very worst of humanity. Ultimately, we are primarily left with their life's work to help fill in all the blanks for a more accurate picture of who they really were. Problem is, defining a person's character based solely on the gravity or artistic value of their body of work tends to eliminate their *profane* side. We are then left with only a shadow of who they were as opposed to a portrait of who they are. Which is a shame because, sometimes, it's okay to learn the truth about our famous figures. We're all human, after all. We make mistakes and we grow. In some ways it would make them more relatable. But sometimes, no matter how great their contribution, some people deserve to be forgotten.

The good news is times have changed. The Internet and social media have made it virtually impossible to hide the truth. *Generation Now* is hungry for information, short on sentimentality, and couldn't give a fuck about your legacy. It's not enough to be a great actor and director if you're an anti-Semite, racist, and a bigot. It's not enough to be a racial barrier–breaking trailblazer and one of the greatest comedians of all time if you're a serial rapist. It's not enough to be one of the most recognized television personalities of the last forty years if you're a pedophile. You can fill in the blanks. Don't get me wrong, things are nowhere near perfect and there are plenty of idiots who still use their fame to evade justice, but as Fox Mulder would say on *The X-Files,* "The truth is out there," and it's just a Google search away.

Here's what I didn't know about Bruce before he walked into the room. It might not have helped that just weeks before I interviewed him, Demi was rumored to be dating *cocksure* new action hero Colin Farrell. Basically, the new (much younger) Bruce Willis. With a full head of luscious brown locks.

Also, Bruce's own director on *Tears of the Sun,* Antoine Fuqua, had publicly called him "a pain in the ass" to work with. Nobody ever snitches on each other in showbiz; the business is too small and nobody wants to burn a bridge. Unless the person is an absolute monster, and even then it's tempered. "Pain in the ass" was likely an understatement. That's why we rarely know what a star's real personality is like. Though sometimes it rears its ugly head organically. Take Christian Bale and that now-infamous audio leak. In my mind, Christian is unquestionably one of the best actors of our time and absolutely one of my favorites. I mean, if you weren't mesmerized by his disturbingly sexy performance as serial killer Patrick Bateman in *American Psycho,* then I think we've now identified the huge void in your life that makes you feel like you're always the dull one in the room. Fix it!

The first time I ever interviewed Christian was for a small film nobody's ever heard of. On a half-assed, makeshift red carpet on which three of the six journalists covering were photographers.

I innocently asked him, "What made you want to be in a small indie film like this?"

To which he sneeringly responded, "First of all, I don't appreciate you calling it a small indie film!"

All righty then! (In my best Ace Ventura.) I instantly knew I had had enough. Every time I interviewed Christian after that, he always came across as surly and took himself way too seriously. Of course, nobody ever made issue of what an unpleasant interview he was because we all just hid it under the all-encompassing veil of "method acting." So when someone on the set of *Terminator Salvation* leaked an embarrassing, expletive-laden audiotape of him going ballistic on a crew member, I couldn't help but smile. I guess we all have lessons to learn. By the time *The Fighter* came out, it was clear to me that a brilliant and smart publicist who wasn't afraid to speak her mind must have told him, "If you want an Oscar, you need to play nice." And surely enough, at that junket, everyone walked out of the room going, "Who the fuck is that guy?" Christian was friendly, smiling, and sweet, and gave all of us press everything we wanted. And guess what? He won the Oscar. Funny how that works, isn't it? And he's remained cool ever since. He's actually fun to talk to now. Whether it's an act or real, it doesn't matter because it shows respect and appreciation, and that's more than enough. His *profane/dark* side is what makes him good at what he does, and I am down with that. But his ability to control it is what makes him someone worth rooting for again.

Some people in this business just take themselves too seriously and lose sight of the fact that it's called entertainment because that's what it's supposed to be. Bitching about it makes about as much sense as dedicating your entire life to working in the underground *Brazilian fart porn* industry only to complain every single day about all the excessive flatulence you're being exposed to. What part of *Brazilian fart porn* did you not understand?

But most of the time, nobody knows when an actor or actress is a *turd sandwich* in real life because of this veil of secrecy. Let's face it, the Mafia's got nothing on showbiz when it comes to keeping secrets. I'll give you two blind examples (call me a coward or someone who isn't quite ready to throw in the towel on their career): this award-winning actor, considered by many to be one of the most beloved actors of our time, is super saccharine on camera but an absolute monster behind the scenes who berates and humiliates those around him as soon as the cameras stop rolling. Another huge female star of beloved romantic comedies has a reputation for hating women with a vengeance. No, it's not Katherine Heigl. She's always been sweet to me. In fact, here's a side of Katherine Heigl you may have never seen before in a press interview. Boisterous, bawdy, and beaming with joy, she'll flip the switch and make a believer out of you. I was excited about her hilariously dirty film *The Ugly Truth* and had some important questions. Lucky for me, she had all the answers:

Katherine: I know that was fun; we get to say COCK! They kind of forgot how far we went.

Me: Blowjobs always first?

Katherine: Blowjobs trump everything else!

Me: As they kind of should . . . I mean really.

Katherine: I guess.

Me: Quick and dirty. *(slapping hands.)*

Katherine: I know. Right!! *(With a huge smile on her face, about to laugh.)* Oh, god . . . starting to blush a little.

Me: Anal sex is jah . . . you know, I don't know, I think I'm gonna put that last. I'm gonna keep that one . . . cause lingerie . . .

Katherine: I think you can have your delusions, if you want them. But you're gonna have to go out there and take one for the team. *(Laughing out loud.)* Find out! Find out the truth!

Me: It'll be a pain in the ass. *(After which I flash a big smile.)*

Katherine: *(Just leans forward and starts laughing hysterically.)* NICE!! NICE!!

Me: I feel like I can help. *(Laughing.)*

Katherine: *(Really enjoying this moment.)* That's really fuckin' clever!

Then I just had to ask about the over-the-top orgasm scene. I mean come on . . . if not me, then who? If not now, then when?

Me: Tell me about um . . . you know . . . sort of getting off in this film . . . on this film. You did . . . quite well. *(Katherine starts to chuckle.)* I was very impressed.

Katherine: It was a long day. Let me tell you. They were fake, but even if they were real, you wouldn't wanna orgasm that many times in one day. You may think it would be awesome; I don't think so.

Fuckin' see this movie . . . that's fuckin' not fuck but you know, you get it!

I've never understood "historically" *douchey* actors and actresses. The ones who act like the press and fans are a nuisance and claim all they care about is "the work." Uh, excuse me, but without fans and the press, there is no work. And if you don't want any of the hoopla that comes along with being on TV or in movies, I'm pretty sure there are some community theater companies and public-access TV stations, all around the country, who would love to have you perform on their stages. Hell, you could even get involved with the bake sale after the show!

I have an idea. Since you've made it this far into the book, I think it's safe to assume that we're now friends. So, just between us, I'm going to tell you a little secret. I'm going to reveal two ways that you, sitting at home, can tell exactly who the divas are while you're watching your favorite talk show. First, look for what is commonly referred to as the *"one-reply bitches."* For the unfamiliar, *ORBs* those are celebrities that answer questions with one or two words or a short useless sound bite. I bet you already have a list in your head of potential candidates. Second, look for those who appear to be suffering from what is universally known as *"post-fartum depression."* This is, essentially, the projection of an overall sense of disappointment or anger that the world is not recognizing your fart with the level of enthusiasm you feel it deserved. *PFD* is very easy to spot and tends to reveal itself in either a facial expression, body language, or both. Please feel free to speculate, and tweet or Instagram me using the hashtags *#OneReplyBitches* and *#PostFartumDepression*. It'll be our little inside joke.

Anyway, it truly is ridiculous how lucky those of us who actually get to work in this business are. Especially considering what other people have to do to make a living in this country. I couldn't fathom the idea of walking around treating people like I'm trying to win a game of *Asshole Bingo*. It's too much work. I had heard about prima donnas ruining interviews, but I always thought that my carefree approach would cut right through that shit.

Nope! *Douchebag* trumps *friendly* almost every time.

I don't mean to burst any bubbles here, but there are more than a few celebrities that try to shove their false sense of entitlement and abject misery down the throats of relatively harmless junketeers. Because why be satisfied with having your ass kissed all day in four-minute increments when you can have these powerless people wear it as a *hat*, too? One guy I have no problem calling out is Tommy Lee Jones. Alas, this is not much of a revelation. He's done such a masterful job of alienating so many people that there have been many articles written about what an insufferable bore he is. He used to get off on scaring people (he's done it to me twice). I heard he's flipped over tables and refused to be interviewed based on what a journalist was wearing. I've seen so many people run out of his interview room in tears, and yet in the public eye, he's respected and revered as a serious ac-TOR. Where he gets the energy and why he ever felt the need to do this is beyond me.

I mean for fuck's sake! It's just a movie we're there to promote, right? Not the reemergence of the black plague! We, the press, all show up to celebrate these films. Whether they are great or horrendous, we extend you the courtesy of pretending that each one is a *celluloid miracle*. Then we enthusiastically come to you like eager little children desperate to be acknowledged. We then graciously listen to you pontificate about the backbreaking and laborious nature of acting in a movie. We wholeheartedly empathize with your poetically Shakespearean reflections on the emotional razor's edge that your artistry demands of you to walk on, in every performance. Never once bringing up the fact that all this pseudo-philosophical rhetoric seems pretty heavy-handed for a Steven Seagal film. We let it go. That's right, Tommy—we even let THAT go. So, perhaps, the very least you can do is to chill the fuck out and display a modicum of human decency, a breath of humility, or even an *ass-hair* of graciousness! And I'm not just talking to Tommy. You all know who you are, *A-listers Gone Wild*. Swallow your pride occasionally; I've heard it's not fattening.

But in the case of "The Press vs. T. L. Jones," all his ridiculous theatrics, rude behavior, and general contempt toward the press have made them turn on him. For the huge blockbusters he appears in, a lack of press support is of marginal importance, but on personal passion projects and small movies he's directed, where press support is essential . . . it's a room full of crickets. Nobody cares. The press finally figured out that interviewing Tommy Lee Jones is like fucking a toaster! You go in all wide-eyed and curious. Inevitably, you get trapped and scared. The only way out is to use your tears as lubrication. And as sexy as that sounds, I think you'd agree that it's just a little too much look! We'll pass. What goes around, Mr. Jones . . .

Nobody warned me about Bruce Willis before I went in, and nobody apologized for his behavior after. They just left me standing there *shit-struck!* So I was stuck in a vacuum of self-loathing. All I kept thinking was that I sucked at my job and I shouldn't be doing it. I had insulted my idol by making a stupid joke, by being myself, and in the snap of a finger, everything derailed. I wasn't good enough. A month after Bruce walked out on me, the whole Tony the Tiger mentality was out the fucking window. I couldn't hold in all the pain and feelings of worthlessness anymore.

Insecurity is a silent and invisible monster. A lurking shadow mocking you at every turn. A crime of opportunity patiently waiting for its next victim. It creeps into your mind the instant your guard is down: while you're sitting at a traffic light staring into the distance, ignoring its routinely changing colors punctuated by the rising cacophony of car horns. It slithers down into your heart the second the tears begin to well up in your eyes: when you're at work alone at your desk picking yourself apart as you force yourself to watch your own interviews to make sure you've made a mental note of every flaw. It permeates your soul at the break of dawn after you've lain in bed awake all night, numb to the sore and swollen aftermath of convulsing lament. I was suffocating with inadequacy while I choked on the fumes of a career that was burning down around me. Powerless against its grip, alone and isolated, I gently began to fade. I was emotionally compromised and on the verge of a mental breakdown. It was not a question of if, it was a question of when, and sure enough, the timing didn't disappoint.

I had to cover the junket for the mockumentary *A Mighty Wind*, a synonym for a fart. Should have been a piece of cake for me, right? As Kourosh drove me to the interview at the Four Seasons in Beverly Hills, we started going over my questions, and I went to an uh-oh Spaghet-tiOs place in my head.

We'd heard that writer/director Christopher Guest could be on the unfriendly side and a bit more than intimidating. And that you had to be on your A-game to keep up with his cast of genius improv actors, like Eugene Levy, Michael McKean, and Harry Shearer. *These people are too fucking good at what they do*, I thought. *And they take what they do very seriously. They're going to eat me alive.*

Suddenly, I couldn't breathe. The pressure of failing again was more than I could handle.

"Stop the car!" I screamed. "I'm not going!"

Kourosh looked at me like I had two heads, and I proceeded to have a nuclear meltdown that was, on a scale of one to ten—Chernobyl.

"You cannot make me do this!" I shrieked at the top of my lungs. "I can't do it! I just can't!"

I was crying uglier than Rose Byrne in *Bridesmaids*—I'd now graduated to rejected *Bachelor* contestant—and punching the car window with my elbow. Makeup, spit, and snot rolled down my face. It wasn't exactly a good look. There was no way I could be on camera, but we had to show up. Kourosh—unshaven, in sweats and a T-shirt—left me in the car, walked into the hotel, and did the interviews.

I was done. I didn't want to do this anymore. I didn't want to be in front of the camera or the stars. After that breakdown, I stopped doing interviews completely. I stayed in the dark edit bay and out of sight. Kourosh would periodically come and gently ask me if I was ready to come back. I'd say nope. I was happy being an editor holed up in a dark room all by myself.

I'd never been a quitter—except for one time in my life. When I was eleven, I took gymnastics classes. I really loved gymnastics. One day after practice where I was learning how to do a backflip off of the uneven bars, my mom came by to pick me up to go to my dad's birthday party. I was super tired from the umpteen times I'd practiced this flip but so excited to show her my new skill so we could tell Dad what I did. I got up on the bars, swung myself to a standing position on the lower bar, and did a glorious backflip. While I was in the air I felt my body contort from exhaustion, but I couldn't correct it in time to stick the landing. My feet slipped on the mat. One leg jackknifed and an arm waved about as I tried to catch myself before my ass kissed the ground. I broke my wrist in two places.

We spent the next several hours in the emergency room, and my dad missed his own birthday party. Not only was I a terrible gymnast, but I was a terrible daughter. I felt so guilty and defeated. Do you think I wanted to try another backflip ever again? Nope. After that, I hated gymnastics. I couldn't even watch the Olympics without having flashbacks. Then, in 1996, that little fireplug Kerri Strug showed me the light. On her first attempt on the vault, she fell and hurt her ankle. Did she give up? Hell no! She limped down the runway then stuck the landing on her second vault on one leg, ensuring a gold medal for the United States and the cover of the Wheaties box. I bet her dad was proud.

Listen, I still never did another backflip off the bars ever again in my life, and I don't intend to in the future. But that's *my* choice. I'm the decider. Bruce Willis doesn't get to make any decisions about my life.

After months of hiding out in my cave, eating Doritos and ice cream and watching zit-popping videos on YouTube, I was sick of feeling sorry for myself. And to be honest, I was sick to my stomach! I intimated to Kourosh that I longed for the good ol' days of cussing it up with everybody. If this was a movie, you'd now see a montage of me studying *The Big Black Book of Very Dirty Words*, drinking raw eggs, and running up hotel front steps like Rocky Balboa. But it isn't a movie; it's a book. So you'll just have to picture it in your head. For the record, I've asked Sly about the raw egg thing. He says it's gross.

Kourosh knew that to be eased back in, I'd need to interview someone sweet and warm, the equivalent of a mug of hot chocolate. So he booked me on *The Rundown* junket, which starred Dwayne "The Rock" Johnson. Before I left he gave me a pep talk.

"Carrie, none of this matters," he said. "We are masters of our own destiny."

It was so true. In my heart it mattered, but it didn't matter to the point where I was going to drive myself crazy. I needed to find the right balance—how the fuck do you not give a fuck and give all the fucks at the same time? It's the key to life. This was our business; we were the bosses. We weren't chasing a sound bite or a breaking news headline; we were chasing a magical moment that may or may not happen. I just needed to go into these interviews, have a good time, and come out alive. Over the years, that would be the only advice that would snap me back from the edge.

"This is *fun*," Kourosh would tell me. "When it stops being fun, we're done."

Fun was the key word. This whole business is supposed to be an exercise in fun. It's privileged people with privileged lives doing privileged things that most of us can only dream of. There is no reason why any of us shouldn't be spreading joy, laughing, and thanking our lucky stars for each day in this business. The ones that take themselves too seriously and behave like its God's work or they're curing cancer ruin it for all of us and could use a harsh lesson in humility. We're not doing God's work or curing cancer. And neither are Bruce *"Look Who's Talking"* Willis and Tommy Lee *"Black Moon Rising"* Jones.

Remember my high school boyfriend, Pete, from Chapter 3? He actually had cancer. That was a serious situation that definitely deserved gravity. Let me share with you what that looks and feels like. It's a memory I hang on to to remind me to remember what's actually important.

I remember pulling up his dressing gown for the first time after his surgery. I asked if I could kiss his boo-boos. He reluctantly said yes. As I lifted it, I saw thirty-seven staples right down the center of his body, from his sternum to just above his pubic hair. I counted them. Inspected them. I was fascinated by how they went in, how symmetrical they were, and how they went around his belly button. I loved Pete so much I wanted to know every part of him. He was freaked out at me seeing his incision. I think he was freaked out about sharing most of this whole process with me. He could barely process it himself.

The day he lost his hair was the day I was going to ask him to prom. I went over to his house. He was in the shower, so I turned on *Star Trek: The Next Generation* and started making us my customary grilled cheese sandwiches. He didn't come out. I knocked on the door. No answer.

"You okay?" I called to him.

I could hear the water running so I got a little concerned that maybe he'd fallen or passed out and couldn't answer. I knocked again, and when it was still silent, I just barged in, expecting to see him face-down in a tub of water. Instead, through the steam, I could see him standing in the shower, staring down at his hands, which were filled with clumps of his beautiful long brown locks.

My eyes stung with tears. I quickly grabbed a towel off the rack and dabbed at them. I didn't want him to see me crying. I approached him, patted him down softly with the towel, then wrapped him up. He put his hair in the sink and we stared at it. I went back into the kitchen to give him some space. I remember him standing in front of the mirror for quite a while. A little later, I could hear him gagging, again, while he was brushing his teeth. They were all terrible side effects of the chemo.

When Pete finally came out of the bathroom, his waist was wrapped in the towel I'd given him, and his head was wrapped in the white T-shirt he had been wearing before his shower. He didn't speak. He just sat down on the couch next to me and ate his grilled cheese with mustard hearts. I felt helpless. There was poison coursing through his body. I found one of those containers you use for a make-your-own-salad at the grocery store, went back into the bathroom, and put the pile of hair inside of it. I don't know why; it just felt like it was the right thing to do, in case he wanted to mourn the loss later, or something.

I didn't ask him to go to prom with me that day, but after much convincing by his friends and family, he ultimately agreed to be seen in public with no hair. We did our best to make it count. We wrapped his head in a black silk scarf, and I had a dress made. I remember taking pictures outside his house before driving away in our rented limo for his one evening away from the misery. I can still see the smiles on his mom's and sister's faces.

I'm only telling you this story because it gave me perspective. I take what I do very seriously, but nothing we do is cancer-serious. We are entertaining people, hopefully dulling their pain from time to time, putting a smile on their faces, and making them forget their shitty days.

The Rock understood that; bless his big heart under those big pecs. He's a wonderful human being, so funny and charming. Everything I hoped Bruce Willis would be. The Rock made it so easy for me to get back in the saddle. We got along so well; he infused me with energy and confidence again. It was like, "Oh yeah, this is a blast. I can do this."

Slowly, I eased back into it, with Kourosh taking on any interview that had the potential to go sideways to protect me. But Bruce the *buzz-kill* kept popping up because it seemed he had a movie coming out every time a bear shit in the woods.

We got offered *The Whole Ten Yards* junket.

"No fucking way," I told Kourosh.

We were asked to cover *Hostage*.

"No fucking way," I told Kourosh.

Bruce kept releasing movies, Kourosh kept asking me to interview him again, and I kept turning him down. Until finally, nearly three years after the original fiasco, Kourosh had had enough. Bruce was releasing *16 Blocks* with rapper Mos Def, the junket was in New York City, and he didn't ask me if I was going; he told me I was going.

"Fuck you, no," I said.

"Fuck you, yes," Kourosh said. "You are doing this."

It wasn't like I was a depressed disaster anymore, but we both knew that I'd never have Bruce out of my system until I saw him again. He'd been orbiting around me for years, and my hatred for him had festered like a puss-filled zit that needed to be popped. Like the ones I'd studied on YouTube during my downtime. Sorry, that was a really gross image but so necessary to move this story forward.

"This is the therapy you need," Kourosh added. "You need to get back in the room and face your fear. And you're going to realize it's not as big a deal as you think it is because you left it in your head for so long."

"Fine! I'll do it."

The NYC junket couldn't have been more opposite from the California junket. Pasadena was lush and beautiful; the opulent Ritz was like a castle. Manhattan was cold and dreary; the rooms at the Regency on Park Avenue were small dark little boxes. My frame of mind was 180 degrees, too. I was so happy to be there last time and so *not* happy to be there this time. I tried very hard not to have a massive panic attack in the elevator on the way up. The only way I could wrap my head around going in was I knew I didn't even have to be good. I just had to get through it.

After so many years had passed, Bruce would forgive me for the "get lei'd" comment, right? I mean, he couldn't possibly be mean to me again . . . could he?

When I walked into the room, Bruce was slouched down in his chair and had a baseball cap pulled down low over his eyes. He didn't acknowledge me, shake my hand, or get up and walk out, nada. He had no fucking idea who I was. I meant absolutely nothing to this guy, but I had let him destroy my life.

With his very best *resting asshole face* on full display, it was very obvious Bruce didn't want to be there. Great, neither did I. Finally something in common to talk about! If I had the balls I have now, I would've made the exact same joke as last time about getting lei'd. But the truth was I was scared shitless. All I wanted to do was get out of there without my head exploding. I also needed to confirm that whole "It's not me, it's you" thing.

Thankfully, I received that confirmation. Though I was a professional and suppressed every ounce of my desire to be passive-aggressive, he mumbled incoherently (or, maybe, intentionally. Who knows?) through the entire interview. I don't even know what I talked to him about, and I'm not going to bother looking it up. It's irrelevant. What matters is that I made it through my four minutes, and a huge weight was lifted off my shoulders.

So to answer my own question, yes, he could be mean again.

But I don't regret going back at all. It was the best thing I ever did. I realized that nothing I could have said or done then or now would have made a difference. All that time stressing and questioning myself afterward was such a waste. Sometimes you win and sometimes you don't. As Mark Knopfler once said, "Sometimes you're the windshield; sometimes you're the bug." Everybody has that "I carried a watermelon" moment. You know, remember the scene in *Dirty Dancing* when Baby met Johnny Castle for the first time at the staff party?

Johnny: Yo, cuz, what's she doing here?

  Billy: She came with me. She's with me.

  Baby: I carried a watermelon.

Johnny: *(He glares at her then literally shimmies away.)*

Like, why did I just say that out loud? I'm an idiot! Baby didn't hold on to that though. She got over it quickly and ended up *schtupping* Johnny. They'd say *schtupping* in the Catskills for sure.

I was never going to *schtup* Bruce Willis for sure. My biggest regret was letting him have such a profound and prolonged effect on me. Hell, I almost quit and walked away from my career for fuck's sake! Would I have been fine if I had just thrown in the towel and done something else with my life? Of course. But I chose to take the harder road—faced my fear—and I became better for it.

Every scar has a story; every broken bone makes you stronger. The best thing about Bruce throwing me shade was that it strengthened my game. Now when I walk into a room, I'm hypersensitive to the vibe and react accordingly. My gut told me the first time that something was off, and yet, I still asked him that question. Nowadays, I don't think about Bruce Willis when I walk into a room anymore, but don't think, for a second, that he's not three thoughts behind. There's always the possibility that it could happen again. True, I'll never react to it the same way I did, but there is little doubt in my mind that someone I admire could pants me again. It's an unsettling feeling, but I've learned to live with it.

But you know, this dude has been mean to *so many*. He's been leaving *shit tickets* everywhere, all over town, throughout his career. I shouldn't have taken it so personally, but that's really hard to do. You have to be an extremely evolved human being. I'm not there yet. I remember watching the weirdness in action during Kourosh's interview with Bruce and Matthew Perry, who were paired together, at *The Whole Ten Yards* junket. There's an uncomfortable competitive thing happening in the room between the two of them, and you could clearly see that Matthew was literally rolling his eyes in frustration throughout the interview and looking like he wanted to choke Bruce out. It was unusual to see a celebrity lose their cool like that, but I guess being trapped in a room with Bruce Willis for an entire day will send you to the nuthouse.

Over the next few years other celebs started going public with their traumatizing interactions, and I felt part of a not-so-special club who'd been bullied by Bruce and survived. By far my favorite confessional was Kevin Smith's, who directed him in *Cop Out*. He described the experience as "soul crushing" and Bruce as "the unhappiest, most bitter, and meanest emo-bitch I've ever met at any job I've held down. And mind you, I've worked at Domino's Pizza." If you haven't seen Kevin's twenty-to-thirty-minute play-by-play decimation of Bruce Willis during one of his TV specials, you're missing out. A poetic, passionate, and detailed *colonic* delivered with the force of a fire hose. A master class on the art of celebrity master-cleanse. Even Sylvester Stallone, one of the genuinely nicest A-listers I've had the pleasure of getting to know, called out Bruce for being "lazy" and "greedy" on Twitter, kicked him off *The Expendables 3*, and replaced him with Harrison Ford. Bruce was even made fun of on *Dancing with the Stars*, the most saccharine show there is, for being a cranky sourpuss while watching his daughter Rumer perform. The dancers imitated the scowl on his face on camera.

People who are assholes are one thing. It's inexcusable, and to me, there's nothing funny about it. But the people who take themselves so seriously and in a manner that is so over the top that it borders on insanity, are tragically hilarious. I'm talking to you, Eddie Murphy. There's not a single laugh today that doesn't somehow originate from one of your jokes or bits from back in the day, and yet, I haven't seen you break a smile in over twenty years. If you can have the life and career that you've had and end up looking as miserable as you do, then what fucking hope is there for the rest of us? What the hell happened? Please say alien abduction. It has to be alien abduction. Just fucking say it! I need to hear it, Eddie!

I know! I digress.

So, somehow, after winning the social lottery of life and being given the gift of worldwide fame and untold riches, my man Bruce, in his infinite wisdom, decided to dedicate his life to becoming that guy at the gym who has his spray tan set to Snooki, wears half-shirts, and is in a constant state of flex? The kind of guy who probably looks at his sphincter with a hand mirror every day just to make sure it's not getting flabby. *Good on ya, mate!*

Alas, I will never see that scowl again in this lifetime (unless Kourosh and I finish our documentary *Searching for Bruce Willis's Sense of Humor* and enter it at Sundance). I refuse to interview Bruce anymore. I don't want to, I don't have to, and I don't need to. When *Live Free or Die Hard* came out, I interviewed his costar Justin Long and simply added in snippets from a stock interview with Bruce provided by the studio. Anyway, it all worked out perfectly for us on that movie thanks to the ever reliable and always fucking hilarious Justin Long:

Justin: He does say "Yippee-ki-yay motherfucker" in the movie. He does say it, and it's the weirdest situation. It's actually while he's inside me.

Bruce: All the stunts are done manually.

Justin: I can't believe Fox went there with that. I think after the success of *Brokeback Mountain* it's going to be a little bit easier for people to be able to handle this kind of subject matter.

Then we showed a montage of slow-mo clips of Justin and Bruce staring into each other's eyes and touching each other, to the *Brokeback Mountain* soundtrack.

Me: Was he slapping your ass while it was going down?

Justin: That's really something that . . . I'm not sure what cut they left in. If it was the one where I had the ball gag in and he was slapping me . . .

Bruce: Hard core . . .

Justin: Or if it was the one that he just had the riding crop and he was wearing the ball gag. We did a couple different . . . for the censors, you know, we did a couple different variations. So I'm not sure what they're going to leave in.

Bruce: We did it. I wouldn't say it if it weren't true.

Me: Now when a cop comes knocking at your door, and he doesn't
have a badge on . . .

Justin: A vag on?

Me: A BADGE. Are there things you shouldn't say to him? That you
might get arrested for?

Justin: Like, "Fuck you, bald prick"?

Exactly!

I owe you one, Justin!

We all have our Bruce Willises to overcome. I know I learned a lot
from mine. It cost me a great deal of heartache, and I wish I knew then
what I know now, but I guess I needed to slay this dragon and learn to
trust myself. So my advice to all you future Don Quixotes is to go forth
and let your heroes fall because those windmills ain't gonna slay themselves. Endure the pain and persevere, but don't spend too much energy
worrying about the *lobotomized fuckwits* of your world. When it's all said
and done, they're not worth it. It's like giving a snowman a blowjob. All
that's waiting for you on the other end is a brain freeze!

16

GEEKGASMS AND THE INFINITE PRECLAPULATION

**Happiness is when what you think,
what you say, and what you do are in harmony.**
—*Mahatma Gandhi*

Anyone under the impression that their religious friends aren't enjoying their lives as much as you are, I urge you to acquaint yourself with *"saddlebacking."* It's the *dernier cri* amongst Christian teenagers. It empowers them to maintain their "virginity" while competing for the title of *"Anal Queen"* of their junior high or high school. Because, let's face it, Homecoming Queen is so passé! Gospel-sanctioned and no pesky condoms. Damn! Talk about a religious experience. No doubt you're asking yourself the same question I am: How the fuck is it possible that they're having more fun than me, and who is this *"Theocratic Zoolander"* that's guiding the devout these days? I need him in *mah* life! Clearly, the Church's centuries-long (aka *shlong*) obsession with what's going on in our pants has led to what can only be described as "sexually ridiculous behavior." Remember the good ol' days when the only thing kids had to worry about were *knock-around nuns* and *pervy priests*? Now we have "butt-stuff for Christ!" Hey, it's somebody's happy place!

Being happy. Two words that can cause a lifetime of anxiety and disappointment or, for those who find it, total and utter . . . bliss. The truth is, finding a happy place just might be the greatest journey of our lives. A place to color outside the lines without admonishment. A place where interpretive dance need not meet the definition of interpretive nor dance. A place where the drugs you take have only one side effect . . . **hope.** I've always believed that until you find the happiness within you, you'll never be able to unlock the potential within you. Knowing how to be happy can be the difference between a life that feels like a consistent daily never-ending full-body orgasm or a life that feels like a nonstop *cinnamon challenge* where every day you're forced to eat a spoonful of ground cinnamon in sixty seconds with no water. Hence, the difference between a life of relentless shakes, delightful quivers, and moans of ecstasy, or gagging, coughing, and vomiting. No doubt about it, the stakes are high and the results range from the dangerous to the bizarre to the incredible to the unexpected. As you can see, finding a happy place is a tricky son of a bitch.

"Tits, balls, ass, and I fuckin' love it! It's fucking great!"

—*Jason Momoa*

I've been really lucky in my life. I've found more than my share of joy. I would have to say that my happiest place is when I'm playing with my nieces, Kira (*my monkey butt*), Piper (*my mini-me*), Alexis (*my chicken*), and Scarlett (*my little supermodel*), and my nephews, Rhys (*my Reese's Pieces*) and Kian (*my Special K*). One little smile, one great big giggle, and the inevitable *Dutch oven* and I'm ten years old again. When people use that expression "to your heart's delight," I'm pretty sure what they mean is the feeling you get when you're playing with kids.

But for you to understand my other happy place, you need to appreciate the two different sides to me that I enjoy cultivating. One is working hard to be a *badass chick*, 'cause that's the only way for a girl to find her true self in a business that doesn't always want her to. And the second is to keep my inner dork alive and fulfilled because I wouldn't have it any other way. You see, I'm a card-carrying geek, and my life is just one crazy fucked-up awesome twisted hell of a *geeksploitation* movie. It's filled with lots of action, heaps of comedy, a fair amount of thoughtful dialogue involving gaseous anomalies, a smattering of male and female full frontal nudity, and of course, stars yours truly as Power Girl! You have to experience it with the wild abandon that I do and rest assured that my happy place is just as powerful as our churchgoing friends, but admittedly, it has a lot less anal sex!

It's never really been a choice for me. Because when I was a child, I was rescued by members of the Rebel Alliance who revealed to me that my true identity was that of a galactic princess named Leia. This, of course, was quite a shock, but somehow it all made sense once Luke Skywalker, disguised as my cousin, and Han Solo, disguised as my brother Lucas Sean, explained to me how they had infiltrated the *Death Star*, cunningly made to look like my bedroom, in order to rescue me from my prison. And so they did . . . breaking a window, a table, two chairs, and a support beam in the process. They were so brave. Once Sean and Lucas had discovered *Star Wars*, it was *Star Wars* for the rest of our lives. Well . . . at least, until I got older and discovered *Star Trek*.

So you want to know what I could talk about for hours, bursting with joy, like our church-going friends? *Star Trek: The Next Generation*, season 6, episode 4, entitled "Relics." For those of you who don't remember, it's the Scotty episode, as played by James Doohan. Anyway, in the final scene, the *Enterprise* with Picard and crew is trapped inside a Dyson sphere (an artificial biosphere surrounding a star). Scotty and Geordi are on board Scotty's ship the *Jenolan*. They've wedged themselves into the gateway of the Dyson sphere and are blocking it from closing using their ship with the shields activated, waiting on the *Enterprise* to make a run for it and escape. As the *Enterprise* makes its getaway flying through the opening, they beam up Scotty and Geordi right before their ship buckles and blows up. You see the problem, of course? How the fuck did they beam these guys out with the shields up? I mean, what were they thinking? That we, the same people that own the blueprints to every ship in Star Fleet and carry a pocket Klingon-to-English translator so we can enjoy Shakespeare in the original Klingon would not catch this HUGE contradiction? Do they consider us *"nuch qoH je"*? When we are *"SuvwI' yoH"*!! No! I don't think so! That would be patently absurd.

Nevertheless, it has been the subject of great discourse over the years between me, my friends, and complete strangers who work on other starships in the same quadrant. Naturally, as any loyal fan would, I have an incurable desire to resolve these inconsistencies because one of the simple pleasures of this world is to use your innate knowledge to problem-solve for the greater good of mankind and because my intergalactic A.D.D. demands it—it's the Advanced Directive for Dimensionalization. I'm sure you've heard of it. So, to that end, we postulate theories that could provide the explanation. Some of the more flawed hypotheses from my colleagues are: "Oh, the ship was blowing up and the beam-out coincided with that final moment as the shields fell," or "The *Enterprise* matched the frequency of the shield and beamed them through it," or "The registry of the ship was NCC2010, so it was a super-old ship, making the ship faulty." Well, to that I cry, "Bullshit!"

Let's be real! The only plausible explanation is that Scotty must have diverted shield strength to the port and starboard, where the force of the pressure from the closing gate was greatest, leaving the minimum shield requirement at the bow, thereby facilitating their escape. Yet, even though I have clearly put this subject to rest, my friends and I have been arguing about it for years. I've been meaning to bring it up with my friend Brannon Braga, one of the executive producers and writers from the show, each time I see him, but he and I still need to work through the whole Captain Kirk death scene in *Star Trek Generations,* which he co-wrote. But I'm still not emotionally ready for that. It's only been twenty-two years and you can't rush these things. Despite the intensity of these frequent debates, to quote Loverboy, I assure you, my friends and I were "lovin' every minute of it!"

That's where it all begins. A conversation about the impossible in the company of the improbable. A powerful connection between people from all walks of life, with disparate beliefs, religions, and sexual persuasions, all finding each other on a road heading in the same direction. All around you the loners, the disenfranchised, the weirdos, the oddballs, the socially awkward, the sexually ambivalent, the technical poets, the toy scientists, the unexpected artists, and everyone else who didn't fit a mold and couldn't find a place to belong . . . finding each other. Our destination? A brand-new world of our own intelligent design. No judgement, no violence, and no hate, where we all stand separate but equal. It's kept me company most of my life and provided a safe haven to reignite my faith when I needed it the most.

It's a place that previously only existed in a land far, far away, beyond the endless reaches of your imagination. A world where differences are celebrated and creativity encouraged, with a civilization so advanced that their mental and physical powers have been developed to the peak of perfection. A world where communication and censorship are mutually exclusive. A world where a warped mind is a terrible thing to waste. A magical place that always restores your faith in humanity and in all that is good in the world of entertainment. A place where your state of mind is constantly aroused and on the verge of climax. Don't take my word for it. Take the word of Loki, Tom Hiddleston, himself:

> It's not just a hammer, but the hammer of Thor. It's, like, embarrassing. You probably have to leave the room, but you can't leave the room because your boner is so big. That gravity is going to weigh you down, and you'll fall over trying to cross the room. Like THAT kind of boner. You'll fall over. It'll unbalance, like we'll go back to being apes. Ya know what I mean? Like it's no longer possible to stand, the boner is so big.

What more could you ask for? This world, my friends, is called FANDOM. It's a community populated with fanboys and fangirls from all over the globe who share a common bond over our mutual obsessions with film, TV, comics, anime, books, etc. It is where I find my joy.

It is where I find my people.

It is where I get to dress up in costumes.

It is where I get to be a kid again.

It is my ultimate happy place.

And, as if that wasn't enough, on top of everything else, it also happens to be a place where cursing for joy is the national pastime. More exaltations of "Holy shit!" "F-U-C-K ME!" "My fucking lord!" "M-O-T-H-E-R-F-U-C-K-E-R!!!" "Well, fuck me sideways!" "Did you fucking see that?!" "Can you even fucking believe this?!" are catapulted into the atmosphere from the world of Fandom than anywhere else. It is such a quintessential necessity that it's not limited to the languages of this earth. Here we are all connected through our profane and, often, verbose reaction to the incredible world all around us. And I assure you, you'll encounter no cool indifference here because everybody's carrying two shits and a rat's ass and cannot wait to give them to you!!

And when we gather to celebrate its awesomeness around the world, it's a wonder to behold. Two of the largest gatherings take place annually in New York City and San Diego, California. They are attended by over 280,000 people, collectively, and are known as Comic-Con.

Comic-Con: San Diego is a four-day convention/tailgate party where 130,000 of the most diehard fans in the universe converge on the *"Whale's Vagina,"* so they can geek out with the stars of their favorite franchises. It's not just for Trekkers and Warsies. It's the ultimate buffet of anime, books, cartoons, comics, video games, TV shows, movies, collectible toys, and everything in between. It's for the genre-obsessed fans of everything from Pokémon to Assassin's Creed to Marvel Comics to *Family Guy* to *Game of Thrones*. Every fan base shows up in full force!

On the next page, I've created a fun little crossword puzzle to test your knowledge of fan community nicknames. You just might find your secret life in here somewhere; I won't tell!

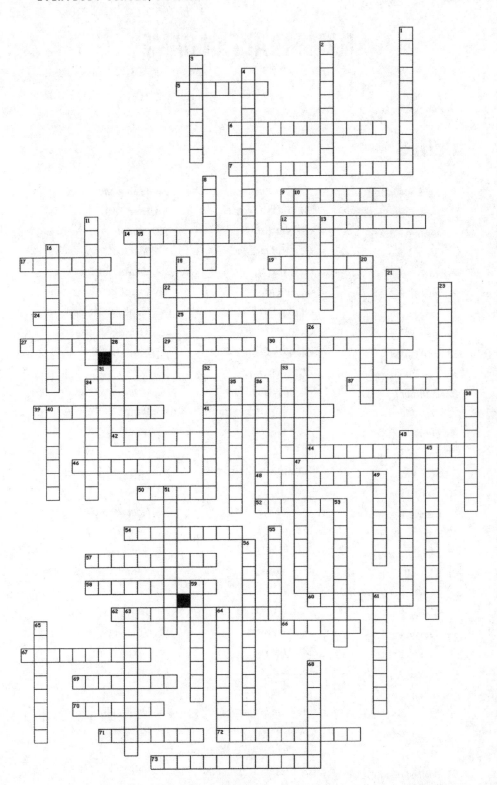

NAME THAT FAN GAME

CLUES

ACROSS

5. Xbox One Fans
6. Stephen King's *Dark Tower*
7. *Dexter*
9. *Twilight*
12. *Fringe*
14. *Jaws*
17. *Torchwood*
19. The Flash
22. *Hannibal*
24. *True Blood*
25. *Heroes*
27. Joss Whedon
29. Star Wars
30. Henry Cavill
31. Carrie Keagan
37. *Tron*
39. *Metalocalypse*
41. Marvel Comics
42. Buffy the Vampire Slayer
44. The Mortal Instruments
46. *Stargate*
48. *Arrow*
50. *Mystery Science Theater 3000*
52. The Sims
54. *Battlestar Galactica*
57. *Ghostbusters*
58. *Galaxy Quest*
60. Nightwing
62. *Orphan Black*
66. *Once Upon a Time*
67. *Firefly*
69. *Avatar: The Last Airbender*
70. *Back to the Future*
71. Chris Pine
72. *Sleepy Hollow*
73. John Barrowman

DOWN

1. Kamala Khan/Ms. Marvel
2. *Pirates of the Caribbean*
3. *Babylon 5*
4. Dragon Ball
8. *Sailor Moon*
10. *Doctor Who*
11. Pokémon
13. *Robotech*
15. *Divergent*
16. Harry Potter
18. *Transformers*
20. *Game of Thrones*
21. *The Walking Dead*
23. *The Hunger Games*
26. James McAvoy
28. Star Trek
32. *Grimm*
33. *The X-Files*
34. Gears of War
35. Carol Danvers/Captain Marvel
36. Teenage Mutant Ninja Turtles
38. Loki
40. *Quantum Leap*
43. Benedict Cumberbatch
45. *Starhunter*
47. Sherlock Holmes
49. *Farscape*
51. *Hobbit/Lord of the Rings*
53. *Supernatural*
55. Xena: Warrior Princess
56. Tom Hiddleston
59. Christopher Nolan
61. Karl Urban
63. *Lost*
64. Batman
65. *Daredevil*
68. *Red Dwarf*

The celebs that appear at Comic-Con appreciate their rabid fans and vice versa. Even though it's a mutual love-fest, more than anything it's a tribute to the regular folks. It's a chance for them to get close to the stars they feel so connected to through their work. It's a divine interchange between strangers who don't know each other at all yet rely heavily on each other every day. It's such an incredible moment that's best described by the words of Irvine Welsh from the film *Trainspotting*, "Take your best orgasm, multiply the feeling by twenty, and you're still fuckin' miles off the pace."

There are still a lot of people who seem to have trouble understanding what this whole Comic-Con thing is and why its fans are so "committed" to it. To those people, I say: It's a lot simpler than you realize. It's a vacation from the harsh realities of the world we live in. The wonder of the experience is that you get to be you, you get to not be judged, you get to feel connected, you get to feel safe, and you get to be happy. It's the one place where if you were going down on your girlfriend and she accidentally yelled out Kirk as she was cumming, instead of having some jealous fight, you'd be high-fiving! It's a world with its own rules that gives you a *happy ending* without the shame or fear of being arrested in some shitty massage parlor in North Hollywood.

Comic-Con is a period of infinite excitement. Cosplayers from around the universe are shining their plastic armor, mixing their green body paint, and packing their limited-edition mint-in-box treasured collectibles for the epic yearly pilgrimage to the epicenter of awesome. It's the biggest tailgate party for all geek kind, and I always set my face to stun and party my *Oola* tentacles off! I've attended Comic-Con seven times; at least that's all I'll admit to—anything more would just be showing off! I have moderated panels in and out of character, but between you and me, I prefer to do it in costume.

Being up on that stage in the Indigo Ballroom and looking out into the sea of cosplayers always gets me thinking. If there can be a Disneyland, there can most certainly be a Comic-Conville! The Con is, actually, the happiest place on earth, and I see it on all of the fans' faces. Whenever I can, I try to hang with my wonderful *amazeballs* fans and take a few pictures. They are the greatest! I'm a very lucky girl!

I have taken the endless walks from hall to hall. I have navigated the insanely crowded red carpets and engaged in impromptu celebrity interviews while standing in line for the women's restroom. I have survived that smell you can taste that fills the exhibit halls. You know, the smell that can only occur when you jam a hundred thousand people into a space intended for only ten thousand. I've attend all the super-secret, by-invitation-only parties where the only way to get in is to be on a list where they can never find your name. Fortunately, I always bring *Ben Franklin* as my plus-one. He can talk his way into anything!

I danced with my horror hero Bruce Campbell at Comic-Con! I discussed *imagination chubbies* with James Cameron. I nibbled on Emma Stone, had an arm-flexing battle with Mark Wahlberg, and examined the phallic nature of their spaceship *Destiny* with the cast of *Stargate Universe*. I've spent every night barhopping through the Gaslamp Quarter like it was Halloween only to end up partying to exhaustion with celebrities who are too busy having fun to realize that they're actually down there working . . . also, I don't think they knew who was in the Chewbacca costume.

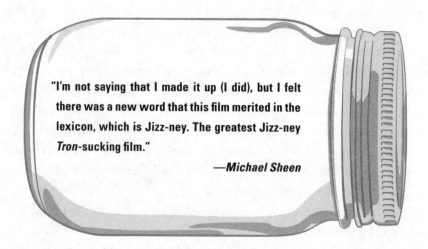

"I'm not saying that I made it up (I did), but I felt there was a new word that this film merited in the lexicon, which is Jizz-ney. The greatest Jizz-ney *Tron*-sucking film."

—*Michael Sheen*

I come back every year because this is where I find my joy. These are my people. This is where I feel normal, even when I just happen to be clothed in head-to-toe latex body paint. That's the secret of Comic-Con because as much as it's a celebrity maze and a studio-driven commercial marketplace, it's still really about the people, and the fans getting close to the celebrities and shows they idolize. Those who travel from all over the world and spend their hard-earned money just to tap into the pure joy that is Comic-Con. Remember that smell you can taste I mentioned earlier . . . well, it's actually joy that emanates from an amazing group of people dedicating their blood, sweat, tears, passion, and love for four days to take it all in and have the most amazing time of their lives. I'm proud to stand with this *geekalicious* bunch!

My not-so-secret survival tip is to prepare as one would for the zombie apocalypse: recording device, comfy footwear, bottled water (which can be vodka disguised as Smartwater, but you didn't hear that from me), hand sanitizer and/or wet wipes, and protective garments, but seeing as how your costume probably already gives you super powers, you should be fine. The only way to avoid the wrath of the CON is to understand the art of the CON. Work hard, party harder! There will be no rest for the wicked!!

Here's what a typical magnificent day for me at Comic-Con might look like:

7 A.M.: Wake up, drink mimosa(s), and eat croissant(s) shaped like the *Millennium Falcon*.

7:30 A.M.: Cover myself in liquid latex head to toe, or a skintight superhero costume, preferably white.

8 A.M.: Pack bag with a recording device, vodka-spiked water, and hand sanitizer, and head to convention center.

8:30 A.M.: Spot cosplayers in assless chaps and body paint and double-check that I haven't accidentally stumbled into a fetish convention.

9 A.M.: Fight over premium seat with a Bioshock Infinite steampunk kid at *The X-Files* Q&A with David Duchovny (Mulder) and Gillian Anderson (Scully).

10 A.M.: Stalk *Gravity* star Sandra Bullock as she walks the floor, looking for free swag.

11 A.M.: Host "Comedy Legends of TV Land" panel starring Roseanne, Wayne Knight (Newman from *Seinfeld*), and—drum roll, please—William "Captain Kirk" Shatner. Become friends with "Bill." Hanging with William Shatner is like being Buddy the Elf with Santa Claus. I kept saying to myself, *I know him! I know him!* Then, almost faint when the king of Comic-Con tweets me.

12 P.M.: Get attacked by an animatronic Godzilla in a warehouse converted into a theme park.

1 P.M.: Attend *The Hunger Games* cast panel. Dive under chair when I mistake thunderous applause for Jennifer Lawrence for a 9.0 earthquake.

2 P.M.: Get lost in *The Vampire Diaries'* Ian Somerhalder's hypnotic blue eyes. Forget to take selfie with him. Slap selfie in face and scream, "You panty waist!" throughout the day.

2:45 P.M.: Pose in front of *Carrie* movie poster and hope everyone sees. Make it my profile pic and post on Instagram, Facebook, Twitter, Pinterest, Tumblr, Vine, Snapchat, LinkedIn, Flickr, Tinder, and Classmates.com.

3 P.M.: Loosen James Cameron up, then sit back and let him explain what the MF stands for in the HMFIC embroidered on his baseball cap (Spoiler alert! It's not *Mezzo Forte*).

4 P.M.: Drink whiskey with Ben Foster, who stealthily smuggled it into the convention center.

5 P.M.: Dress up as Princess Allura from *Voltron*. You don't have to ask me twice.

6 P.M.: Take pedicab to the first of thirty parties all happening at the same time. Scream-sing like a drunk white girl, "There ain't no party like a Comic-Con party because a Comic-Con party REFUSES TO STOP!"

7 P.M.: Attend *Game of Thrones* party. Smash chalices with the cast. Try to accidentally bump into Jason Momoa.

8 P.M.: Party with Aubrey Plaza and Rachel Bilson at *Maxim* and *Playboy* shindigs, and fight off drunken fanboys with liquid courage and more hands than the Watcher in the Water.

9 P.M.: Sip fairy blood with *True Blood* star Ryan Kwanten at makeshift Fangtasia club. Remember to take pic. Post and make people jealous.

10 P.M.: Corner Joss Whedon at *The Walking Dead* bash and give him my horror script, *Helen Killer*.

11 P.M.: Stuff my face with cake at *Supernatural* star Jared Padalecki's birthday bash.

12 A.M.: Try not to get trampled at the *Superman* party, which is so packed that I get five anonymous butt-feels. Hope at least one was Henry Cavill.

1 A.M.: End night with fierce game of Pokémon in a smoky room at the Hard Rock Hotel. Lose shirt. Use your imagination.

In true NGTV style, when we first covered Comic-Con, we didn't know what we were doing (next time we bought our own sheets at Kmart to bring to the only fleabag motel we could afford), but what we lacked in knowledge we made up for in tenacity. The first year, Kourosh, Ken, and I did about 150 interviews in three days. You know why? Because if our fans couldn't make it, we wanted them to feel like they were there. Even if I couldn't talk, walk, or breathe for a week afterward, damn straight I was going to sprint three miles to get that last Robert Downey Jr. *Iron Man 2* interview. That's the sacrifice I'm willing to make for my art, and it's worth every blister and toe-mangling disfiguration!

The best thing about the geek franchises is that there truly is a special relationship between fans and stars. The celebs know what they're signing up for when they agree to do it, so they're willing to go the extra mile to connect with their uber-fans!

I like to pretend all interviews are created equal, but the truth is I probably put some extra special sauce on the fanboy ones because I'm one of them. Besides, whenever I get a superhero, vampire, werewolf, YA-novel heroine, or geek icon to curse, it sends ripples the size of tidal waves through the geek-o-sphere. It gets dissected a thousand times over and disseminated globally in a celebration that feels like the Fourth of July! See why I feel so connected! So I work hard to really give them what they (I) want—which is to see their heroes as human beings they'd love to kick back with and have a beer.

I mean where else are they going to go to see David *"I wrote the best DC movies"* Goyer have a fictional casting session for *The Dark Knight Rises* where Eddie Murphy ends up playing the Riddler but in white face just like when he did it on *SNL*? Genius! Or Edward James *"Frakin'"* Olmos cussing up a storm before revealing that his character Admiral William Adama in the latest incarnation of *Battlestar Galactica* was an ancestor of Gaff, his character in *Blade Runner*! Or Tim Burton discussing how when he's a producer on a film someone else is directing, like on *9*, he sees his job as the guy to slap around and beat up studio executives who are interfering with the director's vision!

Where else would you turn for a master class from directors Quentin Tarantino and Robert Rodriguez and actress Rose McGowan on the importance of the word "fuck" in a grindhouse movie and how to say it right?

Me: How important is the "fuck" word to a grindhouse movie?

Quentin: OH HELL . . . very . . . very important!

Rose: Fuck fuck!

Robert: It's fucking ridiculous!

Rose: The word "fuck" is very important. Quentin and Robert both have a love for the way I say it.

Me: *(To Q and R:)* [Rose] does say "fuck" really well, doesn't she?!

Robert: Really well!

Rose : They both decided that they love how I have "—ck" on things.

Quentin: Rose knows how to use the "—ck." Right? She can really pull out the "—ck."

Rose: Everyone would come running in, "Oooh, oh, oh, I have a change; I have a change to your line." Okay what? "We want you to say 'fuck' another time here at the beginning and then here at the end."

Robert: 'Cause I liked how she said "fuck" so I had the character say that, "I like the way you say 'fuck.' "

Rose: Fuck. Fuck!

Me: "Cunt" is probably a great word coming out of her mouth!

Quentin: Actually she says that very good!

Robert: She says that very good.

Quentin: "Cocksucker" she's very good at.

Rose: Cocksucking . . .

Quentin: He ran with "fuck," I ran with "cocksucker," and she just nails it! *(Doing an impression of Rose impersonating him:)* "Quentin likes the way I say 'cocksucker.' "

Rose: Well, it's a good rhythm. He knows rhythm.

Quentin: It's a great fuckin' movie, all you cunts—come out and see it!

Who else would have the real lowdown on *Pacific Rim*? Director Guillermo del Toro described his film as robot porn before screaming, "Fuck that shit," while laughing so hard about all the rimjob jokes he was responsible for that he's now sore. Here's *Sons of Anarchy* star Charlie Hunnam and *Luther* star Idris Elba talking about double penetration and answering the most important question:

Me: If the Jaegers are defending the rim, does that mean the Kaiju is defending the taint?

Idris: Well . . . yeah!

Charlie: Or attacking the taint! Coming out of the taint to attack the sphinct and we are the Rim God!

Idris: *(Laughing.)*

Me: Nice! We're putting that on the poster. You know that's going to happen!

Charlie: Good. Good!

Me: *(Acting like myself:)* I am a Rim God!!

Charlie: Yeah . . . *(Realizing I didn't understand him.)* Guard. GUARD!

Me: Oh . . . Guard! Oh!

Charlie: But God. I never really thought about that. Rim God!

Me: I like it better!

Idris: *(Turning to Charlie:)* Now you are going to be considered a rim rod for the rest of your life, bro! That's pretty badass!

Charlie: PSSH! Don't call this a comeback. I've been here for years! *(Looks like Charlie likes himself some LL Cool J.)*

Hard to imagine now, but when the first *Twilight* came out, the cast was all a bunch of unknowns, and there was a possibility it'd be a huge flop. Remember The Mortal Instruments? Exactly. It can happen to anyone. Kristen Stewart had been in *Panic Room* with Jodie Foster, and Robert Pattinson had a small recurring role in *Harry Potter*, but Twihards were furious he'd been chosen to play Edward. It was like when Tom Cruise was cast as Lestat for *Interview with the Vampire*. I think I actually cried. Brad Pitt? Fine. Tom Cruise? I'm out—fuck all of you!

The studio was very enthusiastic about us sitting down with these extremely attractive youngsters. At first, we discussed doing an *In Bed With* with Rob and Kristen because the first time they met was in director Catherine Hardwicke's bed. She made the pair do a "chemistry reading" to get the parts, which meant making out passionately even though they'd never met. According to lore, Rob's kiss was so *boom-chicka-boom*, Hardwicke didn't even show it to the studio execs for fear that it was too risqué and they wouldn't get the parts. Likewise, after some back and forth, we ditched the *In Bed With* idea because *Twilight* was a YA novel aimed at a younger audience, and it could seem a tad inappropriate. In hindsight, not getting those two in the sack with me is one of my bigger career regrets. Oh, what could have been!

Turns out, I didn't need to get horizontal with Rob and Kristen for a great interview. Back then, they were so open and not even self-aware at all. They were just a bunch of kids being themselves. They knew this movie would either make them the next Bieber or it'd be the last thing they ever did. They had nothing to lose. KStew, who sometimes seems uncomfortable, was anything but; she was totally down-to-earth and more than okay talking about how she loved objectifying the shirtless boys in the film, and more important, vampire sex:

Me: I think that parents should change their minds a little bit about their daughters dating vampires—the chance of your daughter having sex is probably zero.

Kristen: Yeah, it's true. 'Cause they're, like, impotent.

Me: It just takes forever to even get close. So you'll be, like, thirty before you even actually have sex with him, if you could. So I'm gonna start this petition that vampires should be okay.

Kristen: Yeah, it's perfect for the Catholic schoolgirl.

Me: Now, because this is a vampire movie, is it fair to say this film totally sucks?

Kristen: Yeah, yeah. You are so unoriginal, by the way. That's been said a million times.

Me: Ah, come on! And here I was thinking of that all day! Since this film is now the biggest thing on the planet, have you run into some crazy people?

Kristen: Rob's got the good stories. He has people just, like, chillin' in front of his house. I get sort of the opposite. There are occasions where a girl walks up and the look of disdain on her face is overwhelming.

Me: Just because they're jealous of you!?

Kristen: Yeah! Yeah! Totally! It's like they want to convey, *"Look, I know you think you're great because all of this great stuff is happening to you, but we all know differently . . . and Edward DOESN'T love you."*

Me: Oh YES HE DOES! Tell them something that will make them feel better.

Kristen: I'm sorry?

Rob, in all his tousled-haired glory, was equally great. The *Twi*-highlight of his interview was him admitting vampire sex is "the best type of sex. It's sex where you end up killing the person afterward." For the second film, *New Moon*, it was anything-goes again with the cast, and they took full advantage of their freedom. Rob, that sexy scallywag, drank tea with his pinky finger in the air while saying, "Fuck that!" and admitted that Kristen dictated the sex scenes: "I'm just the big hard tool." I also did raucous interviews with the vampires and the wolf boys. Arh-woooooooooooooo!

Me: So I feel like this is the ultimate showdown of the ultimate VILF and the ultimate WILF.

Kristen: Fuck yeah!

Robert: What are . . . oh! Hahaha.

Chris Weitz: Hotsy-totsies, yes.

Me: I'm callin' them . . . *(Clear throat.)* VILFs.

Chris: VILFs? Hahahahaha.

Peter Facinelli: *(Trying to decipher what VILF stands for.)* Vampires . . .

Ashley Greene: Vampires you'd like to fuck.

Nikki Reed: Um . . . that's weird to, like, say that about yourself.

Kellan Lutz: I wanna be one!

Robert: I think it is, yeah. I like how all the werewolves have to go around naked all the time. It's like, ya know, you always win then when you're a vampire.

Me: *(To the wolf pack:)* Are you guys the ultimate WILFs?

Bronson Pelletier: Whoa . . . what is a WILF?

Chaske Spencer: WHOA!!! Wolf I'd like to . . .

Bronson and Chaske: *(In unison.)* Fuck!

Alex Meraz: Oh, definitely the ultimate WILFs!

Taylor Lautner: Oh yeah, definitely.

Alex: *(To me:)* What would you say?

Me: I would say yes, you have definitely brought your doggie style.

Wolf pack: Oh whoa!!! *(High fives all around.)*

Alex: Love it!

Me: That's good, right?

Chaske: This is the best interview ever!

Peter: Yeah, I'd rather be a VILF than a WILF.

Chaske: Motherfucker!

Is it wrong to ask a bunch of young men playing werewolves why they needed to wear shirts—or pants? The people demanded answers.

Me: I think it's quite a sexy showdown that we have going down.

Kristen: I don't take credit for any of that. It's cool. We objectify the boys in this movie, and I am so down with that!

Me: Me, too!

Kristen: Yeah.

Wolf pack: Fucking awesome!!!

Bronson: Fucking awesome!

Kristen: I really fucking like it.

Me: Can we get a little wolf pack "hooowwwwwl"?

Wolf pack: Yes! "Hooooooowwwwwwwwwl!"

Me: And can we get the shirts off?

(The wolf pack pauses and then:)

Chaske: You first.

Bronson: *(Stands up to undo his buttons then sits back down.)* You first!

Chris: I mean, there's what I think every fan of the books would want, ummmm.

Me: A lot of male upper-body nudity?

Chris: Some ab-bage . . . some ab-bage for your cabbage.

Me: Thank you for that!!

Bronson: Sorry, we only do pants . . . we only take pants off here.

Me: Oh, hey, we can have a pants-off interview. That would be awesome!

Liz: I don't understand why they have pants on, and I don't mean that to be inappropriate, I just don't . . . why are their shirts off?

Peter: Because . . . let me explain . . .

Kellan: Why can't they just be naked?

Me: Because all of a sudden it would be an R movie . . . and all of MY friends would go. . . . Well, 'cause you can't wear clothes as a wolf, right?

Taylor: There you go.

Nikki: Okay then, Liz, they're not going to wear pants anymore, all right? In the behind-the-scenes, they will get them to not wear pants.

Liz: Fantastic!

Me: DVD extras, right??

Chris: DVD? Oh yeah! Big time. Yeah.

Me: Awesome!

The interviews felt like a daylong party. Everyone seemed to be letting off steam and just going with it. A side they could never really show anywhere else, and their fans fucking loved it! Then came a nugget of information that would surely set the fanscape on fire from Robert Pattinson.

Robert: There is one nude scene though; there was . . . there . . . there was one . . . there . . . there . . . actually I don't know if I should be revealing that . . .

Me: Tell me where the Easter egg is! I'm gonna go back, and I'm gonna pause.

Robert: Taylor is naked in one scene.

Me: Niiiice.

Robert: Um-hm.

Again, thank me later! And I have to say Elizabeth Reaser really upped the ante at the end, when she promoted the film with a word you don't really hear that often: "Go see *New Moon*, ya cockfuck!" And Kristen Stewart brought it home with: "Go see the fuckin' movie! We all really like it," throwing a subtle two thumbs up! I've said it before and I'll say it again, Kristen Stewart is a smart girl who knows who the fuck she is, and she's awesome!

The response to my interviews from *Twilight*ers was off the charts. Millions of views, and a ton of the diehards stole our interviews and posted them on their personal sites. We always felt that it was the highest form of flattery. So it was kind of a bummer that as the series blasted off into supernova, we suddenly got shut out of the junkets. We never got an official reason, but we had a few educated guesses. Most likely, it was the

Disney-fication of the franchise, and we were just too damn dirty. Also, the author of the *Twilight* series, Stephenie Meyer, is a devout Mormon. The director of *New Moon*, Chris Weitz, did a filthy interview with me and said his favorite swear word was Godfuck, which, by the way, his two-year-old daughter had created. "If [Stephenie] hears this, I'll never work on these movies again." He laughed. "She's going to kill me!" He didn't come back, either, but I have no idea if that had anything to do with me!

When I was absent from the last few junkets, there was a big up-roar from fans on their message boards. "Where's NGTV?" they cried. Or whatever the equivalent of crying is online. All caps? No, that's screaming. In any case, it was pretty cool that this wonderful audience remembered us. They loved our real and uncensored interviews with their favorite characters. I'm telling you, these fans are the best because they're as loyal as a new puppy. I'll never forget my interview with Jennifer Lawrence, Josh Hutcherson, Liam Hemsworth, and the rest of the cast of the first *Hunger Games*. We covered the only issues the fans really wanted to know. First Josh:

    Me: What's your stance on manscaping?

Josh: Uh . . . I think there's a certain duty that every man has that he needs to, you know, maintain his business, without getting too crazy.

    Me: Oh yeah.

Josh: At the same time, you don't want hardwood floors. That's just kind of awkward.

Then on to Jennifer Lawrence:

    Me: What is all this stuff I keep hearing about on the set? Woody Harrelson had sex swings going on. There's like sex dolls hanging out in your bathroom. What's going on?

Jennifer: It wasn't a sex doll. Let's straighten that out. Right quick.

    Me: These are the rumors I'm hearing.

Jennifer: *(In her newscaster voice with her hands up.)* Jennifer Lawrence has a sex doll in her trailer! *(She smiles.)* I bring it with me on every set! My requirement is a double-banger trailer and a sex doll in every room! No, it was a mutilated corpse.

Me: Oh, okay.

Jennifer: And it was sitting on my toilet, and I don't think anybody would want to use that for a sex doll.

Me: You know what, everybody's got their own fetish. We don't have to get into it.

Jennifer: And to straighten out the sex swing for you, Woody. It was a yoga swing.

Me: Aah . . . because somehow they're different?

Jennifer: I've never actually seen a sex swing. I just . . . I figure how they work. They hang from the wall, and it's in the middle of the trailer. And I was already really nervous about how to meet him. And then I walked into his trailer and prepared to, "Hi, I'm Jen," and then I came out with, "Is that a sex swing?"

Me: *(Doing an impression of her in that moment with Woody.)* Nice to meet you.

(And when it was time promote, she turned to the camera.)

Jennifer: It's a fucking amazing movie! Can't wait for you guys to see it!

Well, needless to say, my interview about sex swings with Jennifer Lawrence got posted everywhere and went viral. Even Perez Hilton got in on the action and posted it. It spread like wildfire, to the point that our server crashed and our facilitator in Germany called us up and said, "What just happened?"

These fanboy audiences are as powerful as they are obsessive. They've already read or watched almost everything there is about these characters on- and offscreen. They've left no stone unturned. So that's why I try so hard to give them something they've never heard before. "Tell me about your character" isn't going to fly with these aficionados. I also can't pull out some obscure factoid I'm not really schooled on fully. These diehards can smell a phony from a million galaxies away. So I go with the third option, which is to make them laugh.

For the *Star Trek* movie, the cast was so big the studio had ten rooms of interviewees. We were one of the select few outlets that got everybody—Chris Pine, Zachary Quinto, Zoe Saldana, John Cho, director J. J. Abrams, and down the line. Unlike *Twilight* or *The Hunger*

Games, the true fans were in a higher age demographic, so technically the conversations could be more adult. They were, and yet, they were also so incredibly immature! What can I say, I love what I do.

When I sat down with J. J. Abrams, it was our first time, and I don't think he believed I was going to swear. It was so awesome! "Are you ready?" I said, smiling. "Seat belt on," he replied. Then I gave him the most enthusiastic "*Star Trek* is the fucking shit!" and his eyes just lit up in amazement, and he responded, "Holy shit! I cannot believe you're swearing," with a huge smile and a look of sheer delight. It could have had to do with my first question, which was, "Is it true that they've invented *Star Trek* diapers 'cause everyone is going to shit their pants when they see this movie?" But I have to say . . . I so enjoyed the responses:

Chris Pine:	Keagan, that's disgusting. (*He says it with that fatherly look 'cause he knows I'm dragging in the shit now.*) It's really . . . I hope people don't defecate in the theaters because that would be awful!
Zachary Quinto:	As long as they have his face on them (*points to Chris*), I'm happy!
Chris Pine:	(*Looking at Zach.*) Mean, mean, mean!
Me:	(*To Chris and Zach.*) And now we're going to battle. (*I love egging on Chris.*)
Karl Urban:	(*Laughing hard.*) It's pretty ballistic!
Zoe Saldana:	Actually, I'm wearing my own *Star Trek* Depends right now!
Eric Bana:	I love that! That's my favorite line today.
Clifton Collins, Jr.:	Just give me a second to compose myself 'cause I just lost my shit! (*Making a wacky gesture with his hands.*)
Bruce Greenwood:	What the fuck!!
J. J. Abrams:	First of all, I do have to go to a psychiatrist now. (*Really hamming it up.*) Seriously, this is, maybe, the most uncomfortable I've ever been. (*Too bad he couldn't stop smiling and giggling.*)

Me: I get paid for these jokes. *(In a very dramatic, "How dare you, sir?" voice.)* I just want you to know.

J. J.: You do? Oh my God! What's your boss's name again? *(Huge mischievous grin while I'm laughing.)*

Me: Kourosh.

J. J.: Kourosh. *(He looks at the camera with a funny look.)* We should talk, Kourosh. Long conversation. *(He breaks down laughing.)*

I so enjoyed taking J. J. on his first NGTV pleasure cruise. He was such a blast. He's incredibly smart yet completely unassuming, and has this awesome childlike quality with that mischievous look that came flying out and charging at me, especially when he agreed that the film would be best described as "the tits!" I take full responsibility for—and great pride in—that.

[Oh and, Kourosh, you're welcome! You're in the *Star Trek* section. *Yadick!*]

Seriously, isn't that way more fun than, "How does it feel to step into these iconic characters' shoes?"? I much preferred to talk about intergalactic love triangles and break down Spock's eyebrows into two F-word categories. Or discuss that *pussy-magnet* Captain Kirk grabbing some booby. My old friends Zachary Quinto, who used to party at NGTV, and Chris Pine, who was also a buddy, were all about it. If they heard, "Were you a fan of *Star Trek* growing up?" one more time, they were going to gouge their own eyes out with a Mek'leth. "I'm supposed to be on my best behavior," Chris said when he saw me, "but now I'm not going to be able to."

Me: As Kirk and Spock, there are two things that are very important. *(Looking at Chris.)* You have to have a look that says, "I want to have sex" and . . .

Chris: I practice that often. *(Laughing.)*

Me: And the up-look that says, "Go fuck yourself." And Spock *(looking at Zach)*, you have to have the eyebrow that says, "Fascinating" or "Go fuck yourself."

Let's be honest, as a fan, in fifty years this has never been broken down so efficiently.

Zach: *(Laughing with Chris.)* Or "Go fuck yourself!" That was the entire foundation upon which my performance was built: "Go fuck yourself!"

Chris: Wow!

Then, in an inspired moment, Chris and Zach turn toward each other and bust out their best "Go fuck yourself!" in character. Or was Chris saying, "I want to have sex," and Zach replied, "Fascinating"? Hmmm.

Zach: *(Making a bizarre facial expression.)* Then get both in there and you look . . .

Chris: You look like you're stoned or something.

And you're a better man for it, Chris! We gave the Trekkies exactly what they wanted—a side of these actors that you never get to see—and the interviews were gangbusters for us. It's the coolest way to cover the superhero genre. What I try to do is take off their masks metaphorically. Damn, that's deep! Somebody write that down. When you ask the *Spider-Man 3* cast, "Is it true once you go black you never go back?" because Spidey spends a part of the movie as Venom in the black costume, their priceless reactions and responses break down that wall between us. It also prompted Thomas Haden-Church to dub me "the smart Pamela Anderson." Thank you, I think.

This particular junket had some memorable moments, like Topher Grace saying, "Fuck yeah, America!" a number of times in the edit. He always brings it up when I see him. Kirsten Dunst using "cunt" to promote the film sure raised eyebrows and got it featured in the big article written about us in *The Hollywood Reporter.* But above and beyond that, it was the controversial opening we shot for it that had us worried. We had this funny and super-profanity-laced idea for this riff on the famous Abbott and Costello bit called "Who's on First?" My cohost Shark Firestone and I assumed a ridiculously awkward positon where he was upside down and I was right side up. Then we performed this bit where we say "fuck" a lot while doing muscle poses and pretending to shoot webs from our arms like Spider-Man, which we added later in post. It was called "Who's Fucking Spider-Man?" It was sooo dirty, and we put it together with a superhero film. It could have gone horribly bad but it didn't. Quite the opposite.

Me: Shark, I saw fucking *Spider-Man* last night. Jealous, you little fucking bitch?

Shark: Baby, I was fucking Spider-Man last night!

Me: So you were fucking Spider-Man? Or you were fuckin' Spider-Man?

Shark: I was fucking Spider-Man!

Me: So you were fucking Spider-Man?

Shark: Fucking Spider-Man? You're fuckin'-A right I was fucking . . . Spider-Man??

Me: Fuckin' swingin' all over fuckin' town, huh?

Shark: It's what they call a sticky fucking situation.

Me: Let me fuckin' guess. Another fuckin' groupie suckin' the fuckin' venom out of your fuckin' Hobgoblin?

Shark: Actually, the fuckin' bitch stopped fuckin' short last night, which left me with no other fuckin' choice.

Me: So you fuckin' kicked her to the curb, right?

Shark: Let's just say I fuckin' showed her that with great fucking power comes great fucking responsibility.

Me: Fuckin' spoken like a true fuckin' superhero.

Shark: More like a fucking guy who fucking jerked off and sent hot stinky fuckin' ropes all over her back and he kicked the bitch out!

Me: The fuckin' Spidey Special fuckin' strikes again!

Shark: Fuck yeah!!

Me: You fuckin' okay?

Shark: Other than my nuts being up my ass and Sandman being up my crack, YES!!

It was so fucking dirty for no reason, and it did so well with our audience. The fans loved it. The viewer numbers were huge, and that was all anyone cares about.

One of my absolute favorite fanboy interviews was an accidental gem that I unearthed during the junket for *What's Your Number?* It took place right after *Captain America: The First Avenger* came out and became a hit. In addition to Anna Faris and Tom Lennon, it features three actors, Chris Evans, Chris Pratt, and Anthony Mackie, who would all go on to become major forces in the Marvel universe. At the time, I was messin' around with these guys I'd known for years, but now, looking back, I found myself having a really dirty conversation with Captain America, Falcon, and Star-Lord.

Tom and I go way back, and Anthony and I are always on the same fucked-up wavelength during interviews, so you knew some dick jokes were going to be on the table early on. Chris Pratt was caught in the middle in the beginning but caught on quick when Mackie got a lesson from me in French that I don't think he was expecting.

      Tom: Hey, Carrie, you know what's weird is, you just came in, but you're the third person who [Anthony Mackie] fucked in their shoulder blades.

      Pratt: BULL! *(Chris is caught off guard and thinks this is serious. Almost makes it funnier.)*

      Me: That's just uncomfortably weird. *(Playing into it.)*

Anthony: I have a long reach! *(Yelling.)* You know what I mean! *(Makes a suggestive gesture with his hands.)*

      Me: So technically . . . *(In a low sexy voice.)* I didn't just come in. He just CAME in!!

    Group: Whooooooooaaaaaaaaaa.

                  (Now I have their attention.)

      Pratt: Hahaha I get it. *(Chris just realizes we were fucking around.)*

We then launch into a long conversation about doggie-style sex and the best way to look good doing it because it can be undignified.

      Tom: You don't find that if you're having doggie-style sex, that it helps to have a large mirror in the room somewhere? Also so that you can give yourself a thumbs-up.

      Me: Can you give yourself, like, an *Eiffel Tower*? *(I had to go there.)*

Anthony: *Eiffel Tower! (Shakes his head in disbelief.)*

      Me: When have you crossed the line?

      Tom: She asked a man who just fucked her shoulder blades. *(Shakes his head.)* . . . I believe on, like, the first or second meeting.

Anthony: Yeah. I don't know how to tell you . . .

      Tom: Had you guys met before that?

Anthony: Nah.

      Tom: Okay!

Me: Great! Now you don't remember the last two times!

Anthony: I don't remember you from the front.

Me: You're such an asshole.

Anthony: What the fuck!?

Tom: You guys . . . by the way, knowing you a little bit *(pointing at Anthony)*, and knowing you a little bit *(pointing to me)*, this is what I call a perfect storm.

Then I switched gears to get Cap's and Star-Lord's opinion on the art of the 69. Turns out our Chris Evans was not a fan, but Chris Pratt had an entire theory:

Me: Sixty-nine is something you do when you're sixteen and you're in a hurry because your parents are coming home?

Tom: Wait . . . well, that's not inaccurate.

Evans: I totally agree. I could not agree more.

Anna: Yeah.

Evans: It's the most ridiculous thing.

Anna: Yeah.

Pratt: It's like that old adage: The young bull and the old bull on the hill, and the young bull says, "Hey, let's run down the hill and fuck one of those cows," and the old bull says, "Let's walk down and fuck 'em all!" Ya know? When you're a kid you're trying to get as much sexual activity in at every given moment as you can, and the sixty-nine is like, "Oh my God, I'm doing two amazing things!"

Me: It's double the pleasure, double the fun!

Anna: Fair enough. Fair enough.

Pratt: But as an adult you're like, I'll tell you what, we'll do both those things, but we'll take about eight hours instead of ten minutes, and we'll take our time. Ya know what I mean? Maybe not eight hours . . .

Finally, it only seemed appropriate to get Falcon's, Star-Lord's, and Cap's opinions on blowjobs vs. hand jobs during marriage and why it's important to be in a rental car if you decide to give yourself a hand job on a long drive.

Me: Hand jobs are out?

Pratt: Yeah.

Me: Ah, but blowjobs are marriage material?

Tom: Right.

Evans: Wait a minute, wait a minute . . . hand jobs are out?

Tom: Do hand jobs have to be out for part two [blowjobs] to be true?

Anthony: I've heard that before . . . and not never . . . I mean, if you're driving, you're on a long drive . . . ya know what I mean?

Pratt: Give yourself a hand job.

Tom: Wait a second, what did you just say?

Pratt: Give yourself a hand job when you're on a long drive?

Evans: That makes sense. I thought you meant that blowjobs were only for marriage . . .

Me: No, no, we are not saving it 'til marriage . . . No, that would be weird!

Evans: This is horrible!

Me: Yes! All of a sudden this became the worst life ever!

Tom: Is it called a hand job when you're the worker?

Me: I suppose it still is if you use your left hand?

Tom: I don't think it is.

Group: Oooh!!

Tom: The left hand.

Anthony: But then you get it on the door.

Me: Ooooh!! . . . uncomfortable. *(Gesturing a jerking motion with left hand, thinking it through.)* Then who cleans up?

Anthony: Exactly!

Me: Oh bleh!!

Tom: The people who rented you this car!
(Group laughs.)

Tom: What do you mean? What are you talking about? There's no way you're doing this in YOUR car! But the second you get a rental car . . . *(Gestures jerking off and making a clicking noise while doing it.)*

Me: Blowjobs are good. Hand jobs are good. No matter what happens, it's all good. Right?

Evans: Yeah, any type of job is . . .

I don't know where else you're ever going to hear a conversation like that. Thank me later!

One of the amazing side benefits of having some really fucked-up conversations with well-known people is that every so often, I'll end up getting some insight into the real person. Sometimes that insight comes from them, directly, and sometimes it comes from a friend or colleague. In an interview with comedians Paul Provenza and Penn Jillette, I asked them who in their experience had the dirtiest comedic mind and went the furthest. They threw out a couple of comedians, as I expected, and then settled on, of all people, Carrie Fisher, whom they'd worked with on a documentary Penn had produced and Paul had directed called *The Aristocrats*. At the time I remember thinking . . . *What?? Huh!!* Princess Leia was the one who went the furthest:

Penn: Carrie Fisher . . . because she brings in real people who really are related to her. When she talks about Eddie Fisher blowing a goat and her mother being a golden showers queen, it's astonishing because . . .

Paul: Mickey Rooney huge with fisting—it's comedy gold.

Penn: I mean Carrie Fisher was kinda like . . . what the fuck!

Paul: Yeah, that was a little surprising. In fact, we even asked her afterward if we can really say all that [in the documentary]. She said, "Yeh, yeh. My mother'll be a little bit upset, but go for my father, all the way; go, go for him. He's an asshole! Give it to him."

As if I didn't have enough reason to love Carrie Fisher. A dirty sense of humor, too. Game over!

One of the more special encounters I remember was with Paul Walker, who sadly passed away in 2013. I had interviewed Paul several times over the years, and he was always really cool and really sweet. Almost a bit shy, which made him very endearing. He was an outlandish personality, although you could tell there was mischief in him. On the occasion of the junket for *Fast & Furious*, which reunited the original cast and rebooted the series, he was in great spirits and super playful. So, of course, we spent a little time discussing nude racing, what else?

Me: Dude, it was so nice to see everybody all together again.

Paul: Yeah, it is. It's like a high school reunion.

Me: Except this time the reunion was like a raging kegger.

Paul: Yeah, you can imagine, huh.

Me: This one you're gonna go fully naked, right?

Paul: Yeah, the whole time. Nude racing! It's a new trend in Japan. It's awesome! . . . Holy shit, we're coming back to make a fourth one? Yeah!

Me: YAY!!!! . . . I'm thinking that the last few *Fast & Furious* were so intense that they actually raise the hair on the back of your neck, right? I mean, they were great!

Paul: Yeah.

Me: This one, it upped it a little bit.

Paul: Really?

Me: This one is so intense that it raises the hair on your balls.

Paul: Wow!! *(He starts giggling to himself.)*

Me: Would it be fair to say that?

Paul: Well, I'm pretty clean right now, but yeah . . .

Me: Okay, maybe not YOURS.

Paul: *(Giggling.)*

Me: It did for me. It worked for me!

Paul: That chicken skin starts sprouting, ya know. *(He wipes the tears of laughter from his eyes.)* Wow. This really is uncensored, isn't it? *(Still laughing.)*

Me: Yeah, a little bit. *(Laughing.)* How's that feel? Is it okay? Did I give it enough energy?

Paul: It feels good. Yeah, it felt real. . . . Now all my religious friends are going to be mad at me. I already talked about the chicken skin. *(He smiles.)* Go see *The Fast & the Furious*, dammit!

Paul was just about as nice as they come. A genuine salt of the earth good guy. Someone who never changed with all his success. I'm glad to have gotten a chance to know him a little.

This chapter would not be complete without a James Cameron story. He is arguably one of the greatest cinematic visionaries in the history of film and someone I am a huge fan of. But everything I could dig up about him spoke to his passion, determination, and intensity about his craft. He was someone that no one fucked with ever! Fuck! These are not

the most encouraging things to hear before you fly to England to interview him for the very first time for this new, technologically groundbreaking film called *Avatar*. So I was concerned. We wanted a great
piece, but I did not want to walk into a Tommy Lee Jones situation with
some guy on a tear. That would be such a buzzkill. Then, a couple of
nights before I left, I caught some interview he did on TV and it was all
very serious, but there were fifteen seconds where they briefly touched
on a baseball cap on his desk, which had the acronym HMFIC on it.
That's all I needed. I knew exactly who this guy was.

And he did not disappoint. We got on perfectly. We went together
like "ramalama" and "ding dong!" So much fun. He's a fascinating guy
with the gift of swear. He was one of us! So you damn well know we
were going to talk about some serious shit the others were afraid to ask.
So I set the tone with, "Is it fair to say that this is the most expensive
porno for the imagination for the Viagra Ecstasy generation?" That's all
he needed to hear to instantly bond with me. Then it was all about what
I took away from the film and why it mattered. I explained that, from
what I could see, this was about *blue balls* and finding a cure. Very no-
ble. It was the simple tale of a boy who's *hung like a donkey* but suffers
from a terrible case of *blue balls*. He falls for a girl and spends the entire
film literally chasing tail to find some relief for his balls. The rest is
just random camerawork, some green bullshit, a couple days of ani-
mation, and some minor effects. Two hundred million dollars and five
years of your life. Congratulations! He had so much fun fucking around
with me, he even created a new Na'vi word just for me: "*P'taoung*," which
means *douchebag*. "Fuck yeah, America!" said Topher Grace. ☺

As they started to wrap me in the room, I brought up that infamous
baseball cap, and just as I suspected, he revealed that it stood for "Head
Motherfucker in Charge." I fuckin' knew it from the moment I saw it. That's
when I knew that I was free to be me. Before it was over, Jim paid me the
very best *No Good* compliment: "I like the way your mind goes right into
the gutter. It's refreshing in a woman, I have to tell ya." That was the beginning of a wonderful relationship. He would ask for us to be invited to his
press junkets, and any time I'd see him on a red carpet, he'd always come
by and say hi and tell whoever was around how much he loved No Good
TV. We hadn't just made a friend; we made a fan. Now that was fuckin'
cool!!

NGTV was built for this audience, and I have always been proud to be its ambassador. The celebs obviously get a kick out of what I do, and the fans fuckin' love it because we feed their obsession with crazy treats! I have to say, no one is happier than me, except maybe Ryan Reynolds, about the massive success of the R-rated *Deadpool* movie. It's triggered a major movement towards more edgy and hardcore superhero films. And if there's any audience who appreciates more color in their language and violence, it's this one. So it's about fucking time. Let's hope the studios do it right and don't unload a bunch of shit and kill its potential. An R-rated supercut of *Batman v Superman: Dawn of Justice* is a great start!

I'm also super excited to see Ryan Reynolds embrace this side of his personality more definitively, and find so much success. After all, he was the man who delivered my jam, "cock-juggling thunder-cunt," with the conviction of Sir Laurence Olivier, way back when. He and I have danced on the edge in our interviews many times over the years. In more of a sarcastic battle of *"wits and shits"* than a full frontal *"butts and fucks."* It's been fun, but I always felt like he was holding back; I just knew there was a twisted motherfucker in there that he was keeping at bay. Guess I was right. Well, seeing Ryan taking ownership of that and getting down with his *profane* self brings real joy to my heart. (Oh wait, what's going on here, Ryan? I smell burnt toast!!)

Well, now you know where I go to find myself, and if that's not a happy place, then I don't know what the fuck is. There's no question that I've been really lucky in finding my happiness within. It's played a crucial role in every aspect of my life. One wrong decision or one momentary lapse in judgement and it all could have gone another way. So, in a fucked-up way, I totally understand what the "saddleback" teens are doing: just being teenagers and doing the dumb things they do. I really feel for those girls. I don't mean to be funny, but they are definitely getting the *raw end* of the deal. It's a sad situation, and these kids are completely misguided. But from their perspective, they're just working the system like any other teenager would once they become sexually aware. They're just trying to make it through a shitty adolescence by creating brief moments of happiness and acceptance through sex within the confines of a pretty bleak existence. Except their world is filled with nonsensical misinformation presented as fact, which is just about the most dangerous thing in the hands of a *dumb-as-fuck* teenager. And when you're surrounded by idiocy everywhere you turn, well, you're bound to make some idiotic decisions. So, inevitably, your decisions about sex appear to have been heavily influenced by Wile E. Coyote's super genius. Except in your case the anvil won't hit you in the head. It gets jammed up your ass!!

My Catholic-school experience could have easily left me upside down, too. It was a learning experience like no other, where logic and compassion were harder to find than a *dildo with foreskin*. We were taught to practice tolerance. It didn't matter if it was verbal bullying, social bullying, or physical bullying; it was to be tolerated. We were also encouraged to embrace our fears and use them to move forward in life. In fact, we were urged to embrace new fears that we didn't even have because we were told not all phobias were bad. Like homophobia—that was one of the *good* ones. And, boy, did these nuns practice what they preached because nothing helps fortify the tenets of a belief system like seeing it in action. And trust me when I tell you, there was a lot of nun-on-student action. But perhaps the greatest wisdom imparted to us were in the tools we needed to navigate puberty. Priceless insights about my sexual urges being the disgraceful thrusts of *demon cocks* fucking my soul really helped me through my teens. It truly was remarkable. An education provided with the intellect and depth of a thrown tomato and the subtlety of a rectal suppository. I **unlearned** so much!

Luckily for me, it was just a small part of my life, and I had a lot to balance against it. Now, if I didn't have parents who were open-minded and not criminally insane to lean on for perspective, who knows, I may have turned to using my butthole to find a little escape and acceptance. But thanks to them, and despite all my efforts to the contrary, I never compromised myself to find a little fake bliss. And ultimately, I put my energies into moving away and starting a new life.

But I'll tell ya, there's a part of me that's convinced that adolescent girls come preprogrammed with just enough sense to make only one good decision during our entire time as a teenager. So we have to fucking make use of it wisely. Our instincts are terrible, we have no knowledge or experience, and we're basically just one raw nerve 90 percent of the time. So, of course, every other choice we make is going to be utter shit. And we don't have any way of knowing at the time, but the best use of our one good decision should involve sex and/or our bodies. Mainly because teenage guys come preprogrammed with ZERO capacity to make a good decision. So we're not getting any help there. Hence, the *adolescent anal invasion* sweeping the Christian nation. So, to all the girls going through this right now, first of all, *keistering* your guy isn't going to make you *happy*, but it will make you *messy*. Sort of like *ipecac for your butt*. And there's nothing that'll fuck up your self-esteem like the gift of blood and chocolate. Secondly, hang in there. It's going to suck for a long while, but then it's going to get a whole lot better!

Anyway, this search for a happy place begins in your discombobulated teenage years and proceeds to consume the rest of your life. So we all get busy collecting joy. It could be a job, a cute boyfriend, a killer pair of shoes, an action figure, a severe addiction to *butt chugging*, or a cool fetish like being a *furry*. Some things satisfy you for a while, some things land you in the hospital, and other things get you arrested. But, hey, it's all in the name of happiness.

Now what would this chapter be if I didn't take you down a *rabbit hole* and "learn ya's sum'in"? Unfortunately, happiness is not reserved for the deserving, and there are a lot of demented people out there looking for their inner smile, too. And unfortunately, what's great about the United States is that there is something here for everyone. No matter what kind of sociopath you are—aliented, disaffiliated, hostile, cheated, aggressive, dysocial, or just your common garden variety—we have the cure for what ails you. Happiness is within reach!

So if your idea of a good time is firing a shoulder-launched missile at God knows what, you should head on down to South Carolina, where it's totally legal. Just a quick permit from the Aeronautics Division of the Department of Commerce, and you and your FGM-148 Javelin with its built-in infrared homing device are ready for a party in the sky at Myrtle Beach. This "fire-and-forget" missile with lock-on before launch and automatic self-guidance will make sure no one forgets your next Independence Day family barbeque. South Carolina—it's "Just right."

Now if a violent aerial assault isn't quite the *boner-loner* you were looking for, but texting unsolicited pics of your *dong* to strangers anonymously and consistently on a daily basis is more your speed, then have I got the vacation spot for you. Say good-bye to judges, lawyers, and being hassled by the police, and say hello to the progressive state of Georgia. In the Peach State it's perfectly legal to let your *big dick and the twins* do the talking for you, and they're ready to welcome you with arms wide open. And with your daily *cock-shot crusade*, you can make sure that when people hear the song, "Georgia on My Mind," all they'll be thinking about is your *schwantz*!

If photography of the *phallus* isn't quite your speed, and you need something more exciting, like smoking crack, nailing a hooker, and counting cards, then it's time to head to the Garden State and "America's Favorite Playground," Atlantic City, New Jersey. Welcome to your new home away from home, where at least one of those three things is perfectly legal, and the other two are extraordinarily accessible. We guarantee that you'll be in the throes of a torrid love affair with a crack whore, faded from being mounted by the *white horse,* and a hundred thousand dollars in debt on beautiful Baltic Avenue, within twenty-four hours. That's when you'll truly appreciate the biggest secret of this mystical paradise as it becomes clear to you that the tagline for Atlantic City is actually backward. It's not "Do A.C."; it's "A.C.'s Gonna Do You" *bareback* then bounce!

If all these activities don't live up to your more delicately refined *Scandinavian* inclinations, and you're just looking for a little bit of How's Your Father with an animal, you're in luck. It appears that you, the discerning zoophile, have the most options of anyone. It turns out, at the moment I'm writing this, that bestiality is legal in thirteen states, districts, and territories in the United States. Fourteen if you count Michigan, where, up until now, it's been nothing but "Great Lakes" and "Great Times" for paraphiliacs. However, I recently read that the legislature there is *"twying weyal haawd"* to pass a bill making it illegal, so you might have to hurry. But, goddamn Michigan, you were right! There was "More to See."

But it's time to seize the day! When it comes to truculent savagery, the real party's in our nation's capital! So how about heading up to Washington, D.C., where you can have a *romantic animal encounter* with a stunning view of the White House, or there's always beautiful Ka'anapali Beach in Maui, Hawaii, with its captivating sunsets and completely unlit shoreline. But wait, there's more! There are so many other dreamy destinations you should consider that are tailor-made for *sexing animals,* it's gonna make your head spin.

First stop is the "Bluegrass State," the Commonwealth of Kentucky, where if you're attracted to feral animals, "It's that Friendly." How about Nevada? Where the morality of farm sex is "Wide Open" to interpretation. Or New Hampshire, where the battle cry "Live Free or Die" has been protecting zoophilism since 1945. Then, of course, there's New Mexico, where the state animal, the black bear, is just waiting for your amorous advances in their "Land of Enchantment." And there's just "So Much to Discover" in Ohio for the modern-day zoosexual in search of a good old-fashioned *hullabaloo!* And in the great state of Texas, it's simple; if they catch you *balls-deep* in a steer, they don't mess with you, and all they ask in return is that you "Don't Mess with Texas." Ya feel me, *compadre?*

It's funny now that I think about it, but where would be the obvious place to get some serious *mooseknuckle* . . . from a "real" moose . . . that you are attracted to . . . for sexual relations? "Vermont, naturally." Don't forget "Wild and Wonderful" West Virginia: It's an all-you-can-eat *animal sex buffet* for you. I shit you not! It's "Almost Heaven." And don't even get me started on Wyoming! Yellowstone, Grand Tetons—it's quite simply "Like No Place on Earth" for a zoo fetishist looking to score some serious *four-legged poonani.* I think you know what I'm talkin' about?!! And don't dismiss the tiny but beautiful island of Guam. If your thing is to have morning sex with whatever's walking around the house, then "Where America's Day Begins" is where you want to be! As you can see, we are living in a *jizz-inhaling gerbil-fucker's paradise,* so plan your next vacation accordingly.

All joking aside . . . WTF?! There is absolutely no reason in the world why bestiality or zoophilia is legal anywhere in this great nation of ours. If you happen to live in any of the beautiful places I was joking about above, first of all, I'm sorry. I did it out of love. Those are all amazing states that deserve better than to have this blemish on them. Secondly, I ask you to please inundate your congressmen and women, senators, and state legislators with e-mails, letters, phone calls, and/or petitions to get off their deplorable asses and eradicate this nonsense. We're in our 240th year as a nation, so we've obviously navigated some seriously complicated situations. This, of all things, can't be the impossible dream that has perplexed certain lawmakers for this long. It's legal in D.C. . . . how is this even possible??!! Elaborate state affairs followed by some hot *goat-bangin'* action on the South Lawn at the White House. Is that what's for dinner? It's ridiculous! Well, the only logical reason that I can think of for why these fourteen states, one territory, and our nation's capital can't seem to get their shit together to do something this simple is that there's a possibility that a whole slew of politicians in each of these states don't wish to curtail their own personal leisure activities!! Now, I don't have proof, but I've lived long enough to know that where there's smoke, there tends to be a *"You got a hard drive full of what kind of videos?"* **FOUR-ALARM FIRE!**

Before I end this chapter, I thought I'd share with you something that might go beyond words and provide you with a more visceral understanding of this fanscape experience. The power is in the way it captivates you from the inside and transports you to another place. That's the nature of this addiction that makes it so potent. In summer 2015, I decided to attend D23, Disney Studio's own version of Comic-Con. *The Force Awakens* was six months from release, so this was going to be a *Star Wars* celebration. And since I'm sort of batty for *Star Wars*, I just had to go. The entire cast was going to appear for the first time in front of an electrified, sold-out crowd. I remember the experience of being there in incredibly vivid detail. It wasn't my first *geekgasm*, but it sure was one of the best!

When I entered the main-stage auditorium to take my seat, it all hit me, starting with the obvious. I felt a tingling, warm sensation in my torso and belly, almost like butterflies. Then, a tightness in my chest, also warm. It was all incidental, almost unnoticeable in my heightened state of anticipation. I felt attached to my seat, almost wrapped around it. But I was so excited, I couldn't sit still. I was urgently fidgeting around in my seat, which felt good and seemed to calm me. Then the houselights went down and the stage lights came up. I was filled with so much nervous tension that my subconscious was in overdrive. The sensation of movement in my muscles was eclipsed by a slight feeling of weakness in my limbs. All followed by a growing tightness in my stomach. I was a bit faint. The anticipation was killing me! I remember the crowd was so excited that we were clapping before there was anything to clap for. *Preclapulation* is an all-too-common prelude to a full-bodied *geekgasm*!

Suddenly, it began. They started bringing the actors to the stage. I felt more tightness build, and the waves of excitement started pulsating. Slowly at first but creating a creeping sensation. I tried to control them, but as more and more people came onstage, the waves just kept building. So much that I felt close to falling into them. It was the craziest reaction. It wasn't quite falling as much as it was a sense of letting go. Just relaxing into it. I felt like I was on the brink of an amazing giant stretch or a huge yawn that would push relief out through all of my limbs. It was exhilarating.

Eventually, when the original three were all finally out, the flurry of excitement hit my stomach again. Waves of it began running up from there, pushing a sneeze-like relief through my muscles, then quickly washing back down to my stomach. Back and forth. Back and forth. They would start very powerfully then gradually get calmer. It was euphoric. When it was all over, my arms felt so weak. I think I had been

clenching my hands intensely the entire time, and my muscles had begun to ache. I was in a state of release, relief, and pain. Looking back, I
think that in the heat of the moment I was so caught up, having such an
amazing time, that I wasn't breathing correctly and my body was now
paying the price. When I got home that night, I collapsed into bed, feeling completely spent but in a total state of euphoria. Sound familiar?

If you can find something in your life that can make you feel like
that . . . never let it go. One of my favorite authors, Chuck Palahniuk,
wrote in his novel *Choke*, "I think that I shall never see a poem as lovely
as a hot-gushing, butt-ramping, gut-hosing orgasm." I think Chuck
might be onto something here!

17

OF ALL THE STUPID THINGS

> But how the world turns.
> One day, cock of the walk. Next, a feather duster.
> —*Aunty Entity*, **Mad Max Beyond Thunderdome**

"Designer blowjobs," "a fucking M&M," and getting "paid by the fuck."
They could easily be three things your daughter's been raving about
since her weekend in Solvang at a "Sugar Daddy" seminar. Or they
could be three things you found in your son's grab bag after he got back
from trick-or-treating at the Bunny Ranch. But to me, they are sentimental reminders of a few special encounters in my career that I can honestly say my life would not be the same without. People who gave me
shelter beneath their shadow and inspiration from their light. I was incredibly blessed to have spent time with them. (And not in the way
attention-seeking, pious posers have sodomized that word each time
they label an Instagram of their well-garnished plate of eggs Benedict
or a *Photoshop-raped* selfie of their "true self" with *#Blessed*. I guess
#IgnorantSchmuck doesn't increase your followers on social media, but
I digress.) It was a rare privilege to have witnessed a brief glimpse of
their truth as revealed to me by the fractured lens of our unorthodox
conversations. And years of exquisitely profane exchanges with the A-list
led me to discover that, much in the same way that the eyes are the windows to the soul, cursing is a gateway to an intimate connection.

I suppose that's always been the secret of No Good TV. That

somewhere hidden between all the dick jokes and F-bombs, there exists truth and intimacy. Who would have guessed it?! I swear; if you closely watch my interviews, you'll be shocked to discover some of the most honest reflections of celebrities caught on tape. That is . . . of celebrities who know that they are being filmed and are there by choice to have their *balls tickled*. Unlike paparazzi footage, which is a whole other "ball" game. One where all the cupping, tugging, licking, icing, and mouthing are considered "foul balls!" Just ask Alec Baldwin. Truth is, no matter how many interviews I've done, to this day, it always amazes me to see it happen before my very eyes. I can't think of another place where you can get any sort of glimpse of who these public figures really are. I know how that may sound, but don't take my word for it. Take a minute and judge for yourself.

I'm sure, by now, you've figured out that entertainment is a business where reality is seldom real and sincerity is, more or less, a moving target. So you have to question the authenticity of everything you see. Pretty much everything you're bombarded with in the media—from entertainment newsmagazine fluff pieces to heartbreaking revelations on the news networks—is all scripted performance art designed to sell you something. Hell, half of the shit you read in the tabloids is fabricated and fed to them by the very people they're writing about. In a business where Nicki Minaj will showcase her butt exercise ritual on the *Kathy Lee & Hoda* morning show, then dredge up the horrible physical abuse she suffered at the hands of her father a couple of days later on *60 Minutes*, all in the name of selling the same record, there's very little room for spontaneous candor. Just to be clear, there's a place for all of it, and there's nothing wrong with using everything you've got to get to where you want to be as long as you're not hurting anybody. The point I'm trying to make is manipulated sincerity should never be confused with the truth.

In my experience, I've witnessed the subconscious purifying effect of cursing across thousands of interviews spanning well over twelve years. And I'm telling you, that shit is potent! It literally tears down your walls, triggers a reversion to your natural state of behavior, and paralyzes any instinct you might have to sell or pitch yourself. Basically, it forces your *inner assclown* to betray your mask. Because no matter how hard you try to be a media whore and sell *dat ass*, you just can't. Because it's impossible to sell anything when you're busy screaming, "Motherfucking nasty ass bitch!" as Jeremy Piven did, while laughing during our interview for *The Goods*! The only thing you can feel in that moment is the freedom and innocence of joy.

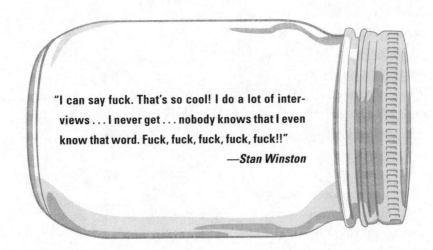

"I can say fuck. That's so cool! I do a lot of interviews . . . I never get . . . nobody knows that I even know that word. Fuck, fuck, fuck, fuck, fuck!!"
—*Stan Winston*

Now, before you give me any of your cynical crap, let me show you when you last had joy and why you've been searching for it ever since. It's that ecstasy you felt when you were still a kid in diapers. Remember when your mom asked you if you needed to go potty and you did that cute little head shake and confidently said, "No"? Then she gave you that loving mom smile, so proud that her little angel was toilet trained, and then she encouraged you to go and play. Remember how getting her approval got you so excited that you decided to tear through the house, screaming and laughing hysterically? Brimming with pure delight while that generously filled-to-capacity gift bag you were carrying left your mom presents everywhere. Now that's the bliss I'm talking about. It didn't matter that your mom didn't understand that "No" didn't mean "I don't have to go," but that it meant, "I already went . . . TWICE." Oh, the memories of youth. That's the joy we spend our entire lives trying to find. It's the same giddy joy you get from cursing, and it's like sodium pentothal for your spirit. It gives your soul a much-needed colonic.

Take for example the time I sat down with Ben Stiller to talk about *Tropic Thunder*:

Ben: *(Very enthusiastic and expressive with his hands out Al Pacino-style.)* Well, I think it's just like FUCKING AWESOME!!

Me: Yeah!

Ben: *(Being a little playful.)* Or motherfu . . . not motherfuck just fuckin' awesome!

Me: Well we don't want to fuck any mothers but it could be . . .

Ben: No we don't . . .

Me: Cocksucking awesome!

Ben: *(Surprised.)* Oh . . . wow!

Me: Also, could be one but a different connotation altogether, really . . .

Ben: *(Smiling but not quite sure what to make of it.)* This is so different than all of the other little interviews I've been doing. *(Starts laughing.)*

Me: *(Hand to chin with a serious but mischievous look.)* What do you mean? I don't understand.

Ben: *(Intrigued.)* Just more . . . again, more freeing.

Me: Ahh! Good! That's a good thing.

Ben: *(With a big smile.)* You're right!

I'm pretty sure I was the first video press interview many of them had ever done where the journalist threw out a *cocksucking* reference during the interview. It should be noted that in this case Ben *motherfucked* first. He started it!! And you can bet your ass, it always made a major impact! Almost immediately a relationship would form between us that would go from shock to disbelief to paranoia to curiosity to fun and then end in euphoria. One way or the other, they would never forget me, and more often than not, they welcomed me with open arms the next time we met. What I was doing was dangerous, rebellious, and liberating, which made me catnip for artists and creatives.

One completely unexpected person I connected with immediately was the incredibly talented actor Michael Clarke Duncan. I was very fortunate to get to know him before he sadly passed away in 2012. He was such an incredible presence and such a kind and gentle soul. He appeared on No Good TV countless times, and it was always lovely to be in his presence. What was so amazing and somewhat surprising about Michael was that he completely got No Good TV and was a huge fan.

The childish giddiness of talking nonsense and letting loose and laughing just really connected with him. He was always tooting our horn as I'd be entering the room to interview him or when I'd be leaving. Who would have ever guessed? It was the coolest thing you could imagine, and what a gift he left us.

I recently discovered that the cameras had caught him doing it at the *Welcome Home, Roscoe Jenkins* junket. He was paired with actress Joy Bryant and was talking to her as we were wrapping up the interview:

MCD: *(Turning toward Joy.)* This is No Good TV, Joy. No good. Okay?
  Me: He knows a thing or two.
MCD: *(Continues talking to Joy.)* It's funny! . . . *(He just keeps smiling and repeating to Joy:)* You gotta watch. You gotta see it. You gotta see this! You gotta see it! *(Then he turns to me.)* Thank you, baby! *(Then right back to Joy.)* You gotta see No Good TV. It's funny as hell, funny as hell, funny!!!!

I'll never forget that day and I'll never forget Michael. I was very lucky to have spent time with him, and it brings me endless joy to know just how much he looked forward to our shenanigans. He was a very special guy.

Over the course of multiple engagements throughout the years, I became privy to a different side of celebrities and formed special connections with some of them that grew out of our uniquely surreal repartees. It was an unexpected gift in an already rewarding life. In the end, I've learned just how lucky those of us who get to sit across from greatness and recount it as a chapter in our own personal histories are. I can attest to the fact that not all heroes disappoint, and neither does the unpredictable hand of fate.

The great irony about crossing paths with fateful events or destiny is the unexpectedly delayed gravity of that moment and how it is often paired with an incomprehensibly frivolous mental reminder. I mean, when I think back to the very first time I thought that I had made it in this business, you might assume I'd think of the day we closed our first five-million-dollar round of financing, or the day we moved into our big new production studio, or maybe the first time our channel became the most viewed network on YouTube. And . . . you'd be wrong. I think of Gene Simmons showing me his nuts!

No, it's not what you think. Gene and I didn't end up in the sack. As Mrs. Doubtfire would say, "It was more of a drive-by fruiting!" He had invited me to the set of his new music video to watch him in action, conduct some interviews, and shoot the making of an uncensored version of his video exclusively for NGTV. The whole scene was a bit surreal. There I was, chillin' with a rock legend that I had spent my childhood dreaming of meeting someday. Now, suddenly, Gene *"It's called business not friends"* Simmons was my business partner. WHAT!! The world had suddenly become our playground and celebrities our Wallholla vertical urban play structure. (Look it up. It's awesome!) Plus, thanks to Mr. "Let's Put the X in Sex," we now had access to an unlimited supply of Diet RC Cola. All that was missing were the MoonPies!

It was an amazing day. Then suddenly, in the middle of shooting a scene in the video that I can best describe as a *boobie car wash*, Gene split his pants, à la Lenny Kravitz, and out popped his family jewels. I remember thinking, *Holy shitballs, what do I do? Do I look away? Do I engage them? Do I pretend his jingle bells aren't on display? What's the decorum for such an occurrence?* And then, in true Gene fashion, and without skipping a fucking beat, he smiled at me as if nothing had happened and gracefully proceeded to give me and the forty-plus member crew on set a fruit basket to remember. And all I could think of was, *WOW! I've finally made it!*

But it doesn't stop there. No! Whether it was a beautiful memory or a devastating tragedy, I honor and treasure it with a silly memento in my noggin. So now you know how my warped mind works; you can see that I'm a gal who loves to live life and collect ridiculous mental artifacts. And of all the stupid things I remember, this chapter is dedicated to a few of the ones that meant the most.

As an entertainment journalist, you frequently find yourself at the center of events that shape our culture, interacting with the very people who are bringing about that change. It's a remarkable experience with marked limitations. You can look but you can't touch. Your job is to observe and report. It doesn't matter if it's for the *Today* show, *Entertainment Tonight,* or an online outlet like People.com; your job is to bear witness. Your voice is not your own. It's never about you. You're just there to look pretty, read the prompter, and smile. Trust me. I've been there smiling so hard I couldn't feel my fuckin' face. Truthfully, it's a good gig if you can get it, but it's a hollow experience.

The best way I can describe it is like being a ghost surrounded by remarkable objects but unable to hold, touch, or feel any of them. Without realizing it, you begin your descent into transparency on day one of your job and complete your transition on the day you retire. And it doesn't discriminate. Even Mary Hart, arguably the best in the biz, after twenty-nine years of time in, was, in the end, completely invisible. I was very fortunate that I was with No Good TV because I wasn't there to witness and report. I was not a *"ghost host."* I was there as a surrogate for our viewers, who wanted to feel the moment, interact with it, and experience the insanity. So that's exactly what I did.

As a result, I would have to say that the single most extraordinary thing about my career, besides the fact that I have one, is that not only have I had a front-row seat and a backstage pass to pop culture history, but that I actually got to touch it and feel it. And perhaps, more importantly, I was touched by it. Not in the way your bathrobe belt sometimes falls into an unnervingly full toilet without you realizing it, only to slap its marinated mass against your leg once you stand up, but it was still very impactful. And when I look back on the most profound experiences I've had, the ones that pierce you to the bone and leave you forever changed, I remember my brushes with the brilliant few who wandered into my life, touched my soul, and left too soon. The ones who made me laugh, made me cry, made me kiss my self-doubts good-bye.

In the summer of 2007, after years of hard work and preparation, I was finally being seen and heard as my interviews for No Good TV started to light up the most-viewed charts on YouTube daily. My take-no-prisoners approach to interviews and my potty mouth were starting to crack the aging veneer of the Hollywood press machine. Whether publicists or studio reps were comfortable or not with my methods, millions of people were watching online, so the madness could not be denied. One thing about the movie business you can always count on is that they'll promote a family film and sell you food and drinks during a violent and bloody crucifixion if they think a lot of people will be watching. Does anyone remember seeing the trailer for *White Chicks* before diving into *The Passion of the Christ*? I swear, truth is stranger than fiction. But maybe some things are best left in the past.

Anyway, I was having a fucking blast, but that didn't mean that I wasn't taking my role as a strong female voice in the media very seriously. In the beginning, there were always those who looked at me funny or questioned my motives, but I ignored them. After all, who could blame them? They didn't know who or what I was about. I knew I had to earn their respect. As far as I was concerned, nowhere was it said that cursing and integrity were mutually exclusive. I knew I was trampling all over certain people's comfort zones and pushing the boundaries of acceptable behavior, but I wasn't doing it to make a statement; I was just being me.

I admit there were times when I wondered if the path I had chosen had a future or was just an explosive act of self-sabotage. But my path was set and there was no turning back. In time, whatever doubts I had would, ultimately, be laid to rest after a series of mystifying encounters with three iconic figures resulting in astonishing consequences. I can't explain how or why these things happened. And I'm not sure that I can do them any justice here with words. But if "designer blowjobs," "a fucking M&M," and getting "paid by the fuck" don't deserve to be paid forward, then I don't know what does!

Lucky for me, No Good TV has always been a place to see the unexpected appearance from legendary figures. People who you might assume would avoid taking a dip in the *verbal-gangbang-Jacuzzi-joust* we call a format. But the truth is, we've long considered our greatest accomplishment to be my sit-downs with the Hollywood establishment. Those celebrities that make you say, "Who the fuck did she blow to make this happen?" Such as the NGTV appearances by icons the likes of Morgan Freeman, Robert Redford, Jane Fonda, Alan Rickman, Peter Falk, Dame Julie Andrews, Dame Helen Mirren, Dame Judi Dench, Harold Ramis, Larry David, Sir Michael Caine, Sir Ben Kingsley, Sir Anthony Hopkins, Robert Duvall, Alan Alda, Cher, Madonna, Diane Keaton, and filmmakers Rob Reiner, Sydney Pollack, Ron Howard, Robert Altman, Sidney Lumet, and Francis Ford Coppola, to name a few. Sadly, some of the immeasurably talented artists I've encountered are no longer with us, but I am extremely honored to have spent a little time in their presence.

Those are the interviews that I wear like a badge of honor. Without question, they have always served as our greatest validators and powerful evidence that our format appeals to everyone. Now, I'm not saying that every interview is a *wall-to-wall fuck-fest*. All I'm saying is that not being able to say whatever is on your mind and not being able to describe your experiences without censorship is the "CON" in conversation that traditional media has hoodwinked us with. Profanity is the common jargon that unites all people because, like I've been saying, everybody curses. I swear! And if you judge me by the sheer number of the who's who that have appeared on NGTV, then you can safely assume I've blown everybody!!

DESIGNER BLOWJOBS

No matter how many iconic celebrities I interviewed, I always went into each one with a certain degree of trepidation. For me the stakes were never higher than in those situations. So when legendary author Jackie Collins walked into No Good TV to tape an interview with me in July of 2007, it was no different. I had no idea what to expect. In my mind, I was preparing for the worst. I was afraid she was going to be an intellectually dismissive snob possessing all the social graces of a sharp-clawed gay man. Behind my cool exterior, my anxiety mirrored the alarm you feel when you accidentally walk in on your cat in mid-diarrhea, only to find yourself in the middle of a *Mexican standoff* where one wrong move leaves you needing a new couch and a full set of new bed linens!

What if this almost-mythical literary figure in her late sixties, who had witnessed the sexual and cultural revolutions of the past fifty years, found our brand of cool shit to be a little too . . . well, SHIT! What if she took one look at us and thought that she had just walked in on a bunch of fourteen-year-old boys at a college panty-raid? And by US, I mean ME. I have to admit, it was a bit daunting. Let's face it, rejection is tough, but rejection from someone you admire is like a blunt-force trauma to the crotch! But I pushed my fears aside because I REALLY REALLY wanted to meet her SOOOOO BADLY. Let's face it: A possible hit to the dick was a small price to pay for a little quality time with JC.

Jackie Collins breezed into our studio and into my life with the elegance of a Hollywood starlet from its golden age and the refined prose from the life she ferociously devoured. She was the epitome of cool and the embodiment of grace. She was exquisite in conversation and exuded an effortless sense of style that reflected her powerful and independent spirit. I was completely mesmerized by her warmth and captivated by her charm. In a word, she was absolutely GLORIOUS. I was instantly smitten.

I should never have doubted that if there was anyone who was going to get what I was trying to do and what No Good TV was all about, it would be Jackie Collins. Her entire professional life was an unorthodox journey across a misogynistic literary jungle that she resolutely macheted her way through. She captivated and riveted readers worldwide with gorgeously filthy and graphic stories of lust, money, power, revenge, sex, sex, and more sex. She had been fearlessly pushing boundaries, redefining acceptable behavior, and fighting for female empowerment for over fifty years, with thirty-two bestselling novels and over half a billion books sold. She was my hero.

We clicked instantly and got along like we had known each other forever. When I looked into her eyes, I could see myself in forty years. She was so youthful and vibrant. She reminded me so much of my crazy aunt Betty, whom I adored. Both of them were a force of nature and didn't give a shit what anyone thought. They were soundly resolute in who they were and beautifully unique. Jackie was wonderful to talk to. She loved our uncensored format and my love of cursing. In some ways, you could say we were the digital modern-day embodiment of gratuitously filthy entertainment geared for mass consumption. This was Jackie's domain. So when she was with me at NGTV, she was home, and she loved letting the viewers know it: "I'm with Carrie on No Good Television and you know what that means? It means a lot of FUCK YOU!!" I was very fortunate to sit down with her a number of times, and each time, I found myself laughing and learning something new about who I was and could be. She was always incredibly supportive and helped me understand that what I was doing was, in no small way, pushing forward the very same agenda she had been for her entire career. It connected us and gave me a lot of courage. It also made me very proud.

I was always so impressed and captivated by her wonderfully relaxed conversational manner. She never let her culture and status become an obstacle in connecting with people. She was easy and accessible, which made her even more delightful. She sure knew how to tell a story and could, all at once, be funny, lewd, off-the-cuff, campy, elegant, and blunt. Her razor-sharp wit gave her raunchiness a touch of elegance and charm. She had a gentle voice, a beautiful smile, and a contagious laugh. She had a kindness to her that was almost maternal that lured you into her world of incalculable mischief. And the way she owned the word "Darling!" you'd think it was invented for her and completely wasted on others.

Our interviews were dirty as fuck. They always went long and were extensions of the conversation we had begun at our bar as soon as she would arrive. We would then take our drinks over to the set, sit down, and pick up where we'd left off, chatting each other's ears off until the cameras ran out of tape. Then, afterward, we'd have another drink and continue until we were completely caught up. It never felt like work. It was pure fun. There were never any topics that were out of bounds. Jackie was quite fluent in the worlds that she wrote about, so we would have the most graphic and honest conversations about everything.

We had a lot of crazy conversations, and she was always giving me the lowdown on the latest sex craze in the Hollywood underground. Jackie liked to lace her novels with outlandish ideas that were based on real-world occurrences. So she was always researching the latest dirt on the streets. My favorite Jackie research story that fits the "so insane, it has to be real" category was, of course, "designer blowjobs." So, apparently, some well-placed Hollywood acolyte had been painstakingly cataloging the blowjob techniques of famous celebrities. He was gathering the information either from personal sexual encounters or from interviewing sexual partners for the play-by-play on the details. And from what she understood, his list of celebrities read like the guest list to the Academy Awards, so there was some concern about his intentions.

Funnily enough, his intention wasn't to write a book or expose anyone, although who knows at this point. His objective was to form a private escort service that would provide designer blowjobs! The service would train their girls in the various fellatio techniques, per his research, so that clients could call and request a specific celebrity blowjob! So, hypothetically, if you were a huge Megan Fox fan, you could call and place an order for the "Fox Experience," and they would send a girl who looks like her to give you a blowjob with all the dazzling style, tip-nibbling technique, and masterful ball handling you might fantasize about getting from this A-lister. At least that was the working theory.

But what Jackie found the most fascinating was that the drama behind the scenes with the starlets had nothing to do with the fact that this sexual catalogue had been created. Far from it. The starlets' primary concern was with the accuracy of the information regarding their individual blowjob technique and how it might reflect poorly on them in any way. Mainly because they didn't want to look bad with potential casting agents, producers, and filmmakers who might utilize the service to order their specific blowjob before hiring them only to discover it was lacking. Apparently, starlets across Tinseltown had fears that they might lose work this way. So they were aggressively attempting to rectify any potential problems that might be created by their catalogued oral work by requesting a redo in order to optimize their performance. Only in Hollywood!!!

Conversations with Jackie were hard to forget. And after a while, I started to realize that there was method to her madness, and that she had a subtle but poignant agenda in everything she wrote and spoke about. I remember one particular conversation we once had about the correlation between *tits* and *balls*. She had very specific views on men and their testicles. She thought if society encouraged women to get breast implants to attract men, then men should be urged to get silicone testicle implants to attract women. She was of the opinion that women deserved a sexy and solid set of balls to look at and hold, and the very least men could do is enhance the depth and weight of their balls for them.

I recall she really got on my case and made fun of me because I wasn't as *ball-knowledgeable* and *sac-sophisticated* as she expected me to be during our deep *ball-talk*. What can I say? I've always been more of a dick girl! Then, later, when she tried to get me to take my top off. That's right. Jackie Collins tried to get me to take my top off. I told you she was awesome! Anyway, I declined because I didn't have a cute enough bra on, so she declared to the world, "She knows nothing about balls, but she knows plenty about bras! That's our Carrie! That's why we love her." And that's my Jackie, and that's why I loved her. Every perverse discussion we had was in some way really about sexual equality between men and women. Her books were designed in the same way. Her words were dirty, but they always had a greater purpose.

This simple truth has been a great source of inspiration for me, and I've always felt that Jackie and I were kindred spirits. The more I've learned about her, the more I think of how lucky I was to have had the chance to know her. I had been following in her storied footsteps without knowing it, and it gave me great relief when I found her. She pushed boundaries forward with her salacious and sexual novels in much the same way I pushed boundaries forward with my uncensored interviews and irreverent approach. Which, generally, would result in another thing Jackie and I had in common. The shared experience of having ridiculously bizarre creative discussions about the work we did and how people would interpret what they thought was indecent and what wasn't. And not necessarily strangers because, quite often, these people were close to us. I remember her being left a little dumbstruck by an odd conversation she had recently had with a new editor she talked about in an interview: "I had a new editor and she said to me, 'You have too much cleavage on the back of book.' And then she said to me, 'Why can't the blowjob start the book?' and I go, 'But it's not about blowjobs.' So she said, 'Yeah but it's a great blowjob. Can't we have that?' I said 'Wait a minute—what are you talking about? You're telling me I have too much cleavage in my picture, and you want the BLOWJOB to start the book?!'" I could definitely relate to that. Jackie was always ahead her time, as I have been. I can only hope that I have the perseverance and tenacity to stay the course as she did, unrepentantly.

She was a feminist literary dynamo. She wrote about powerful, rich, and sexy women before the book market was ready for them. She was dropping F-bombs in her work and getting banned all over the world before it was cool and hip. She wrote about women in control who were engaging in what were then considered to be "sordid acts" when no one else was. In a strange act of irony, her early works were published around the same time birth control pills were first gaining acceptance and feminism was taking ambitious form. In fact, some of the ideas in her books came to life. In her novel *Lovehead*, later retitled *The Love Killers*, published in 1974, she wrote about the prostitutes in New York going on strike, and a few months after the book came out, guess what? The prostitutes in New York went on strike. It was remarkable. In a crazy way, she wrapped women's lib inside what some might call smut. In my experience, smut is what ignorant cowards call colloquialism when they don't understand it.

Her genius was that she took control of the very thing that was being used to objectify and diminish women and utilized it to empower them. The most fascinating part of it all was that she wasn't plotting and scheming. This wasn't some grand design. It was completely organic. She was just being herself. In that way, we are the same. We both use entertainment and relatability to push women's rights forward. Not because we're political animals but because we don't like being told no, we really don't give a fuck what anyone thinks, and we truly can't help but be who we are. Two women who didn't need anyone to tell them that equal rights across the board are nonnegotiable. We already knew!

Jackie Collins's brilliance existed in her inexhaustible ability to dance on the tip of a literary needle. A needle of light she used to sew a beautiful tapestry of powerful female characters into the fabric of pop culture. She didn't do it with elitist verbalism. Rather, her message was delivered on the back of a communal vernacular filled with vulgar truths and beautiful lies. Gritty stories from the real world elevated to fantasies of raw sex and violence, all masterfully manipulated for a population desperate for a gratifying release. Her real life was an audacious reflection of her art, filled with equal parts frivolity and purpose. All designed to mask a hidden resolve. For with every word she wrote, she edged forward the ascent of feminism in her own way. Sometimes with a gentle nudge and sometimes with a violent thrust.

The last time I spent time with Jackie was in February of 2013, when she graciously appeared on my VH1 morning show for the second time. It was a momentous day for me and the show as that morning marked our transition from our tiny set in the lobby of VH1 to the magnificence of the historic *TRL* studio overlooking Times Square. I was beyond ecstatic to share that with her. It was amazing that, by that time, we had known each other for almost six years . . . WOW! There was a calming familiarity between us as we gossiped during the break. I remember how incredibly excited she was for me when I told her the news that I was going to write a book. She could not have been more proud. She was like that, you know—supportive of other women. I was deeply touched.

Of course, I had no idea that she had been diagnosed with breast cancer in 2009 and that each time I had seen her since then, she had been bravely battling it in complete secrecy. Her energy, warmth, and lyrical swagger never once betrayed her. In her final interview with *People,* she said, "I didn't want people's sympathy. I think sympathy can weaken you. I don't live my life that way." Perhaps it was in her obstinacy that she was the most inspiring. She was one of a kind and remarkable in every way.

We were setting a date to see each other again in the fall of 2015 to promote what turned out to be her final book. But, alas, it was not meant to be. My beloved Jackie Collins passed away on September 19, at the age of seventy-seven. On that day we lost a beautiful soul and an extraordinary woman. While the time I spent with her might only amount to specks of dust across the infinite void, I am forever changed by it and eternally grateful. She was one of the kindest and most generous people

I've had the pleasure of knowing. She lived as she wrote, beautifully and fabulously! That was who she was. That's who I aspire to be.

Thank you, Jackie.

A FUCKING M&M

In life, sometimes profound insights are born of unanticipated consequences resulting from unimaginable scenarios. Sort of like the time I fell madly in love and ran away with a wild and sexually adventurous guy who pushed my boundaries and excited me more than I ever thought possible, only to discover that *mah* Prince Charmin' preferred to orgasm while defecating into a diaper. (Yeah . . . it's a thing. Take a minute if you need it . . . Fuck it! Take two . . .) Well, you'd be amazed at how quickly it led me to reevaluate my priorities; ditch Romeo's swaddled ass, knee-deep in his own *mud*; and get my life back on track. 'Cause you don't need to get fucked, just 'cause you got kissed! Which, naturally, brings me to the sweet memory of a curious encounter with a complicated but kind actor, many years ago, the effects of which multiplied over time and rippled across my professional life. He may have sealed the deal with an M&M, but it was his incredible warmheartedness that made *waking up* with Heath Ledger such a bittersweet affair. Again, it's not what you're thinking, and I don't mean to pump your *grundle*, but you can trust me when I tell you that an inconceivable quickie with Heath led me to an earth-shattering revelation. And I've had a special connection to him ever since.

The crazy-sweet irony of this story is that it should never have happened. Heath and I came from two different sides of the Hollywood tracks. I was a simple girl with complicated inclinations. He was a complicated actor with very specific tendencies. I was, generally, a happy person and easy to get along with. He was generally pensive and took a long time to warm up to you. I had a filthy sense of humor and I loved to laugh . . . a lot . . . at pretty much anything . . . to the point of being annoying. He was pretty modest and his humor was reserved for his close friends.

In strictly technical terms, I saw him as a foreign exchange student who was having a hard time understanding our culture, and he probably saw me as one of those Asian hip-hop junkies with the sick dance moves. We understood that we didn't understand each other, if we understood anything at all. But if you know your *West Side Story* then you understand that the Jets and the Sharks don't mix. At best, it was an uneasy truce. Of course, there was the occasional bit of no-contact dance fighting, which was a pretty accurate way of describing our previous interviews together. I always found it easier to connect with the playful celebs, and he always played his cards very close to his vest. We had been running into each other for years, and let's just say very few *"bruhs"* were exchanged. So if anyone was going to profoundly impact my life, it wasn't going to be him. Plus, he wasn't exactly a fan of the press.

Heath was a very nice person and we got along. But some of the most amazing actors in the world are notoriously press shy and detest doing interviews . . . with anyone. They're all about the work, and the rest of it is just invasive and unnatural. For some it's easier playing a character than playing themselves. They find comfort in fiction and anxiety in everything else. All my experiences up until that point made me consider Heath to be press incompatible, which meant that the best outcome I could ever hope for in an interview with him was a stalemate, so I stopped pushing.

And by the way, for anyone just starting out, until you figure out which actors are in this group and adjust your tact in the interviews, like I eventually did, get used to being a ball in the pinball machine of awkward experiences. You're about to enter the junket equivalent of *The Twilight Zone*. You'll get to experience everything from the uncomfortable, demeaning, and insulting to the rude, condescending, and bizarre, and that's before you've even asked your first question. From there it's kind of like a *BDSM session* but without the complimentary *suck 'n' fuck*! It's made up of ducking and weaving with a solid bit of dodging and skeeving. But don't expect anyone to take pity on you and explain that it's not your fault. You'll be left to stew in your own failure and insecurity. As far as anyone is concerned, you signed up for *ferret-legging* as your elective this semester, and by God, you're going to see it through. So why do we, the press, tolerate this? Have you sampled the buffet at the Four Seasons Hotel? Round-trip airfare and free popcorn? We may be whores but we're not stupid.

All kidding aside, I've never had issues with the more serious and self-analytical artists, but I've always found those relationships to be far too complex to allow any room for joy. In the beginning, I quickly came to realize that in those interviews, it was next to impossible to get close and connect with those celebrities. They were so guarded that there was no clear path to finding any truth. There was never any opportunity for fun. It always made me feel like I was lost on the *ass side of ball town*. Those sit-downs were more like cerebral expeditions into the outer reaches of an emotional abyss. Wonderful if you're Charlie Rose, but it might as well be a documentary on Dutch hegemony in the 1600s for us. I couldn't understand what place these more introspective interviews would have on NGTV. I didn't know it then, but the answer would turn out to be right in front of me.

When I'm able to break down that wall or take off that mask with the most closed-off stars, it's the best feeling in the world. But Heath Ledger had never been an easy interview. He was never rude. He was never unpleasant. But he could be pretty introverted and reserved. I liked him. There was nothing not to like. He was a very sweet and gentle guy, but I swear to God, it was like pulling teeth trying to get him to open up. I always thought he just didn't enjoy the constant self-analysis that went hand-in-hand with doing press. Even my light touch suffered the consequences of his pathologically press-shy nature. On the plus side, he wasn't media-treated or a press whore, for no other reason than because he just didn't give a shit. Every time I'd seen him in the past, like for *The Brothers Grimm* or *Lords of Dogtown*, he was super polite. "Nice to see you again," he'd say, and then we'd do another interview that felt like a staring contest . . . with words, only to be occasionally saved by a boisterous cast mate like Matt Damon who was paired with him.

However, all that was about to change when I went to interview Heath in November 2007, at the junket for the movie *I'm Not There*. He'd already finished filming Christopher Nolan's *The Dark Knight* and was waiting for it to be released the following summer, and the future seemed brimming with possibilities. Our truly unforgettable final sit-down together was elegant, simple, and profoundly poetic. The impact of our conversation would be almost immediate. Opening my eyes and expanding my perception of my role as a journalist. And within a few short months, it would alter my entire perspective on the true power of No Good TV as a guardian of historical record for the fans.

From the moment I walked into the room, I noticed Heath was not himself, and I mean that in a good way. He appeared to have gone through a cataclysmic change in attitude, which I found both exciting and alarming. Sort of like going to a nude beach in the Middle East. Now, he wasn't about to do cartwheels and scream out "Suck my nutsack!" He just seemed really relaxed.

As I sat down, the crew was still going through final preparations before we could start rolling. So Heath and I started chitchatting, which was unusual for him. During the interview, I could feel a sense of calm in his demeanor as if he was actually enjoying his time with me. He appeared whimsical and open, almost at ease. You could see the fascination in my face. All I could do was sit there and watch this moment unfold and do my best to just be in it with him and enjoy the ride. None of it made any logical sense, and there wasn't going to be any logical way to edit this, but I knew what was happening was very special. How special, I had no idea at the time.

Me: *(Reminding him.)* We're uncensored.
Heath: Do you just swear because you're allowed to swear?
Me: Sometimes. Sometimes it's just better for emphasis.
Heath: *(Laughing heartily.)* That's funny. Do you want a *fuckin'* M&M?
Me: I would love a fuckin' M&M! Thanks, man! This is gonna be my Dylan M&M!

My inner voice lit up, screaming: *What the fuck is happening here? Why is he enjoying himself? Why am I? Who the hell is this guy and where the hell is Heath?* Followed by the next logical thought: *Clearly, this is an alien abduction!* I had come prepared for oral surgery with a sweet but very uncooperative patient and not this delightful charm-bashing I lay victim to. When you're the battered wife in a junket relationship, the absence of hope is your oxygen, and you keep breathing it in like it's running out. So I naturally concluded: *It must be a trap.*

I felt like I was living out the knock-knock joke where you're painfully put through: *"Knock knock! Who's there? Banana. Banana who?"* countless times and then, when you least expect it, you're hit with, *"Knock knock! Who's there? Orange. Orange who? Orange you glad I didn't say banana!"* Yes, you get the sweet relief of finally getting a fucking orange before you pull all your hair out. But, in the end, what happens? You still get hit over the head with another motherfucking banana!!! Now, isn't that just the way life is!! And this is coming from me, the architect of the original banana theory from the intro! So how could I possibly know if Heath's orange wasn't really a banana, and why on earth would I take that chance?

So I decided to stay the course and not get too excited. No doubt it was an unexpected start to the interview, but the odds were he would step back into his normal, more subdued comfort zone. So as tempting as it was to get in there and cuss it up, I knew that a sudden move on my part to pick up what *mah* man Heath was throwin' down could be a mistake that would leave my ass hanging out in the breeze.

That hesitation proved to be a revelation. I lay back and let it play out with nothing but some gentle nudges here and there, following his lead. And I couldn't believe it; he continued to aimlessly banter with me. He touched on some vagaries and bullshit about Bob Dylan with almost an ambivalence toward any sort of journalistic Q&A protocol. A structure that had, in the past, always been something he adhered to. He wasn't one to reveal much, but what he did say lacked the casual disregard of today. After years of playing the pseudo-intellectual equivalent of *shin-kicking* at junkets worldwide, I simply couldn't believe that we were now just a couple of girls playing double Dutch in the courtyard. And yet, that was exactly what we were doing.

Then at one point in the conversation, and much to my bewilderment, Heath suddenly got up and walked out of the interview and over to the other side of the room. Of course, in my mind, I instantly began to wonder if he was about to Bruce Willis my ass, but no. Heath was a class act. He just grabbed his pack of smokes, then came back and sat down, all the while continuing our conversation, which led to another out-of-character exchange:

Heath: You know, I think I had the easiest task of anyone else in the movie . . . (*He gets up and walks off camera while continuing to talk.*)

Me: Uh-huh.
(*I follow his movements, trying to figure out if security is seconds away from dragging me out.*)

Heath: I can smoke? Right?

Me: Absolutely! (*In a total sense of wonderment.*)

Heath: If you can say "fuck," you can smoke a cigarette!!

Me: I think you're probably right!! (*We both laugh.*)

> *(He then proceeds to light up on camera, and we continue to just talk about all kinds of random shit. Some of it just fuckin' around and every so often a little gem.)*

Me: Do you think it's ever wise to argue with a woman about pain? And who feels more pain?

Heath: It's not wise . . . No. *(With a knowing grin.)*

Me: Probably not so much! Do you think you could ever win that battle?

Heath: Not me. No. I wouldn't start that battle, either. *(I could tell he was talking from experience.)*

He never stopped smiling. He was chuckling the whole time. He never got awkward. He never withdrew. He never disengaged. It was a very atypical interview for him and me. We were both engrossed in a stream of consciousness and just rolled with it. Like a couple of stoners, we had a lovely chat about I don't even know what, for five minutes. Honestly, I didn't even care. After years of polite avoidance and artful dodging, Heath and I had finally found our happy place. It's not somewhere that I had ever been before and it sure wasn't anywhere that he'd ever been before, but it was a place where we both, somehow, belonged. He even cursed . . . in his own way and at his own pace, but he did it:

Me: Your particular version of Dylan though, you kind of got to be the one that maybe most people didn't know about. He was kind of the jerk of the six characters. How did you feel about playing sort of the asshole Dylan?

Heath: Oh . . . FUCK!

Me: That works, too.

Heath: Umm . . . yeah. There you go. It popped out. It was natural.

Me: It feels good.

Heath: Yeah! Run with it!!

And there I was in the presence of one of the most notoriously shy, uncomfortable, and unyielding actors, just hanging out, shooting the shit, and smokin' a cigarette. I remember walking out of the interview lost in the moment with a big dumb grin on my face. I didn't know what to make of it then, but I loved every second of it.

I called Kourosh afterward, feeling very reflective, like I had just witnessed something rare but indefinable. "I wouldn't say it was the most eventful day, but it was special," I told him. "I don't know if anyone else is going to get it. I don't know if it's going to resonate. How do we make this work in the context of our edit? What the fuck do we do with this? I just know what it felt like in the room, and it was different. It was really special." When I got back to LA, we all got together in an edit bay to watch the footage that had left me speechless. There were, maybe, six of us in the room. All of us were quite familiar with the numerous interviews with Heath that had come before and how difficult it had been to engage him. So everyone watched intently, and when it was over, there was a distinct and prolonged silence in the room. We were all thinking the same thing: *alien abduction!*

Then Kourosh turned to me and said, "That was somethin' else. You've never been there before. It was so honest and so intimate." Everyone in the room nodded in agreement, still somewhat stunned. "I say we run it almost as-is. A straight back-and-forth from the second the footage starts to when it ends, even if it's a bit sloppy." He continued, "People are either going to get it or they won't, but we don't want to fuck with what happened in the room!" So we made the cut and posted it online. It really wasn't an interview exactly; it was just a special moment in time, and we elected to just let it be. *I'm Not There* was a small movie, but we were eight months out from Heath's much-anticipated role as the Joker in *The Dark Knight* so our piece did well and got a good amount of traction online. But we had no clue how well, and no one could have anticipated the tragedy that lay ahead or the surprising role that we would play in keeping his memory alive.

Two months after our all-too-brief encounter, Heath Ledger was found dead in his apartment in SoHo from an accidental drug overdose at the age of twenty-eight. I found myself engulfed in a deep melancholy. I felt like we had just been introduced for the first time in New York, and I was so looking forward to the next time . . . but now it would never come. You couldn't help but feel this great emptiness. But this horribly sad incident had turned the whole experience into an even more beautiful gift. My immediate thought was to take down the video because it felt opportunistic to leave it up, plus with all the cursing, I didn't want anyone to misinterpret it as disrespectful. But a couple of weeks later, something completely unexpected happened.

We started to get inundated with Google alerts about my how my interview with Heath had been posted on dozens and dozens of sites. Needless to say, we were a little concerned about how this was happening because it was not under our control, and more importantly, how it was being received. And that's where I received the most heartwarming news. It turns out that my interview was quite a hit with Heath's fans, who had recorded it off of our YouTube channel and started reposting it. We discovered they were including it at the top of their tribute pages and as part of their top five lists of favorite interviews ever with Heath.

It didn't end there. Over the next couple of months, we received countless e-mails thanking us for the best interview ever captured with Heath. I'd definitely never seen him like that before, and apparently neither had his fans. It was an incredible affirmation and one of the most extraordinary things I had ever witnessed. Seeing his fans take such ownership of the video and respond to it so powerfully was beyond words. I knew it was special to me and to us, but I had no idea that I'd captured something so intimate and transcendent. They'd never seen him with his guard down completely, and this was the closest they'd ever felt to him on camera. It made me so happy to think that I may have played some small role in keeping his memory alive. That was, without a doubt, the most humbling and gratifying part of this entire affair.

Heath and I barely knew each other. We briefly engaged in maybe half a dozen pleasant but unremarkable exchanges over the course of five years. Yet somehow, during the course of five astonishing minutes in November of 2007, it culminated in an awakening that changed everything for me and No Good TV. In *Star Trek* terms, the extemporaneous convergence of our two lives is the causal nexus between my past and present as well as that of NGTV.

The entire experience with Heath had opened my eyes to the greater possibilities that lay before NGTV. We were uncensored, yes, but our format wasn't just about swearing; it was a blueprint for free expression. It began with cursing because that was a bridge to connection and intimacy, which is the path to truth. So our endgame has always been about truth. And through this experience, I came to better understand the nature of truth in the moment, and letting the moment take you to wherever that is. I didn't need to focus on whether an interview would edit together or if it was funny enough or dirty enough. There are no rules. It didn't matter if the film was serious or if the actor was solemn and restrained. All I needed to do was to find each person's happy place, their truth, and spend my time with them, there. The rest would follow and it has ever since.

The big reveal is that truth is in the dead space, the breathing, and the pauses, not in the questions and answers. So many of us journalists walk into interviews with the questions we need to ask and the answers we want to get, and if we don't come out with both then it's a failure. For me, after Heath, neither has ever mattered; it was about the space between, which is where truth lives. I no longer feel any pressure to drown a conversation with phatic expressions or to justify my presence with endless *aizuchi*. The silence is where the magic happens. That's where the real person emerges and the deluge of media treatment and bullshit disappears. Even when the interviews are sparse, awkward, or uncomfortable, the celebrities are still being more true to themselves than at any other time.

I've learned that more often than not, it's not about what is said, but rather what is not said and what's left hanging in limbo. The true penetrating thought is not found in the din of an exchange but in the repose, a gentle glance, and a short breath that pierces the soul and fills the heart. In that moment, everything we are and hope to be surrenders into an oblivion of choices never made and intentions unfulfilled. The greatest of artists, orators, and statesmen and -women across time are not purely defined by what they said or did but by the very nature of their hesitations. It is in these sculptures of their negative space that we are given a brief glimpse of their truth. It is only there that we connect with the full measure of who they were and ever hoped to be.

It makes me really proud that so many of the most intimate and honest moments you'll ever see with stars are in interviews with NGTV. We may fuck around and curse and act ridiculous sometimes, but we also do so much that means something to a lot of people. That's the main reason why we started doing this in the first place. And the times we do it the best are when we are obviously doing it for the people who feel the exact same way we do. You, the fans.

PAID BY THE FUCK

Of all the stars I've ever interviewed, there's one guy who always lived up to his legendary status. An artist I revered equally for his brilliance and his generosity. A rare combination for a man who made his bones as a stand-up comic: a profession that relishes a healthy ego and a taste for selective savagery. He always brought out the best in me as an interviewer because facing him meant I had to have my fluency *on fleek*! The man had *oral* skills that would make your head spin.

He'd appreciate me saying that. Come to think of it, we'd probably end up in a lengthy conversation about his other *aural* skills as well. I can just see him riffing on how comedy was basically an exercise in fucking your ears or making love to them, depending on the quality of the stand-up. A good comic would pick you up, give you flowers, open doors, and take you to a five-star restaurant on your way to a penthouse suite at the W, where you'd find a bottle of bubbly on ice. On the flip side, a shitty comic would have you meet him at the St. Marks Hotel, foreplay would be you watching him shave his taint, then he'd throw you against the wall for the best three minutes of his life and afterward offer you a wet rag to squeeze into your mouth if you're thirsty. Then we'd laugh about how the good comedians can't find steady work while the shitty ones all seem to have development deals with Comedy Central. I miss doing that with him.

Now, I'm not going to pretend that he and I were close and that I have some incredible insight about him to add to his collective mythology. No, this is not that kind of book. When you touch as many lives as he did during his career, it's impossible to ever really know the depths of your impact. Because of my career, I got to experience his spark in a way most people could never imagine, and for that I'm grateful. So this is my story, about a little girl who saw a bright shooting star flying closely over her head, reached up as high as she could, and somehow touched its tail before it disappeared into the night and found herself dancing in a rain of its sparkle. That was my Robin Williams.

To me, he was the Bruce Lee of verbal kung fu, who disposed of his opponents with such precision, style, and bravado that they left better for it. Going toe-to-toe with him were the great privileges of my life. The anticipation would get my blood pumping and my mind battle-ready as if I were entering the lexiconic Hunger Games. And without fail, each time, I would find myself front row, center at a livestock auction facing the full force and magnificence of his ferocious comedy *cattle rattle*. But no matter what combination of vocal Jeet Kune Do theories I employed, including timing, trapping, rhythm, distance control, and the element of surprise, I would find myself helplessly outmatched against the master. Much like a sexy and hairy-chested Chuck Norris in the climactic fight to the death against the smooth and glistening Little Phoenix in *The Way of the Dragon,* I fought well and earned a respectful nod, but there was no way I was going to survive the close-up shot of the kitten!

The first time I interviewed Robin, I was petrified that I was going to get swallowed up. I'd seen him on talk shows a million times, where he'd go off on one of his signature manic monologues. Very few hosts could keep up with him. Even the late Johnny Carson, who had him as a guest on his penultimate *Tonight Show* episode, just sat there giggling while Robin made jokes about abortion, his baby boy's giant balls, and the Rodney King riot looters. "We're outta here tomorrow night, what do I care?" Carson said, doubled over with laughter. But the truth was that if you were brave enough to step into the eye of the tornado with Robin, you'd be surprised to discover just how much he embraced you and welcomed you into the fray. When you're that good, the only person you're ever competing with is yourself.

Robin had this uncanny ability to grab a silly thought from midair and smack you around with it 'til you were laughing so hard you didn't know your head from your ass. He was a genius at being a satirical asshole, or as I prefer to call it, a *sass-hole.* And he was my kinda *sass-hole!* A charismatic and sarcastic lyrical gangster that made you want to dedicate your life to becoming a *sass-hole.* Unfortunately, the movie he was promoting for my first interview with him, *The Night Listener,* was one of his serious roles, about a gay radio host who forms a friendship with a sexually abused teenager with AIDS. I wasn't expecting a raucous interview, and to be honest, I wasn't sure what the hell to talk to him about. When we sat down, I started the way I always start, by saying:

Me: We're uncensored.
Robin: You're uncensored? *(Eyebrows raised hopefully.)*

The darkness of the shooting suite seemed to brighten as I saw those oh-so-familiar crescent-shaped eyes and that big cheeky smile take over his face. Little did I know that the tiny turn of phrase from my twisted mind would ignite the spark in an unexpected relationship with my idol that would last for years and change my life. Not to mention the fact that we turned an incredibly serious press day into nothing short of an all-out bathhouse tickle fight.

Me: Yeah, I get paid by the fuck. (*Ad-libbing.*)

And that's all it took—Robin proceeded to go off on a *fuck-filled verbal jamboree*, the likes of which I've never seen again. I got to play straight man in one of his legendary rapid-fire riffs. He was having a grand ol' time, and I couldn't help but join in and instigate.

Robin: New game show: *Paid by the Fuck!*
Me: You just won the ten-thousand-dollar prize!
Robin: That's right; it's a really expensive fuck!
Me: Yes, but can you spell it, sir?
Robin: Expensive or fuck? In the south, F-U-C. *FUK. FAA-KU,* F-A-Q-U-E. *FAA-KU!*
Me: *FAA-KU!*
Robin: *Faqui!*
Me: *Faqui!*
Robin: (*French accent*) Or French, *FAA-KOO.*
Me: (*French accent*) *Fo-Quoi.*
Robin: (*French accent*) *Faquerr!* Which is someone who makes something. A petite *faquerr.* A little *faquerr* like this, come on. They say *le facteur. Le facteur? . . .* No, no, a petite *faquerr,* a little guy who doesn't get paid by the fuck who works for free.
Me: Can you do it in Russian?
Robin: (*Russian accent*) *Nostrovia soukha! Yovinaya soukha.* That fucking hooker! *Yo vinaya betinki manah dekonaya.* These fucking shoes are killing me! *Yop ti pollodura.* Fuck you, halfass! Let's learn some more phrase. *Yopt viyamot.* That's easy. One word is mother. Do the math. *Yop ti.* Fuck you! Now people at home in Russia are going, "So, American TV is changing!"
Me: A little bit!
Robin: (*Russian accent*) Yeh, *Nipnoshkeh Tgovanoh.* It's total shit! *Tolkeh Gavnoh.* No Good Television goes unnoticed. Watch No Good. Why? It's NO GOOD!! Why? We're SHIT!

That interview was the beginning of a beautiful relationship. I interviewed him about eight times total, and each time was better than the last. I'd show up and he'd instantly pep up. "Woo! Let's go!" he'd bellow with that knowing gleam in his neon-blue eyes. Even though Robin was an A-list superstar who did family-friendly movies like *Mrs. Doubtfire* and *Night at the Museum*, when I walked into the room, the gloves were always off. I could never get over that! He would always remember me and assume the position for our semiannual game of Turn Your Head and Cough.

Now that I think about it, our liaisons were a lot like seventies porn. We'd always rendezvous in upscale hotel rooms in LA or New York, performing in front of hand-crafted sets designed with an eye toward the exotic. We'd both be wearing the same amount of makeup and dressed to impress because we were there, after all, to give *face* and get down! Our bodies awash in forgivingly soft lighting that left our faces with a suggestive glisten in the way only the life-threatening heat of quartz lamps and no ventilation can create. All the *action* took place only when the cameras were rolling, and we left nothing on the table except . . . what we left on the table.

The intensity of our performances never betrayed the false illusion of intimacy created in spite of being surrounded by far too many people crowded into far too small a space. Sorta like *triple anal* or flying coach on Lufthansa. Our illicit encounters were typically intense one-on-one sessions but for the occasional ménage à trois because . . . well . . . whatever's clever, baby! Our engagements were all about sophisticated decadence, relentless teasing, and erotic symbolism, both lusty and ironic. Our exchanges were filthy but authentic and not a banal collection of the ins and outs of cliché sexual stereotypes. Okay, maybe a little. And if you happened to be standing outside the door listening, the moans, groans, gasps, indiscriminate yelling, and waves of laughter ending in a climactic plaintiff howl would lead you to conclude that we ended with one hell of a *money shot*! Like I said, Robin and I could well have been the John Holmes and Seka of the junket world. I think you get where I'm going with this. Although I did just throw up in my mouth again!

When I showed up to interview him for the film *License to Wed*, in which his character was a pious reverend who counsels couples, it didn't stop him from shouting "Nice tits!" like a rowdy sports fan the minute the cameras started rolling. And all I remember thinking was, *Oh, I see, Robin.*

Game on! That was the nature of our relationship. We were comfortable and familiar—enough to get into trouble but not enough to need lawyers.

Me: I'm trying to get sex advice from a man who's never had sex before?

Robin: Well, good luck, it's like getting a facial from Ray Charles. *(He launches into full-on Ray Charles character, squinting his eyes, waving his head back and forth, and holding out his hands as if grasping for a face. But he aims lower, toward said tits.)* I think everything's looking good.

Me: That's not my face, Ray.

Robin: *(Doing Ray Charles impression)* Oh! I was saying, boy, your eyelids were pouty. You put a lot of collagen in your eyes, and I must say, you got two things stuck on your eyeballs. And you're cryin', 'cause it's all over my hands. HA HA! LAWWRDD, love a woman! . . . Mmmmhmmm, Geooooorgiaaa, mmm, it's all good, all good. Have you been married, my dear?

Me: *(Joining him in character:)* Um, um, I'm getting married in six months.

Robin: So, it's your future husband?

Me: Yes!

Robin: Oh, I sense a certain . . . a certain trepidation. Do you live together now?

Me: We haven't had sex yet. It's gonna be the first time.

Robin: Lyin' bitch! You dress like that and go, "We've had sex in the butt. We haven't had sex."

Me: Ha! How did you know?

Robin: Well, you're Catholic!
(Did it show?)
(We give each other a solid high five.)

Robin: In some states . . . *(He switches into high gear, mimicking a priest from the South.)* I'm from Georgia! That's a crime! Unless of course you slip. I'm SORRY, BABY! I was driving toward the back and something got lost! Next thing you know I'm like WOW, DAMN! BOY, DO YOU HAVE A TIGHT BOX! DAMN, WHAT SMELLS? *(He immediately snaps out of character and looks back at me.)* So, you haven't had sex? Okay, we'll go with that premise . . . We're here with Mrs. Pinocchio!

Down the road, during our interview for *World's Greatest Dad*, we talked about *chili-dogging* (shitting on your sex partner's chest) and his nickname for himself, "Tiny Vagina."

Robin: Sounds like a great new dog. This fall, *Tiny Vagina*! She's just a little friend.

  Me: And she comes in a little box!

Robin: If you're lucky! *Tiny Giny*, pull her string and hear her sing, oh!

Robin really enjoyed my line, "She comes in a little box." He laughed so hard about it and even repeated it twice. Damn, that felt great. There was something about making him laugh that made me feel like I had accomplished something. Fortunately for me, it didn't go unnoticed. It caught the eye of a producer at *The Tonight Show*, which resulted in one of the most amazing opportunities to have ever come my way.

So, my reputation as "the Naughty Critic" was making a mark, and the media was taking notice and giving me some attention, good and bad, each of which was exhilarating in its own way. In one corner, *The Hollywood Reporter* was hailing me as the movie studios' new secret weapon to attract a younger demo. In the other corner, the master of ceremonies for those who can't think for themselves, Mr. Bill O'Reilly, seemed convinced that I was Lucifer's disciple, hell-bent on bringing down the walls of society. Either way, I was getting a reputation for doing something . . . something worth talking about . . . although what that was I had no fucking idea at the time.

I did learn something very funny about human nature as a result of all this crazy rhetoric. There's no question that when decent, open-minded people embrace you and dig what you do, it's an incredible feeling, but man, does it pale in comparison to when the fascists are yelling and screaming about you because they're uncomfortable. For some reason, that's the only validation that matters.

So there I was, getting some pretty kick-ass coverage—in national publications, no less—and my friends and family were thrilled for me, and everyone at work was, you know, politely congratulatory. But when the O'Reilly *shit-piece* hit, the place lit up like a meth lab on Good Friday. I started getting calls from all over the country. Strangers I hadn't spoken to in ten years were in a *pant-filling frenzy* and dying to tell me about the bashing I had just taken at the hands of the official *rape whistle* of the

GOP. It was crazy, even the energy at NGTV was so palpable you could almost feel the building shaking as if all one hundred employees were leaning against the walls and furiously masturbating in unison.

In fact, the whole company stopped to go and find the piece online and then proceeded to watch in amazement and disbelief as *Billy the O-ring* plated his own *hot carl* and served it with a light garnish. What the fuck!! The whole segment was Mr. *Inside Edition* and some ignorant Internet chick taking the longest *group poop* all over NGTV and me. Droning on and on about how lowbrow, unprofessional, inappropriate, filthy, and disrespectful it was and how it was yet another example of how showbiz is the really painfully sharp ridges on the *devil's cock*. Of course, Bill's been riding that same *hog* for forty years, so I suppose he would know. But the whole time these two *flibbertigibbets* were yapping away, the producer had cut together the most amazing montage of my interviews featuring a nonstop roster of A-list talent with every one of them just laughing and being bleeped. It was the single greatest commercial for NGTV ever, and featured front and center was none other than the amazing Robin Williams.

Anyway, so all this commotion eventually reached the people at *The Tonight Show with Jay Leno,* and one of the producers reached out to talk about having me come on. I was spinning with joy. I couldn't believe it was happening, but that wasn't even the best part. Anytime you go on talk shows, there's a fair amount of preparation and planning that goes into it. It starts with the pre-interview and ends with what they hope will be a killer segment. In my case, the producer had a big idea.

She had done her research on me and watched a ton of my interviews. In particular, she had seen several of my interviews with Robin and had noticed the chemistry we'd had in interview after interview. Of course, he was a legend and I was, well . . . YouTube famous, which at that time was cutting edge and risky but didn't carry the majesty and respect that it does today, where only true artists and poets gather to connect with other true artists and poets. Back then, it was just a place for desperate people with uniquely unmarketable talents and severely lacking social skills to court fame and fortune by showcasing their vulnerabilities and insecurities to a racist, bigoted, homophobic, and violently intolerant audience. And those were just the YouTube premium partners. Good times.

So the producer came back with the most amazing plan. They

thought it would be a riot to have me on as the second guest on the same night Robin was going to be on so we could recreate the chemistry that our interviews had become famous for. Fuckin' brilliant! Of course, it hadn't occurred to them that when Robin and I got going, it inevitably would take a noticeable left turn into the gutter. But as the old Polish proverb goes, *"Not my circus, not my monkeys!"* I was beyond floored. Not only was it the first time in my career that I was asked to appear on one of the biggie late-night network shows, but I was going to have the chance to joke around with the legend himself on national television. Well, fuck me senseless!!

And no sooner had I asked, they delivered! You know how on *The Price Is Right* they play that sad pathetic horn when a contestant loses? Well, you might as well cue it up right now. The date was set to be around Thanksgiving and everything was in order, then two weeks before the day, the Writers Guild of America went on strike. And that was that. *The Tonight Show* shut down and the moment was gone I never made it to *The Tonight Show* and I never got to play *Tickle-Tickle* in front of millions of people with my hero. It was just one of those things that wasn't meant to be.

Robin meant so much to me, as he did to so many people. Without even really knowing it, he touched us all. But for me, he was the Holy Grail. He was brilliance personified, yet he maintained a certain humility that made him magnanimous in his art. I am eternally grateful for that because, as a result, I was able to share time with him. And more importantly, I was afforded a more candid glimpse of the man because we never played media games. We just shot the shit and laughed. Or I should say, more accurately, he shot the shit and I laughed! But during that process he welcomed me in. He encouraged, nurtured, and supported me with his willingness to let this neophyte sit at his table and drink from his fountain. A rare honor that I shall remember forever.

I was devastated when he took his own life in 2014. It was an immeasurable loss for anyone who had even remotely grazed his existence and a heartbreaking tragedy for his close friends and loved ones. My heart goes out to them, for they are the ones who truly knew the full measure of his wonder. I was just a lucky girl who got to meet him and spend a little time talking. He was a genius and, unbeknownst to him, had become a mentor to me. I always walked away from our "conversations of

the absurd" with great stories, great memories, and even greater confidence. I am better for knowing him. We all are.

NUMBER OF NOTHING TO ENCODE

I didn't know Robin personally, but I was heartsick to learn of the tremendous amount of pain and isolation his depression and addictions
caused him, and how his family and friends were powerless to help him.

Unfortunately, it's something that I can relate to all too well. My
best friend and business partner, Ken Stroscher, wasn't just the heart
and soul of No Good TV, he was my greatest inspiration. Despite all his
flaws and creatively self-destructive behavior, he helped me find the
truth of who I am, be brave enough to own it, and find the inner strength
to fight for it. Not a single day goes by where I don't miss his eccentric
idiocy, which I firmly believe is an essential ingredient for a life well-
lived. There is nothing that we have ever created or continue to create at
NGTV that doesn't have his fingerprints all over it in some way, and his
DNA within it. This whole thing was always an exercise in sheer will
and faith, in one way or another, by three friends who saw the world in
the same uniquely fucked-up way and decided to turn that into a business. Plus, that funny fucker turned out to be my human spirit animal.

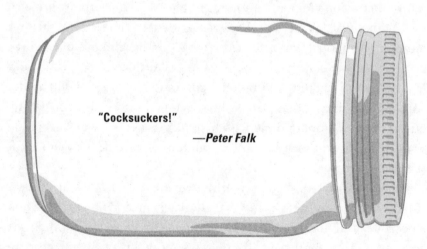

"Cocksuckers!"

—*Peter Falk*

He may have influenced me more than anyone because he was there
when it was the hardest. When we had very little and dreamed so very
big. Kourosh will forget to have fun if you don't remind him, but Ken was

all about the fun—any chance he got. Ken was my savior when things got tough and I couldn't see my way through. I don't know where I'd be without "naked editing" and the countless other stupid things he'd come up with to make me smile and keep moving forward. I just assumed I'd be there to save him if the time came, as well. But it turns out that, in life, things don't always turn out the way you'd like them to.

Sadly, the more successful NGTV became, the more Ken seemed to turn to drink. He wasn't handling the pressure well. On top of whatever else was eating at him that he wouldn't tell me about. Then, somewhere along the way, a casual drink turned into drowning in two liters of booze a day. Of course, he hid it so well that I had no idea how bad things had gotten. Until one day when I quite accidentally came across the most curious thing as I went to grab something for him from his car. Conveniently nestled in the driver's center cup holder was a crystal tumbler, filled with liquor like he was Dean Martin or James Bond. Assuming James Bond had traded in his Aston Martin for a used 1979 beige Volvo. I mean, who the fuck uses glassware as a to-go cup?! It was so dumb and very much a "classic" Ken move to conceal a terrible addiction under the veil of living the fabulous life. His mom was going to kill him when she found out where her missing Waterford crystal set had gone.

I really didn't know what to think. But I found the casual and brazen nature of it very alarming. So I made a point to quietly check his car as often as I could, and sure enough, I found the same thing every time. I confronted him about it only to have him play it off as a little bit of harmless fun that wasn't affecting his work. I wasn't convinced. Not surprisingly, soon enough, Ken's drinking started to affect his work. He started being chronically late, showing up intoxicated, and blowing off his responsibilities. This became a huge problem because he was heading up production and training newly hired editors and producers. He was essential to making them understand our vision and editing style. Plus, he was central to the biggest location shoot we would ever do just on the horizon.

So there we were, heading to our first-ever Toronto Film Festival. Ten days of on-location shooting in Canada, where we had over a hundred celebrity interviews lined up. Just writing that makes me want to punch Kourosh in the gut. A hundred interviews!! Who the fuck books that many? Had we made a deal to start feeding E!'s entire programming that I didn't know about? Fucking *Entertainment Tonight* wasn't doing that much! Even carnival organ grinders gave their dancing monkeys a rest!

He was trying to give me a heart attack! But what I hadn't anticipated was that Ken was going to give him one first.

Ken was terrified of flying the way Kanye West is terrified of humility. But when it's just the three of you and you've got to fly somewhere, you do what you have to do. And in Ken's case, it was like getting B. A. Baracus from *The A-Team* on a plane. So we brought some Xanax and figured we'd give him two of those on the plane and he'd be out for the duration. That would have been too easy! Once we checked in for the flight, we headed to the Friday's to kill the forty-five minutes before we boarded. Where we ended up was at the equivalent of a one-man frat party where we witnessed Ken chug down ten Long Island iced teas in thirty minutes. We watched him casually cruise by the state of *rat-assed* on his way to *obliteration station*. Stunned into a state of abject horror only comparable to the first time we heard Kanye's remix of Michael Jackson's "Billie Jean," it was in that very moment that Kourosh and I had the realization that this was not Ken's first rodeo.

We were worried they wouldn't board him if they knew he was wasted. Which really didn't matter because how the fuck was he going to stand up, let alone walk to get on the plane?! Then came the next surprise: Ken stood up and walked as if he'd been sipping on a lemonade. Who was this guy? So we rolled with him into the crowded boarding line. As we boarded the plane, we kept an eye on him and thought he was right there with us, but when we got to our seats, Ken was nowhere to be found. "He must've stepped into the bathroom," I said to Kourosh. "I mean, where else could he possibly be?" He agreed, but we gave each other that "This is Ken we're talking about, so let's pray he's not passed out on the toilet" look, and patiently waited for twenty minutes . . . no Ken.

Calm changed to panic when we noticed the flight attendants were about to close the door. We grabbed their attention and explained what had happened and begged them to look for him before leaving. They held that plane at the gate for almost thirty minutes before Ken finally strolled on, flanked by two security guards, and sat down next to us, a bit frazzled. It turns out he had somehow wandered onto the plane right next to ours, an international flight to New Zealand. Which would have departed with him on board had we not raised a red flag, having already closed their doors and been about to taxi. Only Ken could find himself at the center of a real-life *shit-show* worthy of a network sitcom! Word to the wise: Everything tragic begins as something stupid and funny.

And that, as they say, was the beginning of the end. The year ahead would test the boundaries of logic and reason as Kourosh and I tried to cope with the challenges ahead and Kenny struggled with his pain. Within a couple of months of our return, the shit hit the fan and things began to escalate and spiral out of control. What had started out as a bit of insanity and craziness turned a dark and tragic corner. I started to get calls late at night, from the weirdest places, like Disneyland and Universal Studios, asking me to come pick him up to avoid their calling the police, after he'd passed out on one of their benches. He would graduate to getting arrested on a couple of occasions. Each time we'd get him a lawyer, bail him out, and check him into rehab. Only to find out that after a couple of days or a week, he checked himself out of rehab, checked into some random motel, and got blitzed before the motel would kick him out and he'd end up on his mom's doorstep. His alcoholism was approaching *Leaving Las Vegas* levels. I don't think I had ever been more scared.

The bigger our business got, the more lost Ken got. He was doing everything to just fade into the background. He was producing very little and barely even showing up. Before we left for our second Toronto Film Festival, Ken was M.I.A. We couldn't get him on the phone, e-mail, nothing. He had gone completely off the grid. We had already made commitments with the studios, and not knowing what to do, Kourosh and I took our scheduled flights and hoped to solve the situation on the fly. On the way to the airport, I sent two coworkers to his apartment complex to get to the bottom of the situation. It took them an hour to figure out how to get into his building and another hour to convince the building manager to let them into his apartment without calling the police first. What they discovered once they gained access looked like a crime scene in a horror movie. The apartment was a disaster zone, with broken furniture everywhere and Ken passed out in a huge pool of blood. For a moment, it looked like he was dead, but then he started to come to. Apparently after a night of hitting the bottle really hard, he had accidentally slipped and smacked his head on his air-conditioning unit and knocked himself unconscious. He could have bled to death.

Kourosh and I were incredibly relieved that he wasn't dead, but we were so fucking mad that we wanted to kill him. When we got back from the festival, we had a long, intense conversation with him. "Ken, you're not musketeering!" Kourosh pleaded, dumbfounded. "All those years we struggled to get anyone to give a damn about what we were doing, and now they do and you don't care. It used to be the three of us in the dark, trying to get the power going, rubbing nickels together to get through the day. Where the fuck are you now? You got a date with two liters of jet fuel a day? Why are you ruining this? Why can't you enjoy it?" The situation had clearly escalated far, far beyond our ability to overcome it.

Ken's problems were bigger than we could ever understand or handle. Ultimately, we all agreed that it might be best for him to take a leave of absence and take all the time he needed to heal himself and try to get his life back on track. His job would be waiting for him whenever he decided to return. No matter how long it took. It was a very sad day. It was as if we were losing a limb, and no matter how big we had gotten and how many employees we had, Ken was irreplaceable. But we held on to hope because we knew Ken was a survivor of the bizarre, so anything was possible. After all, I remember him and his mother telling us the story of how, when Ken was a teenager, he survived a middle-of-the-night encounter with the legendary Lawrence Welk, who was driving through their neighborhood armed with a rifle and had decided to shoot up their house. They even showed us the bullet holes. I figured if he could survive something as random and farcical as that, he could survive anything.

Sadly, I saw Ken infrequently over the next couple of years as he went in and out of several rehab facilities, but I stayed in close contact with his mom and kept close on tabs on him. The highs and lows of his addiction were beating the living hell out of him. Eventually, his body started to aggressively show the wear and tear two decades of alcohol abuse had inflicted. He would go on to suffer a few mini-strokes that left him slightly impaired and requiring a cane to walk but still filthy and whip smart. But inevitably his liver couldn't take it anymore. Two years after he quit NGTV, his mother, Gertrude, called us and said he was in the hospital and wasn't going to make it much longer. Kourosh and I rushed to his bedside. I almost passed out when I saw him. He was unrecognizable: bloated beyond recognition and yellow from jaundice.

It was a terrifying sight, and I can only imagine that it must have been a horrifying ordeal for poor Ken. Kourosh and I stayed and visited him daily, and miraculously, somehow over the course of the following weeks, he started to get better and eventually got well enough to go home. He had been given one last chance for a do-over. The doctors warned him that his liver function was dangerously low and that any drinking would kill him. I remember thinking maybe this was the rock bottom he needed to hit to finally make a change. He had come so close to a painful and terrible death and I could tell that he was shaken by it, so there was hope, I thought.

A couple of months later, we got the same call from his mom, and again, we rushed to the hospital to be met with the same scene as before. Only this time, Ken had slipped into a coma. His eyes were sealed shut, his mouth crusted with blood, and he had a million tubes going in and out all over his body. One by one all of his organs were shutting down. It was utterly devastating. I'll never forget his mom's shattered, expressionless face and vacant stare. She was broken. For days, we waited in silent vigil. I would sit by his bedside, rub his hand, and talk to him in the hope that he might hear my voice and wake up or at least know that I was with him. It was a futile gasp for courage to avoid choking on my fears, but it did little to stop my heart from bleeding out.

Sadly, his condition continued to worsen, but for some reason, he refused to let go. Deep down inside, I just knew that even though his body was giving up, he was holding on . . . for us. He knew how much we needed him, how much I could not let him go. Whatever flaws he had, honor and integrity weren't amongst them. My brave boy. My Kenny bear. One last stand for the three musketeers. In many ways, he was the best of us. He deserved better. And I simply couldn't bear to watch him suffer any longer.

I remember sitting next to his hospital bed, slowly reaching for his hand, and holding on to it for dear life. Desperately, I tried to find the strength to let go, as if the choice were mine to make. All the while, I could feel my heart purging its twisted wreckage through my rib cage and spilling all over my shattered soul. I squeezed his hand, took a deep breath, leaned over, and whispered in his ear, "If you're holding on for us, just go. It's okay." As soon those words left my mouth, my eyes erupted in an uncontrollable flood of tears. Until you hurt, you just don't know how deep it can go. I tried but couldn't prevent them from falling on him and sliding down his cheeks as he lay there, peacefully. And then, for a brief moment, I saw his face catch the light and glisten with my grief like an angel. I told myself that maybe this was meant to be some sort of parting baptism to declare to whoever was listening that this boy was loved, that he mattered, that he made a difference, and that he would never be forgotten.

Ken passed away shortly thereafter.

He was thirty-nine years old. "The heartache and the thousand natural shocks" was all that remained for those of us that were left behind. *Hamlet's* lament proved all too real. He was survived by his family, his loyal friends, his NGTV family, his best friends (Kourosh and me), and as a cofounder of No Good TV, a legacy that will last forever.

Ken was my best friend. I loved him like a brother. I tried to help him. I tried to fix him. But there was nothing I could do. My heart has been held hostage since the day he left with the sweet poetry that was his gentle soul. I couldn't save him, and I carry that with me every day.

At his funeral service, Kourosh gave an incredibly emotional eulogy to a packed church filled with friends Ken had known since high school, family, and a large collection of past and present employees of NGTV who had all come out to say farewell to a friend they admired. He ended his speech with a grand gesture that few will forget. Having asked everyone to stand, he recited the words from Admiral Kirk's farewell speech to Captain Spock from *Star Trek II: The Wrath of Khan*. "In accordance with the traditions of Starfleet and of Article 184 Starfleet Regulations, we are assembled here today to pay final respects to our honored dead." The church fell completely silent as Kourosh said good-bye to a fallen Musketeer. Ending with, "Of my friend, I can only say this: Of all the souls I have encountered in my travels, his was the most . . . human." Kourosh and Ken's friendship of twenty years had started from their mutual love of *Trek*, and everyone there knew that. There wasn't a dry eye in the house.

Later at his burial service, I searched for the strength to ease my trembling silhouette long enough for me to bare my soul and honor my friend with a walk through the beautiful wreckage of "Green Grass" by Tom Waits. But the finality of seeing Ken's casket descend into the ground shattered what little hope of that I had. And though I felt the words "Don't say good-bye to me" flow through my veins, they could not find form in the vacuum of my despair. No longer able to breathe, I handed my notes to Kourosh to share for me as I tried my best to keep my pounding heart from tearing a permanent hole in my chest.

Ken, in his own way, like Robin, was so brilliant, and yet, so tortured. He took his own life, too. It just took more time. Left behind are fragments of thought, splinters of memory, and misplaced photographs of doppelgangers trapped in time and space. What are they so happy about anyway? The only thing remaining that feels real is the discomforting feeling of unfulfilled déjà vu; a haunting reminder that this wasn't how it was supposed to be. It's little consolation as you struggle to stay on good terms with a life that continues to unfold at the same pace as his memory continues to fade.

A Scooby-Doo doll in a Zorro mask, Care Bear Christmas cookies, a giant ball of tin foil, a column on a worksheet labelled "number of nothing to encode," Mr. Dizzo, a bus-stop poster for *Star Trek VI: The Undiscovered Country* signed by the entire cast, "the Nelson tradition of hot-tubbing," McRib, the Tidal Wave ride at Magic Mountain, and a car horn that sounded like a kitten meowing are just some of the stupid mementos I cling to that remind me of my times with Ken. He's never far from my thoughts. But of all the stupid things that bring him to mind, I will never forget the French kangaroo with huge balls.

To this day, when I think about Ken, I cuss him out aloud, almost involuntarily, as if we were sitting next to each other editing an interview at 2 A.M. "Whatever, Ken," I say. "Asshole! Fucker!"

If you really think about it, what is life but a strange and wondrous place filled with beauty, belligerence, and all-you-can-eat sushi buffets? Some people journey through it in private jets overflowing with rose petals and cocaine while others find themselves trapped in the back of a packed Greyhound bus with an overflowing shitter and a talking Kylo Ren toilet brush. Either way, we are all just tourists here. Tourists in exciting and unfamiliar surroundings, frantically rushing around trying to see and do as much as possible before our temporary visas expire and this bizarre trip comes to an abrupt end. If we're lucky, the most we can hope to do is collect a few mental souvenirs along the way to remind us of those defining moments that caught us in their wake as we passed by. Much like a collection of snow globes that each depict a point in time from an experience and are designed to activate the entire memory perfectly.

Ironically, we don't get to choose the mental markers that remind us of the most profound and impactful events in our lives. Our subconscious does. And that's why my emotional scrapbook seems as though it has been heavily influenced by a drunken David Lynch. But no matter how ridiculous, disturbing, sweet, or abstract my mental souvenirs are, they are as much a reflection of me and my incredible journey as the memories themselves.

EPILOGUE

Kourosh, Ken, and I met when we had nothing. We joined forces because we believed in something. Only to realize along the way that within each other, we had everything. Losing Ken felt like the end of our *No Good* creative unit we affectionately called the *dickshow,* but as he was in life, so he was in death. Which means this story can only end one way: *complimentary reach-arounds for everybody!* (Probably somewhere in Koreatown.) So, boys and girls, it was only the beginning. It was just a matter of time before someone showed up with a *milking table* and a new era of *dick-handling* would begin.

However, one knock on the door became five, and a lone table at our local Buddhist meditation hut transformed into an international showroom for horizontal glory holes. It turns out Ken had decided to fill his void with more than one person, and additionally, he was looking to expand our *circle of jerks* by five.

Beth Spruill *(Writer/Producer):* a born *hose slinger* from D.C. She can *double-dick* and *triple-dick* with the best of 'em and has. Anytime we've needed *dick,* day or night, she'd have it coming at us from every direction. She's funny as fuck, has the biggest heart, and is a complete jackass! Together, we tried to answer many of life's most perplexing questions, like can you get a Brazilian wax while on your period or, more importantly, should you? She's my right hand, and I've hated everything about her from the moment she walked into my life. She's both my giant and my mini-giraffe. She's like the little sister I never had nor wanted and not a single day goes by that I'm not grateful we found each other. Like they say, keep your friends close . . .

Michael Ore (*3D Motion Graphics Artist*): a professionally trained *hot-cocker* from Baltimore, Maryland! Nobody can make a *cock* look as hot as Mike can. I go to him with an inordinate amount of *cocks* that need attention, and he makes it look like child's play. What can I say? The man is an artist! We met each other on a mustache Friday and we've been partners in crime ever since. Together, we "fucked" Spider-Man, discovered the wonder that is Campari (btw . . . it doesn't need a mixer because is just as good served straight and at room temperature), appeared in the movie *Miss March* and have seen each other naked more than any "brother and sister" should. He gave life to Shark Firestone, the greatest seventies porn star that never was, and taught me the true definition of CLASS: Come Late And Start Sleeping.

Avi Kipper (*Chief Audio Engineer*): a *cocksolid ear-fucking* dynamo from Israel. A highly skilled audio Ninja, lingual assassin, and trained master of aural manipulation. A formidable street hustler with two streams of consciousness running parallel to each other creating the blurring effect of his frenetic presence. With no regrets from the past and no fears for tomorrow, he exists in a continuous state of death and rebirth. This motherfucker is biblical in his aspirations, and I'm talkin' Old Testament!

Quentin Owens (*Wardrobe Stylist*): an internationally renowned hypno-dazzling *packaging* connoisseur from Oceanside. He knows how to put a bow on your *business* like nobody's business. His *cocksure* persona is the lovechild of Grace Jones, Diana Ross, and the Marquis de Sade. A brutally kind and perversely fun fashion Messiah in the form of a six-foot *cock rocket*, he regards haute couture as something to covet at all costs and then wipes his ass with it the first chance he gets. He's my drinking partner, social concierge, and body man.

Natasha Hamidi (*Finance Guru/Line Producer*): a Cirque du Soleil–trained *master ball juggler*. Able to manipulate any number of *balls* of any size from any position. With all the *double-dickin',* *ear-fucking,* and *hot-cockin'* in play, somebody had to juggle all the *balls.* She's fluent in multiple disciplines including object, method, trick, and team juggling. Her style skills dominate circus, comedy, gentlemen, and sports, with a PhD in street! An intelligent, proud, and powerful woman who exudes grace and compassion, and I am honored to call her family.

I call them: The Five Cocksmen of the Ken-ocalypse!

18

YOU GOTTA STAND UP TO GET DOWN

**What I'm saying might be profane,
but it's also profound.**
—*Richard Pryor*

When was the last time you experienced a teachable moment that was as impactful as accidentally swallowing a blood clot during oral sex? Okay, Okay, Okay. Calm down. Shhhhhhh. It's okay. Take a DEEEEP breath. In . . . out. Now, slowly shake it off. It's going to be okay.

Now, in my opinion, it could have only happened in two situations. Either when you were physically faced with a calamity like the time you pulled the anal beads out of your girlfriend's ass too fast and triggered a horizontal *fecal-fountain* so forceful it stained your teeth, or when a stand-up comic told you about it. In either situation you learn the lesson. Except in one scenario, you're laughing your ass off and high-fiving your friends and in the other one, you're scarred for life and may never kiss another person again. And that, in an extreme nutshell, is why stand-up comics play such a critical role in all of our lives. And why they have always been such a great source of inspiration in my career.

I'm not a stand-up. I've never had the urge to publicly castrate myself for other people's amusement. And this is by no means a criticism. Quite the contrary, I could sit here and discuss the pros and cons of public self-mutilation for days, and we would laugh and laugh and laugh. And, to some extent, that's exactly what we're doing right now.

The truth is I've just never experienced that life-altering event that skews your view of the world. Like coming home early on a school day and finding your dad standing butt-naked on the dining room table, squatting with his hairy balls in a bowl of chicken soup, while your sister blows bubbles in it through a straw screaming "Ballcuzzi!" That's the kind of shit that turns a cute little kid into a dark twisted mother-fucker with a mental limp . . . better known as a stand-up comic.

They're the hot teacher, the bizarre street philosopher, and the sarcastic prick who tells it like it is, whether you like it or not. They are the whistle-blowers of pop culture. Speaking uncomfortable truths to help remove that bunk of denial you've been subconsciously hanging on to like a used condom that's been sitting inside you for two days. Tearing into your brain, gnawing at your pudendum, and when necessary, throwing up in your mouth to give you a line of that straight dope. Their comedy acts fill the only textbooks in our fucked-up society that we actually retain any information from. In five-minute bursts, they do the real schooling like a hotshot into your jugular.

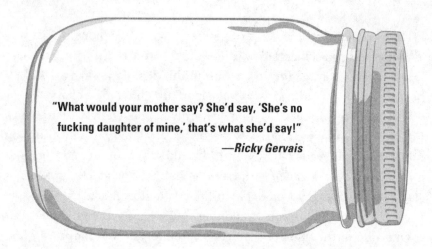

"What would your mother say? She'd say, 'She's no fucking daughter of mine,' that's what she'd say!"
—*Ricky Gervais*

If I have a fatal attraction for anything, it's stand-ups. They're like hot firemen. We don't think about them as often as we should, but when the world is burning, they're the first ones running in to save us and hose us down with their powerful spray. They are the brave and suicidal fuckers who stand on the front line of the battle for ideological progress. While the rest of us are casually accepting our fate, they are the ones that are changing the world with one seriously fucked-up joke at a time. We laugh. We cry. We're offended. We move forward.

They all pay a heavy price because everyone's a critic. And some of them don't survive the battle. But at the end of the day, how the fuck else does society address the horrors of pedophilia, rape, racism, misogyny, homophobia, politics, abortion, stereotypes, and what women really think? (Wooooh . . . that last one is a real bitch to deal with!) Through the lens of comedy, which gives its operatives the right to shoot all the *up-skirt shots* they need in order to reveal the different assholes hidden all around us. You'll learn more about what's fucked up with you and the world around you by browsing through the *candid photos* of Roseanne Barr, Dave Chappelle, Chris Rock, Eddie Murphy, Sam Kinison, Natasha Leggero, Bill Maher, Wanda Sykes, Jon Stewart, Rosie O'Donnell, Redd Foxx, Lisa Lampanelli, John Oliver, Tig Notaro, Don Rickles, Amy Schumer, Mitch Hedberg, or Robin Williams than from anything in schoolbooks or on the news. Or even by reading that daily diary your mother has been keeping on your secret masturbating habits since you turned twelve. Yeah, she knows about the curling iron accident that left you on a donut pillow for two months.

They are the verbal gymnasts that redefine the boundaries of language. It's their routines that bulldoze the soundproof walls that society insists on building around us. In some small way, and in my own way, I try to follow in their footsteps. I'm all about free speech, binging on the things that make us uncomfortable, eliminating stereotypes, looking at life with a sense of humor, pushing buttons because what else are they there for, changing perceptions, empowering women, and most important of all, I'm all about the funny. And I owe a lot to the ones that paved the way for me.

Anyone who curses onstage owes a debt to counterculture innovator Lenny Bruce, who was arrested several times in the 1960s for saying these simple words onstage: ass, balls, cocksucker, cunt, motherfucker, piss, shit, and tits. Anyone who curses on TV or other media is only paying forward the "fuck the system" social commentary of George Carlin, also arrested for his infamous monologue "Seven Words You Can Never Say on Television." What about Richard Pryor, who demolished all preconceived notions of what was okay to joke about and turned cursing into poetic slang? Or Andy Kaufman, who turned stand-up into what-ever the fuck he wanted it to be while *raping* our minds in our comfort zone? And, of course, Joan Rivers, who set a new standard for truth in comedy and bravery in real life, for men and women alike. She mother-fucked the system that motherfucked her through sheer will and audac-ity. She's my fuckin' hero, may she rest in peace.

So when I have the chance to go toe-to-toe with stand-up comedi-ans, I'm in heaven. I love those fearless fuckers who aren't afraid to play. Their lack of inhibition is something most of us wish we were brave enough to have but are too worried about what other people will think of us. I've had the good fortune of going to the dance with some of the best, including Kevin Hart, Adam Sandler, Chris Rock, Bob Saget, Ced-ric the Entertainer, Margaret Cho, Jeffrey Ross, Chelsea Handler, Whit-ney Cummings, Judah Friedlander, Paul Provenza, Loni Love, Martin Lawrence, Joy Behar, Eddie Izzard, Sandra Bernhard, Tracy Morgan, Penn Jillette, Kathy Griffin, Steve Harvey, Bernie Mac, Jim Carrey, and Lewis Black, to name a few. I also had the privilege of being Ken Jeong's first-ever video interview.

Want to hear about the most important lessons I learned from all these amazing stand-ups? Well, Dr. Ken taught me that if a gynecologist offers you a *happy ending*, then he's probably not a gynecologist. Marga-ret Cho taught me that if you fart during anal sex, the force is so strong that your guy will experience something similar to slipping on a tread-mill at high speed, falling on his face and being tossed against the wall. Yeah, those would be the big ones. Thanks, guys! Now, let's take a Vespa down the long and dangerous Spanish Steps of depravity with some of my favorite filthy exchanges with the men and women who stand up to get down!

I had been a Dr. Ken fan for years, so when we had the chance to have him in-studio, I jumped at the opportunity, and he did not disap-point. It's ironic because when you see him in movies like *The Hangover*, you're left with this fucked-up impression of this crazy twisted perverted asshole. But when you get to hang out with him and really get to know him, as I did, you realize that that's just the tip of the iceberg and that you might really be in danger, wishing you had your grandma's Life Alert necklace because there's a good chance you're going to be falling and he's not going to let you up!

Of course, I'm kidding. When this sweet unassuming guy showed up, I was beyond curious. How would we start his very-first-ever on-camera interview? Maybe a biographical journey through his past career as a doctor or a retrospective on his comedic career followed by a quick workshop on style and flow? Nope, he wanted to start with shooting something called "bukkake Asian style." Well, I love Japanese food so I was down to taste his family *noodle-and-broth* recipe. As it turns out, he's Korean and that wasn't the *bukkake* he had in mind. So after a bit of back-and-forth, we settled on him just teaching me the blowjob technique he used to get his role in the movie *Role Models*, in the hope that it might help me get more work:

Me: Do you often talk to your friends about how much you love their comedy?

Ken: Yeah, I do actually.

Me: Are you like, *"Dude, I love when you said that thing!"*

Ken: Yeah!

Me: When you see Paul Rudd, you're like, "Dude!"

Ken: Oh absolutely! It gets me work so it's good. You know. *(He shows me how he talked to Paul Rudd to get the job.)* "I love your work!" *(Pulls his clenched left fist up to his mouth and starts simulating giving a blowjob, with his tongue pushing on his right cheek while his fist goes up and down and he makes guttural sounds.)* "AARRR ARRRR GHGHGH. You're a genius! Such irony! AARRR ARRRR GHGHGH. Can I please be the king? I'll suck more cock to be the king!"

Me: You know, I've tried that. It hasn't really gotten me any work.

Ken: Really?

Me: Am I doing something wrong? Can you show me what you do?

Ken: I think you are . . . *(Cheekily . . . we both turn toward the camera and amusingly stare and hold.)*

Me: Are there tips you can give me?

Ken: I've never seen you suck cock so I don't know. *(Looks at camera.)* I don't know you that well.

> *(Ken then begins to physically demonstrate and share his personal method.)*

Ken: You know this, right? Counterclockwise . . . you know you start at eleven o'clock. A lot of people start at two, which is fuckin' hack!

Me: Oh?

Ken: You gotta start at eleven o'clock, and like, go, work your way . . .

Me: All the way around?

Ken: *(Demonstrating with both hands how the tongue works the rim of the penis.)* In that kind of area. And then, a lot of people think they stop at, like, once. That's just like the initial rim . . . you just have to . . . you know, make it a good pacific rimming. Then you gotta do it over and over again.

Me: Pacific rimming?

Ken: Pacific rimming. That's my style. I've actually copyrighted that term. I mean . . . you know. Seriously . . . it's a thing that I'm very passionate about . . . is pacific rimming a guy's cock!

Me: What about pacific rimming the asshole? *(Making a circle in the air with my finger.)* I mean, there is that as well.

Ken: That's a personal question.

Me: Oh . . . sorry. I didn't mean to go too far 'cause we don't do that at No Good TV. We don't get personal.

Ken: We just talk about . . . I talk about cock and I . . . leave the ass alone.

Watching Ken Jeong's career explode has been such a joy. Every time we run into each other, it's like seeing an old friend . . . pretending to like you because he knows you've got a very compromising video of him. "Bukkake Asian style" Ken!! I didn't say we didn't make the video; I just didn't reveal whose *noodle* was on the receiving end of the *broth*!

As I've discussed in other chapters, my *In Bed With* show never failed to create some truly groundbreaking moments. Let's face it, for a celebrity, lying in a bed for a press interview is a bit bizarre and could be pretty discombobulating. Add to that an uncensored format and a host who thrives on the crazy and unpredictable, and your standard press opportunity has now morphed into a Las Vegas stunt show. You've really got to be a fun-loving free spirit who's willing to bring your A-game. When all the stars align, it can be truly amazing. But when a stand-up comic enters the ring, all bets are off. These guys live to fuck around, and it's a recipe for pure delight. So when I jumped into the sack with Eddie Griffin, I was fully expecting the big "D," and he gave it to me in the form of some afternoon D-light.

I started the interview the same way I start all interviews, by asking for a sperm sample:

Me: Hey, before we do this, would you mind doing me a favor?

Eddie: What's that?

Me: *(Reaching back over to the nightstand, grabbing a glass bowl with a lid, bringing it over, and taking the lid off.)* I was wondering if you could put a little sample in here just so we can prove that you're not shooting blanks?

(Eddie looks at me with a puzzled stare. One that only a blond white girl lying in bed next to you surrounded by lights and cameras could inspire. A stare that posed a dilemma: "Are we shootin' porn?" or "Are you a cop?")

Me: *(Reassuring him.)* It's a family thing.

Any great stand-up knows a win-win when he sees it . . .

Eddie: Oh good. No problem. *(Grabbing the glass bowl from me, he pulls up his T-shirt and slides his hand down his sweatpants. Sweatpants: the uniform of choice when attending a buffet, strip club, or press interview brought to you by Cotton, "The fabric of our lives.")*

Me: We just gotta send it to our lab . . .

(He starts fake masturbating aggressively under his pants. He seemed pretty committed, and I wasn't about get in the way of art. At this point, I was just waiting for a Fox exec to charge in and shut it down. But, instead, I could hear her screaming laughter from the other room. Then, Eddie goes into overdrive.)

Me: Oh god!

Eddie: It's gonna take a minute.

Me: Thank you. Thank you.

Eddie: All right, go on and ask the questions.

Me: Okay.

Eddie: Turn around and let me get some inspiration.

I turn around and bust out laughing as Eddie continued to mock-jackhammer his crotch. For someone else, this may have been the perfect example of the warning: "Be careful what you wish for . . . ," but I wasn't someone else so I played along with this off-the-rails ridiculousness because I wanted to see how far it would go. Unlike the three guys behind the cameras who may have been wondering if they were about to add a porno to their IMDb profiles. After some interesting and very personal visual gymnastics only fit for the reaction shots in *Skinemax* movies, Eddie brought his robust performance to an energetic climax.

Naturally, after giving him a moment to gather himself, I thought it was time for some sweet, sweet pillow talk. He was sufficiently distracted and perfectly primed. So I snuggled up next to him and put his arm around me, and thus began the hilarious and filthy conversation the studio reps had come to expect. And as the interview came to a close, Eddie decided to give it an ending that blew all over the face of everyone's comfort zone, gave everyone at Fox something they still talk about to this day, and risked setting back racial relations by thirty years. Here we pick up close to the end:

Me: The tits on the back. That could actually come in handy, No?

Eddie: No. Nah, you don't wanna see the back of somebody's head and there's a tittie. You know. You just wanna see da ass ripple! That's why brothas like a lotta ass. You know what I'm sayin'. You hit it. It fight back! You know what I'm sayin'. It fight back!! I like dat.

Me: What if it talks back?

Eddie: Shit . . . I make it talk . . . that motherfucker.

Me: Wooooo.
(We both see the "wrap it up signal" from one of my producers, and we lie back to make the final comment to the camera.)

Eddie: Now, y'all go on in and we'll be back in a minute. But right now we gonna make some little *niglets*. *(He rolls over and mounts me and starts going to town. Like I said, he's committed to his craft.)*

As it ended, Kourosh told me the Fox people finally came into the room with that look of: "Okay. So that happened" and were trying to make eye contact with me, looking for a social cue or the sound of a rape whistle. I, of course, was too busy hugging and thanking Eddie for being such a good sport and killing it. The laughter in the room had started with a hint of uncertainty but ended in uproarious celebration, with everyone drinking some of the champagne we had forgotten to use in the interview. From my perspective, Eddie did exactly what a great stand-up does: embrace a situation and throw it on its ass. I was just happy that we could do that together.

Full House star Bob Saget is one of those fearless comics. Penn Jillette once described him to me as the "filthiest motherfucker cocksucker that ever fucked the face of the earth!" He's my kinda guy and I adore him. He came to NGTV once in the early days, and we spent a couple hours on camera together. When we bellied up to the Shark Tank, everyone in the office gathered around, knowing it was going to be a doozy. It was mostly young people along with the fifty-year old mother of one of my producers, who was visiting from Kansas and excitedly pulled up a chair right in the front row.

Unlike the rest of us, who knew Bob was dark and depraved, she only knew him as Danny Tanner on *Full House* and as the original host of *America's Funniest Home Videos.* She had planned her trip around this date so she could attend her favorite TV star's taping and get the chance to meet him up close and personal. It was such a gift to get a front seat to watch her baby daughter at work in her new Hollywood job! Too bad her daughter had failed to mention this was more of a Hollywood-adjacent gig . . . if you get my meaning!

What took place next, besides being fucking hilarious, was nothing short of a full frontal attack on this poor woman's entire moral infrastructure. I can't even begin to tell you how many shades of pale her mom turned during the interview. But you can imagine how her daughter, our producer, came face-to-face with her own mortality while witnessing this verbal assault. Of course, Bob was completely unaware. As far as he knew, he was appearing at some underground speakeasy. Her visit to a Hollywood taping was about to turn into a game of Cry Uncle. The only question was, how long would she last?

Some interviews take a while to build up momentum, but not this one: Right out of the gate, Bob came loaded for bear! He, Shark, and I started with a little anal sex:

Bob: How do you get the most exposure on the Web? I was talking to Lewis Black.

Me: I usually moon.

Shark: Take off your pants!

Bob: Lewis and I figured out the way to get on the Web with a billion hits is to come out with something on YouTube that says, and I told him he can have first billing, "Lewis Black and Bob Saget fucking." I said, "Everybody's gonna want to see that shit." He said, "It's the best thing that could ever happen to our careers!" So I think we're gonna do it.

(Laughter.)

Bob: *(Making physical gesture like he's fucking.)* "Whoops! I'm in your ass . . . BOIINNNGGGG!" That would be great on *America's Funniest* whatever it is. When some guy falls into another man's ass.

Me: Fat Man Falls on Ass.

Shark: Wah . . . wah . . . wah.

Bob: Fat Man Falls into Thin Man's Ass!

Me: Bob Saget is the good guy that's gone wrong.

Bob: Fuckin' A!

Me: Danny Tanner is dead! No. He's not. He will live on in the asses of a lot of men! I have to say that I am very proud to have you on the dark side.

Bob: I love your dark side. What? No . . . You can't have a kid that way! You remember that!

It was at this point where Mom was starting to wiggle around a little in her front-row seat. Then to keep things going Bob hit up the happiest place on earth with a fun story about his *Full House* costar:

Bob: I like Disneyland. I'm a Disneyland kinda guy. It makes me kinda queer but what ya gonna do? Do you like the roller coaster?

Me: Fuck yeah!

Bob: I used to go there with John Stamos all the time. Two years ago we went together.

Me: Uh-huh.

Bob: And he's one of the, "Sit with me on the fuckin' Matterhorn." And we did! It was the gayest thing I've ever done in my life; getting off the Matterhorn with John Stamos.

Shark: Did he hold you when it got scary?

Bob: He wouldn't let go of me. When we got off, he was in me! It was odd. He made a log flume in my ass.

Shark: That, my friend, is the Magic Mountain.

Bob: It is the Magic Mountain.

Me: Weeeeeeeeeee! It's not a small world after all!

Oh boy, Mom was definitely lookin' around! Of course, now that we had opened the *Full House* "back door", so to speak, it was inevitable that someone brought up the Olsen twins, and party favorite, *bestiality*:

Bob: Don't bring 'em up, dude!

Me: Ohhhhhhh.

Bob: No, I can't, I can't go there 'cause that's the only thing that's taboo to me. That . . . and fucking a chicken in the back of the head.

Me: In the back of the head?

Bob: You don't Zapruder a chicken! No, you know what I'm sayin'. Some people believe in the "missing chicken fuckin' theory" where there was a third cock going into the chicken's head. What the? I've never, ever, ever talked about chicken head fucking and there's a reason.

Shark: Why's that?

Bob: Because it's offensive. Chicken head fucking.

Right about this time, Mom realized she wasn't in Kansas anymore. But Bob wasn't done. It was time to take a quick sojourn into the world of snuff films:

Bob: You know . . . someone took, years ago, they took all the clips of all the sickest shit from *Faces of Death* and they had me narrating it from *America's Funniest Videos* and they intercut it. It was like terrible shit, like the bullfighter getting gored by the thing and I was like, "Here's another thing that happened." *(Makes a gun with his hand and puts it in his mouth and pretends to shoot himself.)* It was fucking horrible! I laughed at it for like two minutes and then I realized that I can't look at that footage. I can't. I can't look at snuff. I've stopped makin' it! I can't do it! The only good thing about snuff is there's no second take. You get it . . . *(snaps fingers)* . . .

you get it in one. It's hard to get the tractors to rev up 'cause you get 'em to go zero to eighty . . . I'm sorry everybody . . . I don't know. I just pulled up and thought I was supposed to be on!

I could see Mom was beyond uncomfortable and was attempting to signal our producer to get her out of there but not before Bob upped the ante, went for the jugular, and let loose with his semen:

Bob: I ejaculate gallons of semen a day!
Me: Yay!
Bob: Literally, it's like the water cooler at the office. It's unbelievable the amount of seed . . .
Shark: Seed . . .
Bob: I could be in a truck going to Palm Springs and you'll know my path. It just drains all on the ground. You'll think it's some kind of a, you know, transmission spill. That's how I roll. Always spotting, always draining, always dripping . . . all the time!

Suddenly, he stopped and looked at the old lady. "Someone's mom is here!" he said, pointing right at her. Then, without missing a beat, he dove right back into his seed soliloquy. Mom was mortified, but wasn't about to walk out and make a scene. But her daughter couldn't take any more of watching her mom hear the vilest jokes that could never be unheard. She walked over to her and whispered in her ear and took her upstairs. Sorry, Mom!

Then, of course, there's the interplanetary comedy collision known as Russell Brand. Disguised as a glam-metal junkie Jesus with his painted-on leather pants, long wavy brown hair, scruffy beard, a puffy pirate shirt with vest open to his navel, he was a funny motherfucker with no boundaries, whatsoever!! PERFECT! On top of that, the town was entranced with stories of him being a *sex maniac* who was *fucking* everyone and everything in sight, and they dominated the gossip rags and rumor mill. Minds, hearts, insecurities, and even the occasional "chi," was being disrupted. If you were to believe everything being bandied about, then nobody's body, mind, or spirit was safe. Every "*whole*" was in danger of being *Branded!*

I had been following his career (for the obvious similarities to mine) and was a huge fan for quite some time, so when I got the invitation to meet him and conduct an interview for *Forgetting Sarah Marshall*, I just wasn't sure if I should. I didn't want to find out that he was really a *dick* in real life. Let's just say, I had had my fill of *dicks* at that point. His image didn't bother me at all. From where I was standing, I got the impression that Russell had worked pretty fucking hard to cultivate it, a big part of which was his reputation as a lothario that had bedded countless women. Something he had attributed to a crippling addiction to sex. And in much the same way the mere mention of Diner's Club International opens doors for high society's elite, his admission to being a sex addict, while no laughing matter, only served to further enhance Russell's brand. It was a stroke of genius.

But was I actually going to risk ordering myself another *meet your hero's butt sausage omelet,* heavy on the *butt sausage*? I was filled with about as much titillation as I was with sheer panic. But I had to make a decision and I could feel the pressure rising inside me. With my bladder about to explode and my senses heightened, I almost felt like an omorashi fetishist caught in the desperate final moments leading up to a *pissing orgasm* doubleheader! I'm sure you've been there. It was a terribly odd feeling, though for a hot second, I would have to admit that I could, possibly, see the appeal of its sweet relief. Not that I would ever do it or recommend it. I mean . . . you know . . . not unless it was ABSOLUTELY necessary . . . medically speaking or what have you. But, you know, that's not important right now.

So I thought about it for maybe thirty seconds, which was pretty much all that stood between Kourosh and a front-row seat to an impromptu show-and-tell on water breaking and the modern woman! At which point, I yelled out, "FUCK IT. YES! LET'S DO IT! I WANNA MEET HIM!" Before gunning it to the bathroom for a *screaming orgasm* . . . I mean, to pee.

On my way to Hawaii, where it was all going down, I felt myself getting really excited about the whole thing. I was well-prepared to do my thing with the cast, especially Russell, who seemed extremely intelligent and unpredictable. I was expecting a light and whimsical interview, but were he to suddenly segue into a discussion about Schrödinger's cat, let's just say, I had a *pussy* on standby. The studio seemed equally pumped and had specially requested an additional *In Bed With* shoot with Russell and Jason Segel, along with one-on-one's with the cast. So the big idea was to create an *Eiffel Tower* with yours truly as Lucky Pierre!

No doubt, it was going to be a big and bawdy couple of days, which was just fine by me. I was always down to mess around with the talent and play these parlor games. Most of the time it's super fun! Occasionally, they can feel a lot like getting caught up in some sort of sexual sacrifice ritual. Especially if the people setting it up get a little too excited about getting me together with the talent. That's when you start wondering what looks off and hoping the talent turns out to be more like Ferris Bueller than Machine from *8MM*. Fuck! Please, never Machine!

When I finally met this tall skinny dude with big hair and even bigger balls (not the ones between his legs) for the first time, it was kismet and a relief (he wasn't Machine). It turned out we were kindred spirits. As I sat down and got comfortable for our interview, it felt like the peaceful beginning of a very wild roller coaster ride. I was very excited and looking forward to a few unexpected twists and turns. What came next is best described as a magnitude 10 earthquake with an English accent:

Russell: . . . there's nothing I wouldn't do to you. You strike me as an adventure playground for my cock. Now . . . you, young lady, you're the reason I went through puberty . . . for women like you.

Me: Awww, thanks, that's the nicest thing anyone's ever said to me!

Russell: It's not going to get any better than this. That's it. You've peaked . . . carpe diem, seize the moment. You know what awaits us? The grave. All we have now is this moment.

Me: Isn't that called necrophilia?

Russell: In a way, yah, only if you have sex with dead bodies. Which I don't recommend. Not while you and I . . .

Me: But not in the grave?

Russell: If you had an asma attack now and keeled over, I would take advantage. (*Amused and amazed at how far he's going with this, I start laughing.*) I would decorate your corpse!

Me: Russell, you're a sick fuck! (*A little positive reinforcement never hurts.*)

Russell: Yeah, well . . . let me tell ya! Sick in the sense that I'm jolly good. I mean I'm a jolly good fuck! I've got the moves . . . as it were.

Me: Well, yeah . . . I've heard that about you, actually. You show them off quite nicely in this film. There were things that you were showing the men how to do that I wasn't quite sure of the positions and the angles. You can bend; you're flexible!

Russell: Right, because being good at sex is what I do for a living. The comedy is very much a front for my sexual antics. I only do that to facilitate opportunities like this. Opportunities that I'm not going to let slip through my fingers. Although, you will slip through my fingers over the course of the next few hours, when I make bells ring in your stomach, when I make your eyes dance like fire, when I make you forget your name! Which I'll never do, Carrie Carrie Carrie! A word that rhymes with marry! But why worry, why bother, why should we even take conjugal rights when we could have marital nights? Coital fireworks dancing between our thighs. Let me be shipwrecked with you. Let me be a pirate king. Let us dance subaquatically, let us lose our identities in a glorious union. Our nations aren't so different. If we can attack Iraq, let's attack back. Let's open each other up. Let's orgasm, let's spasm, let's fire, why deny her.

Me: *(Pointing to my breasts with both fingers.)* Can you protect this rack?
(He gets caught a little off guard that I didn't back off from his advances but rather moved further in, and fumbles a bit to find a response.)

Russell: . . . Yeah . . . that is a . . . yeah . . . that, I mean . . . I must say, that's part of the attraction.

Me: *(Laughing.)* Good. I think they've *(making a circular motion around my breasts with my hand)*, you know, they've brought countries together . . . these.

Russell: Well, what they've done is . . . they've torn me apart.

Me: *(Laughing.)* I kinda . . . like you a whole lot.

Russell: Well, I'm an interesting man.

Me: *(Laughing.)* Yeah, you might be . . . yeah . . .

Russell: This is just a small fraction of my personality. After this, you know, I have to make you cum right! And cum and cum and cum and cum. And cum! If I have to, I'll sleep with Hitler to get to you. I've trolled through an endless stream of human flesh only for this climactic moment. I'd commit genocide with my cock to make you cum!

I had just been serenaded by the "Shakespeare of bullshit" and it was spectacular! The whole time he was on his sexual rant, I was thinking, *Wow, it really is like what everyone says it is!* He was this tornado of energy, hormones, and testosterone. He'd throw everything at you, and if he didn't get you with his humor then he'd try something else. It was overwhelming at times, but pretty fucking captivating. He was a "sexual Cookie Monster!" He just had to have it all and wasn't afraid of making a mess.

I realized, from the moment we met, that I was in the presence of an all-powerful *Jizz-Wizard* (which is a lot like a Jedi Master but with a significantly greater amount of *jizz*), so there was a good chance I might get some unwanted spray on me. But he was like a *porno-Gallagher!* It was part of the show, and if I really got worried I could always wear my Duran Duran poncho. Talk about a wet mess! Unless you want a handful of wet spots on your clothes around the waist area, do not forget to take it with you the next time you go see Simon, Jon, Nick, and Roger. Think of it as added protection. It's just like carrying an American Express card except this protects you from female ejaculation. So don't leave home without it.

Speaking of insane experiences, there are crazy moments in your life and then there are fucking crazy moments. But when I traveled to Lake Tahoe to interview Craig Robinson and Rob Corddry for their movie *Hot Tub Time Machine*, I was in store for a motherfucking crazy memory that we still get high from. Craig came from stand-up and Rob came from sketch comedy. They are both seriously funny fuckers, so I knew it was going to be every bit worth the long drive. But when you get to play with "bullshit artists" of this caliber, the only boundaries on what you can do are in your imagination and with hotel security.

After an exhausting road trip up a mountain in a blackout snowstorm, a near-death experience almost driving our crew van off of a cliff, and hours and hours of backtracking due to zero cell service in what felt like a re-creation of *Planes, Trains & Automobiles*, all eight of us finally arrived, slightly worse for wear, at the location, sometime in the wee hours of the morning. What was meant to be an intimate interview with just the three of us in a quiet hotel suite got moved, for some reason, to the center of the hotel's main restaurant. We were assured by management that the place would be very quiet during our scheduled interview time, so we were free to be as *No Good* as we wanted to be without fear of unassuming families being offended to the point of tears as they snack on their holiday clams casino. We took over the fireplace at the center of the restaurant and set up shop.

An hour past their scheduled time with us, there was no sign of the guys, but there was an influx of parents with their kids starting to trickle in. I started to get a little nervous. What I was planning on doing during this interview was very much in line with the sordid nature of the film and was, most definitely, TV-MA. When Craig and Rob finally arrived at the restaurant two hours late, it landed us smack dab in the middle of happy hour. At that point, what seemed like a restaurant at capacity immediately transformed into standing room only once my celebrity guests were spotted. The place was a fucking madhouse! Kourosh led the boys through the craze over to me at our sectioned off area. We were all so happy to see each other, it felt like a full-on family reunion: all big hugs and kisses. Rob scopes all the onlookers and says to me, "We're gonna do your dirty interview here, in the middle of these . . . families?" Craig upon hearing Rob's question simply says, "This is kinda interesting." I sat them down, handed them each a cocktail, and assured them that we had taken the necessary precautions of blocking the views and that the place was so noisy no one would be able to hear us anyway. Of course, I had no idea how much of that was actually true.

Their publicist, who knew us well, came over and stood with Kourosh about four feet away from the action, which I'm sure was just in case she didn't like something going down. Leaving Kourosh within *dick-punching* distance. We all took a minute to enjoy our cocktails and assess the situation. Then, with a very mischievous look on both their faces, we mutually decided to just go for it. What ensued was a game of How Far Can We Push This? And before it was over, we would find out. I had a surprise ending in store, inspired from the snowstorm the night before, that I was, mostly, sure would work. I looked at Kourosh inquisitively to gauge if it was time to bring out the big guns, he looked around the room and gave me a reassured wink, and my inside voice said *Fuck it!*

Me: It's goddam happy hour and somebody needs to black out.
   (Rob, Craig, and I all raise and clink our glasses.)
   When there's a bunch of guys in a hot tub together . . .

Rob: Whoa! I just got hard, right! *(Very loudly.)* When you said that I got immediately hard! Did that show up? *(He inquisitively looks down at his crotch.)*

Craig: And that just got me hard. *(Very loudly.)* Oh my goodness!

Me: Wait, wait, was it a full chub? Because that seems overzealous.

Rob: You said four guys in a hot tub and I immediately got erect.

Craig: Stop doin' that, Rob! *(He blushes as he checks out his own crotchel area.)*

Rob: Four guys in a hot tub.

(Craig's face lights up.)

Craig: Stop! *(He yells with a huge smile on his face.)*

Rob: What's happening? Is it getting . . . *(He makes a gesture with his finger of a growing penis.)* . . . flaccid and then . . . ?

Me: You have to be careful because he is going to poke me in the eye.

Craig: No, it's hard!

Me: Let's make a toast to two men going down on each other because they lost a bet.

(I introduce them to the blowjob shot. We all raise our shot glasses and toast.)

Me: Here's to the blowjob.

Craig: True dat.

Rob: Cheers.

Me: I was really excited about coming to Tahoe for one reason and one reason only . . . *(I reach over to the table, covered in empty shot glasses, and pick up the lid of a silver serving dish that had been sitting there since before they arrived.)* The amazing powder . . . *(I lift the lid, revealing a ginormous mound of a cocaine-looking substance on a beautiful eighteen-inch, circular mirrored tray. It looked like a scene from the movie* Scarface *and they did not see it coming.)* . . . that they have here in Tahoe.

(Both Craig and Rob stare at it in bewilderment. I'm try to gauge whether this is too far for them by looking at their publicist, to see the expression on her face. She was laughing so I continue.)

Me: This is the reason why we are here.

Improvising what could have been a deleted scene right out of the HBO series *The Wire,* Rob pokes a finger into the powder and touches it to the tip of his tongue assessing the quality of the "cocaine" set before him. I pick up what he's putting down and snap into character, reaching in with my finger and rubbing it on my gums. Craig works himself into a frenzy.

Craig: Oh that's real!

  Me: My shit's numb. *(A bunch of it falls off my finger and into my lap.)* I think my whole crotch is numb.

And then the unthinkable happens. We had pushed the boundaries of language and good taste and cocaine use in a public setting. Now it was time to see if we could get ourselves kicked out.

Craig: Powder fight!!! *(Yelling.)*

      (Craig picks up a pile of the "cocaine" and throws it at me and Rob. Oh, it's on. We in turn grab handfuls and fling them at Craig. Mayhem ensues. The powder goes everywhere. All over the walls, the fireplace, the chairs, the table, the floor. And it keeps going on and on until the three of us are completely covered in white powder. I end up snorting lines off of Craig's cheek and Rob's bald head. Cocaine is flying everywhere. It's like a New Jack City *Christmas special.)*

  Me: *(With powder covering my nose and mouth, I settle back into my chair feeling accomplished . . . and a little bit of a sugar high.)* I love Tahoe.

  Rob: *(Covered in powder.)* I actually don't think it's cool that you guys used real cocaine for this.

Craig: *(His blue T-shirt is completely coated.)* I think it's very cool! What's wrong?

  Rob: *(Defending his argument.)* I don't think it's cool . . .

Craig: *(Cutting him off and speaking very quickly like he's coked out of his mind.)* What's the problem? It's very cool. It's all good. Everything is good!

      (We all laugh uncontrollably at the spectacle and the mess we just made inside this nice family establishment.)

Their publicist was laughing so hard, she was doubled over. The scene, when it was over, was surreal. Mission "Fuck Shit Up" accomplished!

When we see each other now, we can't help but reminisce about the "The Great Cocaine Battle of Lake Tahoe." The only downside is none of us have had a healthy relationship with powdered sugar since.

From the outrageousness of Rob and Craig, it makes perfect sense to head over to the brutal honesty of one of my favorite female stand-ups, Margaret Cho. To me, Margaret has always been a trailblazer. She'll talk about anything, no matter how disgusting, personal, or fucking bizarre it may be. I love sitting down with a comedienne who has no limits on the subject matter or filter in terms of how far she will go.

Margaret Cho came to our studio to promote a comedy special and ended up staying for over an hour, downing cocktails and talking smack about tampons, bestiality, lesbian sex, you name it. Of course, nothing was off-limits. During the entire interview, we found comfort embracing the famous NGTV three-foot-long plush cock pillows. I hugged the red one while she fondled the purple:

Margaret: This is kind of reminding me of when guys kinda won't get hard. That's the worst. When they won't get hard.

Me: It's a coke hard-on. *(Referring to her limp cock pillow.)*

Margaret: Yeah . . . the coke hard-on! You're just workin' that dick. You're like workin' at it like a . . . like a baby bird trying to pull a worm out of the ground!
(I start working the cock pillow up and down while Margaret repeatedly makes a face like she's tugging on something with her mouth.)

Me: For days!

Margaret: You know what? Do they have an uncut version? Then you could just pull it back. *(Proceeds to pretend to pull foreskin back from the head of the cock.)*

Me: That would be . . . you could almost . . . like it would be a foot warmer.

Margaret: Yeah. *(Laughing.)*

Me: You could pull it up over your feet like UGGs. *(Demonstrating it with the pillow.)*

Margaret: I don't know. I'm not always that into foreskin but . . .'cause it's kinda . . . well no, 'cause sometimes it's sort of like jerking off a long sleeve. It's like . . . and it also collects things inside.

Me: Does it now? Tell me what you know, Margaret Cho!

Margaret: It tends to collect some things inside. I don't like . . . Sometimes I have problems with guys just because . . . like . . . all of their equipment, it's just, it's like, it's some, there's a lot of opportunities for dirty. A lot of opportunity, especially balls. *(She lifts up the cock pillow's balls and uses them to illustrate the point.)* Because, okay, balls, 'cause you have the dick . . .

Me: Yeah.

Margaret: But then the balls sort of get the ass and the dick dirt. Not just the ass dirt but the dick dirt. So it's really always kind of gross to suck on balls because you have the best of both worlds or the worst of both worlds of the ass and the dicks so you have a lot, anything in here is a bad idea. I just don't like to lick balls that much, do you?

Me: Okay, well, what! It really depends on the . . . Sorry . . . Yes . . . I know, I know . . . guys really don't like it when you ignore the balls, but, however, I have to ask because some girls really prefer them shaved.

Margaret: Oh . . .

Me: So if you're worried about dirt . . . like maybe . . . maybe waxed is better?

Margaret: I don't know if they need to, like, wax them. I think that they should just kind of trim them. Just be ball-aware. Just check yourself before you wreck yourself and just be ball-aware 'cause it's really . . . it could be gamey down there. It gets, you know . . .

Me: Yes.

Margaret: 'Cause I really enjoy giving head but it's just . . . it can be . . . it can be musty and a little bit bleachy.

Me: *(Nodding.)*

Margaret: And I don't know what it is? It's just bad and guys don't think about it 'cause they want their dick sucked, but they don't think about the reality of their dicks being sucked because they've never sucked a dick, or they haven't sucked a dick in a while!!

Me: Or they're lying!!!
(The crowd howls.)

Me: Hold on, we need to rewind for just a second. She likes to suck dick! Let's just get that out in the open.

Margaret: Do you like to?

Me: Yes. It can be fun. It can be good.

Margaret: I think it's really fun and really great . . .

Me: However, I don't like the earmuff handles. *(Gesturing two hands on each side of my head like most guys attempt during a blowjob.)* I don't like that.

Margaret: Oh.

Me: When there's that whole thing going on . . . *(Gesturing my head being forced to go up and down.)* I don't . . . STOP . . . with the pressure on the head.

Margaret: I mean I know what I'm doing!

Me: I will find my way.

Margaret: Yeah . . . as long as it's clean. Like as long as it's, the area . . . it's . . . I mean I like to eat ass . . . I, I love it! I think it's good. *(We high five to the audience screaming YEAH!!)*

Me: Not many people would admit that on camera, and that's why Margaret Cho is the bomb!

Margaret: Thank you. I think it's important to eat ass. I think it's good. I think it's really . . . I think it's really healing . . . and it's a beautiful thing; it's a beautiful gift.

Me: It's the gift that keeps on giving really.

Margaret: It's a gift that you could give to somebody 'cause then they get into it and then later, you know, they're like still into it, you know, and they think about you and they get a nice warm feeling.

Me: Hold on. Time out. What happens . . . because there needs to be advice to women that would like to eat ass . . . what do you do with the dingleberry? What do you do? You go down there and you're like . . . it happens! One needs to know.

Margaret: Well, they're not as good as chocolate chips so you've gotta dispense, you gotta get rid of them.

Me: Get rid!

Margaret: I'd say flick it! Flicking.

Me: Okay. Flicking is okay?

Margaret: Flicking is good. I think just eat around it. Just eat around. Do it like a vegetarian would, just eat around it. Don't eat that part.

Me: Do you do it on a first date?

Margaret: I eat ass on a first date. Yeah. It sort of depends on the person.

Me: It always depends on the person . . .

Margaret: But yeah, of course! Of course. I'd eat ass, but eat ass last. Eat ass as your last supper.

Me: 'Cause after that you really don't want to make out.

Margaret: No. It's sort of the last . . . it's like an after-dinner mint.

And that was just the beginning. An hour and a half later when the interview was over, I walked Margaret out.

"Do you do stand-up?" she asked me.

"Nooooo. That shit's scary!" I said. "I don't know how anybody does that."

"Well you're funny and you should. We need more girls."

In my mind, stand-up seemed like the most terrifying thing in the entire world. There you are in full view of everyone and in all your glory. Except it doesn't feel glorious. They can see you, but you can't see them. You're, literally, standing under a spotlight while everyone in the room laughs at you as you spill your guts. You might as well be giving everyone a live interpretation of "Goatse." It's finally your chance to shine, but instead of landing who wants to be a millionaire, you've ended up naked and afraid in a room full of people who all fancy themselves comedians, but are too pussy to open up those cheeks and bend over. The air is thick with judgement, jealousy, and drunks who demand laughter— clown!! You're the jester in the court of public opinion. The jury of your peers have just spent the day at a shitty go-nowhere job only to find out, when they got home, their kid got expelled from school for drawing pictures of dicks in art class. Now, having spent the last two hours fighting with their spouse about whether they should finally put granny in a home or continue to let her run around the neighborhood naked screaming "Heil Hitler," are expecting you to make them laugh. Personally, I would rather twist my boobs into a bow tie.

I could never, ever, ever, ever, ever do that . . . until I was given an offer I couldn't refuse.

I was asked to roast Jack Black by the New York Friars Club. Whoa. Again. For a couple of reasons, whoa! Reason number one: The Friars Club is the OG (that's *original gangsta* for those who think MLK Day is a celebration of milk) when it comes to roasting. They were *punching nuts* way before the *Comedy Central Roasts*. A good fifty-four years, in fact. When the feet of their inaugural roastee, Maurice Chevalier were being held to the fire in 1949, Bing Crosby was crooning about how to treat a lady. And when Comedy Central's first victim, Denis Leary, was being served a *chili dog* in 2003, Ja Rule was rapping about how to treat dat ass! This was the house built by Jerry Lewis, Jack Benny, Milton Berle, Freddie Roman, Dean Martin, Bob Hope, George Burns, Johnny Carson, Sammy Davis Jr., and Lucille Ball, to name a few. This was where it all began. And THEY just invited ME to come slay with the best of the best! Me, who was already trying to figure out how to make a bow tie knot with my breasts?

Reason number two for "whoa"? Jack Black. Jack Black and Tenacious D were everything!!! Without the sweet, sweet sounds of the "D" masturbating in our ears for the last decade, NGTV would cease to exist. Their style of funny, filthy, and irreverent, while making everyone feel like they were the after party, was, exactly, what we strived to be. So the idea that the first time I was ever going to get onstage and do comedy was to "honor" Jack *"fucking"* Black was extra *trots-inducing*. This would not be my first time meeting the legend.

No, no, Jack and I have a long history of silly fucked-up encounters. It's always an adventure interviewing him. One of the more ridiculous exchanges we had was when I interviewed Jack and his musical partner, Kyle Gass, at the junket for *Tenacious D in The Pick of Destiny*. Those two, separately, are fucking nuts. Now put them together and you have an extra spicy *kielbasa sausage party* you don't want to miss.

As I walked in I could see both Jack and Kyle were in great spirits. I reminded them that after a long day of doing regular press, No Good TV was in the house, which meant they could revert back to their more fun state of being uncensored. Like moths to a flame, they both came alive. Jack just lit into it from the get-go, while Kyle looked like he was brewing an idea to take the interview to another level. Well, it was safe to say he was *brewing* something:

Jack: Fuckin' fuck fuck. Fuck! Fuckity fuck! Fuckin' fuck. Fuckin' *Tenacious D and The Pick of Destiny*. FUCK!!
(Right as he's finishing up his opening, Kyle starts getting up from his chair, turns around, and bends down.)

Kyle: No Good Television. Check this out!
(He then proceeds to bust out the loudest, beefiest, lengthiest, and smelliest ripple fart you could ever imagine.)

Jack: *(With a panicked look on his face:)* OH . . . NO!! OH NO!!

It was an 8.4 on the *rectum scale* and it sounded like a group of thirty people blowing *raspberries,* and it lasted twenty seconds, which is an eternity for a *rump roar.* The studio reps, publicists, and camera crew all guffawed with amusement and horror. As I looked around I could tell they were starting to smell it and then feel it on their skin like I was . . . and like Jack was about to.

Jack: *(Laughing.)* OH MY GOD! *(Then a dense, moist pocket of shit vapor hit him square in the face, and he reached his hands up to wipe it away and get it off.)*

Kyle: No Good TV . . . you just saw some good TV!

I couldn't stop laughing, and his *turd hootie* was only part of the reason. As I looked around the room, I could see each person, almost in slow motion, swallow the *great brown fecal cloud* for the first time, and the look of abject terror that came across their faces was priceless. Some were grabbing their necks, some were starting to choke, some were heaving, about to vomit, but we were all trapped. And no one knew what to do.

Me: Now it's in smell-o-vision.

Jack: Wooooooo.

Jack was doing his best to smile and keep it together for the cameras, while casually attempting to wipe it away with his hand. But the room just kept getting more and more rancid from the *Frequency Activated Rectal Tremor.* At this point, people around us were panicking. The windows were closed and the AC was off. We had all been *hot boxed* by Kyle Gass, and this *Dutch paperweight* was turning into a death trap.

Jack: It really stinks!
Kyle: It's really bad in here!
  Me: What did you eat? *(Fanning the air across my face, wondering if I was about to get pink eye.)*
Kyle: I have no colon. *(He was starting to feel the burning sensation in his throat that we were all feeling from the ghost turd. No doubt some part of him was starting to think that he just might have, accidentally, committed Dutch oven suicide.)*
  Me: *(Laughing to hide the pain.)*

I could see Jack was just dying and not in a good way. He put his head down and was trying to wipe the sweat off his brow. There was nothing to do. No one dared make a move for the door as it could ruin the interview. It was ridiculous. Not knowing what to do, Kyle tried to move forward with the interview. All the while Jack is desperately trying to avoid another bite of that *air biscuit* by keeping his hand in front of his mouth.

Kyle: Did you ever see *School of Rock*?
  Me: I did.
Kyle: Did you ever see the porno version?
  Me: I did not.
Kyle: Guess what it was called?
  Me: *School of . . . Cock?*
Kyle: No! *School of Sex.*

At this point, Jack, who has this bizarre smile on his face that's trapped somewhere between annoyed and homicidal, pipes up, speaking through his teeth and keeping his lips as closed as possible.

Jack: No, it was *School of Cock, School of Cock.* *(He says impatiently.)*

Meanwhile, the *gaseous anomaly* had evolved into a terror resembling Stephen King's *The Mist* and was slowly eating through all the breathable air in the room, exposing everyone's last nerve. Jack being at ground zero for the *anal volcano* finally broke down.

Jack: Here's the thing: There is a powerful stench in this room!

 Me: *(I just start laughing my ass off.)*

Jack: *(Looks off screen at a studio rep.)* And we're pretending like there's not . . . can you turn on the fan? *(His voice is getting more serious and desperate which each word.)* It's okay if it hurts the sound of the interview, at this point. *(Behind the scenes, people are scrambling to get it done; terror has set in.)* Yeah, leave that door open. *(The fan is on and the PA is being tentative about what she should do with the door.)* For real! For real! *(Jack starts to make motions with his hands as the fake smile on his face turns to a frown as he feels like he's suffocating from Kyle's booty bomb, but the PA isn't sure if he's being super serious.)*

 Me: Is it burning your nostrils?

Jack: *(Frustrated at the PA:)* She thinks I'm joking! *(Throwing his hands in the air.)*

Finally they opened all the doors, turned on the AC, and got all the fans going. We proceeded to complete the interview, but the terror unleashed from Kyle's ass was not to be underestimated. That *triple flutter blast* dogged my entire interview and the rest of the day for every other interview. Rumors persist to this day that that particular room at the Four Seasons in Beverly Hills is haunted, and if you listen closely you can still hear the *brown horn brass choir* take an encore. With memories to last a lifetime such as these, I had to make sure I came to the roast with some game.

Fortunately, I got to collaborate with some seriously killer writers in putting my debut together. You didn't think I was going to write it all by myself, did you? Fuck that. I was going to be too busy trying not to throw up. The challenge for me in writing roast jokes is that I'm not really comfortable making fun of people. That's not my sense of humor. I like people to feel like we're all on the same team, but that is the exact opposite of the typical jokes that you hear at a roast. It took me a few days to try to figure out the right angle, but I finally gave my writers a direction—my tits. I figured my tits could tell jokes that I couldn't, and I was pretty sure that no man was going to be insulted by a message from the girls. So first in was the super-talented and funny Beth Armogida, a former writer on *The Tonight Show,* who taught me how to go *balls deep* without getting messy. Then I mixed in a few gut punches and a couple of chin whacks from two members of the kick-ass pit crew from *Buzz*—the quick-witted Chris DeLuca and the consistently brilliant Andrew Goldstein. Then, I topped it all off with a coup de grâce to end with a bang.

When I accepted the gig, there were a couple of things that set my mind at ease a little bit. First, being someone who likes to drink more than your average bear, I know firsthand that everyone is funnier when alcohol is involved. Booze has always been a good friend of mine, and I thought the roast was going to be just another example of that. Uh . . . not so much! About a week before, I found out that it was taking place in the middle of the week at lunchtime. What the fuck? Look, I'm not against getting drunk on a Wednesday at 1 P.M. (as a matter of fact, it's Thursday at 3 P.M. as I write this, and I'd be lying to you if I didn't tell you that this chapter is sponsored by Jameson), but I was assuming that that would not be the case for most of the people in the audience. They were professionals and businesspeople who had shit to do.

Strike one!

The second thing that I was counting on was a teleprompter. I'd seen the roasts on TV, and everyone read off of a teleprompter. I was taking solace in the fact that, as nervous as I was, I wasn't going to have to memorize my roast. Wrong. When I got there, I was told that there wasn't going to be a teleprompter but that the staff could put my jokes on little cards to bring up onstage with me. Are you fucking kidding me? Tiny little blue cards that had little tiny letters on them?

Strike two!

To top it all off, and the one thing I hadn't even thought of until I got there, was who I would be performing in front of. I guess I was so busy worrying about what I was going to say I didn't even think about who I was going to be saying it to. When I walked into that room, it was packed with comedians, jaded Hollywood muckety-mucks, and people who have been coming to these things for years and have seen the best of the best.

Do you know how hard it is to make a comedian laugh? They've heard every premise, every setup, and every punch line ever. The best you can get out of a comedian isn't even a laugh; if they like a joke they'll just say, "That's funny." Thanks for the truckload of confidence. The Hollywood people and vets of the Friars Club were not going to be any easier. They had heard everything. What in the world was I going to say that could possibly make them laugh?

Strike three!

I felt like shooting horse tranquilizers directly into my eyeballs. Panic had officially set in.

The one thing I was sure of was that I knew I needed to bring a friendly face with me. Someone I could lock my eyes onto when I was up there so I didn't feel alone. Someone who had a calming effect on me. So I brought my buddy Shane Farley, the showrunner and executive producer of my show *Big Morning Buzz Live.* He was someone I trusted would always have my back should airship Keagan take a nosedive into her river of dreams that day. The plan was for him to sit somewhere where I could see him, and no matter what everyone else was doing, he would laugh uncontrollably. Stacking the room in your favor is always a good idea.

I remember when I was in fifth grade, I wanted to be in charge of handing out everyone's Valentine's cards to my class. We were going to have a vote to see who got to be in charge, so a few days before the vote, I brought a bunch of people lollipops, and they promised to vote for me. Well, when the big election day finally arrived, my teacher counted the votes, and I was already walking up to the front of the class to give my acceptance speech when she said, "The winner is . . . Karen Muench." What the fuck? Turns out sneaky Karen had the same idea I had, but her parents had a little more money and she gave everyone gift certificates to McDonald's. "Damn you, McRib! Why did you have to come back?"

The big day itself felt like riding a hurricane on a rubber dinghy. My ridiculously jam-packed morning had me ricocheting from one thing to the next like a pinball in an orgy of thumper bumpers. My head was spinning so fast while we shot my morning show that I didn't have much time to panic about my pending date with the kings of comedy. That is, up until I walked into the Grand Ballroom at the New York Hilton and laid eyes on the over *three thousand* New York Friars Club members, dignitaries, celebrities, and friends who were about to witness my stand-up debut. *Holy fuck!* In that instant, I felt like I had all the *Red Bull and diarrhea!* But there was no turning back now, so I started making my way to the stage. As I walked across the stage to take my seat on the dais, the gravity of the situation hit me like a *donkey punch.* I looked around and saw Amy Schumer; Sarah Silverman; Richard Belzer; Artie Lange; Oliver Platt; Jeffrey Katzenberg; Richard Marx; the "Roastmaster General" himself, Jeffrey Ross; and living legend Jerry Lewis, to name a few, and I thought to myself, *What the hell am I doing here?* Seriously, here I was, a woman with no "official" stand-up comedy experience, except for the occasionally well-placed dick joke in an interview, and I was onstage with legends. Legends! To make matters even worse, they had NO IDEA who I was. To them, I probably looked like the lead actress in a remake of *Faster, Pussycat! Kill! Kill!* All bust, no bite!

As an aside, I have to say that one of the more ironic, gratifying, and completely unexpected things that happened at the event was running into my old friend and former business partner, Gene Simmons. I'd come a long way since the last time we had seen each other a couple of years back, and we ended up having a lengthy catch-up sesh! Gene was an early believer in me, so it was great to have our paths cross at such a prestigious event and to have so much to share. Of course, Gene being Gene, he had plenty of things to say and advice to give. And, me being me, I had plenty of grief to give him in return. No matter what, Gene and I will always have Santa Monica Boulevard!

Anyway, back on the dais, I was somewhere between crying, puking, and pooping—even my insides wanted out of there. Things were spiraling quickly, so I sat down and looked out at the table where my friend was sitting. I needed a friendly face to talk me off the ledge, and when I found his table, someone else was sitting in his seat. No, no, no, no, no, no. That wasn't possible. He'd shown me where he was sitting! That was the table where he was supposed to be sitting. I scanned the audience . . . nothing. Ladies and germs, let the flop sweats begin!

And then, the first bit of good luck shone down on me in the form of Al Roker. He must have sensed how nervous I was. Either that or he saw the waterfall of sweat pouring off of my forehead. "You're gonna do great," he said, and smiled at me. I'm sure I'm not the first person to have ever said this but, "Thank God for Al Roker." If it wasn't for him I think I might have stood up, walked out of the Friars Club, and lain down on the closest train tracks. He kept my mind off of the roast as best he could just by making small talk and introducing me to a few people. Normally, I'd want to stay focused on getting my head straight, but in this case, any small talk was way better than the big talk that was going on in my head, which sounded something like this: *TAKE YOUR STILLETOS OFF AND RUN LIKE THE WIND! GET THE FUCK OUT OF HERE! RUN! RUN! RUN!*

As the show started, I was caught somewhere between trying to listen to these people—who I consider to be some of my heroes—telling hilarious jokes and going over my set in my head. It was honestly hard for me to concentrate because—and this was the final mindfuck they had laid on me when I got there—nobody knew what the order was. For professional comedians I'm sure that's no big deal. For me, it was a pretty big fucking deal. I wanted to be able to prepare myself for when they called my name, so when people looked over at me, I didn't look like someone who had just been seasick on a boat for three hours. Not only that, but to add to the pressure, the people who were going on before me were KILLING! I mean, they were slaying, and with a certain type of insult humor that this crowd was clearly here to see. A certain type of comedy that I, unfortunately, was not about to deliver.

Strike four! In my baseball game there are unlimited fuckups.

And then, it happened. Through a fog I heard Bob Saget say, ". . . Carrie Keagan!" My new best friend, Al Roker, nudged me and said, "You're up." I didn't hear anything Bob said before, just my name, and it kind of echoed, like he was saying it on a mountain five hundred yards away—"Keagan, Keagan, Keagan!" It's just as well that I didn't hear how he introduced me because what that *thingamafucker* actually said was, "I'd like to say something funny about our next roaster but I honestly don't know who the fuck she is. Please welcome Carrie Keagan."

As I walked up to the podium and looked out at a sea of people eating cold salmon and capers (perfect comedy food), something happened to me. I know this is going to sound ridiculous, but I basically had an out-of-body experience. I don't really remember much, but it was like I was floating above the room and I could see myself standing there. I honestly don't remember what I said and I can't find those stupid little blue cards they gave me, but just like Rey in her climactic lightsaber duel with Kylo Ren in *Star Wars: The Force Awakens*, I closed my eyes and let the force guide me.

The first thing out of my mouth was something vile about Bob Saget, and then I went straight into introducing the room to my very intuitive co-stars, my tits. Basically, eight minutes about my tits and what they thought of the people up on the dais.

"Thanks, Bob. It's great to finally have your attention; I usually have to put my finger in your ass to do that!

"I was seven years old when the show *Full House* premiered. Every Friday night, Bob Saget would come into my living room . . . until my parents found out and called the police.

"Hey, Bob, at least John Stamos gave me candy, you cheap prick.

"Bob, I'll let you know when I'm finished, because obviously you wouldn't have a clue.

"I'm very excited to be here at the Friars, mainly because nose and ear hair gets me hot.

"But enough about me. Let's get right to the topic of the night: my boobs. They are amazing. Aren't they? Some of you losers may not know this, but . . . having giant breasts can help your career. Well, except for Jeff Ross.

"My boobs have special powers. They can predict the future. It's true.

"For example . . .
"My boobs predict Freddie Roman will continue to tell jokes that are older and drier than Sarah Silverman's eggs.

"My boobs predict Richard Marx will die in a plane crash. Just kidding. Only famous singers die in plane crashes.

"My boobs predict Amy Schumer will be my friend—my fat, dumpy friend.

"My boobs predict Artie Lange will win the Nobel Prize after saving an entire village from dying of thirst just with his ball sweat.

"My boobs predict Oliver Platt will finally stop sexting me his penis, which is a relief, because my iPhone won't zoom in that far.

"My boobs predict Jeffrey Katzenberg will have lots of success and make an ass-load of money. Hey, my breasts ain't stupid. I heard Mr. Katzenberg likes 3-D . . . Hey, Jeff, I've got your 3-Ds right here. (*I point to my boobs.*)

"My boobs predict Jerry Lewis will make love tonight to his one, true love: himself!"

Who knew my boobies were that funny? Then it was time to pay my respects to the man of the hour. The man who ended every interview we ever did with his filthy version of the Buddhist chant. A beautiful self-affirming chant that we would sing together. Feel free to join in if you know the words: "God Damn Motherfucking Stupid Piece of Shit. HEY!! God Damn Motherfucking Stupid Piece of Shit. HEY!!" Rinse and repeat until you have found your chi. Jack introduces that song to me for the first time, every time. So I sang our little ditty in my head, for courage, and stepped forth deeper into the abyss:

"And my boobs also have a prediction for Jack Black. They predict he will star in a huge box office success called *Kung Fu Panda 14*. *(Turning to Jack:)* Jesus, Jack! Don't you have any self-respect? *(To audience:)* In that film, Kung Fu Panda will get violently fucked in the ass over and over and over again. That's right—George Lucas will direct it!

"There's one thing I admire about Jack Black. Jack will do anything for a movie role, except push-ups and sit-ups.

"In *Nacho Libre*, he wore these really tight pants, and we saw everything, which is really fucking sad. Jack got his whole body completely waxed. Picture something hairless, clammy, and huge—like Madonna's pussy!"

After *clooping* Jack a half dozen more times (that's a backhand to the nutsack, for the uninitiated), it was time for my big finish, where I get to apologize for giving him the public prostate exam and tell him why his ass is the best. The most important things to me were that I wanted to make Jack laugh, and I needed him to know what an influential role he'd played in my life. I thought for days about the right way to end it, and I finally found inspiration in one of my favorite lines from their 2006 movie *Tenacious D in The Pick of Destiny*. It's a subtle but essential thematic element that stemmed all the way back to the very first episode that aired on HBO in 1997. It was a private joke that only he and Tenacious D diehards would appreciate: "Jack, you and the D have been such an inspiration to me in life, and I just want to thank you, from the bottom of my heart, for fucking my ear pussy!"

You know what happened next? Applause. Fucking applause! I couldn't believe it! The consciousness that had left my body when my name was called suddenly floated back into me just as Jack stood up and gave me a huge hug. Sarah Silverman shook my hand and Jeffrey Ross, "the Motherfuckin' Roastmaster General," said to me, "You should seriously consider doing stand-up." It was the perfect ending to a terrifying verbal bungie jump! I made it out with my head held high.

Well, almost . . . as I made my way back my seat, Jerry Lewis stood up, tackled me with a bear hug, then proceeded to *"body slam"* me onto the dais floor, dry humping me. After three whole seconds of pure ecstasy, I walked my new boyfriend back to his chair. "Old and feeble," my ASS!

P.S. I tried doing stand-up a few weeks after that.

P.P.S. I bombed.

P.P.P.S. Fuck you, Jeffrey Ross!

19

ALWAYS OUTNUMBERED, NEVER OUTGUNNED!

. . . by watching her I began to think there was some skill involved in being a girl.
—To Kill a Mockingbird, *Harper Lee*

If you ask me who I am, what I do, how I feel, how's work, how's life, or how's the family, you have my answer. "Always outnumbered. Never outgunned!" It's the simple truth of every obstacle before me and my power to overcome it. It's become a bit of a "battle cry" to remind me that there is no life but the one we make, so get in there and fight, motherfucker, fight!

I didn't set out to change the world; I was just trying to find a sense of purpose. I soon realized that when you try to do things *drastically different* than the norm, the world will try to change you. It will come at you from every direction. It will wound your spirit. It will break your heart and it will not be sentimental about it. But like Eleanor Roosevelt once said, "A woman is like a tea bag; you won't know how strong she is until it's in hot water." So I would not be deterred. Whether you find purpose or purpose finds you, once you have it, it can be a source of great strength and much needed clarity. Plus, isn't life all about taking risks and navigating its hazards with skill in order to find true fulfillment? Is that not the art of living dangerously?

Life is complicated. Show business is a complicated conundrum of contradictions. Like Caitlyn Jenner marrying Kanye West. So you better have a fucking game plan. Either you play the game or the game plays you. As a girl in this business, you are constantly surrounded by unfair limitations, unreasonable scrutiny, unfounded accusations, unprofessional conduct, and unethical judgement. Kind of like asking a flight attendant in coach for a glass of water before take off. All of which only increase with success. Like I've said before, everything in showbiz is counterintuitive.

And it doesn't always come from the obvious places, either. That would be too easy. Instead, it's everywhere. In fact, much of the time, it comes from the very last place you'd expect. Sort of like the fifty-million-year-old sperm they recently found in Antarctica. No one saw that *cumming*! Intricately woven into this game's complex tapestry of challenges is an inbred "battle of the sexes." Now that, in and of itself, is not much of a revelation, except for the fact that I'm not just talking about women vs. men. I'm talking about every other permutation, including something closer to a "battle royale," where it's everyone for themselves. There are days you feel like you're at a rave with DJ "Sun Tzu," working his scratch and scribble on the turntable. So you've got to be mentally prepared.

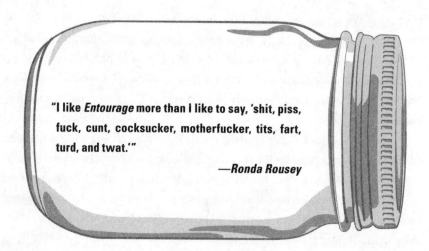

"I like *Entourage* more than I like to say, 'shit, piss, fuck, cunt, cocksucker, motherfucker, tits, fart, turd, and twat.'"

—*Ronda Rousey*

Women kick ass!

Women are born to fight. We've been used as accessories. We've been treated like luggage. We've been owned like property. We are neither the inheritors nor the administrators of legacy. We've never had anything handed to us that we didn't have to earn either before or after receiving it. We've been denied, diminished, devalued, and devoured by an androcentric culture. Let's face it: Women are battle-hardened by design. We are the living embodiment of the old Japanese proverb, "Fall down seven times, get up eight." Each day we seize, each stride forward we make, and each success we achieve is an exercise in pure will. We have always been warriors in an unnecessary war.

I'll say it again. Women kick ass!

From the womb, we're indoctrinated in the art of *mental jiu-jitsu* so formidable it makes sphincters tremble. Our exceptional skill and accuracy with the *side-eye* is akin to that of a Jedi with a lightsaber. We come fitted with X-ray vision so powerful it can see right through dense objects like bullshit. We are created to take that sorry excuse for casual misogyny called "social awkwardness" and shove it *where the monkey put the whistle.* We are formed from ninja rocks designed to smash any glass ceiling built above us. We are masters of a *verbal judo* so powerful that our words and ideas have infiltrated the superhighway of public opinion known as the media. Gender equality is no longer our hope but it is our manifest destiny. I'm not just a feminist by choice; I'm a feminist by voice!

So one more time for the cheap seats . . . women kick some serious ass!

On its best day, the entertainment business is the corporate equivalent of a bullfighting arena filled to capacity with a bloodthirsty mob. All of whom are hiding the awful truth that when the female matadors take the stage, the crowd starts rooting for the bull. Sadly, this business has a wicked way of breeding pettiness and jealousy as everyone tries to protect their square foot of land, both in front of and behind the camera. To be perfectly honest, I can't help but fear that some women have become so proficient in ass kicking that it no longer matters whose ass it is or why. They just need to kick it. And if you know, you know; but if you don't, let me tell you when women turn on each other, there are piranha that look away because it's too damn vicious!!

I wish I could to tell you that the battle against misogyny is inching forward in the capable hands of a sisterhood of single-minded determination for the common good of us all. But I don't want to overwhelm your capacity to process horseshit by delivering it in tonnage you're not accustomed to. The good news is there are many brilliant and brave women who are all of these things every day and in every way. The bad news is that many of them often find themselves unwittingly swimming in chummed-up water, on the wrong end of a documentary on natural selection and the great white shark. But I think, no matter what, women should treat each other well. They should be support systems for one another and root for each other to succeed. Unfortunately, there are plenty of women who think a good heart makes a good meal.

There's a critical aspect of this business, you may be *shocked* to discover, that exploits insecurities and vulnerabilities. It's the perfect enabler for anyone who thinks sharpening your teeth is the perfect Sunday afternoon: men, women, or sharks! Now here's a *shocking* revelation: Entertainment is a business of objectification. Boom! When you're on camera, you're on display, and there's a certain amount of much-needed but generally unwanted attention that goes into getting any display ready. It can be weird and invasive, but if you don't like the process of being prepared for display, then perhaps being on camera isn't right for you. Objectification is shallow, demeaning, and exactly what it needs to be. I say that with no enmity. It's simply an undeniable fact. Anyone who tells you different is probably also trying to convince you that you need a *fifty-five gallon* drum of lube (which, I'm sure, he can get you for a really good price).

Those of us fortunate enough to work in this business willingly surrender our "humanity card" and are handed our "product ID" on day one. From that moment forward, it's a game of Poke and Prod, governed by the Japanese rule of *Nin'i no ana*, which, loosely translated, means "any hole." Not to be confused with the other Japanese game of *Machigatta ana*, which means "wrong hole." But, in all honesty, at the end of a long day of playing Who's in My Hole? and Which One Is It?, it all feels the same.

Everyone you know and love on TV has been focus grouped, product tested, and Q&A'd up the wazoo! Between the general meetings, auditions, group assessments, and postmortems that we're exposed to, your *undercarriage* starts to feel a bit overexposed, if you know what I mean. Probably why "vaginal rejuvenation" has become all the rage in Hollywood! "I swear everyone's doing it!" Truth be told, these vocational *lube jobs* are as much a part of your "career maintenance" as STD testing is for porn stars. So you can't let this mentally trip you up. Accept it, draw strength from the knowledge, and move forward.

Where this can get *challenging* and hurtful is when the poking and the prodding serves no business reason and is just personal, used with malicious intent by a person in a position of power. Imagine you're giving a guy a blowjob, and he suddenly decides to hold your head by the ears like a soccer ball and take control, almost choking you in the process. It's one thing to brutally assess someone for merited reasons, but it's completely another to tear them down because they wouldn't sleep with you or because they're gay or because they're a threat to you or because you think they're too confident and need to be taken down a notch or because you woke up on the wrong side of the bed in the *bitch ward* and need a new ant for your magnifying glass. I think we all come into this business with the understanding that, to a certain degree, we're going to be treated like human pin cushions. But many of us never really grasp that some people are incapable of seeing the fine line between being a human pin cushion and a tortured voodoo doll.

It's not just limited to character assassinations by men trying to control women. Oh no, it's ubiquitous. The truth is no one has an eye for detail like women do, and if you've ever sat around a brunch table gossiping with your friends, then you know, when so inclined, we have the capacity to tear each other apart molecule by molecule. Where guys tend to be sloppy and generalize their comments, women have mastered the art of torture by *verbal acupressure*. They'll use a comment about your fat ankles to send your mind spiraling into self-consciousness. I'd be lying if I didn't tell you that it hurts my heart when I see or hear about women doing this to each other. There's nothing more demoralizing than crawling through the endless horseshit that you sometimes have to in this business, only to then get handed another shovel's worth from a female exec with a chip on her shoulder. Someone you'd think, having been through it herself, would be sympathetic and supposedly understand how terrible it is. How can that happen, for fuck's sake? We're better than that. I know we are. But on those sad days, hope is just a hooker with a dream.

I've had my inexplicable and hurtful experiences with female execs, but I'm one of the lucky ones. I also found the warm embrace of some extraordinary ladies who went to the mat for me throughout my career and in my life. Truth is, every time I've been a little down-and-out at the hands of a female exec, it's always been another girl who shows up and picks me up, dusts me off, and gets me going again. I'm proud to say that some of the people primarily responsible for my improbable and fortunate career have been these incredible women. Which is a pretty wild thing to say when the business is so male dominated. But it just goes to prove that there are still so many wonderful women rooting for each other that it keeps this hooker dreaming.

As much as I've tried to avoid it, there was nothing I could do to prevent having some fucked-up, head-scratching, and ass-backward encounters with women. I hate to focus so much on the women, but with men, I sort of expect "complications" here and there. There's nothing surprising or interesting there. But with women, I'm just fucking baffled. It's never made any sense to me. It's not a part of who I am and how I operate. And boy, does it hurt somethin' fierce when you find yourself at the *ass-end* of a *pile-driver* delivered by a woman. Especially one you thought was in your corner. For some reason, I just never see it coming. I always tell myself that in the end, the girls that defy the odds, surpass your expectations, and go all the way are the only ones that matter. The rest are just noise and, maybe, could use a free hug.

I'm proud to say that the majority of my life and professional career has been cultivated by astounding women. Which is probably why it really fucking bugs me when I see the seedy other side because I'm living proof of how good it can be. You can't come from where I did and not get annoyed with girl-on-girl "corporate" violence. I can't help but be a bit of a hippie chick when it comes to girls supporting each other. I'm proud to have come from a long line of tough independent women who taught me better!

There's nothing I haven't done or wouldn't do to help a girl find her way. I consider it an unspoken obligation. Yet in spite of that, I've had a complicated relationship with women my whole life. I think the girls in school who bullied me left me with some lifelong deeply rooted insecurities and hesitation. So when I connect with a girl and find acceptance, I get really excited because I always start out a bit nervous. To be perfectly honest, walking into a room with just one woman has always been harder for me than walking into a room where there's just one man. For some reason, I'm much more self-conscious about what I'm wearing or even how I say "hello." I always feel like I've walked in with my skirt tucked into my pantyhose. I'm always afraid of being judged.

But I've never let it stop me from walking into any room, especially one with a girl in it, because I figure there's a good chance that she's probably feeling the same way. Plus, connecting from a place of mutual tension is what lifelong friendships are made of. I see it as my responsibility to turn the situation around because that's what girls are supposed to do for each other. Right? In a funny way, it's very similar to when I walk into a room to interview a female celebrity. Neither of us is completely comfortable or know what to expect, and I do my best to take the edge off and assume she will, too.

It would be easy to assume that the early adopters of NGTV in the biz must have been straight guys since it's so edgy and sexually charged. I mean who else would get the humor and invite us? Right? Nope! You could not be more wrong! The vast majority of publicists we dealt with in the beginning—and still do, to this day—are some incredible women, followed by some amazing gay men and women and let's not forget the kick-ass straight guys. It's doubtful we would have ever gotten off the ground were it not for some seriously forward-thinking and incredibly hip female studio publicists and execs. They're the ones that got our humor before anyone else and fought to get us included. At every major studio, women were responsible for and witnessed my inaugural uncensored interviews and F-bomb raids and chose to embrace me.

My first red carpet, junket, in-studio interview, set visit, *In Bed With* . . . were all arranged by fucking awesome women. They risked their reputations to get my foul mouth and crazy questions into the rooms with their A-list stars. They were the ones that validated us and then convinced their colleagues, their bosses, their counterparts, and the all-important personal publicists—again, mostly female—to accept us. In every backfire, misstep, and shit-storm along the way, it was a woman who took the heat for us. A woman who didn't write us off. A woman who understood that when you're doing something different, there are growing pains. A woman who kept bringing us back. I wasn't used to it, but at every turn, I found such warmth and support from these girls. They always made me feel like they were rooting for me. They became my friends, my fan club, my laugh track at the interviews, and they even helped me get other work. They made me feel so accepted. I can honestly say that I wouldn't be here were it not for a multitude of brave and ballsy ladies!!

I owe these incredible women and the amazing men who have supported me throughout my career an enormous debt of gratitude. They all played such a crucial role in helping me prove that the *language* barrier is actually a connecting bridge because, like I've been telling you, everybody curses, I swear! There are so many amazing and wonderful people who helped propel me on this journey, and continue to, to this day, that I swear I could fill an entire book with their names. To all of you, I just want to say THANK YOU from the bottom of my heart for believing that a girl could curse and for taking a chance on me. I salute you all!!

But as they say, you never forget your first, so here's to all the brave and brilliant women and men who were there at the beginning and who went against their better judgment and allowed me to bring some *color* into their lives. I will never forget.

THANK YOU: Alan Nierob, Alex Klenert, Alexandra Greenberg, Alice Zou, Alison Branch, Allegra Haddigan, Allison Johnston, Ame Van Iden, Annalee Paulo, April Florentino, Ariana Swan, Arlene Ludwig, Arnold Robinson, Ava DuVernay, Barry Dale Johnson, Bianca Asnaran, Brad Cafarelli, Brooke Blumberg, Carman Knight, Carol Cundiff, Carol Sewell, Carrie Gordon, Catherine Culbert, Charlie Pinto, Cheryl McLean, Chris Libby, Chris Regan, Christine Foy, Christopher Belcher, Cindi Berger, Clay Dollarhide, Corey Scholibo, Dana Gordon, Danielle De Palma, Danielle Misher, Danni Pearlberg, David Mortimer, David Waldman, Deette Kearns, Denise Stires, Dennis Higgins, Doug Neil, Ekta Farrar, Elizabeth Much, Ellene Miles, Emily Lu, Emmy Chang, Evan Fong, Fredell Pogodin, Gail Silverman, Gary Mantoosh, Gina Soliz, Guido Gotz, Harlan Gulko, Heather Forziati, Heather Phillips, Heather L. Weiss, Hilary Hartling, Ian Shive, Jackie Tulk, James Lewis, Jamie Blois, Jan Craft, Jay Waterman, Jeffrey Godsick, Jennifer Allen, Jennifer Lopez, Jennifer McGrath, Jennifer Sandler, John Smith, Justin Simien, Kara Silverman, Karen Fried, Karen Oberman, Karen Sundell, Kari Lipson, Karina Vladimirov, Karl Williams, Kate Piliero, Katrina Wan, Kelly Krause, Kim Lerner, Kristine Ashton-Magnuson, Lauren Robinson, Lea Porteneuve, Lee Ginsberg, Leslie Sloane, Libby Henry, Linda Brown, Lisa Danna, Liz Rosenberg, Loraine Valverde, Lori Burns, Marina Bailey, Mark Pogachefsky, Matthew Labov, Max Buschman, Meghan Gamber, Melissa Holloway, Melissa Kates, Melody Korenbrot, Meredith Judkins, Meredith Lipsky, Meredith O'Sullivan Wasson, Michael Agulnek, Michael Lawson, Michele Robertson, Michelle Margolis, Michelle Rasic, Michelle Rydberg, Michelle Slavich, Nanci Ryder, Natalie Bjelajac, Nathan Marcy, Ngoc Nguyen, Nicole Canizales, Nicole Perez-Krueger, Nicolette Aizenberg, Orna Pickens, Pantea Ghaderi, Pat Shin, Paul Bloch, Paulette Osorio, Rachel McCallister, Rebecca Fisher, Rene Ridinger, Robin Davids, Ryan Stankevich, Samantha Shuman, Sara Hull, Sara Reich, Sara Serlen, Sarah Greenberg, Seanna Hore,

Shelby Kimlick, Sonia Freeman, Stacey Leinson, Stephan̄
ven Wilson, Stuart Gottesman, Tamar Teifeld, Tara Mar
Herring, Teni Karapetian, Tim Menke, Vivian Mayer, an
McCarthy.

Across the board, these women and men were so amazing ᴛᴏ ᴝ
that I had almost put my bullied days in Buffalo behind me. The ladies
at 20th Century Fox had offered up my name to host a new Saturday
morning show on the Fox Television Network, which I ended up doing
for a couple of years. I also started getting hired for a lot of other fun
stuff, too. I was in a great place and embracing all these new wonderful
opportunities provided to me, so of course, I showed up to everything
that came my way with a smile on my face and bells on my toes. I mean,
what could go wrong?

But there are times when all the best intentions in the world can't
save a bad situation. I suppose that it was inevitable that my *muchachas*
would return to the center of controversy. It's just a damn shame because
I had come so far in coming to terms with them. I like to think of my
jahoobies as croutons on a salad. They aren't the focus of the dish, but a
good crouton can turn a good salad into a great one. But even after I
came to terms with them, that doesn't mean everyone had, and every
now and then in Hollywood, they really work against me.

There was a period of time early on in my career when I was hired
by the TV Guide Network to host their red carpet coverage of all the
major awards shows including the Emmys, the Golden Globes, and the
Oscars. I loved that gig. It really helped me cut my teeth doing live TV.
It was my first real experience on a major cable network and it was the
first time I interviewed celebs and cracked jokes live on TV. Clearly
they liked what I did professionally because they kept bringing me
back, over and over again. Then all of a sudden, one day it stopped. I
never questioned it because shit like that happens all of the time in
this town, and I just figured someone younger filled my spot. It wasn't
until years later that I learned what had really happened.

A few years later, I ran into one of the executives who was at the TV
Guide Network at the time I was working for them. He was actually one
of the people responsible for getting me hired at the network. We ended
up hanging out for a while and reminiscing. I could tell something was
gnawing at him, and eventually he got around to the elephant in the
room and said:

"I'm really sorry we stopped working together."

"Yeah. What's the story with that?" I asked.

To which he responded, "There were a few female executives who were offended by your boobs and made it impossible for me to hire you anymore."

My eyes narrowed, my stomach turned, and I felt like I was in high school again. And you know how much I love that feeling.

"Why didn't they just tell me to dress differently?"

"They didn't want to," he replied.

He was apologetic and a little embarrassed. I had a pit in my stomach. I really want to believe that that is not what happened. What's really fucked up is that I remember, way back when I met everyone, thinking to myself how cool it was that it was a group of women execs and I could feel safe in their hands. How naive I was.

These kinds of letdowns are the worst. WTF, LADIES?! We're supposed to look out for each other! Where was the sisterhood of the magical support I had hoped for?! I was bummed, to say the least, but I was lucky and had moved on to other opportunities. What if it were someone else, and she had been stifled in her career with these irresponsible comments? We already get objectified by men; we shouldn't be doing it to each other. Would these women have been happier if I had gotten breast reduction surgery? Luckily, I knew for every person who was "disgusted" by them there were 745 million people who weren't.

It reminds me of the inane chatter about Christina Hendricks and her tits. Not how great her acting is, not what an incredible run she's had on *Mad Men*, but her tits. It's no wonder that some women have a negative reaction to them, because either they don't have them and are jealous of the attention other women get or they themselves don't want to be defined by them. It's crazy. Guys aren't defined by the size of their nuts. You don't see guys getting nut enlargement surgery, but women get boob jobs. Why? Because, unfortunately, they're the first thing a lot of people judge us by.

Too many women in this town get defined by how they look and their body parts, and I hate that that happens. You can't see me without seeing them, but by the end of my interviews they aren't even an issue. My boobs are part of the party. They are natural. They came with the program. Why create an issue?

Of course, this unfortunate incident ended up being a precursor to the most influential women in my career walking into my life. Beginning with my dear, dear friend, Leah Horwitz. A beautiful, smart, talented, passionate, and remarkable executive with amazing instincts, and one of the kindest people I have ever met. She was the first network executive to seek me out after I appeared in the *Los Angeles Times*. I was so flattered that a senior talent exec at VH1 wanted to meet with me. Needless to say, we hit it off. (It's hard not to with Leah; she's pretty awesome!) In an act of such graciousness and generosity, she introduced me and NGTV to every senior exec at VH1 in New York and Los Angeles. Most of whom turned out to be more really cool women. That started a chain reaction that triggered a seven-year successful working relationship with VH1 and led to my own morning talk show there called *Big Morning Buzz Live* with yours truly! There is no question in my mind that without her continued faith and unwavering support, none of it would have happened. In my mind she is, undoubtedly, the living embodiment of all the ideals that all women should strive for in this business. She always gives me hope and puts a smile on my face. I owe her so much and I am lucky to be her friend. Thank you, Leah.

As crazy as some situations were with the complicated women, there was always enough happening with the beautiful ones that in between the head scratching I had reasons to celebrate, too. The front-page article in *The Hollywood Reporter* that referred to my interviews as ". . . eyebrow raising, even by Internet standards," subsequently launching my career into orbit, was written by a lovely woman named Carly Mayberry. A few months later I was signed to WME by my agent to this day, David Sherman, who I think of as more of a close friend than anything else. He's stood by me through all the shit and sunshine. And guess how he found me? Thanks to his amazing wife, Danielle De Palma, an executive at Lionsgate, who brought me to his attention. Secure and powerful women will do wonders for themselves and each other. Right around this time, another influential woman came into my life as I was starting to get more notice in the press.

You know how you can tell the moment you've made it in show business? When you're ripped to shreds on a "Worst Dressed" list. Which, actually, has nothing to do with what you're wearing and everything to do with whether you're worth talking about. Unless, of course, you showed up to a red carpet decked out in nothing but Ed Hardy and Von Dutch gear. Then you're the only thing worth talking about or you're Jon Gosselin. Anyway, I had reached a point in my career when the tables had turned a bit and suddenly the media was interested in me. I wasn't "sex tape" famous; I was a more "I have fans in prison" famous. And one of the pinch-me perks of this level of notoriety was being invited to go on talk shows. So I was on cloud nine when I started getting the offers to appear on several shows. And guess what. They were mostly hosted by women. AWESOME!

Unfortunately, this led to one of my most frustrating professional disappointments, which came at the hands of a female host who was someone I really admired. She was a hilarious ball-buster whom I thought the world of, and being invited on her show was a highlight in my life. I thought we were copacetic. It never felt competitive or awkward. Joking around with her always felt really organic and fluid. I really looked forward to it because she would let me be myself, joke around, and be dirty. I pretty much enjoyed myself as much as a human being could without involving Marshmallow Fluff and kittens.

But after being invited back over a dozen times, suddenly, the next time I was booked, the whole vibe changed. Where I once was part of the family, I now felt like a stranger. The warm and fuzzy was gone and had been replaced by an awkward discomfort. It was similar to the awkward discomfort Dr. Charlie Shedd's book *The Best Dad Is a Good Lover* triggers. Proof positive that focus-grouping the title of a book prior to publication is always a good idea. But, as they say, hindsight is twenty-twenty. Yes, I was a bit sad and confused, but the taping went well and so I thought it could have been a misunderstanding. When it was over, the host and I said our good-byes and everything seemed fine. I left thinking we were good. I was never invited back on the show again.

It was sad, and having no clue what had happened wasn't helping. Luckily, I was busy at the time, and moved on to something else. Once again, another couple of years would pass before someone in the know would tell me what happened, and it wasn't what I'd expected at all. Apparently, the network was seriously looking at me to host a show there and reportedly, she was not having any of it. So it seems she used her significant power at that network to shut me down.

Here was a chance for a fellow female entertainer to simply reach out her hand and help another female entertainer up the ladder, but instead she kicked the ladder over, threw a hot bucket of shit over the ledge, and walked away. Clearly, she forgot rule #4 of the Sisterhood of the Ladies' Room:

1. Always offer a heads-up if there is splatter all over the seat.
2. Pretend not to hear pee farts.
3. Never let another woman walk out with a wardrobe malfunction. Even if she's a stranger.
4. **Always help another woman move up on the show business ladder.**

I sorta get why she did it. I mean, if your life is one big fight, and you don't know how to stop, you're gonna hurt a lot of innocent people. But what kind of life is that?

Again, just as I was starting to sink into this nonsense, it was two other women who showed up to present me with another much bigger opportunity. Thanks to Leah, I'd been steadily working with VH1 for a few years, and the same female execs who I'd come to know really well were looking to launch a morning talk show in New York City. After some phone calls and meetings, I was offered the job, which started one of my life's greatest adventures. I would move to New York City for the next three years to host my own show, *Big Morning Buzz Live with Carrie Keagan* from Times Square. Unreal.

Most importantly, landing *Buzz* seemed like the ultimate validation. I'd finally figured out who I was and what I was good at, and I felt rewarded. VH1, and the all-female executive team who oversaw the show, obviously believed I was the kind of woman America would enjoy waking up to every morning. When we began, we were shooting it in VH1's lobby on the twentieth floor, but by the end were in the TRL studio overlooking Times Square. The journey would have more ups and downs than any roller coaster and be filled with complications, craziness, and utter bliss.

It was a wondrous experience from the get-go. A journey of key moments in time shifting into one another. Getting the offer, I caught my butterflies and took flight. Landing in New York a week before the premiere, I remember feeling I belonged. Entering the Viacom building for the first time, I felt I had greater purpose. Meeting the crew, I felt connected. During rehearsals, I started to realize my world was about to get bigger. New Year's Eve in the Big Apple, surrounded by all that energy, felt like home. Walking through Times Square in the darkness before dawn with only the gentle snowfall as company was magic. Broadcasting live for two weeks was like swimming in the clouds for an hour every morning. Seeing myself on the Jumbotron in Times Square was an out-of-body experience. Flying back to Los Angeles, I was engulfed by a sense of longing for a future yet to come. Upon entering my apartment, I was filled with enormous gratitude. I would go on to experience a different variation of this for each of the nine seasons we shot the show. But the experience taught me so much more.

As if that wasn't enough, in addition to this crazy personal journey I was on, there was something unexpected waiting for me that put my entire career into perspective and put the show on the map. It took everyone at VH1 by surprise. No one saw it coming. Every new talk show lives or dies based on its ability to book big-name guests, and when you're new, it's tough as hell because publicists are always on the fence when it comes to booking their big clients on a show that might be canceled tomorrow. They play wait-and-see because nine out of ten shows disappear before anyone even notices they were on the air. Now, I had been building relationships with celebs and their handlers for years, but you really don't know if these relationships are in your head or real until something like this happens and it's put to the test. This was the moment of truth, and it blew my fucking mind *and* the colons of many executives on the show!!

It was amazing!!! The support that I got for my show from studio reps, publicists, and the celebrities themselves was off the fucking hook. Here I was hosting VH1's very first morning show ever from the lobby in front of the elevators, of all places. A network that had become known, in those years, for D-list celeb-reality and *train-wreck* TV shows and had not had a talk show on it for ten years—so there was no real bridge to the talent community outside of music. We were seriously outnumbered and desperately outgunned. Sounds like a fair fight to me!!

So what happened? Well, my dear friend Rick Krim's team (Rick was the head of all things music at VH1, at the time) and my team formed the "Legion of Straight-up Motherfuckers" with one mission: Book the shit out of the show! Lucky for me, right under Rick was my constant savior, Leah. Music was handled! Kourosh and I took on the movie and TV talent and reached out to all our friends in the business to come on the show. Typically, it can be a bit of a territorial mess behind the scenes, but here we all knew if the show couldn't book, there would be no show, so everybody did what they had to do. And sure enough, starting from the two-week trial run and into the subsequent first season, we launched a motherfucker of a show that we were all proud of—a pattern that continued on the show all the way through all nine seasons.

And you know what? When we asked our friends in the biz, they fucking came! So many big names came on the show, even during the two-week trial run, that the network wasn't even promoting because they were so afraid it was going to fail. But our friends just kept rolling in their clients, and people's heads at the network were spinning in disbelief. Everything behind the scenes was a learning curve, which was perfectly normal for a new show. So everyone was in the fight. But it wasn't all "Go get 'em, tiger!" On the opposite side of the spectrum, I sensed that the show's day-to-day in-house PR team were straight-up nonbelievers and were not prepared for success, nor were they courting it. I think they were planning on taking it easy during what they assumed would be a quick death. Instead, they found themselves unable to keep up with the show's momentum and spun out as the show pushed forward.

Concerned that they were helplessly outclassed by the daunting task of working a talk show, I brought on my own PR team, led by my ingenious publicist Lauren Auslander, to make sure we were firing on all cylinders. I don't know what I would do without her. The show meant everything to me, but for the in-house PR team, it was one of thirty shows. I never cared for those odds. Boy, were they surprised that despite their best efforts to keep a lid on the show, my amazing PR team blew it wide open. Getting this beautiful unicorn of a woman on my team was the best thing I ever did! There were more than a hundred people working on the show, just giving it everything they had. And don't kid yourself; it's a fucking grind when you're producing five shows a week at the level they were. I am so proud of the creative heroics of our entire crew. I would gladly be a *bottom bitch* for any one of those brilliant and fearless motherfuckers. The lesson here is that you get, maybe, a couple of chances in your life to do something great, so don't let lazy uninspired people and their rubbish drag you down. First, say please, and if they continue to wear their asses as a hat, then steamroll the fuck out of them and work with people that inspire you.

The great bookings created so much positive momentum and

energy behind the scenes—great TV for the viewers and tons of media buzz all around. It established the show as a place to be seen. It was a huge part of the reason why we stayed on as long as we did. When the likes of Aaron Sorkin, Steve Carell, Emma Stone, Nicolas Cage, Seth Rogen, Madonna, Jennifer Lawrence, Sylvester Stallone, Nicole Kidman, Kris Jenner, Judd Apatow, Jonah Hill, and Cameron Diaz appear on a show, that show is a keeper. But what made this so special for me was that pretty much all of our friends showed up, which for me was proof that what I had been doing all these years with NGTV had worked. And, if you payed close enough attention, you could feel the F-U being put back into fun! I had connected with and impacted these celebrities and their teams in such a positive way that they were reciprocating by following me wherever I went. Kourosh and I played a significant role in booking the show during the entire nine seasons. Thanks to our industry friends, my little show wasn't so little anymore.

One of the first of my longtime friends to come on the show was Adam Sandler—the mufuckin' SAND MAN, himself!! It was amazing, plus you couldn't ask for a sweeter guy. Let me just set the scene for you. Remember, we're literally set up in the lobby on the twentieth floor of the Viacom building, right in front of the elevators. So I'm sitting with my back to the elevators, and every couple of minutes the elevators open and people walk out behind us as we're broadcasting live. Then, all of a sudden, as I'm mid-hosting, I hear someone yell "KEEEEEE-AEEEEEEEGAAAAAAAAAAAN!!" There are only two people who greet me that way: the showbiz love of my life, Emma Stone, and the great Zohan, Adam Sandler (and Emma's voice is way lower). I looked back and smiled at him, knowing just how many *broners* were standing at attention behind me. That's a *bro* with a *boner*, for the uninitiated.

Come to think of it, there were more than a few times the guys on my show presented a cornucopia of a *chubbious maximi*. In fact, my recollection of all the A-list guests is pretty much a mental scrapbook of *crew boners*. There was the *jock boner* or the *joner*, when Eli Manning was there. Which was a purely physical arousal and not to be confused with the *intellectual boner* or the *cerebroner* present each time Aaron Sorkin came on. I have to say, there are very few people that have the astonishing *bone appeal* that Aaron has across the gender divide. When he enters a room, men experience *rapid velocity* in the nether region and women suddenly spring *girthy hogs*. It's a gift.

I'll never forget the time I booked Robert F. Kennedy, Jr., on the show. I remember, after the obligatory "how the fuck did you get a Kennedy to come on the show?" that it created quite the commotion in everyone's pants. First of all, there was a solid contingency of *political boners* aka *Chappaquidoners*. Then, there was a surprising array of *confused boners*, aka *coners*, when all the executives at VH1 were freaked out one morning because the president and CEO of Viacom, Philippe Dauman, was coming down to visit the set. Apparently, that was a first. Shocking that the head of this multimedia conglomerate had never really expressed an interest in visiting the set of *Tool Academy*. I was quite proud that something our little show did, early on, brought us to his attention. In those days, every little bit of interest in our show helped. Plus, he and I became good friends. I guess my *executive boner*, or *xoner*, must have been showing.

Then there was the invasion of the *spiritual boner*, aka the *Choproner*, inspired by Deepak Chopra's appearance. I couldn't believe that nine years of *dick humor* had finally brought me together with the father of *"Oprah spirituality,"* available wherever *Oprah* people and products are sold. Last but not least, one of my all-time favorites came courtesy of my friend and all around *Boss Bitch*, Kris Jenner's appearance. When she walked in, interest just peaked, and there was not a loose pant in the house. Nothing really comes close to the dense and thick-headed *Kardashian boner* primarily known as the *Kanye*, which was in full effect. When she was there, there were a lot of tiny, chunky *Kanyes* ready to *spit* without provocation. Now that I look back, it occurs to me that, with the sheer number of awesome guests we had, our studio was pretty much a *boner buffet* and *jizzatorium*. It would get messy.

Anyway, back to Adam Sandler—he and I have known each other for over twelve years, which is a crazy long time when I think about it. We hit it off instantly the first time we met on a beach in Hawaii for a junket on a perfect sunny day while we were both a bit tipsy from all the *hydrating* we'd been doing. I asked him to "Give me fifty fucking reasons why people should go to this fucking movie?" and he obliged with "Yeah, you fuckin' got it, baby!" followed by an *F-bomb bonanza*. Our friendship was born. He always makes the time to appear on my shows and goes out of his way to make me feel special while he's there. He's always generous with the compliments, especially when he's paired with a costar that I may not know well. As he christens the filth about to be unleashed, he's always on the lookout to see how quickly I can organically work a *dick joke* into the forefront of an interview. Here he was with Jennifer Aniston at the junket for *Just Go With It*; he was clueing her in on my whole uncensored thing, but little did he know the game had already begun:

> **Me:** How many times did you get bleeped today? *(I asked innocently as we were getting settled in.)*
>
> **Adam:** Oh, I don't know . . .
>
> **Jennifer:** *(Wanting to help.)* How many . . . I'm sure you're allowed to say penis as much as you want.
>
> **Adam:** Penis is fine.
>
> **Me:** You can say penis on NBC, I think . . . even . . .
>
> **Adam:** Yeah.
>
> **Jennifer:** I think penis is alright.
>
> **Me:** *(I found my opening.)* It's cock. You can't use cock on any other network but this one!
>
> **Adam:** *(Looking at Jennifer with an all-knowing smile on his face, he perks up.)* Ya hear Keagan? She slipped out cock! *(Sounding quite proud.)*
>
> **Me:** *(Everybody laughs.)* There it is!

Observe, the power of the "Sandman." At this point, he's pretty much watched me grow up in this business, which is kind of cool and a little bizarre. I mean, I've been a fan of his since *Click,* and now our relationship is, like, super close! Well, I suppose it's more *super* than close.

Before I forget, I should give a shout-out to Adam's producing partner, Allen Covert. Covert and I met on the set of *Grandma's Boy*. Let me just say that "to know this movie is to love this movie." Aside from laughing your ass off and committing your entire life to a smokin' hot and super-high-maintenance new girlfriend called *Maryjane,* you'll walk away from this film with two lasting impressions you'll take to your grave. First, Jonah Hill bursting onto the scene in a supporting role that almost stole the film, in which he sucks a stripper's naked lactating tittie and delivers the line: "Baby love milky?" A role he was born to play. Second, Covert standing over a toilet, furiously *boxing his Jesuit* while molesting a Lara Croft doll only to be interrupted by his friend's hot mom, whom he accidentally covers with endless *ropes* of his *creamy custard* while screaming, "I can't stop cumming! I can't stop cumming!" Watch the film and thank me later! So, of course, the second we arrived on set, I remember Covert being excited to show me where he was going to be shooting what was clearly going to be a career-defining scene. We ducked into a fake bathroom, and we've been buddies ever since. By the way, not everyone got the memo about the fake toilet because that toilet was all *method!* HOT SET, PEOPLE!!

Anyway, the best part of when I see Adam now is that aside from the *sack punching* during the interview and me trying to sneak in as many *dick jokes* as I can while he's promoting his family movie, we also get to reminisce about old times. Like when I was still a "press person" to him and I, unwittingly, showed up to his private family dinner at the Chateau Marmont with my buddy Rob Schneider, who didn't exactly fill me in on where we were going. That could have been all kinds of awkward, but Adam was nothing but accommodating. He is, hands down, one of the kindest and most generous people I've ever met in this business. I have no idea why he took an interest in me and continues to do so. I can only guess that I must have been his kind of *crazy.*

Being on a television show is an extrasensory event that sends more shock waves of experience through your body and mind than we're built for. Without question, it's extraordinary, but it is also schizophrenic. I came to realize that there are three distinct realities that comprise a life in front of the camera. The first is the fun one, the blemish-free version that the audience sees; the second is the surreal one comprised of hyper-condensed fond reflections that only the talent sees; and last, there's the real one, which is what actually happens day-to-day. Surviving the first one means you put on a good show and found a connection with the audience. Surviving the second one means you were able to feel all the wonder and amazement of the journey without succumbing to the intense pressure. Surviving the third one means you have strength of character and know how to take the hits and keep moving forward.

The distinct honor of becoming one of only a small number of women to ever host her own talk show was a gift that went far beyond the obvious. The community experience of working with a cast and crew with boundless creativity and courage was the most rewarding of all. The challenge of evolving to meet the demands and expectations of a giant TV network that was pushing me to elevate my game was the most satisfying. But by far the most mind-blowing earth-shaking life-altering experience was witnessing firsthand what happens when a group of powerful female executives converge to create and execute an incredibly complicated and creatively challenging project of enormous magnitude. Only that experience could be eclipsed by the extraordinary fact that this dream was brought to life for me by a group of grounded, smart, secure, and decent women.

So much good has happened in my life that I try not to dwell on the bullshit. The memories of those stomach-churning experiences where either I or someone I knew had suffered at the hands of women have always left me struggling to understand why it happens. It's a lot like when women say, "I'm fine," when we're anything but. It's the global disaster of relationship-speak. It's been classified by the government as an E.L.E. *(Extinction Level Event).* I think the roots of it stem from a place of fear and insecurity that has been bred into us by a male-oriented culture that has reinforced this notion that we're not good enough. Thus, having been severely marginalized and made to feel powerless for so long, we've decided to take out all that pain and anger on each other because we can't stand to see any of us rise. If we don't start empowering one another and embracing each other's ambitions and dreams, we may be dooming this generation and those to come to live out their lives in a vicious cycle of criticism, denigration, attack, and sabotage. Pawns in another man's game.

I think if we're going to break the cycle, it's really important to talk about it. Ask uncomfortable questions and take the time to discover all the roads that led us to this point. We women are the inheritors of a powerful legacy. One that was hard earned by our foremothers. And they did not eat shit for hundreds, if not thousands, of years so that we could now throw it at each other like a bunch of monkeys. We women need to remember who we are, where we've come from, and what we're truly capable of.

So I ask: Is it possible that after spending most of our lives kicking, clawing, scratching, biting, and punching our way through the "battle royale" we call a career path, for some of us women, fighting is all we know? Is it possible that women are so used to being on the defensive and blindly beating down the endless attacks on our dignity that some of us just don't know how to stop anymore? Has the perpetual rage torn into the very fabric of unity and support that has been the backbone of our movement? Can we, as women, save the sisterhood that we've been fighting for from being decimated from within? I certainly hope so. I think the answer lies in remembering where it is we came from, what it is we're fighting for, and who it is we're fighting against. In my mind, that's the only way to remove these calluses that seem to have formed over some of our hearts. And it all starts by looking within.

Women, much like men, are creatures of habit, and that predictability in our behavior is undeniably our own worst enemy. I think there is an unheeded flaw in our very nature that is constantly stifling our ability to move past some of our baser instincts. If *The Hitchhiker's Guide to the Galaxy* taught us anything, it's the fact that the only way we're ever going to solve any problem is by "really knowing where [our] towel is." So, basically, we need to face the truth. And strangely enough, we're not going to have to go that far to find it because the truth is a mirror we take with us everywhere but rarely look into. So, ladies, it's time to take out your compacts, wipe off the inexplicable *white powder* residue, and start *reflecting* instead of *deflecting*.

I'm not saying there are any easy answers, but there is plenty of food for thought, some of which reveals itself in the most unexpected places. I recently stumbled across a profound bit of wisdom from a time when wisdom on women's issues was in short supply. Here was an intriguing commentary, published fifteen years before women were given the right to vote, that seemed to dissect this matter with inexplicable clarity. In his intriguingly forward-thinking essay entitled "The Gentleman's Code," first printed in *Sunset* magazine in May 1905, poet, author, and humorist Frank Gelett Burgess observed,

> Most women have all other women as adversaries; most men have all other men as their allies. Women know little of this esprit de corps, this mutual shielding of sex by sex, for the reason that they are not, ordinarily so accustomed to law.

It hit me like Truman's boat hit the horizon of his reality in the movie *The Truman Show*! I realized that from as far back as anyone can remember, women have lived in societies whose very social infrastructure has been designed by men. And much like a zoo, we have been kept on display and told how to behave while they have been our keepers who set the rules. We are maintained in environments created to reflect their idea of the world and how we should live in it. By keeping us separated from one another, with locked ideological doors, they've nurtured an organic insecurity, distrust, and paranoia that is now firmly rooted in our subconscious. And as a precaution against escape and gathering, the zoo is designed as a labyrinth to confuse us and give them a safety net. Now, during the last century, we seem to have found a way to gradually convince our keepers to unlock the doors and let some of us roam freely. But centuries of subconscious conditioning don't just disappear overnight, especially if you're encouraged to believe that all the other animals are out to get you.

Could Burgess's simple and straightforward analysis actually be the root cause of the inconsistency that exists in relationships women have with one another? Is this an illuminating perspective that should have been dead and buried in the past but seems to have transcended time? Is the sad irony of this uncomfortable truth the fact that its words may be no less true today than when they were first written, over 110 years ago? Should it bother us that we're still trapped in this maze that men created a very long time ago? Is this double standard the tie that binds us and, possibly, the insight that can get us the fuck out? Can we use this bit of harsh reality to move forward? I hope we can, and I think we should.

The answer has always been right in front of us and we haven't been paying attention. We need to wake the fuck up and start paying fucking attention. Women need to be cool to each other. We just don't realize how much power we have, especially if we band together. Our first instinct always seems to be to beat the crap out of each other, animal kingdom–style. That's why guys are winning right now—because girls get distracted by each other's BS. It's not in our nature to get along for "some reason." But we can change that. If we turn that around, we can get so much shit done.

We women have always been independent spirits. It's in our blood. It's in our heritage. It's in the very essence of who we are. We've often had to fight our battles alone and in secret. We have had to bear the guilt and shame of crimes committed against us in isolation. To survive, we have had to rely only on ourselves. We have suffered in silence for so long that we're quick to distrust and will attack each other even when unprovoked. Through time and repetition, we've cemented this selfish, defensive, and paranoid legacy into our psyche. Perhaps it's time we eliminated the adversarial culture that divides us and focus on the common ground that unites us. We have always been outnumbered, but we have never been outgunned. We have got to get out of the business of one step forward, two steps back, and get into the business of never going back.

tend to be more graceful and clever with their filthy proclivities and don't actively seek the spotlight the way men do. Or, maybe they do—but with greater panache.

Unfortunately, the primary reason for that has less to do with women being more cultured and more to do with the fact that we live in a society where a woman's reputation is not afforded the same flexibility and resiliency as a man's. Men tend to get a pass for their indiscretions, while women must bear the shame as some sort of Scarlet Letter. Resulting in women adopting an endless defensive posture that has spread its roots far and wide. But the truth remains, to paraphrase the Irving Berlin timeless classic, (feel free to sing it with me), "Anything men can do, we can do better; we can do anything *dirtier* than you."

In my mind, one of the most offensive words used to control women is "reputation." For centuries, it's been a noose that men have placed around our necks when we become teenagers. We then spend the rest of our lives trying to avoid hanging ourselves with it. Very rarely is it a reflection of who we *really* are, but more of a subjective opinion about us that comes with a hidden agenda. And because neither a good reputation nor a bad one requires any sort of actual evidence to support, it's one hell of a psychological weapon. In show business terms, as a woman, whether you're on-camera talent, a producer, or an executive, the way your reputation is held hostage is a lot like an adoption gone wrong. You hand your baby off to an unknown group of industry insiders to raise as their own. But every time they don't like the way you're behaving, they shrewdly imply that your kid could get hurt. Leaving you in a constant state of paranoia and fear. Like winning a scholarship to study sense-memory acting with Bill Cosby.

Take it from someone who knows firsthand. A woman in the business of being edgy and pushing boundaries is, basically, a Vegas casino's wet dream: A gambler who goes "all-in" in a never-ending game of Let It Ride. (Not *infamous booyah* "all-in," just regular "all-in.") There are only two ways we walk away from the table: *quit or die!* The dirty work of trying to get us to quit could fall anywhere between a simple passing comment at the community urinal and an elaborate humiliating story leaked to the tabloids from an "anonymous source." Oh, and in case you were wondering, in show business, an "anonymous source" is slang for "Fuck you, you fuckin' fuck!"

Of course, then there's the *lip-boxing* that takes place behind your

20

THE EMANCIPATION DICKLAMATION

It's all about a girl who lost her reputation
but never missed it.
—*Mae West*

One night, recently, I found myself engrossed in yet another article about
the most insane things found in the butts of college fraternity brothers.
I'm sure you've been there. And after having spent hours analyzing all
the data, I ended up reaching a depressing conclusion: Why do women
not get the same kind of press for their equally reckless behavior as men?
And then, just like the eighteen-inch reproduction of the submarine from
the film *The Hunt for Red October* discovered in one of their rectums, a
powerful epiphany surfaced in my mind. The double standard that exists
in the way men and women are judged is no longer limited to the privacy
of the boardroom and the bedroom; it has now reared its ugly head in
the pop culture garbage dumps of society, as well.

Then, like the fully intact lightbulb removed from another frat bro's
taut butthole, I lit up with the realization that our culture celebrates the
bizarre rituals of male bonding and virtually shuns the dark depravity
of sisterly communions. As if to perpetuate the antiquated notion that
depravity is the birthright of men, and virtue is the sole obligation of
women. Well, if this book hasn't already turned that fucked-up notion on
its head, I'm here to reaffirm that degeneracy is not mutually exclusive—
it belongs to all of us. The only difference is that, historically, women

back or on social media. Short bursts of character assassination delivered with surgical precision, like papercuts to your genitals delivered with a spritz of fresh lime juice. Do any of these comments sound familiar? "That comedienne is too filthy; she has no real talent," or "This actress wants equal pay; she's an ungrateful diva bitch," or "That presenter dresses too sexy; she's a mindless slut," and my personal favorite, "That girl who swears in her interviews is inappropriate and immoral." It always starts small then grows into an endless barrage of unfounded bullshit. Not unlike going to a Westboro Baptist Church anti-gay protest where shoving your head up your own ass is not just a choice; it's your calling. Except here, people eat it up because tearing other people down seems to be the national pastime. It can and often will tip the balance for or against you in conversations you'll never know about, in rooms you'll never be in. So it's only natural to care about your reputation and want to protect it. After all, our parents and teachers told us so. But what they didn't tell us is that it's an anchor that keeps you in your place. To move forward, you have to let that motherfucker go.

One thing I always try to do when I interview women is empower them. Some women don't need it. Some sit down and are so confident in who they are and what they want to do, it's perfection. While other women, quite clearly, are still kind of caught up in how they think they're supposed to act or what other people might think. It's painful to see that. But I get so much personal satisfaction from the experience of witnessing someone blossom in front of me. It's become kind of a mission for me to do everything I can to help that happen. If I can be the one to help nudge someone out of that protective shell that's been placed around them, I feel compelled to do it. Why waste precious time when those opportunities are so important and so rare? The few times I've gone against my gut and hesitated still haunt me. But none more than when I sat down with a member of the Jackson family quite a few years back.

For me, regret is a Jackson named Janet. They're like American royalty. We don't have a royal family; we have the Jacksons! She's a tough interview to get, and this wasn't for NGTV; it was an exclusive fan event for a major brand that was backing her tour. Janet Jackson doesn't do many one-on-ones, so I wanted to make sure that I got it just right. I knew what I wanted to talk to her about, but for some reason, my brain was telling me to treat her differently than I had treated everyone else I had interviewed. It could've had something to do with the people in my ear the whole week leading up to the interview, saying things like, "Ms. Jackson doesn't like it when you do this . . ." and "Ms. Jackson won't talk about that . . ." Everyone around me was so fucking freaked out that it started to freak me the fuck out! (It also occurred to me that, man, a lot of these people are nasty.)

You know what it was like? Shots. Not *doing* shots but *getting* your shots, like when you were a kid. I remember the buildup to my doctor's appointment freaked me out so badly that I would do anything to get out of it. Like putting the end of a thermometer on a light bulb so it would heat up and I could pretend that I had a fever (side note, that worked really well until the day I left it on the lightbulb a little too long and ended up being rushed to the ER, with a temperature of 105, by my panicked mother. That was not a good look). Or the time I pretended I was so scared that I faked passing out whenever someone said the word "shot." And then there was my personal favorite, the "bulletproof" scheme where I told my mom I couldn't go to the doctor because I was "waiting on a really important phone call" in my best business voice. Yeah . . . the whole being seven years old at the time made that one especially tough to pull off.

I was getting so mindfucked by the overly intense production that I ended going against everything that I *knew* would work from experience. I've said it a million times: Most famous people respond the best when you don't talk to them like they're famous people. They get their asses licked on the daily, so when someone talks to them like a normal person, the hypnotic monotony of *anus-tickling* gets disrupted and springs them into action. Unfortunately, I decided to check my instincts at the door when I got to the shoot and got caught up in "Jacksonmania." The producers wrote out all of the questions for me, all of which were written from a fearful and defensive place. They not only didn't want to risk offending Janet or anyone in the world, they also didn't want to risk creating something people might actually want to watch. A brilliant strategy from all perspectives. Honestly, why the fuck even bother?

Now, I'm not saying Janet and I needed to *drop trou'* and start freestyling dick jokes on our way to the local *cunt-fest* to get in touch with our lady parts. But did it have to be the most boring sterile interview of all time? This was Janet *"Motherfucking"* Jackson! One of the hottest most talented fascinating gender-barrier-breaking women on the planet! People should have been able to emotionally masturbate to this interview, but instead, it came across like listening to your friend talk to you about her gluten allergy . . . until the last question.

During what ended up being the last question, it finally dawned on me that I was blowing one of the greatest opportunities of my life because I'd decided to conform to what other people thought I should do. So I thought-whispered *"Fuck it!"* and went off script and started to talk to her like we were just a couple of girls laughing and shooting the shit. Instantly, her energy changed, she sparked, and a casual side of her I don't think anyone but those close to her see suddenly emerged. It was subtle, but wow did she become a different person. And just when I had finally broken through, they wrapped us, and it ended. Oh, what could've been! I can only blame myself. I was an experienced soldier on the front line of *oral* battle. I should've let my instincts guide me. Instead, I allowed other people's fears to control me. I had failed her, and I had failed myself. *"Never again,"* I swore to myself. Never again would I stop being me and doing what I do.

My celebrity interviews are supposed to be a retreat from the status quo. A sanctuary to escape the arbitrary moral boundaries of polite society. A place to let your *inner idiot* get naked and run free without judgement. But, for women, it needed to be much more than that. It needed to be a place where they could stop being what our male-driven society was telling them they should be and start being who they really are. To accomplish this, an act of law was required, and since one was not available, I took it upon myself to create the *Emancipation Dicklamation*. A proclamation conceived to protect the rights of female celebrities wanting to break free from all the *dicks* in the world who try to manipulate them. The *dicks* who try to tell them who to be, how to act, and what to say. A sanctuary where they are given the power and support to NOT conform to what is expected of them. A retreat where they are encouraged to breach those gates and embrace the new "hot shit" in the streets called "freedom of expression!" Won't you join us?!

I'm here to tell you that our numbers are strong and that more and more women are bending rules and breaking balls than ever before! I have been freeing the hearts, minds, and mouths of women for well over a decade. Tweet me to declare your support and join our movement by adding the hashtag *#EmancipationDicklamation*. Ignore what you may have heard, forget what you think you know, and let's celebrate the girls who go all the way!

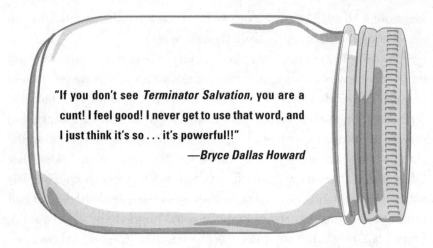

"If you don't see *Terminator Salvation*, you are a cunt! I feel good! I never get to use that word, and I just think it's so . . . it's powerful!!"
—*Bryce Dallas Howard*

Some of my all-time favorite girls to interview are Cameron Diaz, Emma Stone, Kerry Washington, Rachel McAdams, Taraji P. Henson, Carla Gugino, Charlize Theron, and Drew Barrymore, and the list goes on and on and on and on and on . . . Why, you ask? Because they are down to play—open, vibrant, and fearless. They are bold, brilliant, and beautiful women who feel secure in who they are. They've realized that being themselves is the power move.

And if anyone loves *girl play* . . . it's me.

Truth be told, I'm very proud to say I've had mostly positive experiences with female stars and vice versa. Kate Hudson, who I've had a ton of fun with across many interviews, did me a genuine kindness. I was there to interview her and Matthew McConaughey for a movie, and unbeknownst to me, the camera caught her whispering to Matthew, "Oh, you're going to love her," as I was walking into the room. Hearts came out of my eyes for like a week after I saw the footage.

When I sat down with the lovely Carla Gugino to interview her for the movie *San Andreas*, she said she was so excited to see me because she had something she was just dying to tell me. And she literally blew my mind! One of our mutually favorite words is "fuck." She started to explain to her castmate Alexandra Daddario, who was also in the room, right as I sat down. "And so when I had the one [fuck] in the movie," she said, turning to me and smiling, "I thought of you. I actually honestly did." I couldn't believe it. I had made a lasting impression. I was so touched and filled with a sense of joy that I could only find the words "I love you." It was beyond flattering to learn, firsthand, how my potty mouth had infiltrated the hearts and minds of Hollywood's elite even when they were away from me on set. "Shit the fuck yeah!"

When I get together with my girl Emma Stone, all bets are off; anything can happen and usually does. There's a connection she and I have had from the day we first met at the *Superbad* junket, and it's been all downhill since . . . in the best way! She's a kindred spirit, always ready to throw down and go to town. I've done everything from putting honey on her lips to examining Spider-Man's ass to playing the Asshole Game. But at the *Gangster Squad* junket, we decided to forgo our traditional shenanigans in favor of taping Hollywood's first-ever Kegel exercises for the A-list. Once she knew I was getting men to do it, her curiosity got the better of her:

Emma: How do men do Kegels? (*Looking at me intensely.*)

    Me: The same way I'm doing them right now. (*I start focusing real hard, while I tighten and loosen my muscles. All the while maintaining eye contact.*) There it is.

      (*Emma then takes my cue and starts focusing while tightening and loosening, nodding her head with approval. This continues for a while, back and forth in an almost Zen fashion.*)

      Feels good, right?

      (*Emma starts laughing loudly.*)

      Instantly this junket got better!

Emma: You always take it to another level.

    Me: Why not?

Emma: You always do.

    Me: That's what today has brought me. So, you know, thank you.

Emma: A lot! You've really milked today.

Emma Stone, my eternal girl crush!

For *Bad Teacher*, Cameron Diaz and I talked about so many dirty things, but the highlight was what it was like to dry-hump her then-boyfriend and costar, Justin Timberlake, or should I say "Timbersnake."

      Me: You know Justin brought sexy back in 2006. And I feel like now he's bringing dry-humping back.

Cameron: We strived to make the least sexiest sex scene ever. And we succeeded, I believe.

Me: Prince says there are twenty-three positions in a one-night stand. I'm wondering if it's the same for dry-humping.

Cameron: Let's just face it: This is a PSA for safe sex. Okay? If you keep your jeans on, seriously, you can't get pregnant!

Me: Nobody gets hurt, well, except for the chafing.

Cameron: I was going to say there's a bit of chafing involved if I remember correctly back in the day when I was in seventh grade.

Me: What were we doing back then? And why did we do that?

Cameron: I know why we were doing it! It's very clear why it was happening!

Me: I was wondering, does it creep you out at all to know that the whole world has now seen you having fake sex?

Cameron: Justin and I will clearly do anything for a laugh. There's no question about it, obviously!

Me: And that is to our benefit. Then, of course, the other benefit to dry-humping, just to close it out, cleanup is a snap.

Cameron: Ain't my problem, buddy! You deal with it!

Forget the stereotype that girls can't be as dirty as the guys. The actresses I've met over the years—and this started way before *Bridesmaids* and *Broad City*—are not delicate little flowers. They may be super-feminine, but they've taken Hollywood by the balls. They made it to the top, so they have confidence oozing out of their pores, can hold their own, and can do whatever the fuck they want. And what they want is to have fun and be themselves.

And it's not just limited to a handful of actresses who are trying to cultivate an edgier image. This isn't about the pretend version of the actresses you see in movies; this is about who they actually are in real life. They're just like you and me. They feel the same heights of elation and depths of pain. What's better than language to do it with? Filthy, frosty, tasty, and delicious curse words. And by the way, it's a proven scientific fact that cursing diminishes pain. So the next time you accidentally scald your *hoo-ha* with that steam-powered vibrator your aunt gave you, feel free to bust out "Motherfucking-cum-guzzling-cock-nibbling-sheep-shagging-sphincter-sweat!!!"

Speaking of stupid shit, here's a lesson in don't-believe-the-hype. I'd been warned by other women that certain superstars—like Julia

Roberts, Jennifer Lopez, Scarlett Johansson, and Halle Berry—have a reputation for being "difficult" with other women. But in my experience, they've been wonderful. In fact, J. Lo and Halle, who don't need anyone's approval to bust a verbal move, have a penchant for the word "motherfucker," so deal with it! Don't listen to a fucking thing anyone says. That's that whole manipulation thing I was talking about earlier. I would suggest ear muffing that kind of chin wag and forming your own opinion.

I interviewed Jennifer Aniston for *He's Just Not That Into You*, right in the thick of the gossip mag bullshit that pitted her against Angelina Jolie and turned her into this pathetic victim. A few weeks later, I watched with awe as she stood onstage as a presenter at the Oscars, with Brangelina sitting under her nose in the front row. The tabloids were praying that "Jen" would lose her shit in front of a billion people, but she was all grace and poise. Balls, I tell ya!

That day, she was teamed with Drew Barrymore, who is the original barnstormer who flashed her *bewbs* for David Letterman on national network television. Drew and I have gone many-a-round in the caged "Fuck-Fight" circuit; we're both *"profanity"* professionals with masters' degrees in *"verbal atrocity."* The two of them were so funny and secure in themselves throughout a pretty dirty interview, as evidenced by their great advice about men giving a shit:

> **Me:** If he says he doesn't give a shit, does that mean he actually doesn't give a shit?
>
> **Drew:** If he says he gives a shit but isn't behaving like he gives a shit then he doesn't give a shit.
>
> **Jennifer:** Yeah, if he says he doesn't give a shit, but then he doesn't behave as though he doesn't give a shit then I don't agree with him.
>
> **Drew:** Or he says, "Oh, I give a shit. I really do."
>
> **Jennifer:** Yeah, yeah.
>
> **Drew:** But then he's acting like he doesn't—guess what. He doesn't!
>
> **Jennifer:** That's it!
>
> **Me:** What if . . .
>
> **Jennifer:** Pay attention to the actions . . .
>
> **Drew:** Not the words.
>
> **Jennifer:** Not the words!

> **Me:** Kevin Connolly said there are times when he says, "I don't give a shit" but he doesn't mean it?
>
> **Jennifer:** But he does give a shit, so that's what I'm saying is the . . . I don't know anything!
>
> **Drew:** Interesting. Kevin . . .
>
> **Jennifer:** Kevin just threw us a curve ball.

Just like with the guys, a rare few girls are not comfortable going blue. Also, like clockwork, some women turn into schoolmarms right after they have babies, in my opinion. I think they probably feel like now that they're mothers, they have a responsibility to be proper upstanding citizens. Courteney Cox was the exception to the baby-birthing rule. She held her five-month-old baby, Coco, on her lap while cussing up a storm, no big deal, and when I interviewed her the next time, she cemented it: "This is my favorite thing that I get to cuss and talk about drinking. I mean why don't we just do the rest of the interviews this way? CNN, fuck YEAH! What? OH! I thought that's the way we did it now."

My girls will always return to the *dirty hive*, and more often than not push the limits of my interviews even further. Secure in their sick sense of humor, here come three more super-cool chicks who are just blowing up right now. No inhibitions, ready to have fun, and totally comfortable diving into the deep end of the pool are Elizabeth Banks, Rashida Jones, and Emily Mortimer. It just took a mere hint from me about the *grundle* that made its theatrical debut and they were right there when I sat down with them at the junket for *Our Idiot Brother*:

> **Me:** Now Steve Coogan introduces something into this movie, and possibly, into the world . . .
>
> **Elizabeth:** His balls. Yes.
>
> **Me:** I don't know if we've seen the back of anyone's balls in a while.
>
> **Rashida:** The taint.
>
> **Emily:** His arsehole, in other words.
>
> **Me:** He did introduce that as well.
>
> **Emily:** Yeah.
>
> **Me:** The full-on. We got everything.

Rashida: Yeah. There was, like, taint and ass crack, maybe, like, a little sphincter even.

Me: We may have gotten a little hole.

Rashida: It was pretty graphic. I was like "AAHHHH!!" when I saw it.

Emily: His hairy balls and his A-hole.

Elizabeth: His ball work in this movie is . . .

Me: Genius.

Elizabeth: Really good.

Emily: Totally fucking awesome.

When it was time to promote the movie, the ladies did not disappoint.

Elizabeth: You fucktards better go see this fucking movie!

Emily: *Our Idiot Brother* does the opposite of chafing my anus. It's the film that least chafes my anus of any film I've ever seen.

Rashida: I really like the word. I like ass bag. I like ass rash. Ass rash is a good word, right?

Me: Maybe you won't get an ass rash if you see *Our Idiot Brother*!

Rashida: No, more like . . . Paul Rudd is an ass rash! In *Our Idiot Brother*. Not in real life, in the movie. Ned is an ass rash. Ass bag.

Me: I like it.

Rashida: Dickhead.

I will never forget the day I sat down across from actress/comedienne Mo'Nique for her movie *Welcome Home, Roscoe Jenkins*. She would go on to win an Academy Award for her powerful performance in the movie *Precious* and host her own talk show on BET, but before that she brought down the motherfuckin' house with me. Making such a stir that her costar Martin Lawrence stormed into the room to see what the fuck was going on. She was paired with Mike Epps, but poor Mike didn't realize that he was about to be sucked up into the one-woman-whirlwind called "Hurricane Mo'Nique." Why this was so special to me was that it perfectly illustrated why No Good TV connects with so many people . . . because we were familiar, or should I say familial, just like your fucked-up dysfunctional family:

Mo'Nique: See what you're doing right now? That is exactly what we went through every day, every second of the day. A ball of laughs, a good time, and it was just family. I feel like you just family! You just came right in. You a cousin . . . through marriage. We gon' have to explain some shit. But through marriage, you came on into the family and we love her. *(Looking at Mike.)*

Me: I've been accepted! *(Hand on my heart. Mike makes a displeased face.)* What? What was that face? You're not accepting me!

Mike: Yes, I am. I'm just . . . whooo. *(Looking at me all leery.)*

Mo'Nique: He wanna see your ATM card.

Me: *(Looking at Mo'Nique.)* He's just pissed 'cause now I'm in the family. It's like blood. *(Looking at Mike.)* Now he can't have any!

Mike: *(Unhappy look.)* No, I can't!

The interview just took off from there and continued to escalate. The cussing was outta control, and the room was on fire. As I looked around I could see there as not a single person who wasn't just dying with Mo'Nique and Mike's tour de force, wall-to-wall "fuck" fest. And just when I thought it couldn't get any more insane, Martin Lawrence blew in while Mo'Nique was motherfuckin' the room like a T-shirt cannon:

Mo'Nique: *Welcome home, Roscoe Jenkins* is the best muthafuckin' film you'll ever see in your muthafuckin' life! *(Mike's arms are crossed, and he's looking menacingly into the camera.)* If you've never gone to a muthafuckin' film, this is the muthafuckin' film to go to!
(Mike loses his shit, laughing, and starts slapping his knee and laughing 'cause he sees Martin Lawrence has just run into the room.)

Mo'Nique: 'Cause we do it the muthafuckin' . . . haaaaaa!
(Martin runs into the interview and jumps in the middle of them. He sits back and puts his arms around them in a tight embrace and they're all fuckin' losing it as the room explodes in chaos, screams, and laughter. Across from them, I'm laughing my ass off, stomping my feet and clapping like a damn fool. It was awesome!)

Mike: *(Screaming while Martin is squeezing them.)* What's up! We got Martin Lawrence in the muh'fucker!

Mo'Nique: *(Screaming.)* It's the muthafucka who did this muthafuckin' thing! Come on, baby!

(Martin kisses her on the head and fucks with Mike.)

Me: *(To Martin:)* You couldn't have picked a better mother-fuckin' time to come in!

(Martin starts to leave.)

Mike: *(Screaming.)* Where you gonna go, Mar?

Martin: *(Screaming from across the room.)* Is she lettin' you cuss as much as you want?

Mo'Nique: *(Screaming back.)* As much as we muthafuckin' want to!! *(Mike is just laughing and clapping.)* I appreciate this mutha-fucka right here! *(Adjusting her hair and looking to the camera.)* You see I'm staring into this muthafuckin' camera! Keep it on me! When you say "muthafucka," there's a way you got to say it to mean dat . . . okay? See *(softly)* mother-fucker . . . that don't mean shit . . . you say MUTHAFUCK DAT!! I meant dat shit, you feel that? You see how I'm turnin' 'round in this chair. Getting my body situated right. Putting my leg up. When you do dat shit, MUTHAFUCK DAT BITCH! Das' gon' make him come back in that mutha-fucka more!

Mike: *(Looking down at her ass in the chair as she's positioned herself on her side.)* And look, there's a little bit'a ass jus' hangin' out over the side.

Me &

Mo'Nique: POW!! *(Everybody is laughing and clapping and almost falling off their chairs.)*

There's no denying it. Girls can hang with the boys in every way imaginable. They can hang, and they're better than any pair of balls THIS girl has ever seen. Hell, we've always been able to. We just haven't always been allowed. We were raised to think that boys are supposed to act a certain way, and girls are supposed to act another way. But that was then and this is now. People didn't think women could be funny. . . . Well . . . Amy Schumer is one of the most bankable comedy assets in this town. They thought a woman couldn't headline a hugely successful primetime network show alone . . . well Kerry Washington is about as hot as they get. There was always a stigma that a woman couldn't be the lead in a movie and have it be a huge success . . . uh, Melissa McCarthy has firmly planted her foot into the ass of that idea with four number one movies: *Identity*

Thief, The Heat, Spy, and *The Boss.* And, of course, there's the enigmatic gem that woman will never be able to host a successful late-night TV show . . . Chelsea Handler was not only better than the men but can also probably drink them all under the table. Do I need to go on?

Of course, the problem with late-night TV is that it's still stuck in the seventies. The rest of television has changed—the rest of the world has changed—and yet, somehow, women are still a question mark when it comes to late-night. Well, this little lady brain is mad as hell and not gonna take it anymore.

Don't get me wrong: I love the seventies. I never experienced it first-hand, but I love almost everything about it. The music was awesome. The clothes were fabulous—from the four-inch-thick belts that were basically a boob job for your pants to the terry cloth leisure suits that were hip to wear even if you weren't in prison. Random sexual encounters were totally copacetic, and the term "big bush" didn't refer to George W.'s dad. The hair didn't stop there, either, because there was shag everywhere. They even made shag toilet seat covers—because nothing absorbs pee like a nice luxurious coat of carpeting.

Okay, so the seventies weren't perfect, but everyone sure had a great time, right? Actually, to truly appreciate the decade, I guess 50 percent of the population would have to first get past the rampant sexism in the media, misogyny in the workplace, and general treatment of women as second-class citizens. Television, in particular, was a man's world. Everything you needed to know was presented to you by men. Middle-aged white men. They were the voices of authority. They were the voices of reason. They represented all that was white—I mean right—in the world.

And yet, things looked a lot different at the end of the seventies than they did at the beginning. This was the decade when Barbara Walters became the first female co-host of the *Today* show; Katharine Graham, of the Washington Post Co., became the first female Fortune 500 CEO.; and Gloria Steinem founded *Ms.* magazine. They were women—hear 'em roar!

And look how much has changed since then! We've had Diane, Katie, Oprah, Ellen, Christiane—the list goes on and on. Somehow, though, none of that change has trickled down to network late-night TV, a place that is clearly in need of a little facial reconstruction. And while it doesn't have to be surgical, it certainly does feel like pulling teeth. Having said that, I have a sneaking suspicion that a powerful storm is coming. I'd say we're in the early stages of a full vaginal penetration in late-night.

The days of networks claiming that there simply aren't any women with the right experience for the job after hanging yet another late-night show on yet-another Y chromosome are long fucking gone. Ignoring the cornucopia of killer female talent "engorging the business" right now and clearly visible to anyone whose eyebrows aren't in desperate need of threading is about as intelligent and well thought out a move as when guys attempt a quick and stealthy *crotch-swipe* and *butthole-check* when they think no one's looking. And, unfortunately, there are still quite a number of television execs in high-ranking positions who continue to ignore the obvious female currency right in front of them, opting for further self-analysis of their *bonch.* Apparently, they remain convinced that the next big thing is hiding out on the *ball-side of ass-berg,* so while no one's looking, they continue to hit the *durf.*

Newsflash, motherfuckers!! We're always looking! Women don't have the luxury of turning away. That's when stupid shit happens. Usually involving you . . . with your hand . . . going where it's not supposed to be. In fact, we're born with a built-in motion sensor that alerts us when a guy in our vicinity is *dry-scrubbing his taint.* And yet, regardless of whether you're at your niece's dance recital, your sister's wedding, or just waiting in line to buy popcorn at the movie theater, you can't help but double check the fine shellac on your *rusty sheriff's star.* And don't give me your hair-brained bullshit about how it's Tourette's or OCD! What it is, is a *fecal injustice* that needs to end. It's so fucking disgusting, and no matter how many times you get caught, and I tell you women are born with *buttfingersniffing* peripheral vision, you can't help yourself. Why can't you be more like us girls and *sniff the whiff* in private?

Today, we're living in a bit of a renaissance for the "dirty" girl (or the *Keaganaissance,* as I like to call it). It's awesome to watch more and more talented and brazen women like Amy Schumer, Jennifer Lawrence, Taraji P. Henson, Sandra Bullock, Aisha Tyler, Tina Fey, Kerry Washington, Amy Poehler, Queen Latifah, Emma Stone, and Wendy Williams, to name a few, cut the umbilical cord of "reputation" and forge forward. But there is no progress without consequences. So we can't forget that while Joan Rivers broke all sorts of barriers, her success placed her reputation in the crosshairs of a high-powered rifle named Johnny Carson. And while

Roseanne Barr tore through all preconceived notions of female stand-ups on her way to becoming an icon, it's hard to ignore the devastating public blows her reputation had to endure. And there are many, many more . . .

It's a dirty business that can be really daunting. There are plenty of women who are marginalized and manipulated by this very male attitude who then, unknowingly, contribute to it by perpetuating the reputation game to protect their territory. It's a wicked cycle that has to stop. I believe that it's every woman's responsibility to cut that cord, if for no other reason than to honor the pioneers that came before us, like the very first female stand-up, Jackie "Moms" Mabley, who pushed the edge, in her own way, at a time when the edge carried a shotgun.

I, in my own small way, have been in the business of not giving a shit what other people think for fifteen years and counting. Believe me, it's very liberating. I couldn't tell you whether it's the courage of ignorance or stupidity that powers my undying conviction. But I can tell you that I'm not trying to be brave. I'm just trying to be me. A truth that is always worth fighting for.

For I am not just the creator of the "Emancipation Dicklamation"; I am a card-carrying member. Never underestimate the power of a woman when she sets her mind to something. NEVER!

EPILOGUE

One night, a few years ago, I was in a bathroom stall at Club Cock, trying really hard to ignore the three guys engaged in a *Devil's pitchfork* in the other stall, when something caught my eye that really bugged me. Right next to me on the wall was written "profanity is the linguistic crutch of the inarticulate motherfucker." I'm pretty sure this phrase has been passed around, in one form or another, more often than Jared Fogle's *birdhouse* (polite for gaping butthole) in federal prison, but you gotta love the motherfuckin' irony. I remember thinking three things. First, *that's some heady shit written in a toilet stall that I doubt gets used as a toilet very often!* Second, *Jesus Christ! Is that an actual glory hole under it?* And third, *where the fuck am I? I'm going to punch Quentin for bringing me here!* And, *fuck my life! I think all three of these guys next door are cumming at the same time and Quentin better not be one of them!!* Not funny! I mean, funny now but not funny then. Anyway, there was one thing about the saying that really bugged me; my hope is that, at this point, if nothing else, I've proven to you that I am not inarticulate!

Language is power. Language is art. It can shape our experiences and the experiences of those around us. Cursing is a grand expression in the time honored tradition of challenging the norm. Possibly the single most important action humanity must never stop taking. Not to mention that it also happens to be the best fucking eighties high school party ever! I mean, was there ever another time where we were more culturally disparate and fashionably ridiculous? And yet we had so much fucking fun. That's right, swearing isn't just this amazing connective tissue that ties all people together; it's also a constant reminder to fight the status quo. Every great accomplishment in history began with challenging that which was forbidden. And it is our responsibility to keep that candle burning and never surrender to the *bag of dicks* the so-called *moral majority* have deemed to be the rules of conduct. Every time those *fuckheads* rear their ugly heads, I get a bad case of *Deja Moo*—you know that feeling you get when you've heard this bullshit before! So now that you know you hold the future of progress in your hands, please curse openly, curse freely, and curse often!! And do me a fuckin' favor: Swear with a some style, a little panache, and a fuck-ton of gusto!

Believe me when I tell you, "Dirty words are sacred; dirty words endure. When your soul has constipation, dirty words are the cure!" I hope our little journey through my wonderland of very bad words further opened your eyes to the wondrous joys of swearing and unshackled your imagination's untold, potty-driven potential. Between our tasty exchanges of "fucking" delicacies, your newfound verbal "fucking" dexterity along with the release of your inner *dirty birds*, I consider it the *dog's bollocks* to have helped you laugh, cry, and kiss your preconceived notions good-bye!!

Your new grasp of profanity will be your life preserver when you least expect it. Remember the time you took your parents out to a fine restaurant and ordered the *duck butter* and *goose cheese* for the table to impress them? How were you supposed to know *duck butter* refers to the thick and creamy emulsion found on the *grundle* and *butthole* created by the accumulation of sweat and filth from an unwashed *ball sack* and *anus?* It's not your fault that you insisted the waiter explain everything. You could not have possibly known that *goose cheese* is its equally sinister counterpart but exclusive to the vaginal area, specifically the *gooch*, and best described as more of a rémoulade in both texture and appearance. Sadly, some nights last forever, and your poor mother may never feel the same way about a spicy rémoulade, but you will never look like a *fucking asshole* again! Like they say; the more you know!

Take a long hard look at these fifty terms, commonly used by history's idiot brigade, to denigrate the inescapable delight of dirty words: *Accurses, anathemas, bawdiness, bedamnings, blasphemies, coarseness, crudities, curse words, debaucheries, degeneracy, depravities, desecration, devilry, execrations, expletives, filthiness, foulness, grossness, immoralities, impieties, improprieties, indecencies, indecorousness, invective, irreverences, lasciviousness, lewdness, libertine, licentiousness, lubricities, maledictions, no-no's, obloquies, obscenities, perversities, profanities, raunch, roguery, sacrilege, salaciousness, scurrilities, slang, smuttiness, swear words, transgressions, vices, vilifications, vituperations, vulgarities, and wickednesses.* I find these words to be far more fuckin' offensive than any curse word I know. So much energy wasted in a foolish pursuit by ignorant people who regard all cursing as imprecation, never realizing that it's actually all about the implications. Two different words, two different meanings, and one motherfuckin' truth!! These words are not born negative, they're born neutral, and it's we, the people, who give them purpose. And they have no greater purpose than when we want to celebrate, communicate, giggle, weep, innovate, and fight . . . for our right . . . to party!!! So next time you're looking to harsh our mellow, please stop to consider that you may not know what the fuck you're talking about.

Mathematics may be the more sophisticated and elegant language of the universe, but down here on planet earth, it doesn't hold a candle to cursing, its way cuter and far more relatable, colloquial cousin (twice removed). It's got swagger for days, and that *motherfucker* can dance! Hell, even when mathematics wants to hit the town, meet some hotties, and get its fuck on, it turns to its favorite cousin, who can talk about the Pythagorean theorem like it's the geometry of sex! So how's that hypotenuse treating you now?! Shiiiit!! The Euclideans ain't got nuthin' on C-Money! $(\sqrt{-shit})^2$ **Shit just got real!!!**

Congratulations on completing Volume I of the *The Encyclopedia Hysterica for the Cursing Connoisseur*. I hope you enjoyed reading it as much I enjoyed proving the infinite monkey theorem by writing it.

It's been one hell of a ride. I've said and done some incredible things, in inconceivable places, with incomprehensible people. I've created the impossible, perpetrated the improbable, and orchestrated the unimaginable. Some days I'm a sorceress, some days a witch, other days a fairy, but most days I'm a *cunning linguist*. And through it all, I learned these two important lessons: 1) Fame is fickle, a never-ending pickle. With profound consequences, disguised as a tickle; and 2) the only thing worse than stepping in a fresh turd on live television is finding out it's yours.

Your greatest enemy throughout your entire life will always be apathy. Any time you're faced with the challenges of forging your own destiny and following your crazy-ass dream, you'll find it waiting for you outside your door. Like a pair of comfortable shoes with cruel intentions, it will gracefully guide you down the path of indifference on your way to irrelevance. It's a little something I call the casual acceptance of fate.

Aristotle once said, "You'll never really know the true measure of who you are and what you're capable of until someone *pressure-washes their quiver bone in your bitch wrinkle!*" (That's Aristotle Benchod, my fish guy.) A situation that not only fucks you up, it fucks you down, and right before it's over, it fucks you sideways, for good measure. Sorta like bailing your mom out of jail for trying to kill your boyfriend because she caught him fucking your dad! It ain't a pretty sight, but then again, transformative moments rarely are.

Fortune favors the bold. So be bold. It all begins and ends with you.

There is a fuck hidden deep inside of each and every one of us.

It's up to you to find it and give it!

—CK

PROFANITY INDEX

CELEBRITY INDEX